Outgrowing God?

Outgrowing God?

A Beginner's Guide to Richard Dawkins
and the God Debate

By Peter S. Williams

CASCADE *Books* • Eugene, Oregon

OUTGROWING GOD?
A Beginner's Guide to Richard Dawkins and the God Debate

Cascade Books
An Imprint of Wipf and Stock Publishers
199 W. 8th Ave., Suite 3
Eugene, OR 97401

www.wipfandstock.com

PAPERBACK ISBN: 978-1-5326-9346-5
HARDCOVER ISBN: 978-1-5326-9347-2
EBOOK ISBN: 978-1-5326-9348-9

Cataloguing-in-Publication data:

Names: Williams, Peter S., author.

Title: Outgrowing God? : a beginner's guide to Richard Dawkins and the God debate / by Peter S. Williams.

Description: Eugene, OR: Cascade Books, 2020 | Includes bibliographical references.

Identifiers: ISBN 978-1-5326-9346-5 (paperback) | ISBN 978-1-5326-9347-2 (hardcover) | ISBN 978-1-5326-9348-9 (ebook)

Subjects: LCSH: Dawkins, Richard, 1941– | God | Irreligion | Atheism | Religion | Apologetics | Faith

Classification: BL2747.3 W55 2020 (print) | BL2775.3 (ebook)

Scripture quotations marked (YLT) are taken from the 1898 YOUNG'S LITERAL TRANSLATION OF THE HOLY BIBLE by J.N. Young, (Author of the Young's Analytical Concordance), public domain.

Manufactured in the U.S.A.   10/15/20

This book is dedicated to:

The colleagues and students I've met through
NLA University College at Gimlekollen, Kristiansand, Norway.

&

My goddaughter, Sophie Alexandra McKerracher,
born 27th September 2019.

The foundation of every state is the education of its youth.

—Diogenes Laertius

Scepticism can sometimes be as dogmatic as fundamentalism.

—John Dickson, *Is Jesus History?*

Contents

Author's Preface

I agree with Paul Copan when he says:

> There is a "secret infidel" in every believer's heart, a kind of internal dialogue between one's "believing self" and "unbelieving self." The wrong response to doubting and questioning youth is to keep them in a "Christian bubble"—or simply to dismiss their questions and exhort them to "pray harder," "read the Bible," or "just believe." The right response is to teach them to doubt wisely. Christian leaders and parents should give the young people entrusted to them ample room to grapple with doubts—to ask questions around the supper table or over a cup of coffee. The next generation should receive direction in honestly working through these questions. We should seek to sharpen their minds and strengthen their faith so they can embrace it as their own.[1]

I hope engaging with the dialogue between the characters in this book will equip young people (as well as older readers) of all worldview persuasions to doubt and to believe with wisdom.

This project was completed after the 2020 pandemic hit the United Kingdom. I'd like to offer my thanks to Dr. Sarah Campbell, for inviting me to move into her spare room for an indefinite period of co-isolation.

For commenting on and responding to questions relating to chapter 7, I'd like to give thanks to: Douglas Axe, Maxwell Professor of Molecular Biology at Biola University; Ola Hössjer, Professor of Mathematical Statistics at Stockholm University; David W. Swift, MSc; and Steinar Thorvaldsen, Professor of Information Science at the University of Tromsø.

1. Copan, "Learn How (Not) To Doubt," para. 8.

I'd also like to express thanks to: Highfield Church's "Apologia Lunch" group for having me to speak about *Outgrowing God* on October 6th, 2019; both of my church home-groups, for their encouragement and prayers; Ellie Robinson, for a conversation about knitting; Mark Towers, for helpful comments on an early draft of chapter 1; Caleb Shupe, for his copyediting; Calvin Jaffarian, for his typesetting and facilitation of post-publication tweaks; staff and students of NLA University College at Gimlekollen in Kristiansand, Norway, for their encouragement; and last but not least, my parents, for their constant support.

My website has a page for this book that carries various resources, including an extensive list of meeting specific recommended resources. See: www.peterswilliams.com/publications/books/outgrowing-god/.

Biblical quotations are from the English Standard Version (ESV) unless otherwise stated.

Peter S. Williams,

Southampton, England, Autumn 2020.

First Meeting

One God Isn't Much like Another

T he snow made a satisfying scrunching sound under Hiromi's combat boots as she walked towards *The Campus Coffee Cup Café*. Her first year abroad had been enjoyable, but also a little lonely. This year, she'd joined a student book club. It would be a good way to meet people, and the book they were going to discuss dealt with a topic of genuine interest.

Arriving at her destination, Hiromi stopped to remove her headphones and facemask, pocketing them inside her black leather jacket. Peering through the window, she could see why the café would be glad to fill some tables after lunchtime. The place was fairly empty, with a scattering of students absorbed by their phones or typing away at laptops, and several people sitting at a table in the corner opposite the barista station. That must be the club. Hiromi inhaled a deep lungful of cold air before pushing at the door and stepping into a warmth flavored by coffee beans and steamed milk.

Stamping the snow off her boots onto the sodden welcome mat, Hiromi heard a voice inviting her to take a place at the corner table. The voice belonged to a lady Hiromi recognized from the group's Facebook page as Professor Sophie Minerva, a tall woman with a calm, businesslike expression and a warm but penetrating gaze.[1] As Hiromi settled into the only remaining seat at the table, the professor asked everyone to introduce themselves, and what they thought about "the God Question." Around the table were:

- **Hiromi:** An international student from Japan, studying music and philosophy. She explained that while she could see the attraction of belief in God, she had questions about the rationality of affirming or denying God's existence. She wanted to see if Dawkins would change her mind.

1. See Book I of Anicius Manlius Severinus Boethius's *Consolation of Philosophy*.

- **Thomas:** An undergraduate studying classical antiquity. He described himself as "a skeptic and neo-atheist." He'd brought some knitting with him.[2]

- **Douglas**: A postgraduate student of philosophy. He described himself as "a classical atheist."

- **Astrid:** An international postgraduate student from Norway. She described herself as a Christian. Inspired by studying communication and worldviews at NLA University College's Kristiansand campus,[3] she was now studying theology.

Some general chat ensued (about their studies, their countries of origin, and the snow) whilst drinks were procured.

Sophie: Thanks for coming everyone. Permit me to open with some brief remarks: In these divisive days of "post-truth" and "fake news,"[4] it's more important than ever to remember the ideals at the heart of the university: A communal commitment to the wise pursuit of truth, goodness, and beauty. In particular, we must join in the philosophical quest to know and defend true answers to significant questions by thinking carefully and arguing well: "to mediate and speak forth [truth] and to refute the opposing error."[5] This quest demands "the critical examination of the basis for fundamental beliefs as to what is true, and the analysis of the concepts we use in expressing such beliefs."[6]

Of course, people disagree about which fundamental beliefs are true and how best to express and defend them. So we must always seek to be "speaking the truth in love,"[7] remembering both the importance of tolerance and the fact that toleration isn't celebration. Indeed, we can only tolerate that with which we disagree! This means we also need to *listen* "in love." We need to listen to those whose views differ from our own as a prelude to a rigorous but respectful dialogue aimed at the intellectually virtuous pursuit of knowledge and wisdom.

---

2. See Williams, "Outgrowing God?"; Duan, "Dudes, Why Aren't You Knitting?"; Theo Merz, "Men's Knitting."

3. See www.nla.no/en/; NLA Høgskolen, "Kommunikasjon og livssyn"; NLA Høgskolen, "Velkommen til NLA Høgskolen." See also Mon Amie, "KRISTIANSAND, Norway."

4. See "Post-Truth and Fake News"; Guinness, *Time for Truth*; Kakutani, *Death Of Truth*.

5. Aquinas, *Summa Contra Gentiles*, 60–61.

6. Crofton, *Big Ideas in Brief*, 8.

7. Eph 4:15.

There is, then, a sense in which we should welcome disagreement, as a means to the end of discovering truth; for "As iron sharpens iron, so one person sharpens another."[8] As Charles Taliaferro says: "philosophy is best done among groups where there is an authentic spirit of friendship or camaraderie."[9]

I hope we will find that spirit of friendship as we discuss the fifteenth book by Richard Dawkins: *Outgrowing God: A Beginner's Guide*. I see you all have electronic copies. How modern.

Professor Dawkins is one of the world's most prominent atheists. He's a leading light of the so-called "New" or "Neo"-Atheist movement that arose in reaction to the "9/11" terrorist attacks in America.[10] He's an evolutionary biologist, an Emeritus Fellow of New College at Oxford University. He's a Fellow of the Royal Society, which is a fellowship "of the most eminent scientists, engineers and technologists from the UK and the Commonwealth."[11] In recognition of his books explaining scientific issues to the general public, Dawkins was received into the fellowship of the Royal Society for Literature in 1997.[12]

In his review of *Outgrowing God*, paleontologist Neil Shubin says that: "With wit, logic, and his characteristic flair for expressing complex ideas with uncanny clarity, Richard Dawkins separates myth from reality.... His book is more than a beginners' guide to atheism: it is a primer that liberates us to see and explore the beauty of the Universe free of fables and fantasies."[13]

Oh, there's no need to put your hand up to ask a question in an informal setting like this, Hiromi. As Homer says: "Speak out, don't hold it in buried in your heart."[14]

Hiromi: Thank you, Professor. I would like to ask, what is the difference between "atheism" and "neo-atheism"?

Douglas (using his phone)**:** Well, first of all, *atheism* is the belief that no deity of any kind exists. Philosopher Michael Ruse says the term "is applied . . . to

8. Prov 27:17 (NIV).
9. Taliaferro, *Philosophy of Religion*, xi.
10. See Winston, "'New Atheists' Emerge From 9/11."
11. See https://royalsociety.org/fellows/.
12. See https://rsliterature.org/about-us/.
13. See www.penguinrandomhouse.com/books/601964/outgrowing-god-by-richard-dawkins/ for the endorsement by Shubin.
14. Homer, *Illiad*, 1.363.

those who deny any and all gods."[15] *Neo*-atheists, like Dawkins, generally combine atheism with three other beliefs: First, that the only real things are the sort of things describable by natural science. That's a view about what exists, called "naturalism" or "physicalism." Second, that knowledge comes only from science. That's a view about how we know things, called "scientism." And third, that religious faith isn't just *intellectually* wrong, it's *morally* wrong and bad for society.[16]

Hiromi: Thank you.

Thomas: Hang on. Isn't an atheist just someone "who doesn't"[17] believe in any deity, as Dawkins says?

Douglas: The thing is, if you define atheism as "a lack of belief in anything supernatural,"[18] as Dawkins does, you erase the distinction between atheism and agnosticism.

Astrid (using her tablet): Philosopher C. Stephen Evans says an agnostic "neither affirms belief in God (theism) nor denies the existence of God (atheism) but instead suspends judgement."[19] He also distinguishes "the 'modest agnostic,' who merely claims to be unable to decide the question of God's reality, from the 'aggressive agnostic,' who claims that no one can decide the question and that suspension of judgement is the only reasonable stance."[20]

Douglas: Right; an "agnostic" says either that they don't, or that we can't, know if God exists. Dawkins say that while "We can't know for sure . . . most of us are confident enough to say we are 'atheists' with respect to"[21] the gods of polytheism. It's clear that by "atheism" here he means a positive belief that there are probably no gods. He doesn't claim certainty, but he certainly expresses a negative opinion on the matter.

15. Ruse, *Atheism*, 8.

16. For an introduction to and critique of neo-atheism, see: Williams, "New Atheism"; Ganssle, *Reasonable God*; Glass, *Atheism's New Clothes*; Williams, *Getting at Jesus*; Williams, *C. S. Lewis vs. the New Atheism*; Williams, *Sceptic's Guide to Atheism*.

17. Dawkins, *Outgrowing God*, 5.

18. Dawkins, *Outgrowing God*, 95.

19. Evans, *Pocket Dictionary of Apologetics & Philosophy of Religion*, 8.

20. Evans, *Pocket Dictionary of Apologetics & Philosophy of Religion*, 8–9.

21. Dawkins, *Outgrowing God*, 95.

Astrid: And that means he has to defend his opinion, just as the theist has to defend theirs.

Thomas: I see.

Hiromi: I am agnostic in the "modest" sense. I have no opinion to defend.

Astrid: I'm glad you're not apathetic as well as agnostic.

Hiromi: Apathetic?

Astrid: It means not caring about something. Many people are apathetic about God. But you said you wanted to see if reading Dawkins would change your mind, so you're clearly interested in forming an opinion about God's existence.

Hiromi: Yes. I think the existence or nonexistence of God makes a big difference to the kind of world we live in and the kind of life it makes sense to live. There are many questions about life it is hard to answer when you are in two minds about God. I would like to arrive at an informed opinion about God and about my life. I have been reading the agnostic philosopher Mortimer J. Adler, who said: "More consequences for thought and action follow the affirmation or denial of God than from answering any other basic question."[22] He also said: "The philosopher ought never try to avoid the duty of making up his mind by merely entertaining opinions or advancing them lightly."[23]

Astrid: Did you know Adler became a Christian late in his life?[24]

Hiromi: Interesting.

Thomas: Dawkins says atheists "don't believe in anything supernatural."[25]

Astrid: Do you think he means that while he doesn't believe in souls or angels, they may be real for all he knows? Or do you think he means that souls and angels probably don't exist?

22. Adler, *Great Books of the Western World*, 561.
23. Adler, "Technique of Philosophy," para. 10.
24. See Samples, "Christian Thinkers 101: A Crash Course on Mortimer J. Adler."
25. Dawkins, *Outgrowing God*, 7.

Thomas: I guess he means that, like gods, souls and angels probably don't exist.

Hiromi: Yes, because if a god or a soul existed it would be a supernatural thing, and according to Dawkins, atheists do not believe in supernatural things. That is to say, they believe supernatural things do not exist.

Astrid (using her tablet): But I think Dawkins has that back-to-front. It's not that you have to disbelieve in anything supernatural in order to be an atheist, but that people who disbelieve in anything supernatural are automatically atheists. Atheist philosopher Julian Baggini says: "The atheist's rejection of belief in God is usually accompanied by a broader rejection of any supernatural or transcendent reality. For example, an atheist does not usually believe in the existence of immortal souls, life after death, ghosts, or supernatural powers. Although strictly speaking an atheist could believe in any of these things and still remain an atheist."[26]

Douglas (using his phone): I agree. That "broader rejection of any supernatural or transcendent reality"[27] comes from having a naturalistic worldview,[28] which is "a general picture of all reality as consisting of nothing but the operations of nature."[29] According to naturalism, "no transcendent, supernatural, divine being or superhuman power exists as creator, sustainer, guide, or judge. Such a universe has to exist . . . not by design or providence but by purposeless natural forces and processes. There is no inherent, ultimate meaning or purpose."[30]

Hiromi: Naturalism is "nihilistic." That is, it denies the existence of any objective purpose or values. For the nihilist, everything is ultimately pointless and lacking in objective meaning.

Douglas (using his phone): Atheist philosopher Alex Rosenberg writes:

> Is there a God? No. What is the nature of reality? What physics says it is. What is the purpose of the universe? There is none. What is the meaning of life? Ditto. Why am I here? Just dumb

26. Baggini, *Atheism*, 3–4.

27. Baggini, *Atheism*, 3–4.

28. See Craig and Moreland, *Naturalism: A Critical Analysis*; Goetz and Taliaferro, *Naturalism*; Rosenberg, *Atheist's Guide to Reality*.

29. Smith, *Atheist Overreach*, 46.

30. Smith, *Atheist Overreach*, 45.

luck. . . . Is there a soul? . . . Are you kidding? Is there free will? Not a chance. What happens when we die? Everything pretty much goes on as before, except us. What is the difference between right and wrong, good and bad? There is no moral difference between them . . . life is meaningless, without purpose, and without ultimate moral value. . . . We need to face the fact that nihilism is true.[31]

That's my "creed."

Thomas: Well that's depressing!

Douglas: I'm afraid depressing things can be true. Rosenberg says: "if this seems hard to take . . . there's always Prozac."[32]

Sophie: Hiromi, could you tell us why you're agnostic in the "modest" sense?

Hiromi: Sure. The "aggressive" or "hard" agnostic disagrees with both theists and atheists, claiming to know that humans *cannot* know whether or not God exists. I used to be a "hard" agnostic.

Douglas: Why'd you change your mind?

Hiromi: The hard agnostic says it is *impossible* to know if God exists, at least in this life. However, the hard agnostic also admits that God *might* exist.

Thomas: What's the problem with that?

Hiromi: Well, God is usually said to be "almighty" or "omnipotent," able to do anything that's logically possible and consistent with other divine characteristics, like being all-good.

Astrid: That's right. God can't create a square-circle, because that's impossible. The idea of a square-circle contradicts itself. It's an incoherent concept. Likewise, God could never do something evil for its own sake, because God is wholly good, and the idea of doing something evil for its own sake contradicts the idea of being wholly good.

---

31. Rosenberg, *Atheist's Guide to Reality*, 2–3, 19, 95.
32. Rosenberg, *Atheist's Guide to Reality*, 19.

Hiromi: So, *if* an almighty God exists, it would seem that making his existence knowable to us, even in this world, would be something he *could* do.

Thomas: I see. Given what's meant by "God," it seems that *if* God exists, *then* he could make his existence known to, or knowable by, humans. In which case, we can't reasonably claim both that God might exist *and* that we can't know if God exists, though we might still think it a hard question we might fail to answer.

Hiromi: Yes. So, I stopped being a "hard" agnostic. I think it is *possible* to know the answer to the question "Does God exist?" and I hope that discussing Dawkins' book might help me decide whether or not to believe in God.

Astrid: You mean whether or not you believe *that* God exists. That's not the same thing as whether or not you believe *in* God.

Hiromi: Yes; but I think, for me, the one would lead to the other. I suppose other people may feel differently about that.

Sophie: I'm so pleased to see students ready to ask questions, to challenge each-another's thinking, and their own thinking too! Now, Hiromi kindly agreed to summarize the first chapter of *Outgrowing God*, so let's proceed with that.

Hiromi (using her tablet): I think the main point Professor Dawkins makes at the beginning of his book is that we should think carefully about the beliefs we embrace about the nature of ultimate reality. Rather than having blind faith in whatever beliefs we have inherited from our family or our culture, we should think for ourselves.

Dawkins clearly assumes the truth of the logical law of non-contradiction, which states that something cannot both be true and not true in the same sense and at the same time.[33] Having introduced various beliefs about gods, he argues on the basis of this law that: "These beliefs contradict each other, so they can't all be right."[34] This means that Dawkins affirms the existence of an objective reality about which our beliefs are either true or false. And he wants readers to agree with him that knowing the truth about reality is more important than the cultural identities we inherit.

33. Zacharias, "Law of Non-Contradiction."
34. Dawkins, *Outgrowing God*, 10.

I noticed some other claims about knowledge. Dawkins says, "it's impossible to prove that something does not exist. We don't positively know there are no gods."[35] He also says that we should not believe anything, and should not claim to know anything, unless we have a reason for thinking our belief is true. He says that "until somebody offers a reason to believe, we are wasting our time bothering to do so."[36]

I found it puzzling that Dawkins spends the rest of the chapter making many statements he obviously expects readers to believe, but without offering any reasons to believe what he says. He just *asserts* that:

- The monotheism of Christians and Muslims is basically polytheism, because of beliefs about Satan and/or angels, the Catholic view of Mary and/or the Christian doctrine of the Trinity.[37]
- The doctrine of the Trinity was disputed violently.[38]
- The spread of Christianity is a historical accident due to Constantine in AD 312.[39]
- There was no first man called Adam.[40]
- Abraham is a mythical figure.[41]
- Horus and many other ancient gods were supposed to have been born of a virgin.[42]

Dawkins ends with the observation that "plenty of people have offered what they thought were reasons for believing in one god or another. Or for believing in some kind of un-named 'higher power' or 'creative intelligence'. So we need to look at those reasons and see whether they really are good reasons."[43] This is a key subject that interests me personally, so I was disappointed to discover we will only "see some of them in the course of this book."[44] I guess this is a limitation of "a beginner's guide," but unless Dawkins has a knock-out argument for atheism, then even if he is right to discount

---

35. Dawkins, *Outgrowing God*, 13.
36. Dawkins, *Outgrowing God*, 13.
37. Dawkins, *Outgrowing God*, 7–10.
38. Dawkins, *Outgrowing God*, 8.
39. Dawkins, *Outgrowing God*, 6.
40. Dawkins, *Outgrowing God*, 8.
41. Dawkins, *Outgrowing God*, 6.
42. Dawkins, *Outgrowing God*, 5.
43. Dawkins, *Outgrowing God*, 14.
44. Dawkins, *Outgrowing God*, 14.

the arguments for God he examines in *Outgrowing God*, there are other arguments that might provide good reasons to endorse theism.

Sophie: Thank you for that summary, highlighting Dawkins's key message about thinking for yourself, as well as his key assumptions about rationality and reality. As you say, an introductory book can't cover a topic comprehensively. Still, we have to start somewhere.

Douglas: I'd like to start by noting that Dawkins is viewed by many atheists as an embarrassment, a mirror-image to religious fundamentalists. If Dawkins makes a bad argument, that doesn't prove atheism is unreasonable, only that he is. I share Dawkins's naturalism, but I think he's a bad philosopher. For example, his arguments about God have drawn criticism from prominent atheist philosophers.

Thomas: Such as?

Douglas: Thomas Nagel said Dawkins's dismissal of the traditional arguments for the existence of God was "particularly weak."[45] Eric Wielenberg says: "the central atheistic argument of [Dawkins's bestselling book] *The God Delusion* is unconvincing."[46] I could go on.

Thomas: Perhaps that's because Dawkins doesn't write academic papers for philosophy journals, but popular books that try to make a difference in the lives of real people.

Sophie: Philosophers are real people too.

Hiromi: Does popularity excuse bad arguments?

Douglas: I don't think so. Hiromi makes a good point about Dawkins adopting an attitude of authority that contradicts his own statements about the importance of giving reasons. I've read the whole book already, and several of those claims Hiromi listed never get mentioned again. It's supposed to be religious leaders who demanded blind faith, not scientists like Dawkins!

Astrid: Religious faith doesn't *have* to be blind, and some religious leaders *are* scientists.

---

45. Nagel, "Fear of Religion," 25.
46. Wielenberg, "Dawkins's Gambit, Hume's Aroma, and God's Simplicity," 127.

Thomas: Maybe so, but Dawkins is writing "a beginner's guide" for young adults. He wants to keep it short. He doesn't want to clog it up with footnotes.

Hiromi: I like footnotes.

Douglas: He could have given a fuller discussion of fewer topics! He could have included a bibliography, or at least some recommended reading!

Thomas: I suppose.

Douglas: And then there's Dawkins's *scientism*, his belief that science provides our only path to knowledge about anything. Dawkins divides all beliefs into the categories of blind faith on the one hand and "proper evidence-based belief"[47] on the other. As he writes in *The Magic of Reality*: "the only good reason to believe that something exists is if there is real evidence that it does . . . it always comes back to our senses, one way or another."[48]

Thomas: Why's that a problem?

Douglas (using his phone): Because, as Christian Smith notes, the statement that only empirical science gives us knowledge

> is not itself a scientific statement and could never, ever itself be validated by empirical science. It is instead a philosophical presupposition . . . scientism, then, turns out to be internally self-defeating. It depends on a nonscientific position to take the position that only science authorizes us to take positions worth taking. And that is like calling someone on the telephone to tell her that you can't call her.[49]

Astrid: Not to mention counterexamples of things we know without scientific evidence grounded in our physical senses.

Thomas: Like what?

Astrid: Like knowing that truth and integrity *matter*, that naturalism logically entails atheism, that two plus two equals four, that I'm consciously enjoying the smell of coffee, that snowflakes are beautiful . . .

47. Gordan and Wilkinson, *Conversations on Religion*, 120.
48. Dawkins, *Magic of Reality*, 16, 19.
49. Smith, *Atheist Overreach*, 94.

Thomas: I get the picture.

Hiromi (using her tablet): In that *New Scientist* magazine interview Sophie circulated, Dawkins holds back from answering a social question and says: "I'm not a sociologist. I'm not a psychologist. I would only be able to give an amateur opinion as a citizen, which is no more interesting than anybody else's."[50] I wonder why he does not apply the same caution to giving opinions on philosophical and theological issues?

Thomas: Arguments from authority aren't always invalid, are they? Dawkins is a scientist.

Douglas: Being a scientist only makes Dawkins an authority on the scientific subjects in which he specialized. In Dawkins's case, that's zoology and evolutionary biology. It doesn't make him an authority on the philosophy of religion, or mythology, or ancient history.

Thomas: But amateurs can educate themselves on subjects outside of their professional expertise. I imagine Dawkins is well-read.

Sophie: According to Bradley Dowden's article on fallacies in the *Internet Encyclopedia of Philosophy*:

> much of our knowledge properly comes from listening to authorities. However, appealing to authority as a reason to believe something *is* fallacious whenever the authority appealed to is not really an authority in this particular subject, when the authority cannot be trusted to tell the truth, when authorities disagree on this subject (except for the occasional lone wolf), when the reasoner misquotes the authority, and so forth. Although spotting a fallacious appeal to authority often requires some background knowledge about the subject or the authority, in brief it can be said that it is fallacious to accept the words of a supposed authority when we should be suspicious of the authority's words.[51]

Hiromi: Professor, how did you quote so much without looking it up?

---

50. Dawkins, "Features Interview," 38. See video of this interview at New Scientist, "Richard Dawkins Outgrows God."

51. Dowden, "Fallacies: Appeal to Authority," para. 1. See Harding, "Argument from Authority"; Hansen, "Fallacies."

Sophie: In Plato's dialogue *The Phaedrus*, Socrates tells a story about the god Ammon, who offered the gift of letters to the king of Egypt. He said letters would "make the Egyptians wiser and give them better memories."[52] The king replied: "this discovery of yours will create forgetfulness in the learners' souls, because they will not use their memories; they will trust to the external written characters and not remember of themselves . . . they will appear to be omniscient and will generally know nothing."[53]

Thomas (using his tablet): I don't think Dawkins is omniscient, but I trust him to do his research. After all, his whole thing, really, is about taking facts seriously. On page 103 he says: "The only good reason for believing anything factual is evidence."[54] I saw him in a TV interview promoting *Outgrowing God*, and he said he wants to rid the world of "anything that's not evidence-based where factual knowledge is concerned . . . things which are based on . . . authority rather than on evidence."[55]

Astrid (using her tablet): But take Dawkins's assertion that the spread of Christianity depended on Emperor Constantine's decision to patronize Christianity in 312 AD.[56] That doesn't seem to be based on evidence. Indeed, Dawkins doesn't seem to know that: "By the Fourth Century . . . the Church had already spread beyond the borders of Roman rule. There were Christian churches . . . beyond the reach of the Empire, in India, Persia, Japan, Scotland, Ethiopia and Transoxiana."[57] So it seems Christianity spread around the world just fine without Constantine.

Thomas: Trans-what-ia?

Sophie: The Central Asian home of the Parthian State.[58]

Astrid (using her tablet): In that *New Scientist* interview, Dawkins says he wants "to encourage people to think for themselves . . . whilst being keen not to indoctrinate, because that's of course what we criticize religious people

---

52. Plato, *Phaedrus*, 275a.

53. Plato, *Phaedrus*.

54. Dawkins, *Outgrowing God*, 103.

55. Channel 4 News, "Richard Dawkins on Scientific Truth," 1:00–1:25.

56. Dawkins, *Outgrowing God*, 6.

57. Park, *Myths, Lies and Howlers from the Fringes of the New Atheism*, loc. 619.

58. Venetis and Mozdoor, "Establishment and Development of Christianity in the Parthian Empire."

for doing."[59] But it seems to me that in *Outgrowing God* Dawkins relies on people *treating him as an authority* and *not thinking for themselves* about his claims. *Outgrowing God* is an exercise in indoctrination![60]

Sophie: Let's not get ahead of ourselves. To properly assess how trustworthy Dawkins is on these matters, we'd have to examine a representative sample of his claims to determine how often he is mistaken. We won't have time to do that today, but let's bear the issue in mind as we progress. In the meantime, I suggest we look at what Dawkins says about belief in the small "g" gods of polytheism and the capital "G" God of monotheism.

Thomas: Dawkins claims that Christians and Muslims are basically polytheistic,[61] but that ignores important differences between the sort of thing a "god" is within the polytheistic religions of the ancient world, and the sort of thing "God" is within the Abrahamic religions.

Astrid (using her tablet): Philosopher Norman L. Geisler defines polytheism as: "the worldview that many finite gods exist in the world."[62] He notes that "in some forms, all the gods are more or less equal. . . . In another type of polytheism, the gods form a hierarchy with a chief god, such as Zeus. This is called henotheism."[63] Geisler and William D. Watkins explain that in either case, polytheistic gods "are not viewed as being beyond the space-time world . . . these gods are not creators of the universe but are its shapers and transformers . . . polytheists agree that the gods had a beginning . . . many of the gods were products of nature. Still other gods came to exist through the sexual activities of the already existent gods."[64] As journalist Rupert Shortt comments: "The difference between monotheism and polytheism is not one of numbering, as though the issue were merely a matter of determining how many divine entities one happens to think there are. It is a distinction instead between two entirely different kinds of reality."[65]

---

59. Dawkins, "Features Interview," 38. See video of this interview at New Scientist, "Richard Dawkins Outgrows God."

60. Gooblar, "What Is 'Indoctrination'?"

61. Dawkins, *Outgrowing God*, 7.

62. Geisler, *Christian Apologetics*, 222.

63. Geisler, *Christian Apologetics*, 222–23.

64. Geisler and Watkins, *Worlds Apart*, 217, 218, 221.

65. Shortt, *Outgrowing Dawkins*, 28–29.

Douglas: So, unlike the God of monotheistic religions, the gods of polytheism are "finite," having limited power, and so on; and they're wholly immanent beings that came into being and that only exist *within* the universe.

Hiromi: Yes, because the gods of polytheistic worldviews ultimately come from an uncreated universe. That's a major contrast with monotheistic worldviews, where God is the uncreated creator of the universe. A universe-creating God exists beyond the universe, as well as being present to it and within it by his power and knowledge.

Sophie: Theologians express this by saying God is both "transcendent" and "immanent."

Astrid: In the Old Testament, the divine name revealed to Moses is "Yahweh," which means both "He is/was/will be" and "He causes to be."[66] That is, "God's Hebrew name . . . reveals God both as the eternally self-existent ("transcendent") One and, at the same time, as the Creator and Sustainer of all else that is."[67]

Hiromi: If the gods of polytheism are ultimately *products of nature*, is it right to call them "supernatural"?

Thomas: The gods are portrayed as having eternal life and miraculous powers. I guess that counts for something.

Hiromi (using her tablet): Dawkins portrays the Jews as henotheistic polytheists who thought of Yahweh as the chief god. He writes about "Yahweh, the god of the Jews"[68] with a small "g" and says that Yahweh is "today's dominant god (whom I'll therefore spell with a capital G, God),"[69] which suggests the distinction between the gods and Yahweh is just a matter of popularity. He says: "although the Israelites worshipped their own tribal god Yahweh, they didn't necessarily disbelieve in the gods of rival tribes, such as Baal, the fertility god of the Canaanites; they just thought Yahweh was more powerful."[70]

---

66. See Coleson, *Genesis*, 27–28.
67. Coleson, *Genesis*, 27–28.
68. Dawkins, *Outgrowing God*, 6.
69. Dawkins, *Outgrowing God*, 6.
70. Dawkins, *Outgrowing God*, 7.

Sophie: The Jewish Scriptures portray Yahweh as the head of a "divine council" of supernatural beings that later Jewish and Christian writings describe in angelic terms.[71] They also describe Yahweh as opposed to the worship of any created or man-made thing, including "foreign gods."[72] Their critique of idolatry shows that *some* Jews believed in and even worshiped "foreign gods." However, Habakkuk 2:18 asks: "What profit is an idol when its maker has shaped it . . ? For its maker trusts in his own creation when he makes speechless idols!" According to Isaiah 41, foreign gods "are nothing" and "a delusion".

Thomas: In the ancient poems of Homer, the Greek gods all have their own spheres of influence, like Poseidon being god of the sea.[73]

Astrid (using her tablet): Or Thor being the god of thunder in Norse polytheism. That's why polytheism is hostile to science. Geisler and Watkins cite the *Theogony*, by the ancient Greek poet Hesiod, as describing "a pantheon, or group, of gods, each one having jurisdiction over a specific aspect of life or the world. . . . The gods quarrelled with one another, deceived one another, sought to overthrow one another. . . . And although they were powerful, they were prone to many of the same weaknesses that befall humans."[74]

Sophie: As Huston Smith observed: "Whereas the gods of Olympus tirelessly pursued beautiful women, the God of Sinai watched over widows and orphans."[75]

Thomas (using his tablet): I've got a copy of Hesiod's *Theogany*,[76] or "Birth of the Gods," with me. It's an eighth-century BC poem about how the first gods arose, and how later gods came from those gods, until Zeus made himself ruler of the gods. Here's some lines from the opening:

> at the first Chaos came to be, but next wide-bosomed Earth,
> the ever-sure foundations of all the deathless ones who hold
> the peaks of snowy Olympus, and dim Tartarus in the depth of
> the wide-pathed Earth, and Eros, fairest among the deathless
> gods, who unnerves the limbs and overcomes the mind and

71. See Ps 96:4. See Williams, "Do Angels Really Exist?"
72. See Exod 20:3; Deut 32:16–17.
73. See "Odyssey and the Iliad in Just Two Minutes."
74. Geisler and Watkins, *Worlds Apart*, 222.
75. Smith, *World's Religions*, 275.
76. See Evelyn-White, "Theogany of Hesiod."

wise counsels of all gods and all men within them. . . . And Earth first bare starry Heaven, equal to herself, to cover her on every side, and to be an ever-sure abiding-place for the blessed gods. . . . After them was born Cronos the wily, youngest and most terrible of her children.[77]

Astrid: See how different Hesiod's worldview is from Genesis 1: "In the beginning, God created the heavens and the earth."[78] Or Psalm 24: "The earth is the LORD's and the fullness thereof, the world and those who dwell therein."[79] Melvin Calvin, an American Nobel laureate in biochemistry, speaks for the consensus among historians of science when he traces the origin of the foundational conviction of modern science, that nature is reliably and intelligibly ordered, to the biblical idea "that the universe is governed by a single God, and is not the product of the whims of many gods, each governing his own province according to his own laws."[80]

Hiromi: So, while Dawkins thinks the demise of belief in gods like Thor was brought about by scientific thinking, scientific thinking was brought about by monotheism?!

Astrid: That's right.[81]

Thomas: But even if the idea of a reliably ordered cosmos came from monotheism *historically speaking*, that doesn't mean one has to believe in God to do science.

Astrid: Of course not. But it leaves the scientist who doesn't believe in God with a faith in cosmic order and intelligibility that can't be explained.

Douglas: Bertrand Russell said: "the universe is just there, and that's all."[82]

Astrid: Really?![83]

77. Evelyn-White, "Theogany of Hesiod," para. 9.

78. Gen 1:1.

79. Ps 24:1.

80. Calvin, *Chemical Evolution*, 258. See Grant, *History Of Natural Philosophy*; Hannam, *Genesis of Science*.

81. See Williams, "Theological Roots of Science."

82. Russell, "Existence of God," para. 55.

83. See Williams, *Faithful Guide to Philosophy*.

Sophie: I think what you've noticed, Hiromi, is that Dawkins switches between different meanings of the word "god" in order to make it seem that rejecting the existence of Yahweh is the same as rejecting the existence of Zeus. An argument that depends on blurring or switching different meanings of the same term in this way commits the logical fallacy of "equivocation."[84]

Douglas: Yeah, that's just a bad way to argue for atheism.

Sophie: Shall we discuss Dawkins's assumptions about logic and knowledge?

Astrid: I agree with Dawkins that statements about reality are either true or false.

Hiromi: And that means statements which contradict each other cannot both be true.

Sophie: As Aristotle said: "opposite assertions cannot be true at the same time."[85]

Hiromi: And any statement that contradicts itself is incoherent and must be false.

Thomas: Like, if I said: "I can't speak"?

Hiromi: Yes; in that case you are *saying* that you cannot say anything, which is self-contradictory and is therefore a false statement.

Astrid: In which case the contrary statement, that you *can* speak, must be true.

Douglas (using his phone): I like the way Thomas Nagel explains the necessity of trusting in the basic laws of logic. He writes: "Certain forms of thought can't be intelligibly doubted because they force themselves into every attempt to think about anything. . . . There just isn't room for skepticism about basic logic, because there is no place to stand where we can formulate or think it without immediately contradicting ourselves by relying on it."[86]

---

84. See Dowden, "Equivocation"; Pirie, *How To Win Every Argument*, 58–60; Warburton, *Thinking from A to Z*, 61–63.

85. Aristotle, *Metaph.* 4.6.1011b13–20.

86. Nagel, *Last Word*, 61–62.

Thomas: If we can't be skeptical about basic logic without contradicting ourselves, why describe accepting those laws as a matter of trust? That makes it sound like logic involves faith, but Dawkins rejects faith in favor of reason.

Astrid: Dawkins writes as if having faith is the same thing as having blind faith, but that's not true.

Thomas: It isn't? Why not?

Astrid: You can't argue *against* the laws of logic without assuming them. But neither can you argue *for* the laws of logic without assuming them. The laws of logic aren't things we can argue *for*, because they're the things we argue *with*. So, to exercise skepticism about anything, we first have to exercise trust, otherwise known as faith, in our basic intuitions about logic. The fact that Dawkins endorses logic means he endorses faith *in this context*. Therefore, what Dawkins rejects isn't faith *as such*, but *blind faith*, which we can define as faith that pays no attention to what's wise or reasonable.

Thomas: So, you're saying that because Dawkins endorses reason he endorses faith in reason, because you can't give reasons for being reasonable that don't rely on reason. I get that, I think; but this sort of faith is obviously compatible with reason *and* with Dawkins's rejection of *religious* faith, given that what he really means to reject is "blind faith."

Astrid: Well, I'd say Dawkins is wrong to suggest that all religious faith is blind faith. Christian philosopher Paul M. Gould defines Christian faith as "a kind of ventured trust" and says "it's trust in an object that's reasonable to believe in."[87] You can at least admit that people like Gould and myself don't have "blind faith." After all, here I am, engaging with the arguments of Richard Dawkins!

Hiromi: I get what you are saying, but I think there is a difference between having the sort of faith in logic we *must have* in order to be reasonable and having faith in God.

Astrid: I agree. Think of it like this: On the one hand, there are things we believe or trust in a "non-basic" or explicitly indirect manner, on the basis of other things we believe or trust. On the other hand, there have to be some

---

87. Gould and McLean, *Primer on Cultural Apologetics*, 28.

things we believe or trust in a "basic," direct manner. There have to be some things we believe or trust without basing that belief or trust on other things we believe or trust.

Hiromi: That seems right. Otherwise, we would have an infinite regress of beliefs.

Astrid: The things we believe or trust in a "basic" manner can be rational in two different ways. First, they can be things that we can't doubt without self-contradiction, things like the laws of logic or our own existence. Second, they can be things we *can* doubt without self-contradiction, but which it's nevertheless *reasonable for us to accept in the absence of a sufficient reason for doubt,* simply on the basis that *this is how things seem to us.* Philosophers call this sort of experientially grounded basic beliefs "properly basic," meaning they can be "properly" or rationally held without being based in an argumentative fashion on other beliefs we hold.

Sophie: Perhaps an example of a "properly basic" belief would be helpful?

Astrid: Sure. I find myself believing I'm in a coffee shop. I'm not going through an argument in my mind that leads to the conclusion "Therefore, I'm in a coffee shop." It just seems to me that I'm in a coffee shop, and I trust this impression. My being-in-a-coffee-shop belief isn't based on other beliefs I hold, so it's a "basic" belief; but it is grounded in my experience, so it's a "properly basic" belief. This "properly basic" belief *could* be wrong. *Perhaps* I've been hypnotized, or plugged into a computer-generated reality, like in *The Matrix* films.[88] But I don't think so, and it's reasonable for me to trust I *am* in a coffee shop until and unless someone gives me sufficient reason to think otherwise. The burden of proof is on the person who tells me things aren't as they seem to me.

Hiromi: That makes sense. But how does that apply to faith in God?

Astrid: Some philosophers argue that although faith in God's existence doesn't fall into the category of basic beliefs it's impossible to doubt, it can fall into the category of things it's reasonable to believe in a basic way, for anyone to whom it *seems* that God exists. On this account, belief in God is

---

88. See Couch, *Matrix Revelations.*

reasonable for anyone with the right kind of experience.[89] Then again, one might argue that there are good "non-basic" *arguments* for belief in God.

Hiromi: So why do you think *your* belief in God is reasonable and not a matter of blind faith?

Astrid: I think the basic and non-basic paths to rational faith re-enforce each other.

Douglas: I disagree with Dawkins's claim that it's impossible to disprove the existence of anything. Dawkins is so invested in scientific ways of knowing that he misses the fact that you can use logic to disprove the existence of things.

Thomas: How can you do that?!

Douglas: For example, do you think we might discover a square circle one day?

Thomas: Of course not! A "square circle" can't exist, the very idea is self-contradictory.

Douglas: Exactly! So, if we can show the concept of a thing to be self-contradictory, or incoherent, we show that its existence is impossible. Impossible thing can't exist, and therefore don't.

Thomas: Haven't some atheists argued that the concept of God is incoherent, thereby proving that God doesn't exist?

Astrid: Some atheists have offered arguments like that, but I don't think they succeed. Plenty of philosophers, including agnostic and atheist philosophers, defend the coherence of theism.[90]

Thomas: What about the famous question: "Can God create a stone he can't move?" If he can, then he can't move that stone; but if he can't make

---

89. See: Alvin Plantinga, *Knowledge and Christian Belief*; Plantinga, *Warranted Christian Belief*; Williams, *Faithful Guide to Philosophy*.

90. See Williams, "Perfect Being Theology"; Owen, *Christian Theism*; Hebblethwaite, *Philosophical Theology and Christian Doctrine*; Moreland and Craig, *Philosophical Foundations for a Christian Worldview*; Morris, *Our Idea of God*; Swinburne, *Coherence of Theism*.

such a stone, then that's also something he can't do. Either way, there's something God can't do!

Astrid: Yes, but that doesn't mean God isn't "omnipotent." Rather, it means omnipotence should be defined as "the ability to do anything *that's logically possible*." Anything that's logically impossible isn't something that *could* be done, even by an omnipotent being. Like "creating a round square," "creating a stone that God can't move" simply isn't a logically possible thing that anyone, including God, could do. God's inability to create a stone he couldn't move is no more a refutation of his omnipotence than his inability to create a round square.[91]

Douglas: I think it's best to think of arguments about the coherence of divine properties as helping us understand *what it means* to claim that God exists, not as arguments that help us decide *whether or not* God exists. We can always shape our understanding of divine properties so they don't fall foul of any proven incoherence. As atheist Richard Carrier comments, arguments for thinking that "God" is an incoherent concept are "not valid, since any definition of god (or his properties) that is illogical can just be revised to be logical. So, in effect, arguments from incoherence aren't really arguments for atheism, but for the reform of theology."[92]

Astrid: Well, if you admit God's existence is possible, you have to take modern formulations of the "ontological argument" seriously.[93]

Sophie: Let's not get sucked into a discussion of the ontological argument for God, since it's quite complicated and Dawkins doesn't mention it in *Outgrowing God*.

Thomas: Does Dawkins mention any incoherence arguments for atheism?

Hiromi: I guess the closest he comes is his comments about the Christian doctrine that God is a Trinity of divine persons, and about the role of Jesus's death in the Christian picture of God forgiving people.[94] But he doesn't give any arguments. He just ridicules what he doesn't understand.

91. See Menuge, "Can God Create a Rock So Heavy that He Cannot Lift It?"

92. Carrier, *Sense and Goodness without God*, 276.

93. See Craig, "Ontological Argument"; Williams, "Brief Introduction to and Defence of the Modern Ontological Argument"; Williams, *Faithful Guide to Philosophy*.

94. On the latter, see McGrath, *Making Sense of the Cross*; Williams, *Understanding Jesus*.

Thomas: Isn't it a contradiction to claim that there's only one deity *and* three deities?

Astrid: Not if you distinguish between the different concepts of deity involved in the doctrine of God's trinitarian nature.

Thomas: What different concepts?

Astrid: Answering that involves some pretty complex theology, so it's tempting to respond with a reading list! But I'll try to give a brief explanation if you're interested.

Sophie: Not everything can be explained in a tweet. However, I think we should encourage Astrid to have a go at explaining why the Christian concept of God is coherent, because philosophical objections don't get more serious than the objection that one's ideas are incoherent and therefore impossible.

Astrid: All right. As a monotheist, I believe there's one unsurpassably great, personal, divine being. That's one sense of the term "God." And I believe this "God" is composed of *three divine persons*: "God the Father," "God the Son," and "God the Holy Spirit." These *three divine persons* are distinguished by slightly different senses of the term "God," and they necessarily compose the *one divine personal being* we refer to as "the Trinity," "the Godhead," or "God."

Thomas: But Christians call God "he"; doesn't that imply God is one person?

Astrid: It's analogical language that preserves the idea that the one and only trinitarian God isn't an impersonal "it," but a personal being (although God is not a solitary person, but three divine persons in one divine personal being). Christians also refer to individual members of the Trinity as "he," but in either case, calling God "he" doesn't entail that God is biologically male!

Hiromi: Ah, but Jesus was male and you think he was divine.

Astrid: Yes, but I also think he was human! Jesus is one person with two natures. One nature is divine, the other is human. In Jesus, the divine nature of God the Son has a human nature or way of being that's male. But that doesn't make his divine nature male.

Hiromi: I see. I suppose Jesus having two natures would explain how he can be divine but also be born and die?

Astrid: That's right. The traditional theological understanding of the incarnation says "God the Son" remained the same divine individual he'd always been, whilst gaining an additional, sinless, human nature. This is another much-written-about subject,[95] but as Catholic philosopher Peter Kreeft says: "The idea that Jesus is only one Person *and* is two Persons would be a logical contradiction. And the idea that Jesus has only one nature *and* has two natures would be a logical contradiction. But the idea that Jesus is only one Person but has two natures is not a logical contradiction."[96]

Douglas: I'm wondering what stops the three persons of the Trinity being identical to each other and so being one and the same thing?

Astrid (using her tablet): Theologians have traditionally held that each person of the Trinity exists in a different eternal relationship to the others. Kreeft notes that the fifth-century Athanasian Creed "asserts that all three Persons of the Trinity are unmade and uncreated, but differentiates them in that the Father is sourceless, the Son begotten by the Father, and the Holy Spirit proceeds from the Father and the Son."[97]

Sophie: That's in-line with the fourth-century Nicene Creed,[98] which talked about "the only Son of God, eternally begotten of the Father" and "the Holy Spirit . . . who proceedes from the Father and the Son."[99]

Hiromi: But what sense can we make of this language of divine persons being "begotten" and "proceeding"? What distinctions are being described here, philosophically speaking?

Astrid: I guess most Christians are content to leave this as a mystery, but theologians and philosophers offer various models for thinking about how

---

95. See Moreland and Craig, *Philosophical Foundations for a Christian Worldview*; Morris, *Logic of God Incarnate*; Senor, "Incarnation and the Trinity"; Swinburne, *Was Jesus God?*

96. Kreeft, *Because God Is Real*, 86.

97. Kreeft, *Because God Is Real*, 115.

98. See the Nicene Creed at http://anglicansonline.org/basics/nicene.html; Hebblethwaite, *Essence of Christianity*; Polkinghorne, *Science & Christian Belief*.

99. See the Nicene Creed at http://anglicansonline.org/basics/nicene.html.

God is a Trinity.[100] For what it's worth, here's my take: In the first place, we might say that "God the Father" exists necessarily whilst necessarily causing the existence of "God the Son." That means the "Son" depends upon the "Father" whilst still existing necessarily.

Thomas: And "necessary" means "has to," right?

Sophie: Correct. Something has necessary existence if it can exist but can't not exist. Necessary things can't fail to exist. Necessary existence contrasts with contingent existence, where a thing can exist but can also not exist. This mug exists contingently. Since the mug exists, it obviously can exist. But equally obviously, the mug doesn't *have* to exist, as we'd soon see if I were to drop it on the floor from a sufficient height. It would quickly fail to exist. Philosophically minded monotheists have generally thought that *if* God exists, *then* God has necessary existence.

Astrid's also using the philosophical distinction between existing in dependence upon something else and existing without depending upon something else, between "dependent" and "independent" existence.

Astrid: That's right. So, having said that "God the Father" exists necessarily whilst necessarily causing the existence of "God the Son," we might add that "God the Holy Spirit" is necessarily caused by "the Father *and* the Son." So, "God the Father" has necessary and independent existence. The "Son" has necessary existence whilst depending upon the "Father." And the "Spirit" has necessary existence whilst depending upon both "the Father and the Son." Naturally, "the Trinity" shares in the necessary and independent existence of the "Father." And that's one way to unpack what it means to say that "the Father is sourceless, the Son begotten by the Father, and the Holy Spirit proceeds from the Father and the Son."[101]

Hiromi: So, belief in the Trinity is *not* the same as belief in a group or family of polytheistic "gods."

---

100. See Williams, "Trinity"; Williams, "Sermon: Revelation 1:1–8 (On Revealing the Trinity)"; Copan, "Is the Trinity a Logical Blunder?"; Craig, "Formulation and Defence of the Doctrine of the Trinity"; Hasker, "Deception and Trinity: A Rejoinder to Tuggy"; Williams, "Understanding the Trinity"; Crisp, *Reader in Contemporary Philosophical Theology*; Davis, *Christian Philosophical Theology*; Hebblethwaite, *Philosophical Theology and Christian Doctrine*; Moreland and Craig, *Philosophical Foundations for a Christian Worldview*; Morris, *Our Idea of God*; Owen, *Christian Theism*; Senor, "Incarnation and the Trinity"; Swinburne, *Christian God*.

101. Kreeft, *Because God Is Real*, 115.

Astrid: It's not. The trinitarian creator God of Christian monotheism is *very* different to the wholly immanent, contingent, fallible deities of polytheistic worldviews. Unlike polytheistic "gods," the necessarily existent divine members of the Trinity are necessarily unified in mutual love and bound together by eternal relationships that mean none of them can exist or function apart from, let alone against, the others.

Douglas: The doctrine of the Trinity makes Christianity distinct from other forms of monotheism, like Islam.[102]

Astrid: Definitely, although there's a complex continuity with the Old Testament's portrait of God.[103] By encompassing love of self, love of another, and shared love of another, only an explicitly trinitarian concept of God's nature describes a God that encompasses all three qualitatively distinct forms of love.[104] I think that makes the Christian concept of God the greatest possible concept of God.[105]

Hiromi: I think the idea of God as Trinity connects with a question that interests me. I want to know if love is just a meaningless, subjective by-product of nature, or if love is rooted in the depths of objective reality.

Astrid: H. P. Owen wrote that the doctrine of the Trinity "*reconciles the paradoxical affirmations that God is self-sufficient and that he is love.*"[106] It tells us that loving relationships *are* at the heart of reality, because "God is not a solitary monarch but a tripersonal mystery of love."[107] It says something important about what it means to claim that humanity is made "in the image of"[108] a God who "is love,"[109] for loving relationship with God and each-another.

Douglas: That sounds nice; but as Dawkins proclaims: "The universe we observe has precisely the properties we should expect if there is, at bottom,

102. See Williams, "Islam"; Craig, "Who Is the Real Jesus"; "Concept of God in Islam and Christianity"; Beverley and Evans, *Getting Jesus Right*; Licona, *Paul Meets Muhammad*; Qureshi, *No God But One*.

103. See Sanders, "What Does the Old Testament Say about the Trinity?"

104. See Williams, "Understanding the Trinity."

105. See Craig, "Concept of God in Islam and Christianity."

106. Owen, *Christian Theism*, 65. See Williams, "Understanding the Trinity."

107. Pinnock and Brow, *Unbounded Love*, 49.

108. Gen 1:27.

109. 1 John 4:8, 16.

no design, no purpose, no evil, and no good, nothing but blind pitiless in-difference. . . . DNA neither knows nor cares. DNA just is. And we dance to its music."[110]

Hiromi: And yet I *observe* that love really *seems* to be something that *ought* to shape the dance of our lives.

Thomas: That's beautiful.

Sophie: Christians down the ages have offered various analogies for the Trinity. Do you find any of these analogies illuminating, Astrid?

Astrid was staring out the window. She didn't seem to be looking at anything in particular.

Sophie: Astrid?

Astrid: Mm? Sorry. What was that?

Sophie: I was asking if you thought there were any useful analogies for the Trinity?

Astrid: There's a musical analogy I find quite helpful.[111]

Hiromi: A musical analogy? That sounds interesting.

Douglas: Pun intended?

Astrid: As you know, a musical chord is composed of three different notes sounding at the same time. For example, the chord of C major is the notes C (the "root" of the chord), E (the third from the root), and G (the fifth from the root). Each note is "a sound," but all three notes played together make up a richer "sound." A chord is both three individual sounds and one communal sound. By analogy, God is three divine persons in one divine personal being; or one divine personal being essentially composed of three divine persons.

---

110. Dawkins, *River Out of Eden*, 133.

111. See Begbie, "Hearing God in C Major"; Begbie, *Beholding the Glory*. For a different analogy, see Reflexion, "Dr. William Lane Craig."

Sophie: Since an analogy isn't a description, every analogy falls short of the thing it helps us imagine. So, how do you think the chord analogy falls short?

Astrid: First, the notes of a chord aren't persons, divine or otherwise! Second, while each note in a chord can be played without the others, and none of them *have* to be played at all, in the Trinity none of the persons can exist without the other two also existing, and all three *have* to exist. Third, the chord of C major is one chord among many possible chords, whereas if God exists, he's the only God whose existence is possible.

Thomas: Okay, so what if the doctrine of the Trinity isn't incoherent? What I want to know is, why think it's true?

Astrid: Christians developed the doctrine of the Trinity to make sense of data that flowed from their acceptance of Jesus' claim to be the divine Son of God.[112] Later reflection showed that the doctrine follows from the idea that God must have the greatest possible essential nature, and that it resolves the paradox involved in saying God is essentially loving but doesn't need to create.

Hiromi: There is much in the Christian worldview I find attractive, and much I find puzzling, often at the same time. I think I have more questions now than when we began!

Sophie: That's good! Socrates said that "wonder is the feeling of a philosopher, and philosophy begins in wonder."[113] Thank you everyone for working hard to make this a good discussion. Especially you Astrid. We did rather lean on you, for obvious reasons, and will continue to do so. We'll meet again next week, to discuss chapter 2 of *Outgrowing God*, which looks at the historical basis of the claim that God is revealed in Jesus.

After some more social discussion, people began to leave. Hiromi zipped up her leather jacket and stepped out into the snow, carrying with her a warmth that had nothing to do with coffee.[114]

---

112. See Polkinghorne, *Science & Christian Belief*; Williams, *Understanding Jesus*.

113. Plato, *Theaetetus* 155d.

114. An extensive list of chapter-specific recommended resources can be found on this book's webpage at www.peterswilliams.com/publications/books/outgrowing-god/.

Second Meeting

Testing the New Testament

Seeing everyone settled in place, Hiromi placed a gift-wrapped box on the table and announced that she'd brought Japanese sweets for everyone to enjoy. She urged Professor Minerva to open the package, which she did by pulling at the sparkly ribbon bow and folding out the box-flaps. Inside were little dome-shaped confections Hiromi called "Daifuku Mochi."[1] They'd clearly been homemade. Hiromi recommend eating small pieces and chewing well, because "people sometimes choke on them." Everyone thanked Hiromi, who protested that it was nothing. Sophie prompted Thomas to get things under way, once he'd nibbled some mochi . . .

Thomas (using his tablet): Tasty! So, in chapter 2, Dawkins examines the texts of the "New Testament." He indicates that evidence for the historical Jesus is weak, but admits: "The balance of probability, according to most but not all scholars, suggests that Jesus did exist."[2] However, Dawkins argues that since little reliable evidence about Jesus is available, we don't know much about him.

According to Dawkins, the earliest New Testament writings are letters by Paul. They say "a lot about the religious meaning of Jesus, especially his death and resurrection."[3] But there's "almost nothing" about Jesus in these letters "that even claims to be history."[4] Dawkins says this near silence "wor-

---

1. See two recipes for making mochi here: www.japanesecooking101.com/daifuku-mochi-recipe/; https://youtu.be/aZ8BusSvxWw.

2. Dawkins, *Outgrowing God*, 21.

3. Dawkins, *Outgrowing God*, 18.

4. Dawkins, *Outgrowing God*, 18.

ries historians"[5] and "makes them wonder."[6] But he allows that maybe "Paul thought his readers already knew the story of Jesus' life."[7] Alternatively: "it's possible Paul didn't know it himself: remember, the gospels were not yet written. Or maybe he didn't think it was even important."[8] Dawkins talks about "the story"[9] of Jesus' life and not *the history* of Jesus' life, because he doesn't think the Gospels contain much history.

Dawkins discusses the only early historians who mention Jesus: the Jewish historian Josephus and the Roman historian Tacitus. Josephus says interesting things about Jesus, but "Many historians suspect this passage is a forgery, stuck in later by a Christian writer."[10] Dawkins notes that the statement in Josephus about Jesus being "the Messiah" sounds "very like a later Christian forgery," and that this is "certainly what most scholars now believe."[11]

Turning to the four New Testament "Gospels," Dawkins says "nobody has the faintest idea" who wrote them, because "we have no convincing evidence in any of the four cases. Later Christians simply stuck a name on the top of each gospel for convenience."[12] According to Dawkins: "No serious scholar today thinks the gospels were written by eye-witnesses."[13]

Dawkins highlights the "long gap between Jesus' death and the Gospels being written," which "gives us one reason to doubt that they are a reliable guide."[14] Evidently, serious scholars "agree that Mark, the oldest of the four gospels, was written about 35 or 40 years after the death of Jesus."[15] Dawkins says this means the contents of Mark, and even more so the other Gospels, can't be trusted, because they suffered from decades "of word-of-mouth retelling. Chinese-Whispery distortion and exaggeration before those texts were finally written down."[16] He concludes: "even Mark wasn't written early enough to be potentially reliable history."[17]

---

5. Dawkins, *Outgrowing God*, 19.

6. Dawkins, *Outgrowing God*, 19.

7. Dawkins, *Outgrowing God*, 18.

8. Dawkins, *Outgrowing God*, 18.

9. Dawkins, *Outgrowing God*, 18.

10. Dawkins, *Outgrowing God*, 20.

11. Dawkins, *Outgrowing God*, 20.

12. Dawkins, *Outgrowing God*, 21.

13. Dawkins, *Outgrowing God*, 22.

14. Dawkins, *Outgrowing God*, 28.

15. Dawkins, *Outgrowing God*, 22.

16. Dawkins, *Outgrowing God*, 22.

17. Dawkins, *Outgrowing God*, 27.

In this context, Dawkins discusses "how an untrue story spreads be-cause it's entertaining and fits with people's expectations or prejudices,"[18] and suggests this "might have been true of stories of Jesus' miracles or his resurrection."[19] Indeed: "Early recruits to the young religion of Christian-ity might have been especially eager to pass on stories and rumours about Jesus, without checking them for truth."[20]

Dawkins stresses that the "canon," the books accepted as the official contents of the New Testament, "wasn't finally settled until centuries after Paul's death,"[21] and that while the four Gospels "are the only gospels in the official canon . . . plenty of other gospels of Jesus had been written around the same time."[22] The New Testament Gospels "were only four out of a large number of gospels doing the rounds at the time of the Council of Nicea," in AD 325. According to Dawkins: "Any of them could have made it into the canon, but for various reasons none of them made it."[23] Indeed, he says: "it was little more than chance which books got included in the canon."[24] Again, he says there were "about fifty" other gospels that were "mostly written down in the first couple of centuries AD" and "might have been included in the canon."[25]

Of the idea that Jesus fulfilled Old Testament prophecies, Dawkins says: "You get the feeling that Matthew was quite capable of inventing an incident and writing it into his gospel, simply in order to make a prophecy come true."[26] He also argues that "A simple translation error"[27] between the Hebrew text of Isaiah and its Greek translation led Matthew to invent the story of the virgin birth. Talking of which, Dawkins points to contradictions between the birth narratives in the Gospels, between those narratives and the Gospel of John's assumption "that Jesus was born in Nazareth,"[28] and between the birth narratives and secular history.

Dawkins draws on an argument against belief in miracles made by an eighteenth-century philosopher called David Hume. He boils Hume's

18. Dawkins, *Outgrowing God*, 23.

19. Dawkins, *Outgrowing God*, 25.

20. Dawkins, *Outgrowing God*, 25.

21. Dawkins, *Outgrowing God*, 25.

22. Dawkins, *Outgrowing God*, 26.

23. Dawkins, *Outgrowing God*, 26.

24. Dawkins, *Outgrowing God*, 28.

25. Dawkins, *Outgrowing God*, 33.

26. Dawkins, *Outgrowing God*, 29.

27. Dawkins, *Outgrowing God*, 30.

28. Dawkins, *Outgrowing God*, 30.

argument down to a rule of explanation that says: "When you have a choice of two possibilities, always choose the less miraculous."[29] In other words, a non-miraculous explanation is always better than a miraculous explanation.

Dawkins notes that Christians don't believe "the fantastic miracles in the infancy Gospel of Thomas really happened,"[30] and challenges them to explain "why not? What's so special about the particular four gospels lucky enough to be chosen for the canon by a bunch of bishops and theologians in Nicea in AD 325? Why the double standard?"[31]

The most important miracle claim in the New Testament is Jesus' resurrection from the dead. But other resurrections are reported by the Gospels, including Matthew's report that "Only three days before Jesus did it, lots of other people bust out of their graves and walked the streets of Jerusalem. Do Christians really believe that? If not, why not? There's as much reason . . . to believe it as there's to believe in Jesus's own resurrection. How do believers decide which far-fetched tales to believe and which to ignore?"[32]

Dawkins concludes that while Jesus "probably existed . . . the claims that his mother was a virgin, and that he rose from the grave, are very extraordinary. . . . So the evidence had better be good. And it isn't."[33]

Sophie: Thank you for that detailed summary.

Thomas picked up his needles and began adding to his current knitting project.

Douglas: That's "game over" for *Christian* theism, isn't it?! There's hardly any evidence for Jesus outside the Bible and little inside it. The four Gospels are lies and legends written long after Jesus died, and were randomly selected from a bunch of other gospels that Christians don't take seriously because they didn't get a stamp of approval from some fourth-century bishops. There's no good historical evidence that Jesus' mother was a virgin, or that he rose from the dead. But even if there were, evidence should never convince us a miracle has happened, because any non-miraculous explanation of the evidence would be more plausible *by definition*.

---

29. Dawkins, *Outgrowing God*, 40.
30. Dawkins, *Outgrowing God*, 38.
31. Dawkins, *Outgrowing God*, 38.
32. Dawkins, *Outgrowing God*, 38.
33. Dawkins, *Outgrowing God*, 39.

Astrid: Honestly, the only thing I thought was "over" as I read chapter 2 was any hope Dawkins might have bothered to learn something about ancient history or modern New Testament studies.

Sophie: What do you think, Hiromi?

Hiromi: Dawkins says claiming Jesus rose from the dead is "very extraordinary indeed. So the evidence had better be good. And it isn't."[34] But he doesn't *really* care about evidence.

Thomas: What makes you say that?! Remember what Dawkins said on TV about wanting to rid the world of anything that's not evidence-based.[35]

Hiromi: Yes, but Dawkins also says that, faced with testimony for a miracle, even if you'd say "it would be a miracle if he was lying or otherwise mistaken,"[36] you would "surely admit" that the occurrence of the miracle in question would be "even more miraculous."[37] When I read that, I asked myself: "*Why* must I 'surely admit' this?" Dawkins doesn't argue from a detailed comparison of explanations in this or that *particular case*. Instead, he *begs the question* against miraculous explanations *in general*.

Thomas: How come?

Hiromi: Because to say, *apart from investigating the evidence*, that non-miraculous explanations are always better than are miraculous explanations amounts to assuming naturalism is true.

Thomas: Isn't Dawkins just saying that, when choosing between alternative explanations for something, we should "always choose the less miraculous."[38] Isn't that sensible?

Astrid (using her tablet): It sounds plausible, but its ambiguous. In context, "less miraculous" clearly means *non-miraculous*. When Dawkins says "it would be a miracle if he was lying or otherwise mistaken"[39] he obvi-

---

34. Dawkins, *Outgrowing God*, 39.

35. Channel 4 News, "Richard Dawkins on Scientific Truth," 1:00–1:02.

36. Dawkins, *Outgrowing God*, 40.

37. Dawkins, *Outgrowing God*, 40.

38. Dawkins, *Outgrowing God*, 40.

39. Dawkins, *Outgrowing God*, 40.

ously means "miracle" in the *non-supernatural sense* of "a really unlikely but fortunate natural event." He'd evidently reject the idea of explaining anything in terms of a genuinely *miraculous* lie, or a genuinely *miraculous* observational mistake! In *The Magic of Reality*, he says: "Suppose something happens that we don't understand, and we can't see how it could be fraud or trickery or lies: would it ever be right to conclude that it must be supernatural? No!"[40]

Hiromi: And that makes his naturalistic worldview *immune to testing in the light of evidence*! Given the importance he places on forming beliefs according to evidence, that's inconsistent of him.

Sophie: Philosophers call that sort of failure of consistency a *double-standard*.

Douglas: I agree that Dawkins doesn't do himself any favors by arguing against miracles *on philosophical grounds* even though he says elsewhere that knowledge "always comes back to our senses, one way or another."[41] Nor does he do himself any favors by relying upon Hume's notorious argument against belief in miracles.

Thomas: Why "notorious"? The neo-atheist writer Christopher Hitchens said Hume "wrote the last word on the subject"[42] of miracles.

Douglas (using his phone): That just shows how little Hitchens knew about philosophy. It's generally agreed by philosophers today that Hume overstated his case against miracles.[43] As neo-atheist Jerry A. Coyne admits: "Hume took it too far. No amount of evidence, it seems, could ever override his conviction that miracles were really the result of fraud, ignorance, or misrepresentation. Yet perhaps there are some events . . . when a [miracle] is more likely than human error or deception."[44]

Thomas: But isn't Dawkins right when he quotes Carl Sagan's rule about "extraordinary claims" requiring "extraordinary evidence"?[45]

40. Dawkins, *Magic of Reality*, 262–63.
41. Dawkins, *Magic of Reality*, 16, 19.
42. Hitchens, *God Is Not Great*, 141.
43. See Williams, *Getting at Jesus*, 29–53.
44. Coyne, *Faith versus Fact*, 124.
45. Dawkins, *Outgrowing God*, 39.

Hiromi: I guess you can say any miracle claim is "extraordinary." But what does it mean for evidence to be "extraordinary"? What standard or standards must an explanation meet in order to qualify as "extraordinary" evidence that makes it reasonable to believe in a miracle?

Thomas: I don't know.

Hiromi: Exactly! At the end of the chapter Dawkins drops the concept of "extraordinary" evidence and just says that the evidence for any miracle claim had better be "good."[46] But he fails to define his terms in either case, leaving readers in the dark.

Astrid: Assuming Sagan's rule isn't just another way of asserting a miracle can *never* be the best explanation of anything, it looks like a way of *admitting* "the possibility that a theistic explanation may account *better* for . . . some putatively miraculous phenomena,"[47] whilst *avoiding* any evidence-based discussion of specific cases. Dawkins is basically saying: "I'll believe in a miracle if there's extraordinary evidence for it, but although I'm not going to tell you what would qualify evidence as being extraordinary, whatever evidence you give me isn't going to count. Therefore, I don't need to examine the evidence and I win."[48]

Hiromi: Yes, he's saying: "I am open-minded. Please do not confuse me with evidence."

Thomas: Maybe; but can you provide an alternative to Sagan's rule?

Astrid: Sure! Whether or not an event that's most plausibly viewed as miraculous occurred "should be judged on the customary criteria by which we assess [evidence and explanations], not on the basis of whether it fits a favoured worldview."[49]

Douglas: But what are these criteria?

---

46. Dawkins, *Outgrowing God*, 39.
47. Huston, *Reported Miracles*, 166.
48. Loosely adapted from Birdieupon, "Probability & Resurrection 4."
49. Larmer, *Legitimacy of Miracles*, 130, 133.

Astrid: Well, first there are criteria for establishing the evidence that needs to be explained, and then there are criteria for choosing between hypotheses that aim to explain the evidence.

Douglas: That makes sense. Let's have the *evidential* criteria first.

Astrid: They include general rules of thumb like: Prefer earlier over later sources. Prefer eyewitness over second-hand sources. Prefer multiple and especially independent sources over single and non-independent sources. Look for "enemy attestation," which is corroboration from sources that would otherwise disagree with a given source. Value testimony that's embarrassing to the source sharing it. Value testimony that was open to contradiction by public memory. Check for historical verisimilitude.

Thomas: Veri-what-itude?

Sophie: It means being true to life. Historians want to know if the contents of a document "match with what we know of the place, people and period described in the document?"[50] So, historians who investigate gospels look for "linguistic and cultural features that fit what we know of first-century Palestine."[51]

Hiromi: Such as?

Astrid (using her tablet): When it comes to the canonical Gospels, there are *many* signs of historical verisimilitude. The Gospels exhibit "linguistic verisimilitude" in their retention of various Aramaic words and phrases, as well as "geographic and topological verisimilitude, cultural and archaeological verisimilitude, and religious, economic and social verisimilitude."[52]

Hiromi: Interesting.

Astrid (using her tablet): The more criteria of authenticity someone's testimony passes, the more seriously we should take it. William Lane Craig explains that "these 'criteria' . . . focus on a particular saying or event and give evidence for thinking that specific element of Jesus' life to be historical,

---

50. Beverley and Evans, *Getting Jesus Right*, 22.
51. Neufeld, *Recovering Jesus*, 44.
52. Beverley and Evans, *Getting Jesus Right*, 23.

regardless of the general reliability of the document in which the particular saying or event is reported."[53]

By the way, *this* is why I don't believe "the fantastic miracles in the infancy Gospel of Thomas really happened."[54] It's not just that they didn't make it into the New Testament canon, but that they don't fare well when assessed by the standard evidential criteria. Indeed, it was the failure of these other "gospels" to meet some of these evidential rules that explains why they weren't accepted into the canon!

Douglas: What about the *explanatory* criteria?

Astrid: The strength of an explanation depends on several factors, including: simplicity, explanatory scope (whether an explanation covers the relevant evidence), explanatory power (whether it raises the probability of the evidence to be explained), explanatory plausibility (how far our background knowledge implies the explanation), degree of explanatory ad hoc-ness (the fewer un-evidenced assumptions, the better), and degree of explanatory disconfirmation (avoiding conflict with our background knowledge).[55]

Douglas: Seems reasonable. At least, it's better than just saying we need "extraordinary" evidence!

Sophie: Since our discussion has drifted from philosophical matters to historical matters, let's ask what we make of Dawkins's case against the historical credentials of the New Testament. Thomas, I wonder if your studies in classical literature can throw any light on his criticisms?

Thomas: Well, there *were* a few places where I thought his skepticism went too far.

Sophie: Such as?

Thomas: Dawkins makes a lot of the gap between Jesus' death, in the early 30s of the first century, and the dates of the canonical Gospels. He says Mark is "the oldest" and that it was written "about 35 or 40 years after the

---

53. Craig, *Reasonable Faith*, 298.

54. Dawkins, *Outgrowing God*, 38.

55. See Meyer, "Return of the God Hypothesis."

death of Jesus."[56] He says this means the contents of Mark and the other Gospels can't be trusted.

Hiromi: Why not? Dawkins expects us to believe his own account of becoming an atheist sixty-something years ago![57] I trust the stories my great-grandmother used to tell me about being a teenager in the 1950s!

Thomas (using his tablet): Ancient historian John Dickson says: "a time gap of 20–70 years between an ancient figure and numerous biographical writings about him or her is pretty good."[58] He points out that "the preeminent source for our knowledge of [the Roman Emperor] Tiberius is the account of . . . Cornelius Tacitus, whose *Annals* provide a wealth of information about several emperors of this period. Tacitus wrote his *Annuls* around AD 115–118. That is about 80 years after Tiberius' death [in AD 37]."[59] That means: "The latest source used to study Jesus (John's Gospel) was written 20 years earlier than Tacitus' account of the man who ruled the world at the same time as Jesus."[60] Again: "Roman historians use Livy to reconstruct the history of the Roman Republic several centuries before his lifetime. Classical historians use Plutarch (second century AD) for the history of Themistocles (fifth century BC), and all historians of Alexander the Great (fourth century BC) acknowledge as their most accurate source Arrian's *Anabasis* (second century AD)."[61] So, if we followed Dawkins in considering 35–40 years too long a gap for the reliable transmission of information, we'd basically have to close the ancient history department!

Hiromi: Your professors wouldn't like that! Still, Dawkins says all the stories in the Gospels suffered from decades "of word-of-mouth retelling. Chinese-Whispery distortion and exaggeration before those texts were finally written down."[62]

Astrid: Why does he think that?

---

56. Dawkins, *Outgrowing God*, 22.

57. I owe this point to a tweet by Rebecca McLaughlin (@RebeccMcLaugh), posted on November 20, 2019.

58. Dickson, *Is Jesus History?*, 77.

59. Dickson, *Is Jesus History?*, 77.

60. Dickson, *Is Jesus History?*, 77.

61. Yamauchi, "Current State of Old Testament Historiography," 26.

62. Dawkins, *Outgrowing God*, 22.

Thomas: He doesn't say; and it goes against what we know about how memorization worked in first-century Jewish and Greco-Roman oral culture.

Douglas: What do you mean?

Thomas: People in these cultures had more highly developed memories than most people do today. Besides, the game of one-time-only, *serial* "whispers," which is *designed to corrupt information*, is a poor analogy for the *parallel* process of repeatedly recounting oral information in the ancient world, which was *designed to preserve information*.[63]

Astrid (using her tablet): Dawkins gives no evidence to think the chain of testimony behind the Gospels was like a game of whispers. Theologian John Polkinghorne explains that "First-century Palestine was a society in which oral transmission had an accuracy and importance which it is hard for us to realize today."[64] Theologian James D. G. Dunn comments that the oral history in the Gospels isn't "casual recall across several decades or something once heard and little thought about since [but] a deliberate attempt to implant firmly and rootedly matters of importance in the memory of individuals motivated to listen, to absorb and to live accordingly."[65]

Thomas: Specialists in oral history argue that oral cultures typically have the ability to reliably transmit historical material for long periods of time, even centuries![66] Oral cultures are invested in preserving information that shapes their cultural identity. The people entrusted with the task of retelling the oral traditions of a community are allowed *some* flexibility in how they express the traditional material in any given performance, but the community as a whole typically ensures that each performance retains the substance of the tradition they know. Repeatedly retold stories exhibit this sort of core stability.

Hiromi: I can repeat the stories my great-grandmother told me. I wouldn't use exactly the same words every time. But I would repeat the same key points and use some of the same phrases.

---

63. See Godnewevidence, "Jesus, the Gospels and the Telephone Game"; Craig, "Is the Oral Tradition Comparable."

64. Polkinghorne, *Way the World Is*, 42.

65. Dunn, "Social Memory and the Oral Jesus Tradition," 186.

66. See Eddy and Boyd, *Jesus Legend*, 92, 395.

Thomas: Right. Anyone who knows "Goldilocks and the Three Bears" or "Little Red Riding Hood" knows the stock phrases that should be included. And if you didn't include them, your audience would complain. Goldilocks has to say "Just right!"; the wolf has say "All the better for eating you!" and so on.

Astrid (using her tablet): I think Dawkins assumes his whispers theory to give plausibility to the suggestion that "Matthew was quite capable of inventing an incident and writing it into his gospel."[67] If I may, I've got some relevant quotes.

Sophie: By all means.

Astrid (using her tablet): On the one hand, philosopher Paul Copan observes that:

> Given (1) the importance of memorization and oral tradition in first-century Palestine, (2) the practice of (occasionally) writing down and preserving the teachings of rabbis by their disciples, (3) the fact that the vast majority of Jesus' teaching was in poetic (and easily memorable) form, (4) the importance and revered status of religious traditions in Palestine, and (5) the presence of apostolic authority in Jerusalem to ensure the accurate transmission of tradition . . . we have good reason to believe that the material in the Gospels was carefully and correctly set down.[68]

On the other hand, philosopher Stephen T. Davis points out that if the early church had felt free to invent things about Jesus:

> it is highly probable that sayings would have been placed in the mouth of Jesus that were relevant to the central concerns and controversies of the church in the second half of the first century. But notice that there are no sayings of Jesus in the canonical gospels that are directly relevant to such burning issues in the late-first-century church as . . . the proper practice of the Lord's supper, how churches ought to be governed, etc.[69]

Davis also notes that the Gospels "preserved and passed on 'difficult' sayings of Jesus [such as] sayings about the human failings of some of the

---

67. Dawkins, *Outgrowing God*, 29.
68. Copan, *True for You, But Not for Me*, 103.
69. Davis, "Should We Believe the Jesus Seminar?," 12.

church's greatest leaders."[70] For example, all four Gospels report Peter's threefold denial of Jesus. But people who don't feel free to omit things that embarrass their cause, or to put words in Jesus' mouth that would support it, probably wouldn't feel free to invent events to make prophecy come true. Again, the disciple's willingness to be persecuted and even martyred for their faith in Jesus shows a sincerity and a concern for truth at odds with the suggestion that they invented incidents to write in the Gospels.

Thomas: I don't know if I buy all that; but I can agree that the gap between Jesus and the Gospels doesn't suggest the Gospels are unreliable.

Hiromi: Was there anything else you disagreed with, Thomas?

Thomas (using his tablet): I got the impression Dawkins wants to make readers doubtful about the existence of Jesus.[71] He downplays the scholarly consensus on this, but as Dickson writes: "The claim that Jesus of Nazareth did not even exist has virtually no currency in contemporary scholarship."[72] The standard, secular compendiums of ancient history: "all judge the core of the story—that a popular Galilean teacher and reputed healer named Jesus was crucified in Jerusalem by order of Pontius Pilate—to be beyond reasonable doubt."[73]

Astrid: Hang on, is Dickson an Australian?

Thomas: Yeah, he's a professor at Sydney University.

Astrid: He spoke at a conference I attended at Grimstad Bible School![74] I remember him telling us that he'd issued a public challenge, that if anyone could find a full professor of ancient history, or classics, or New Testament in any real university who argues that Jesus never existed, he'd eat a page of his Bible! He said he'd put it on some toast with vegemite!

Douglas: I'll bite. Has Dickson had to swallow his words yet?

---

70. Davis, "Should We Believe the Jesus Seminar?," 12.

71. See Williams, "Existence of Jesus"; Habermas, "Did Jesus Exist?"; Hannam, "Historical Introduction to the Christ Myth"; Wallace, "Is There Any Evidence for Jesus Outside the Bible?"; Maier, "Did Jesus Really Exist?"

72. Dickson, *Is Jesus History?*, 39.

73. Dickson, *Is Jesus History?*, 39.

74. See https://bibelskolen.no and https://veritaskonferansen.no/#veritashome.

Astrid (using her tablet): Nope. As agnostic New Testament scholar Bart Erhman says: "I don't think there's any serious historian who doubts the existence of Jesus."[75] He calls Jesus' crucifixion "One of the most certain facts of history."[76] Atheist New Testament scholar Gerd Lüdemann says: "Jesus' death as a consequence of crucifixion is indisputable."[77]

Hiromi: If your death is "indisputable," you must have lived!

Astrid: Dawkins says we know Caesar and William the Conqueror existed "because archaeologists have found tell-tale relics,"[78] but he's obviously un-aware we have a first-century limestone burial box from Jerusalem, dating to the 60s AD, bearing the inscription: "James, son of Joseph, brother of Jesus."

Thomas: Really?

Douglas: I read that was a fake. Wasn't the antiquities dealer in whose col-lection the box was discovered prosecuted for forgery?

Astrid (using her tablet): He was, but the case against him collapsed. Plus, more recent peer-reviewed scientific analysis has supported the authentic-ity of the inscription.[79] To quote historian Paul L. Maier: "there is strong (though not absolutely conclusive) evidence that, yes, the ossuary and its inscription are not only authentic, but that the inscribed names are the New Testament personalities."[80] Here's a photo:[81]

---

75. MrShazoolo, "Atheist Refuted by Agnostic Historian," 0:27–0:31.

76. Ehrman, quoted by Licona, *Resurrection of Jesus*, 600.

77. Lüdemann, *Resurrection of Christ*, 50.

78. Dawkins, *Outgrowing God*, 16.

79. See Rosenfeld et al., "Aucenticity of the James Ossuary."

80. Maier, "James Ossuary." See also Witherington, "James Ossuary"; Baxster, "James Ossuary"; House, "James Ossuary."

81. See the "JamesOssuary-1" file on Wikimedia Commons.

Hiromi (using her tablet): Dawkins says that while the letters of Paul are the earliest writings in the New Testament: "Paul says hardly anything about Jesus's life. There's lots about the religious meaning of Jesus, especially his death and resurrection. But almost nothing that even claims to be history."[82]

Astrid: That's not true.

Thomas: Why do you say that?

Astrid: First of all, there's good reason to think that the letter of James is the earliest text in the New Testament. It doesn't say much about Jesus, but it confirms his existence and shows that first-generation Jewish converts to Christianity considered Jesus to be Divine with a capital "D."[83]

Hiromi: Interesting.

Astrid (using her tablet): Second, Paul affirms the *historical* reality of Jesus' death and resurrection! His first letter to Christians in Corinth, about 54

82. Dawkins, *Outgrowing God*, 18.
83. See Williams, "Epistle of James vs. Evolutionary Christology."

AD, contains the earliest testimony we have about these events. Paul refers to testimony he "received" as a formal oral tradition before he'd personally "delivered" it to the Corinthians around AD 51. This fixed tradition, or "creed," mentions Jesus' death and burial before listing witnesses who met the risen Jesus. Scholars think this creed dates to within a few years or even months of the crucifixion. As Jake O'Connell writes: "the pre-Pauline material of 1 Corinthians 15:3–8, which surely dates to within years of the resurrection, and is nearly universally regarded as summarizing extremely early material, ensures that the appearances enumerated there cannot be legendary."[84]

Thomas: Is that what *Christian* scholars think?

Astrid (using her tablet): Not *only* Christians. According to Lüdemann: "the elements in the tradition are to be dated . . . not later than three years after the death of Jesus."[85] Atheist New Testament scholar James Crossley concludes that the 1 Corinthians 15 creed preserves "reliable reports"[86] from "eyewitnesses"[87] that "must be taken very seriously"[88] and provides "good evidence that the first Christians did not invent the resurrection from scratch."[89]

Hiromi: What does Paul say?

Sophie: Paul writes:

> For I delivered to you as of first importance what I also received, that
> Christ died for our sins
> in accordance with the scriptures
> and that he was buried
> and that he was raised on the third day
> in accordance with the scriptures
> and that he appeared to Cephas
> then to the Twelve
> then he appeared to more than five hundred brethren at one time
> (most of whom are still alive, though some have fallen asleep)
> then he appeared to James
> then to all the apostles.

84. O'Connell, "Jesus' Resurrection and Collective Hallucinations," 75.
85. Lüdemann quoted by Habermas, "Tracing Jesus' Resurrection," 212.
86. Crossley, *Date of Mark's Gospel*, 140.
87. Crossley, "Against the Historical Plausibility of the Empty Tomb Story," 171–86.
88. Crossley, "Against the Historical Plausibility of the Empty Tomb Story."
89. Crossley, *Date of Mark's Gospel*, 140.

Last of all, as to one untimely born, he appeared also to me.[90]

Astrid: New Testament scholars universally recognize the material from "Christ died" until "the Twelve" as belonging to the tradition Paul received and passed on. Some also include the phrases "then he appeared to more than five hundred brethren at one time," "then he appeared to James," and "then to all the apostles." Everyone agrees the lines about some of the five hundred still being alive, and about Paul's own eyewitness experience, are Paul's own comments.

Hiromi: That's amazing!

Astrid: I also want to note, contrary to Dawkins, that Paul's letters do contain biographical information about Jesus.

Douglas: Such as?

Astrid (using her tablet): Paul knew that Jesus had brothers (1 Cor 9:5), including James (Gal 1:19); that Jesus was poor (2 Cor 8:9); and that he was a humble man, full of love and compassion (Phil 1:8; 2:6–11). He knew he'd had a ministry among the Jews (Rom 15:8) and that he'd had twelve key disciples (1 Cor 15:5), including Cephas (Peter) and John (Gal 1:19; 2:9).

Paul distinguishes between Jesus' teachings and his own teachings;[91] but how could he do that without knowing what Jesus taught? Paul claims Christ as his authority when teaching Christians about divorce (1 Cor 7:11) and supporting preachers (1 Cor 9:14). Paul knew that Jesus taught about accepting all foods as ritually clean (Rom 14:14), blessing persecutors and not repaying evil with evil (Rom 12:14), and he may have been drawing upon Jesus' teaching when he says taxes should be paid (Rom 13:7), and when he writes about loving one's neighbor (Gal 5:14). Indeed, Paul seems to refer to Jesus' Sermon on the Mount several times in his letter to the Romans.[92]

Paul goes into detail about Jesus' last supper (1 Cor 11:23–25), his betrayal at night (1 Cor 11:23), and his death by crucifixion (1 Cor 2:2). He knew that having been buried (1 Cor 15:4), Jesus was resurrected "on the third day" (1 Cor 15:5; Rom 4:24; Gal 1:1), appearing to Cephas, James, the

90. 1 Cor 15:3–8 (RSV); my brackets and pagination.

91. See 1 Cor 11:1; 4:10–12; and 1 Thess 1:6.

92. See: Rom 12:14, 17; 14:13.

twelve, all the apostles, and to more than five hundred people at once (1 Cor 15:5–7). And Paul writes all this within two decades of the crucifixion.[93]

Douglas: Where does Paul get his information from?

Astrid: Remember, Paul writes as an eyewitness of the resurrection. And he was authorized by the Jerusalem-based disciples to spread the "good news" or "gospel" about the Jesus they'd known out into the gentile world. Paul met with Peter and James in Jerusalem.

Hiromi: Does Dawkins get anything else wrong?

Astrid: We don't have time to go into everything he gets wrong!

Sophie: We noted last week that making an assessment of Dawkins's trustworthiness as an authority would take some time, because we'd have to check a representative sample of his claims.

Astrid: Well, it's rather misleading of him to say that only two early *historians* mention Jesus. That excludes the Gospel writers. And he neglects to mention that Jesus is referenced by early non-Christian writers who aren't historians.

Thomas: Such as?

Astrid: In a letter written around AD 70, a Syrian philosopher named Mara Bar-Serapion mentions the Jews murdering someone he calls "their wise king." That's probably a reference to Jesus. There are references to Jesus in the Jewish Talmud, and he's mentioned by the Greek writer Lucian of Samosata in a satire written about 165 AD.

Sophie: Lucian wrote:

> The Christians, you know, worship a man to this day—the distinguished personage who introduced their novel rites, and was crucified on that account . . . these misguided creatures start with the general conviction that they are immortal for all time, which explains the contempt of death and voluntary self-devotion which are so common among them; and then it was impressed on them by their original lawgiver that they are all brothers, from the

---

93. See Williams, "Paul and Jesus"; Barnett, *Paul: Missionary of Jesus*; Wenham, *Did St Paul Get Jesus Right?*; Wenham, *Paul and Jesus: The True Story*.

moment that they are converted, and deny the gods of Greece, and worship the crucified sage, and live after his laws.[94]

Hiromi: Anything else?

Astrid: Dawkins seems to suggest most historians think the passage in Josephus that he mentions is a forgery.[95]

Douglas (using his phone): Here's a translation of the Greek text of *Antiquities* 18:63:

> About this time lived Jesus, a wise man, if indeed one ought to call him a man. For he was the achiever of extraordinary deeds and was a teacher of those who accept the truth gladly. He won over many Jews and many of the Greeks. He was the Messiah. When he was indicted by the principal men among us and Pilate condemned him to be crucified, those who had come to love him originally did not cease to do so; for he appeared to them on the third day restored to life, as the prophets of the Deity had foretold these and countless other marvelous things about him, and the tribe of the Christians, so named after him, has not disappeared to this day.[96]

You've got to admit, that's suspiciously Christian.

Thomas: Josephus wouldn't say Jesus was the Messiah!

Astrid (using her tablet): True, and most historians do think the reference to Jesus being the messiah is a later addition. But most historians also think this reference comes in a reworking of a passage Josephus *did* write about Jesus. In fact, there's an Arabic translation of this passage, quoted by the tenth-century historian Agapius, that's probably closer to Josephus's original.

Sophie: The Arabic version says:

> At this time there was a wise man called Jesus, and his conduct was good, and he was known to be virtuous. Many people

94. Lucian, *Peregr.* 11–13, quoted by Wallace, "Is There Any Evidence for Jesus Outside the Bible?," para. 28.

95. Dawkins, *Outgrowing God*, 20. Williams, "Josephus on Jesus"; Goldberg, "Coincidences of the Emmaus Narrative of Luke"; Whealey, "Testimonium Flavianum in Syriac and Arabic."

96. Maier, "Josephus and Jesus," para. 5.

among the Jews and the other nations became his disciples. Pilate condemned him to be crucified and to die. But those who had become his disciples did not abandon his discipleship. They reported that he had appeared to them three days after his crucifixion and that he was alive. Accordingly, he was perhaps the Messiah, concerning whom the prophets have reported wonders. And the tribe of the Christians, so named after him, has not disappeared to this day.[97]

Astrid (using her tablet)**:** Cool. Moreover, what Dawkins fails to mention is that there's another passage in *Antiquities* that mentions Jesus! As historian Paul L. Maier explains:

> In *Antiquities* 18:63—in the middle of information on Pontius Pilate . . . Josephus provides the longest *secular* reference to Jesus in any first-century source. Later, when he reports events from the administration of the Roman governor Albinus . . . in *Antiquities* 20:200, he again mentions Jesus in connection with the death of Jesus' half-brother, James the Just of Jerusalem.[98]

Thomas: Okay; but what about the four Gospels?

Hiromi: Dawkins says: "No serious scholar today thinks the gospels were written by eye-witnesses."[99]

Astrid: Christians never said Mark or Luke were eyewitnesses. They claimed Mark got his information from Peter, for whom he'd worked as a secretary. The most they claimed for Luke was that he knew Paul. The Gospel traditionally associated with John indicates that most of its testimony about Jesus came from "the disciple Jesus loved," who sat next to him at the last supper. That this was John remains the best fit for the evidence.

Thomas: You mean to say that only the Gospel "according to Matthew" has been traditionally attributed wholly to an eyewitness?

Astrid: That's right. I think that shows how trustworthy the early church was in handling these texts.

---

97. Maier, "Josephus and Jesus," para. 7.
98. Maier, "Josephus and Jesus," para. 3.
99. Dawkins, *Outgrowing God*, 22.

Hiromi: Dawkins says: "Christians simply stuck a name on the top of each gospel for convenience."[100]

Astrid: If you're attributing a Gospel to anyone you like, you probably use an authoritative name.

Douglas: Your point being?

Astrid: Matthew was best-known as a tax collector who'd collaborated with the Romans. His name wouldn't endear a Gospel to Jewish readers. Neither Mark nor Luke, nor John's editors, lay claim to being eyewitnesses.

Hiromi: Editors?

Astrid: John 21:24 says: "This is the disciple who is bearing witness about these things, and who has written these things, and we know that his testimony is true." Many scholars think there's a distinction drawn here between the eyewitness John, who wrote most of the content of the Gospel according to John, and a group of his disciples, who edited the final version of this Gospel. It may be that John had written as early as the 50s AD, whilst John's Gospel as such wasn't published until the 90s.

Hiromi: Dawkins says that while the four Gospels "are the only gospels in the official canon . . . plenty of other gospels of Jesus had been written around the same time."[101] Is he right?

Astrid: We know of *later* "gospels," but they all date from the second century onwards, and neither the early church nor contemporary scholarship sees them as offering much of anything by way of historically reliable information about Jesus.[102]

Thomas: Anything else?

Astrid: You've covered the problem with Dawkins's skepticism based on the time gap between Jesus and the Gospels. Actually, there's a plausible case

---

100. Dawkins, *Outgrowing God*, 21.

101. Dawkins, *Outgrowing God*, 26.

102. See Evans, "What Should We Think About the Gospel of Judas?"; Green, *Books the Church Suppressed*; Wright, *Judas and the Gospel of Jesus*.

for dating Mark around about AD 49, Matthew and Luke in the early 50s and John in the 90s,[103] but not much hangs on this.

Douglas: Why not?

Astrid: Well, even on the first-century dates for the Gospels used by Dawkins, the fact that they're *first-century* dates make them *early* sources by the standards of ancient history. Moreover, the testimony written down in the Gospels and other New Testament texts probably traces back to eyewitnesses.

Douglas: But even you admit that Mark and Luke weren't eyewitnesses.

Astrid (using her tablet): That's right; but they probably got their information from eyewitnesses. Luke writes that "those who from the beginning were eyewitnesses and ministers of the word have delivered them to us."[104]

New Testament scholar Richard Bauckham argues that the presence of various named characters in the Synoptic Gospels is best explained by the hypothesis that they were the eyewitness tradents of the tradition to which their names are attached. He says that "many of these named characters were eyewitnesses who not only originated the traditions to which their names are attached but also continued to tell these stories as authoritative guarantors of their traditions."[105] He concludes that "in imagining how the traditions reached the Gospel writers, not oral tradition but eyewitness testimony should be our principle model."[106]

Hiromi: I can see there is a stronger case for the historical reliability of the Gospels than Dawkins admits. But I wonder about the evidence for the miracles, like the virgin birth and the resurrection. Are you familiar with Dawkins's points about the birth narratives in Matthew and Luke?

Astrid: I am, but Dawkins doesn't exactly leave readers any better informed. He just makes a bunch of accusations without argument.

Thomas: Such as?

---

103. See Williams, *Getting at Jesus*, chapter 2.
104. Luke 1:2.
105. Bauckham, *Jesus and the Eyewitnesses*, 39.
106. Bauckham, *Jesus and the Eyewitnesses*, 8.

Astrid (using her tablet): Well, take his claim that John's Gospel "assumes that Jesus was born in Nazareth."[107] John never says Jesus was born in Nazareth! In John 1:45 Philip tells Nathanael: "We have found him of whom Moses in the Law and also the prophets wrote, Jesus of Nazareth, the son of Joseph." Well, Jesus was legally Joseph's son, and Jesus and his family lived in Nazareth. Plus, it's obvious in light of what Philip says about the prophets having spoken about Jesus, that John 7:40–43 plays on the irony that while "the people" mistakenly think Jesus was born in Nazareth, *John and his readers know he was born in Bethlehem*: "some of the people said, 'This really is the Prophet.' Others said, 'This is the Christ.' But some said, 'Is the Christ to come from Galilee? Has not the Scripture said that the Christ comes from the offspring of David, and comes from Bethlehem, the village where David was?' So there was a division among the people over him."[108]

Douglas: What about Dawkins's claim that a "translation error"[109] between the Hebrew and Greek texts of Isaiah led Matthew to invent the virgin birth?

Astrid (using her tablet): Dawkins is referring to Isaiah 7:14's use of the Hebrew word *almah*, which basically meant "a young woman of child-bearing age who hasn't had any children." In that culture, an *almah* would have most likely been a virgin; so the Greek translation of *almah* as a *parthenos*, a virgin, isn't necessarily wrong.[110] That said, by referencing Isaiah 7:14, Matthew is highlighting a *typological* rather than a *predictive* fulfillment of Scripture.

Douglas: What's a "typological" fulfilment of Scripture?

Astrid (using her tablet): Theologian Jim Hamilton explains that "typological fulfillment . . . refers to the *fullest expression of a significant pattern of events*. Thus, typological interpretation sees in biblical narratives a divinely intended pattern of events. Events that take place at later points in salvation history correspond to these and intensify their significance."[111] Hamilton explains that this was "a common method of interpretation, as we can see from the words of Matthew's contemporaries."[112] So we can understand Isaiah 7:14 as pointing to a child that will be born during the lifetime of

---

107. Dawkins, *Outgrowing God*, 30.
108. Dawkins, *Outgrowing God*, 30.
109. Dawkins, *Outgrowing God*, 30.
110. See Heiser, "Almah of Isaiah 7:14."
111. Hamilton, "Virgin Will Conceive," 7. See also Garrett, "Type, Typology."
112. Hamilton, "Virgin Will Conceive," 23.

King Ahaz, to a young woman (not necessarily a virgin) of child-bearing age without children, and read Matthew as respecting the historical context of Isaiah's prophecy: "claiming in Jesus a *typological* rather than a *predictive* fulfillment of Isaiah 7:14."[113]

British theologian N. T. Wright points out that "there is no pre-Christian Jewish tradition suggesting that the messiah would be born of a virgin. No one used Isaiah 7:14 this way before Matthew did. Even assuming that Matthew or Luke regularly invented material to fit Jesus into earlier templates, why would they have invented something like this? The only conceivable parallels are pagan ones, and these fiercely Jewish stories have certainly not been modelled on them. Luke at least must have known that telling this story ran the risk of making Jesus out to be a pagan demigod. Why, for the sake of an exalted metaphor, would they take this risk—unless they at least believed the stories to be literally true?"[114]

Douglas: That's interesting; but didn't Dawkins say the story of Jesus' virgin birth *was* stolen from the stories of Horus and other pagan gods who were supposed to have been born of a virgin?

Hiromi: Dawkins says that in chapter 1,[115] but gives no evidence for the claim.

Astrid: That's because *there is no evidence* for such borrowing. Indeed, Jewish stories about the Jewish messiah just wouldn't have been modelled on pagan myths. However, the fact of there being two *independent* birth narratives, written within 60–70 years of the event, that agree on Jesus' virginal conception and birth despite their different perspectives, *is evidence* that must be taken into account.

Still, I doubt anyone becomes a Christian due to the evidence for Jesus' virgin birth, though there's more I could mention.[116] I certainly find it easier to accept the virgin birth in light of the evidence for the resurrection, rather than the other way around.

Douglas: But what's so significant about the resurrection of Jesus if the Gospels report other people being resurrected?

113. Hamilton, "Virgin Will Conceive," 23.

114. Wright, "Virgin Birth and the Constraints of History."

115. See Dawkins, *Outgrowing God*, 5.

116. See Williams, "Nativity"; Ward, "Evidence for the Virgin Birth"; Williams, "Archaeology of Christmas"; Machen, *Virgin Birth of Christ*; Nicholl, *Great Christ Comet*; Redford, *Born of a Virgin*.

Astrid: First of all, the *only* person who has been resurrected according to the New Testament is Jesus.

Thomas: But what about "the raising of Lazarus," for example?

Astrid (using her tablet): The New Testament mentions several people who are *resuscitated*, that is, who came back from death to earthly life. But that's not what the Judeo-Christian tradition means by a *resurrection*. Resurrection involves a transformed embodiment suited to a sinless eternal life in the new heavens and earth; and although Dawkins suggests Jesus' resurrection was an untrue story that spread "because it's entertaining and fits with people's expectations or prejudices,"[117] anyone who understands the cultural context of first-century Israel will find this suggestion laughable.

Jesus' crucifixion was an embarrassing death blow to his messianic pretentions, and the idea of the resurrection of an individual within human history, before the last judgement, cut *against* everyone's expectations and prejudices! As Peter J. Williams notes: "the concept of the bodily resurrection of *one person* in advance of others would have been very odd within Judaism, and therefore it is unlikely that early Christians would have invented it in an effort to continue the Jesus movement after the death of their leader."[118] In fact, as Rebecca McLaughlin points out,

> Dawkins himself notes that the idea that [the crucified] Jesus was the messiah . . . would have seemed 'pretty bonkers' to first-century Jews. Crucified would-be messiahs weren't uncommon in the first century. But crucifixion spelled either the end of the movement or the transfer of leadership to another messiah candidate. Claiming the crucified messiah had risen from the dead was utterly outrageous.[119]

The idea that the Jewish messiah had been *crucified* and then *resurrected* was *not* the sort of thing "recruits to the young religion of Christianity might have been especially eager to pass on . . . without checking them for truth"[120]!

Hiromi: And second?

Astrid: Second?

---

117. Dawkins, *Outgrowing God*, 23.

118. Williams, *Can We Trust the Gospels?*, 135.

119. McLaughlin, "Richard Dawkins's Latest Case for Outgrowing God."

120. Dawkins, *Outgrowing God*, 25.

Hiromi: You said "first of all," so you must have had a second point in mind.

Astrid (using her tablet): Sorry. Oh, yes. I wanted to say that the significance of the resurrection of Jesus lies in the fact that it was *Jesus* who was resurrected. As theologian Michael F. Bird writes: "Jesus made extravagant claims about himself as to his authority, mission, and origin, and the resurrection was a divine affirmation that those claims were good."[121]

Thomas: I for one am not going to take the New Testament writers at their word on this one! I want to know if there's any *historically warranted* evidence for the resurrection.

Astrid: There are several historical facts that one might consider relevant. I say "historical facts" because each fact is firmly established by passing multiple criteria of historical authenticity.

Douglas: And what are these "facts"?

Astrid: Jesus died by crucifixion. His corpse was buried and sealed inside a tomb. On the third day, a group of Jesus' female followers discovered that same tomb to be open and empty. Then multiple individuals and groups of people experienced a protracted, multisensory pattern of what they sincerely believed were meetings with a *resurrected* Jesus. Within days of his crucifixion, Jesus' disciples sincerely believed in and boldly preached Jesus' resurrection, despite a socioreligious context that made their claims both culturally embarrassing and life-threatening.

Thomas: We're not just talking about the conclusions of Christian scholars, are we?

Astrid (using her tablet): Scholars with widely different worldviews agree on these facts, because the evidence is so strong. In his book *Getting at Jesus*, Peter S. Williams shows that Jesus' death by crucifixion and the occurrence of apparent resurrection appearances are both supported by twelve evidential criteria, including having early, independent, and eyewitness sources. Jesus' burial and empty tomb both pass eleven criteria, including early, independent, and embarrassing sources. That the disciples believed in the resurrection soon after the crucifixion is supported by ten criteria, including early, independent, and eyewitness sources.

121. Bird, "Did Jesus Think He Was God?," 67. See Williams, *Understanding Jesus*, chapter 3.

David Mishkin writes:

> Many non-Jewish scholars already have a faith commitment to
> Jesus. This does not mean that their scholarship should sum-
> marily be discarded as biased. It should be evaluated on its own
> merit. Nevertheless, the reality is that presuppositions are influ-
> ential. Jewish scholars begin with a different set of presupposi-
> tions. But, what is interesting to note is that the main historical
> events that make up this discussion are virtually the same for
> both groups: crucifixion, burial, disciples' belief, empty tomb,
> and Paul's dramatic turnaround.[122]

In the words of Eric Metaxas: "it's clear that Jesus really lived and was
crucified and lain in a tomb and that on the third day, that tomb was found to
be empty."[123] And as Jonathan Kendall observes: "That numerous individuals,
including Jesus' closest disciples, had experiences subsequent to the crucifixion that led them to conclude that Jesus had been resurrected from the dead is
a fact accepted by essentially all New Testament scholars, even those that are
most skeptical of Christianity and of the resurrection itself."[124]

Douglas: But why think that Jesus' resurrection is the only possible explanation of this evidence?

Astrid (using her tablet): I don't think it's the only *possible* explanation. I
think it's the *best* explanation. On the negative side of the scale, as William
Lane Craig reports, "Modern scholarship recognizes no plausible explanatory alternative to the resurrection of Jesus."[125] Philosopher Stephen T. Davis
affirms that "no one who denies that Jesus was raised from the dead or who
offers reductive theories of the resurrection has yet been able to account
adequately for [the] widely accepted facts."[126]

Having observed that "the disciples must have been either deceivers,
deceived, or telling the truth about the resurrection," philosopher Lydia
McGrew argues that "The details and context of the disciple's claims pre-
clude the first two options."[127] According to McGrew, it's the historically
established details of Jesus' death, burial, and empty tomb, the protracted
pattern of multisensory resurrection appearances to multiple individuals
and groups of people, and the disciple's firm belief in Jesus' resurrection

---

122. Mishkin, *Jewish Scholarship on the Resurrection of Jesus*, 210.

123. Metaxas, *Miracles*, 100.

124. Kendall, "Hallucinations and the Risen Jesus," 307.

125. Craig, "Contemporary Scholarship and the Historical Resurrection of Jesus
Christ."

126. Davis, *Risen Indeed*, 180–81.

127. McGrew, *Hidden in Plain View*, 221.

despite their socioreligious context, "that give such tremendous force to the apostle's testimony and to their willingness to die for it, for it is from these details that we can conclude with confidence that they were not hallucinating, experiencing some sort of non-physical, paranormal event, having visions, or merely mistaken."[128]

Hiromi: And on the positive side?

Astrid (using her tablet)**:** As Peter S. Williams argues: "The resurrection hypothesis offers a relatively simple explanation of the relevant historical evidence that combines excellent explanatory scope . . . and excellent explanatory power . . . with a fair degree of plausibility . . . and low degrees of ad-hoc-ness and evidential disconfirmation, especially if one already accepts theism."[129]

Hiromi: And that takes us back to Dawkins's philosophical approach to evidence.

Sophie: In which case, that's a good place to finish for today. Whether or not the New Testament and its Gospel biographies contain any reliable information about Jesus is obviously a key question. And we've obviously only skimmed the surface of this question today. Perhaps Astrid can recommend some follow-up materials?

Astrid: Sure. Take a look at William Lane Craig's *Reasonable Faith* website. I can also recommend some short, introductory books: *Jesus: A Very Short Introduction* by Richard Bauckham; *Is Jesus History?* by John Dickson; and *Can We Trust the Gospels?*, by Peter J. Williams.

Sophie: And beyond the introductory level?

Astrid: I'd recommend *Getting at Jesus: A Comprehensive Critique of Neo-Atheist Nonsense about the Jesus of History* by Peter S. Williams. He's an English philosopher who taught me on that "communication and worldviews" course I took.

Sophie: Thank you Astrid. And thank you everyone for such an informative discussion.[130]

---

128. McGrew, *Hidden in Plain View*, 221, 223.

129. Williams, *Getting at Jesus*.

130. An extensive list of chapter-specific recommended resources can be found on this book's webpage at www.peterswilliams.com/publications/books/outgrowing-god/.

Third Meeting

Testing the Old Testament

Astrid slouched her way through the softly falling snow. Each exhaled breath condensed into a ghostly cloud of white. She was beginning to feel as numb on the outside as on the inside. She thought about turning around and heading back to bed; but she kept going, one foot in front of the other.

Astrid found herself settling into a chair at the usual table in *The Campus Coffee Cup Café*. Glancing up, she saw she was the last to arrive. Professor Minerva waved off her apology and offered to buy her a drink. She declined. The professor insisted. Something about putting color in her cheeks. Not wanting to be rude, Astrid asked for black coffee. Unzipping her woolen jumper, she began fiddling with her tablet.

Hiromi noticed that Astrid was wearing a vintage T-shirt displaying cover art from the classic 1994 album *Brave*,[1] by British band *Marillion*.[2] She was about to ask about it when Sophie returned with a tray of drinks, which she began passing out whilst indicating that Douglas should begin his chapter summary.

Douglas (using his phone): Dawkins's third chapter questions the historicity of the Jewish Scriptures, which Christians call "The Old Testament." He describes them as containing stories that mostly belong to "the shadowy realms of myth and legend."[3]

Dawkins's use of the term "myth" is vague, but he seems to mean that "myth" is a non-historical literary genre. He says: "The stories of Adam and

---

1. See Prog Archives Music, "Bridge—Marillion"; Marilliononline, "Brave (2018 Steve Wilson Remix)."

2. See www.marillion.com.

3. Dawkins, *Outgrowing God*, 48.

57

Eve, and of Noah and his Ark, are not history. . . . Like countless such stories from all over the world, they are 'myths'. There's nothing wrong with
myths. Some are beautiful and most are interesting, but they aren't history."[4]
He says much of the Old Testament is myth, and "there's nothing wrong
with that. Myths are rightly valued."[5] He says the people who first told these
myths "might have intended them as moral tales. Like Jesus' parable of the
Good Samaritan. Or like Aesop's Fables."[6] So, while a "myth" might convey
truths about life, it isn't intended to convey *historical* truths, except inciden-
tally. After all, although the parable of the Good Samaritan isn't history, the
Samaritans are a real religious sect.[7]

By "legends," on the other hand, Dawkins means something like an
"exaggerated"[8] retelling of an "original"[9] historical event, a true story ob-
scured by "the Chinese whispers effect" we discussed last week.[10]

Thomas: Like a film "based on true events"?

Douglas (using his phone): I reckon. Dawkins gives the example of the Pa-
cific Island "Cargo cults" that emerged when ancestor-worshipping peoples
saw the technology of soldiers fighting World War Two. For example, the
cult of "John Frum," a vaguely "messiah-like figure who, the islanders
believe, will one day return to take care of his people," appears to take its
name from a soldier known as "John from America," since "(in American
English 'from' sounds like 'frum', rhyming with 'come')."[11] Dawkins draws a
connection between the Cargo cults and stories about Jesus, asserting that
since there was "nothing but word-of-mouth gossip for decades after Jesus's
death, the cult of Christ was able to take off—virgin birth, miracles, resurrection, ascension into heaven and all."[12]

Hiromi: But a key point from last week's discussion was how Dawkins is
wrong about his "whispers" model of ancient oral culture and the Gospels.

---

4. Dawkins, *Outgrowing God*, 56.

5. Dawkins, *Outgrowing God*, 70.

6. Dawkins, *Outgrowing God*, 57.

7. See Merriman, "Modern Trials of the Ancient Samaritans."

8. Dawkins, *Outgrowing God*, 57.

9. Dawkins, *Outgrowing God*, 57.

10. Dawkins, *Outgrowing God*, 57.

11. Dawkins, *Outgrowing God*, 59.

12. Dawkins, *Outgrowing God*, 64.

Douglas (using his phone): Dawkins also asserts that: "The early Christians believed Jesus's Second Coming would happen during their own lifetimes, and his own words, as quoted in the gospels, suggest that Jesus—or at least, the people who wrote his teachings down—thought so too."[13]

Anyway, Dawkins's bottom line is that "biblical scholars don't take [the Old Testament] seriously as history."[14] He spends much of the chapter applying three different arguments to a selection of stories from the Old Testament with the aim of convincing readers to share this assessment. First, he asserts that this or that story makes "an extraordinary claim requiring extraordinary evidence."[15] Second, he asserts an absence of extrabiblical evidence *for* the historical truth of certain Old Testament stories. Third, he asserts the existence of extrabiblical evidence *against* the historical truth of certain Old Testament stories.

Dawkins also discusses some of the evidence against the historical reliability of *The Book of Mormon*, which is a nineteenth-century fake created by Joseph Smith.[16] And he makes some ethical criticisms of God's actions in the exodus story that seem to have escaped from the next chapter, which is about morality rather than historicity. And that's chapter 3.

Sophie: Thank you, Douglas. As you say Hiromi, we discussed Dawkins's "whispers" take on Gospel traditions last week. We also discussed the "extraordinary claim requiring extraordinary evidence" slogan. And we can postpone questions about the morality of Exodus until we discuss chapter 4. So, perhaps Astrid would get things started by commenting on the claim that Jesus and his earliest disciples "believed Jesus's Second Coming would happen during their own lifetimes."[17] Then we can focus on the historicity of the Old Testament narratives.

13. Dawkins, *Outgrowing God*, 60.

14. Dawkins, *Outgrowing God*, 48.

15. Dawkins, *Outgrowing God*, 48. On the so-called "long day" (*Outgrowing God*, 48) in Joshua 10:12–15, see Howard, *New American Commentary*, 238–51; John H. Walton, "Joshua 10:12–15 and Mesopotamian Celestial Omen Texts," 181–90. On the incident that Dawkins describes as "Jonah living three days in the belly of the big fish" (*Outgrowing God*, 48), see Pitre, "Resurrection of Jesus and the Sign of Jonah."

16. See Williams, "Mormonism"; Williams, "Mormonism—An Introductory Critique"; Licona, "What To Say To Mormons"; Wallace, "Mormonism"; Beckwith et al., *New Mormon Challenge*; Beverley, *Mormon Crisis*; Larson, *Quest for the Gold Plates*; Miller, *Leaving Mormonism*; Scott, *Mormon Mirage*; Southerton, *Losing a Lost Tribe*; Williams, *Getting at Jesus*, 374–81.

17. Dawkins, *Outgrowing God*, 60.

Astrid: Dawkins must be confusing Jesus's prediction about the destruction of the Jewish temple *within a generation* and his predicted "second coming" *at an unspecified time* in the future.[18] Mark's Gospel reports Jesus saying *of his predicted second coming* that: "concerning that day or that hour, no one knows, not even the angels in heaven, nor the Son, but only the Father."[19]

Hiromi: *Was* the Jewish temple destroyed within a generation?

Thomas: It was, in 70 AD, at the end of a war between the Jews and Romans.[20]

Sophie: Turning to the Old Testament, I suggest we begin with Dawkins's claim that stories set before the eighth century BC "are not history, and no educated theologian thinks they are. Like countless such stories from all over the world, they are 'myths.'"[21]

Hiromi (producing a paperback book from a pocket in her coat): That turn of phrase about "no educated theologian," is an example of what atheist philosopher Walter Sinnott-Armstrong calls *"abusive assuring."*[22] He says: "People often resort to excesses like . . . 'Everybody who knows anything knows that . . .' or (in the opposite direction) 'only a naïve fool would be deluded into imagining that . . .' Whenever people turn to abusive assurances like these, you should wonder why they adopted such desperate incivility instead of giving evidence for their claim."[23]

Astrid (using her tablet): In popular culture, to call something "a myth" is to call it "a false story"; but as an academic term, "myth" doesn't carry this negative meaning. Egyptologist James K. Hoffmeier explains that "myth, in the technical sense, is concerned with ultimate realities, not fiction."[24] According to William Lane Craig: "Whereas 19th century scholars looked at ancient creation myths as a sort of crude proto-science, contemporary scholars tend more to the view that such stories were taken figuratively, not

---

18. See Copan, *When God Goes To Starbucks*, chapters 15–16.

19. Mark 13:32. See also Matt 24:36; Acts 1:7.

20. See Williams, "Jesus the Prophesied Prophet."

21. Dawkins, *Outgrowing God*, 56.

22. Sinnott-Armstrong, *Think Again*, 128.

23. Sinnott-Armstrong, *Think Again*, 128.

24. Hoffmeier in Halton, *Genesis: History, Fiction, or Neither?*, 27.

literally, by the people who told them."[25] Theologian Tremper Longman III comments that the biblical creation narratives "clearly have a theological and not a scientific, interest . . . the creation accounts . . . use a high degree of figurative language."[26] Creation myths don't map neatly onto our modern concepts of scientific description or explanation; but they can't be dismissed as falsified "proto-science." We might say that creation myths "serve as *guides* to the world rather than as *depictions* of the world."[27]

Douglas: What's the difference?

Astrid: The abstract London Train Map *guides* people through London's underground system without being a scientifically accurate *depiction* of the underground system. In a similar way, a myth is a story that aims to help people navigate their lives within the framework of a worldview. As such, a creation myth articulates truth-claims that can be critically assessed, by philosophical argument if not scientific investigation, once we distinguish the worldview of the myth from the figurative language in which it is expressed.[28]

Thomas (using his tablet): Here's a copy of the "London Underground, Overground, Docklands Light Railway and Crossrail" map:[29]

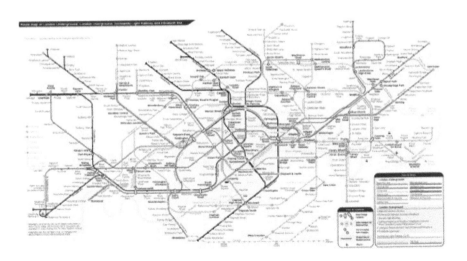

25. Craig, in Caruso, *Science & Religion*, 39.

26. Longman, *Introducing the Old Testament*, 17.

27. Segal, *Myth*, 139.

28. See Williams, "Mythology," 459–60.

29. See "London Underground Overground DLR Crossrail Map."

Astrid (using her tablet): Thanks. Given the popular meaning of "myth," theologian Gordon J. Wenham thinks it's "prudent to avoid the term"[30] when describing the genre of Genesis 1–11. He says:

> These chapters contain stories that both illustrate important social and theological principles, as myths are often alleged to do, yet they tell of unique occurrences. . . . I prefer to describe Genesis 1–11 as protohistory. . . . It is not ordinary history. . . . On the other hand, it is not fiction . . . protohistory shares with both these genres the aim of imparting an interpretation of the world as we experience it. . . . But whereas history could be described as a photograph of the past . . . protohistory is akin to a portrait of the past. It is a valid representation that faithfully portrays the artist's intentions.[31]

He illustrates this distinction by comparing a photograph of the night sky with Van Gough's painting *Starry Night*. The photo and the painting both have reference to the night sky, but in rather different ways.

Sophie: Can you give us a biblical illustration of that difference?

Astrid (using her tablet): Ancient literature sometimes uses numbers in symbolic rather than literal ways, and "both the segments and the sums of the patriarchal life spans represent sums and products based primarily on the sexagesimal (base 6) system of ancient Mesopotamian mathematics . . . the biblical figures in these genealogies are . . . derived from the Mesopotamian mathematical heritage of the biblical narrator/redactor."[32] So, even beyond Genesis 11, we have to be alert to the fact that ancient stories that are meant to tell us about real people don't necessarily communicate truth in the same way as a modern work of history or biography would communicate truth.

Sophie: Thank you. Before we look at Dawkins's specific historical claims, let's think about the general *types* of argument Douglas highlighted. We discussed Dawkins's assertion that extraordinary claims require extraordinary evidence last week, so let's begin with the idea that an absence of extrabiblical evidence *for* certain Old Testament stories amounts to an argument *against* taking those stories "seriously as history."

---

30. Wenham in Halton, *Genesis: History, Fiction, or Neither?*, 84.

31. Wenham in Halton, *Genesis: History, Fiction, or Neither?*, 84–85, 87.

32. Coleson, *Genesis*, 20–21. See also Hill, "Making Sense of the Numbers of Genesis"; Olsen, "How Old was Father Abraham?"

Hiromi: Isn't that a fallacious "argument from ignorance"?

Sophie: It is. Arguments from ignorance make an undisciplined shift from the absence of evidence for or against a proposition to the truth or falsity of that proposition. As atheist Victor Stenger warns, absence of evidence is only evidence of absence "when the evidence should be there and is not."[33]

Astrid: Exactly, and the history of biblical criticism is strewn with long-abandoned arguments from silence overturned by later discoveries.[34] Of course, some believers would *agree* with Dawkins about the stories he highlights being historically false, without taking them to be making historical claims in the first place. They'd read them as "myths" in Dawkins's sense of the term, whilst still believing in God, believing Jesus is the Son of God who died for our sins and rose from the dead, and so on.

Hiromi: If the stories Dawkins says are not historically true are not *meant* to be historically true, their being historically false wouldn't undermine the reliability of the Old Testament. But even if the stories he says are unhistorical are all meant to be historical, or proto-historical, it would only follow that the Old Testament gets *some* of its historical claims wrong. It wouldn't follow that it gets *all* or even *most* of its historical claims wrong!

Thomas: Even Dawkins admits the Jewish exile in Babylon was real.

Hiromi: Exactly.

Astrid: Thinking the Old Testament gets *some* of its truth-claims wrong is compatible with the kind of religious belief that treats Scripture purely or partly as a merely human response to divine revelation, rather than as also a revelation in and of itself.

Douglas: Is that your view?

Astrid: I think the Bible's also a revelation in and of itself. I'm just pointing out that Dawkins's argument only applies to a subset of believers.

Hiromi: Dawkins seems to assume religious believers would be irrational to trust the Old Testament if they can't rebut all the claims he makes about

33. Stenger, *New Atheism*, 58.
34. See Maier, "Biblical History."

its stories being "myths and legends." However, Dawkins continues believing his naturalistic worldview despite admitting it can't explain away *all* the evidence that currently seems to point to the existence of God. I guess this is because he thinks he has sufficient reason to accept naturalism *despite* its current inability to explain things like the origin of life. But couldn't the religious believer offer the same kind of defense?

Sophie: That's an excellent point Hiromi. As Walter Sinnott-Armstrong says: "One can still hold one's beliefs strongly while recognizing that there are reasons to believe otherwise, that one might be wrong, and that one does not have the whole truth."[35]

Astrid: Dawkins seems to assume that religious believers begin by accepting certain texts as having an authoritative status as Scripture before attributing warrant to particular beliefs grounded in that Scripture. He doesn't reckon with anyone whose beliefs move in the opposite direction, from the acceptance of particular historical events that in turn seem to warrant the conclusion that certain texts are a revelation from God.

Sophie: Turning to Dawkins's specific claims about certain Old Testament stories, it's clear that he subscribes to the "minimalist" school of thinking about the Old Testament, rather than the "maximalist" school. As theologian Michael S. Heiser explains, minimalists "basically [believe] the OT has little or no historical value, as it was entirely written during or after the exile. Maximalists, on the other hand, disagree, but on what I'd call a continuum of optimism about the biblical text as a historical source."[36]

Astrid (using her tablet): Historian Paul L. Maier warns that "biblical minimalists . . . base their case almost entirely on what they deem to be the *absence* of archaeological evidence that corroborates material in the earlier eras of the Old Testament."[37] Biblical minimalism takes us back to Dawkins's use of the argument from ignorance.

Douglas: So, you're a "maximalist"?

---

35. Sinnott-Armstrong. *Think Again*, 80.
36. Heiser, "Archaeology and the Old Testament," para. 1.
37. Maier, "Biblical History."

Astrid (using her tablet): With good reason. While there certainly are biblical scholars who "don't take [the Old Testament] seriously as history,"[38] there are plenty who do. As Walter C. Kaiser Jr. comments: "Just when skepticism seems to be making the most noise, we are being flooded with an overwhelming amount of real, hard evidences that demand a verdict opposite to what [minimalists] are clamoring for."[39]

Thomas: What sort of "hard evidence"?

Astrid (using her tablet): Paul Copan reports that "the once-doubted historical claims of the Old Testament—whether the cost of slaves in the ancient Near East, camels on livestock lists during the time of Abraham, the kingship of David, the mines of Solomon, the metallurgy of the Philistines, or the existence of the Hittites—turn out to be anchored in ancient Near East history."[40] Purdue University historian Lawrence Mykytiuk recently listed fifty-three figures from the Old Testament whose existence has been confirmed by archaeology![41]

Hiromi: Is Dawkins right when he says "no serious scholar thinks"[42] Moses wrote the Pentateuch, the first five books of the Old Testament?

Astrid (using her tablet): That's a bit misleading.[43] According to theologians Scott Hahn and Curtis Mitch: "many scholars would insist . . . that a real historical connection between Moses and the five books of the Pentateuch can still be confidently affirmed, regardless of whether Mosaic origin be defined in broad terms, where Moses is considered the primary source and/or author of the Pentateuchal laws, or more narrow terms, where Moses is considered responsible for composing the bulk of the Pentateuch, laws and narratives alike."[44] Likewise, Jimmy Akin says there are scholars who think the Pentateuch "substantially depends on material stemming from or connected with the historical Moses, even if it were not put in its final literary form until later."[45] For example, Professor Daniel L. Bock says he doesn't

---

38. Dawkins, *Outgrowing God*, 48.

39. Kaiser, quoted by Nagtegaal, "Did David and Solomon Actually Exist?," para. 34.

40. Copan, *Is God a Moral Monster?*, 68.

41. See Mykytiuk, "53 People in the Bible Confirmed Archaeologically."

42. Dawkins, *Outgrowing God*, 50.

43. See Bock, "Recovering the Voice of Moses"; Longman, "Who Wrote the Book of Genesis?"; Tilley, "Documentary Hypothesis"; Lawrence, *Books of Moses Revisited*.

44. Hahn and Mitch, *Ignatius Catholic Study Bible: Exodus*, 13–14.

45. Akin, "Who Wrote the Books of Moses?"

doubt "the historicity of Moses, the authenticity of his speeches, nor the fundamentally Mosaic authority behind the entire Pentateuch."[46]

Sophie: Let's start at the top of Dawkins's list, with Adam and Eve.

Astrid: Dawkins doesn't seem to realize that religious believers hold different views about Adam and Eve. Some understand them as archetypal figures rather than historical figures. Others think they're *both* historical *and* archetypal; and some of these believers think the Bible doesn't require us to take Adam and Eve as the first human couple, but as the first humans called into a covenantal relationship with God.[47]

Douglas: How does that last interpretation fit into Genesis?

Astrid: Some commentators argue that Genesis 1 sees the creation of "*adam*" in the "humanity" sense of the word, whereas Genesis 2 tells the *subsequent* story of an individual human called "Adam" who is called by God to serve as a priest within Eden's temple-garden. Reading the narrative this way explains why Adam's son Cain is afraid "whoever finds me will kill me" when God makes him "a fugitive" for murdering his brother Abel.[48] It also explains why, when Cain marries and has a child, he founds a whole settlement rather than a single house. And it allows Adam and Eve's sons to find wives without committing incest with sisters the text never mentions!

Douglas: But doesn't Paul talk about Adam as "the first man"?

Astrid: Sure, in 1 Corinthians 15. But in the same context he calls Jesus "the last Adam" and "the second man"![49] Paul's point obviously isn't chronological, it's that Adam and Jesus represent two different *types* of humanity.

46. Bock, "Recovering the Voice of Moses."

47. See Hos 6:7. See also Biologos, "Human Origins and Adam and Eve"; Barrett et al., *Four Views on the Historical Adam*; Croucher, *Adam: The First Human?*; Charles, *Reading Genesis 1–2*; Gauger et al., *Science & Human Origins*; Hill, *Worldview Approach to Science and Scripture*; Walton, *Lost World of Adam and Eve*; Youngblood, *Genesis Debate*.

48. Gen 4:14, 12.

49. See 1 Cor 15:42–49.

Douglas (using his phone)**:** But when Paul is addressing the philosophers in Athens, he says God "made from one man every nation of mankind to live on all the face of the earth."[50]

Astrid: Actually, that translation makes a particular interpretive choice. What Paul literally says is that God "made of one every nation of men to dwell on all the face of the earth."[51]

Thomas: Wait, the phrase "one man" isn't in the original Greek?

Astrid: Nope. In the Greek of Acts 17:27, the nature of the "one" Paul mentions is left for the reader to infer from context. Translators often try to supply the missing subject in their translations. Some think Paul must have meant to refer to one "man" because they already believe Adam was the first human. Old Testament theologian John Walton suggests the "one man" in question wasn't Adam, but Noah.[52] Other translators think Paul meant to refer to a common human nature or ancestry behind the different peoples or nations on earth, or that Paul's language is and should remain open to interpretation. So, for example, Young's Literal Translation renders Luke's Greek as: "He made also of one blood every nation of men."[53]

Thomas: And that "one blood" could be one man or one ancestral stock or human nature?

Astrid: That's right. The "one stock/nature" interpretation gains plausibility from the fact that the Athenians, to whom Paul was speaking, thought of themselves as a distinct and superior race of humans that had sprung directly from the local soil of Attica. Thus Paul may well have been making a point against Athenian racism.[54]

Sophie: Next comes the flood narrative of Genesis 6–9.

---

50. Acts 17:27a.

51. Acts 17:27a (ASV). For the original Greek of this verse, see https://biblehub.com/interlinear/acts/17-26.htm.

52. See RJS, "From One Couple?"; Walton, *Lost World of Adam and Eve*.

53. The phrase "one blood" is also used by the World English Bible, Webster's Bible Translation, Darby Bible Translation, New Heart English Bible, the King James, New King James, and King James 2000 translations.

54. See Peter May, "Paul at Athens"; Hornblower, *Greek World 479–323 BC*, chapter 12; Isaac, *Invention of Racism in Classical Antiquity*, chapter 1.

Thomas (using his tablet): I've got this article by Damian Thompson at *The Spectator*, who asks: "If Richard Dawkins loves facts so much, why can't he get them right?"[55] Thompson reports on a Twitter thread by George Heath-Whyte, a PhD researcher in Assyriology at Cambridge University, who said: "Reading @RichardDawkins new book 'Outgrowing God', and as an Assyriologist I've had a couple of major face-palms moments."[56] Thompson begins with Dawkins's claim that "the Old Testament story of Noah comes from a Babylonian myth, the legend of Utnapishtim, which is turn was taken from the Sumerian Epic of Gilgamesh."[57] Apparently: "It was this discussion that led Heath-Whyte to cover his face with his palms. Unfortunately for Dawkins, he then removed them and started jabbing out a devastating series of tweets."[58] Heath-Whyte observes that:

> The version of the Gilgamesh story that contains the flood narrative of Utnapishtim is NOT written in Sumerian, but Babylonian (Akkadian).
>
> There are older Sumerian stories about the character Gilgamesh, none of which contain a flood story. There is even a Sumerian flood story too, but it's not the flood story he's talking about.
>
> It seems he's talking about a weird mix of one Babylonian flood story about a guy called Atrahasis and another Babylonian flood story about Utnapishtim (the latter being a part of the Babylonian epic of Gilgamesh) . . . but come on Dawkins, even Wikipedia could have told you that neither of these were written in Sumerian.[59]

Whyte considers Dawkins's claim that: "Arguably the world's oldest work of literature, [Gilgamesh] was written two thousand years earlier than the Noah story."[60] He responds:

> He's just stated that Genesis was written "during the Babylonian captivity" (6th century BC), and now he's stated that (what we assume he means to be) the epic of Atrahasis, or the Babylonian Epic of Gilgamesh, was written 2000 years earlier—so roughly 2,600–2,500 BC.

55. Thompson, "If Richard Dawkins Loves Facts So Much."

56. Heath-Whyte in Thompson, "If Richard Dawkins Loves Facts So Much," para. 2.

57. Thompson, "If Richard Dawkins Loves Facts So Much," para. 3.

58. Thompson, "If Richard Dawkins Loves Facts So Much," para. 4.

59. Heath-Whyte in Thompson, "If Richard Dawkins Loves Facts So Much," paras. 5–8.

60. Dawkins, *Outgrowing God*, 53.

Most likely Atrahasis was written less than 1,300 years before the Babylonian captivity, and the version of Gilgamesh that included a flood story was probably finished less than 1,000 years before the Babylonian captivity. . . .

We know Dawkins has got confused, so maybe he meant to say that some other flood story (there were a few) was "arguably the world's oldest work of literature," and was "written two thousand years earlier than the Noah story."

Well, whatever flood story he was thinking of, there is no debate: no flood story was "arguably the world's oldest work of literature," and the earliest flood stories currently known were only written down (at the very earliest) 1,400 years before the Babylonian captivity.[61]

Heath-Whyte also says Dawkins "mixes up the animals in the Gilgamesh and Genesis flood stories, and claims that the Sumerian flood legend, like the story of Noah's Ark, ends with a rainbow."[62] In point of fact, he says: "There's no rainbow mentioned in any Mesopotamian flood story. Anywhere. There just isn't."[63]

Thompson adds that Dawkins

has misidentified a Sumerian god. . . . And, just when Dawkins must be wishing that a non-existent God would send a flood to cover his embarrassment, [Heath-Whyte] delivers the killer blow. As he says, even Wikipedia would have put the professor right on these matters. So what was his source? "A quick google search suggests that Dawkins' source for a lot of this stuff may be a cute little website called HistoryWiz." I checked, and he's right: this is the version of the Gilgamesh as mangled by HistoryWiz.[64]

Douglas: That's pretty embarrassing.

Astrid: That reminds me to mention how impressed I am that the Old Testament repeatedly passes the historical criterion of embarrassment by being brutally honest about the failings of its characters. Moses committed murder, or at least manslaughter, and tried to avoid God's calling to confront

61. Heath-Whyte in Thompson, "If Richard Dawkins Loves Facts So Much," paras. 11–14.

62. Thompson, "If Richard Dawkins Loves Facts So Much," para. 15.

63. Heath-Whyte in Thompson, "If Richard Dawkins Loves Facts So Much," para. 16.

64. Thompson, "If Richard Dawkins Loves Facts So Much," paras. 16, 18.

Pharaoh. King David committed adultery with Bathsheba and arranged for her husband to be in the front line of a battle so he'd get killed. The nation of Israel repeatedly fails to live up to its covenant with God. And so on.

Thomas: That's an interesting point.

Hiromi (using her tablet): Dawkins says that "All around the world, there are similar myths of a great flood in which only one family survived."[65] Is that true?

Thomas: It is, though it's not like *every* ancient culture has a flood story. The existence of flood stories in ancient cultures from different parts of the world certainly doesn't prove that there was a single global flood! Different ancient cultures suffered different floods and based stories upon them from within the perspective of their own worldview. The ancient Greeks and Romans had a story about Deucalion and Pyhrra, who saved their children and some animals in a giant box-shaped craft.[66]

Astrid (using her tablet): Which would have been unstable in the water, in contrast with Noah's "floating boxcar."[67] But I accept the point. I don't think Genesis 6–9 speaks of a worldwide flood, at least, not literally. I think it uses hyperbolic language to talk about a flood of Noah's "world." As Timothy Keller writes:

> I believe Noah's flood happened, but that it was a regional flood, not a worldwide flood. On the one hand, those who insist on it being a worldwide flood seem to ignore too much the scientific evidence that there was no such thing. On the other hand, those who insist that it was a legend seem to ignore too much the trustworthiness of the Scripture . . . we should remember that the Bible often speaks of the "known world" as the "whole world."[68]

Roger Forster and Paul Marston argue that: "to translate 'the whole *eretz*' as 'the whole earth' is really misleading to the modern reader, for we think of 'earth' in terms of a 'Globe'. To translate it 'the whole land', would much better convey the kind of concept in the mind of the writer—and often

65. Dawkins, *Outgrowing God*, 54.

66. See "Deucalion."

67. The dimensions of the ark in Genesis, as in other near eastern flood accounts, are probably symbolic or hyperbolic rather than literal. See Copan and Jacoby, *Origins*, 161.

68. Keller, *Genesis*, 81.

it does not even imply the whole of the then known world."[69] Moreover: "the term *tebel*, which translates to the whole expanse of the Earth, or the Earth as a whole, is not used in Genesis 6:17, nor in subsequent verses. . . . If the intent of this passage was to indicate the entire expanse of the Earth, *tebel* would have been the more appropriate word choice."[70]

Douglas: Is this a modern interpretation?

Astrid (using her tablet): Not at all. Psalm 104 describes the creation using the same literary structure as Genesis 1. When it gets to the separation between the waters and dry land, it says God "set a boundary that they may not pass, so that they might not again cover the earth." So the psalmist didn't think the flood entailed waters covering the whole earth.[71] The same goes for the author of Job 38:8–11.

Outside the Bible, the first-century Jewish historian Josephus noted how Nicolaus of Damascus wrote about "a great mountain in Armenia . . . upon which it is reported that many who fled at the time of the Deluge were saved."[72] Josephus himself says: "the sons of Noah were three . . . these first of all descended from the mountains into the plains, and fixed their habitation there; and persuaded others who were greatly afraid of the lower grounds on account of the flood, and so were very loath to come down from the higher places, to venture to follow their examples."[73]

Douglas: So how does a non-global flood fit with what Genesis 7 says about the waters covering the mountains?

Astrid (using her tablet): The Hebrew word "*har*" can be translated as "mountain" or "mountains," but it can also be translated as "hill," "hills," or "hill country." Moreover, the Sumerians thought of their ziggurat temples as mountains, "calling them 'É. kur,' which means 'house of the mountain' or 'mountain house.'"[74] Indeed, "the specific Mesopotamian word for 'mountain' (*šadû*) is derived from 'mounds,' and may indicate that the Mesopotamians thought of their high temple mounds on the very flat

69. Forster and Marston, *Reason, Science & Faith*, 297. See Youngblood, *Genesis Debate*, 224–26.

70. Biologos Forum, "Did a Global Flood Really Happen?"

71. See Deem, "Why the Bible Says Noah's Flood Must Be Local."

72. Josephus, *Ant.* 1.3.6.

73. Josephus, *Ant.* 1.4.

74. Hill, "Noachian Flood: Universal or Local?"

alluvial plain as mountains."[75] Now, Genesis 7:20 literally says: "Fifteen cubits upward did the waters prevail; and the mountains were covered."[76] This doesn't mean the water rose fifteen cubits *higher than* the "*har*." It means the water rose to a height of fifteen cubits *and in so doing covered* the "*har*." So the "*har*" might be literal hills or symbolic temple "mountains." Or the description might be hyperbolic.

Douglas: How could the Ark be grounded on top of Mount Ararat by a non-global flood?

Astrid (using her tablet): Genesis doesn't say it was! Genesis 8:4 says: "the ark came to rest on the mountains of Ararat." Now, remember that "the word for 'mountains' and 'hills' is the same in Hebrew"[77] and take into consideration the fact that "Ararat was the Hebrew version of the name, not of the mountain but the country around it."[78] Genesis 8:4 could be translated: "the ark came to rest on the foot-hills of the country of Ararat."

Thomas (using his tablet): In a Babylonian "Ark Tablet" dating from around 1900–1700 BC, a god called Enki tells a man called Atrahasis to make a circular boat. The resulting Ark is basically a 230-foot-wide reed coracle! It's interesting to note that in this Babylonian version, just as in the biblical story, the animals are said to enter the Ark "two by two."[79]

Astrid (using her tablet): James Hoffmeier suggests that: "Given the fact that there were several different traditions from Mesopotamia, and that they have so many points in common with the biblical story, it might be logical to conclude that all the stories recall a common event that was retold to reflect different social, cultural and theological contexts."[80]

Hiromi (using her tablet): Dawkins argues that if "the tale of Noah were true, the places where we find each kind of animal should show a pattern of spreading out from the spot where the biblical Ark finally came to rest

75. Hill, "Noachian Flood: Universal or Local?"

76. RSV translation. See https://biblehub.com/genesis/7-20.htm.

77. Fischer, *Historical Genesis*, 107.

78. Kurkjian, *History of Armenia*, quoted by Fischer, *Historical Genesis*, 110.

79. Weiner, "Animals Went in Two by Two." Genesis 6:14 may refer to "reeds" rather than "rooms/compartments," and "gopher" may refer to cedar wood, or may be an Akkadian loan-word that refers to reed huts. See Hill, *Worldview Approach to Science and Scripture*, 74–78; Longman and Walton, *Lost World of the Flood*, 59–61, 77–78.

80. Hoffmeier, *Archaeology of the Bible*, 38.

when the flood subsided—Mount Ararat in Turkey."[81] But this only argues against a global flood.

Sophie: What about the stories of the Jewish "patriarchs," starting with Abraham?[82]

Astrid (using her tablet): Maier observes that "details in the biblical account regarding Abraham, such as the treaties he made with neighboring rulers and even the price of slaves, mesh well with what is known elsewhere in the history of the ancient Near East."[83] Likewise, M. J. Selman writes that: "the patriarchal customs can be compared without difficulty with a wide range of material from the ancient Near East. . . . From the independent viewpoint of the historian . . . the social parallels make the historical existence of the patriarchs more likely."[84]

Wenham argues that "the complete absence of Baal from the patriarchal tradition points to its antiquity. In the second half of the second millennium BC Baal took over from El as the leading god in the west Semitic pantheon, yet he is never mentioned in Genesis. This is intelligible if the patriarchal tradition originated before about 1500 BC, but not if it comes from later times."[85] He also points out that since Jerusalem "certainly existed in patriarchal times," the failure of the patriarchal narratives to mention Jerusalem as a center of worship "is most easily explained if the patriarchal traditions not only originated, but were committed to writing, before Jerusalem became the principal cultic centre"[86] around the beginning of the first millennium BC.

Douglas: But what about Dawkins's claim that Abraham's camels are an "anachronism" because "the camel was not domesticated until many centuries after Abraham is supposed to have died"?[87]

---

81. Dawkins, *Outgrowing God*, 55.

82. See Kitchen, *On the Reliability of the Old Testament*, chapter 7; Millard and Wiseman, *Essays on the Patriarchal Narratives*; Provine et al., *Biblical History of Israel*, chapter 6.

83. Maier, "Biblical History: The Faulty Criticism of Biblical Historicity." On how the changing price of slaves in the ancient world correlates with the biblical data, see: Kitchen, *On the Reliability of the Old Testament*, 344–45.

84. Selman, "Comparative Customs and the Patriarchal Age," 128.

85. Wenham, "Religion of the Patriarchs," 185.

86. Wenham, "Religion of the Patriarchs," 185.

87. Dawkins, *Outgrowing God*, 53.

Astrid (using her tablet): Dawkins is misinformed.[88] While Genesis doesn't suggest domesticated camels were *widespread* in the nineteenth century BC, it does describe the use of camels in certain settings, including in the story of Abraham. British Egyptologist Kenneth Kitchen comments: "It is often asserted that the mention of camels and of their use is an anachronism in Genesis. This charge is simply not true, as there is both [written] and archaeological evidence for knowledge and use of this animal in the early second millennium B.C. and even earlier."[89]

Hiromi: What evidence?

Astrid (using her tablet): Kitchen lists a bunch of evidence including: a nineteenth/eighteenth-century BC figurine of a kneeling camel, from Byblos; a North Syrian seal depicting deities riding camels, from the eighteenth century BC; and references to camels in a Sumerian text dating to the early second millennium BC.[90] He says: "There are other traces of camels much earlier, e.g. in Egypt and Arabia in the third millennium . . . the camel was for long a *marginal* beast in most of the historic ancient Near East (including Egypt), but it was *not* wholly unknown or anachronistic before or during 2000–1100."[91]

In his comprehensive study of the domestication of camels, Professor K. Martin Heide concludes:

> The archaeological evidence points to the fact that the Bactrian camel was domesticated before the dromedary and was put into use by the middle of the 3rd millennium or earlier. The gradual spread of the Bactrian camel . . . seems to have reached the Mesopotamian civilization sporadically by the middle of the 3rd millennium and more frequently at the end of the 3rd / beginning of the 2nd millennium. . . . The archaeological and inscriptional evidence allows at least the domesticated Bactrian camel to have existed at Abraham's time.[92]

---

88. See Paterson, "Will Camel Discovery Break The Bible's Back?"; Verbruggen, "5 Things You Need to Know about Camels and Biblical Accuracy."

89. Kitchen, *Ancient Orient and Old Testament*. See also Millard, "Methods of Studying the Patriarchal Narratives as Ancient Texts," 43–58.

90. Kitchen, *On the Reliability of the Old Testament*, 339.

91. Kitchen, *On the Reliability of the Old Testament*, 339.

92. Heide, "Domestication of the Camel," 367–68.

Sophie: Next is the exodus from Egypt under the prophet Moses.[93]

Astrid (using her tablet)**:** Kitchen argues that:

> to explain what we have in our Hebrew documents we need a Hebrew leader who had had experience of life at the Egyptian court . . . including knowledge of treaty-type documents and their format, as well as traditional Semitic legal/social usage. . . . In other words, somebody distressingly like . . . Moses, is badly needed . . . to make any sense of the situation as we have it.[94]

Douglas (using his phone)**:** But as Dawkins writes:

> You would think that such a big event as the enslavement of an entire nation, and its mass migration generations later, would have left traces in the archaeological record and in the written histories of Egypt. Unfortunately there is no evidence of either kind. No evidence of anything like a Jewish captivity in Egypt. It probably never happened, although the legend is burned deep into Jewish culture.[95]

Hiromi: Doesn't it strike you as unlikely that a nation would invent the culturally embarrassing claim to be descended from slaves if that claim had no historical foundation?

Astrid (using her tablet)**:** Dawkins doesn't seem to allow any claim made in the Old Testament to count as historical evidence, but I think we should attach some significance to the fact that "There are over one hundred references in the Old Testament to Israel's escape from slavery in Egypt."[96]

Douglas: Dawkins says a real exodus "would have left traces in the archaeological record."[97]

---

93. See Williams, "Exodus"; Hahn and Mitch, *Ignatius Catholic Study Bible*; Hoffmeier et al., *Did I Not Bring Israel Out of Egypt?*; Hoffmeier, *Israel in Egypt*; Hoffmeier, *Ancient Israel in Sinai*; Humphreys, *Miracles of Exodus*; Kitchen, *On the Reliability of the Old Testament*, chapter 6; Pokrifka, *Exodus*; Provine et al., *Biblical History of Israel*, chapter 6.

94. Kitchen, *On the Reliability of the Old Testament*, 295.

95. Dawkins, *Outgrowing God*, 50.

96. Tilley, *Defending the Christian Faith*, 50.

97. Dawkins, *Outgrowing God*, 50.

Astrid (using her tablet): He might think that, but Thomas W. Davis is an archaeologist, and he *doesn't*. Davis says:

> no direct evidence has yet been uncovered to ground the [exodus] in historical physical space. This absence of evidence is often interpreted as a direct challenge to the historicity of the biblical account. However, the formation processes that affect archaeological data in remote desert environments such as Sinai, and the nature of the archaeological signature of a migratory group force a reassessment of this negative conclusion . . . finding direct evidence of a single-use campsite of a nomadic people group that can be dated in isolation in the Sinai is a totally unrealistic expectation.[98]

Thomas: What about the "written histories of Egypt" though?

Astrid (using her tablet): According to Kitchen:

> A tiny fraction of reports from the East Nile Delta occur in papyri recovered from the desert near Memphis. Otherwise, the entirety of Egypt's administrative records of all periods in the Delta are lost . . . and monumental texts are also almost nil. And, as pharaohs *never* monumentalize *defeats* on temple walls, no record of the successful exit of a large bunch of foreign slaves (with loss of full chariot squadron) would ever have been memorialized . . . in temples in the Delta or anywhere else."[99]

Hiromi: An absence of evidence isn't necessarily evidence of absence; and the Bible is evidence in and of itself. Still, it would be *nice* to have some independent evidence for the exodus.

Astrid (using her tablet): Theologian Richard D. Patterson says there's "a growing body of evidence supporting the historicity of the Exodus event, from the departure from Egypt to the Conquest."[100] To begin with, there's plenty of evidence that Semitic people went to Egypt during times of drought and that the Egyptians had Semitic slaves.

Thomas: Such as?

98. Davis, "Exodus on the Ground," 223.

99. Kitchen, *On the Reliability of the Old Testament*, 246.

100. Patterson, "Victory at Sea: Prose and Poetry in Exodus 14–15," 54n45.

Astrid (using her tablet): The tomb of an Egyptian vizier called Rekhimire, built around 1450 BC, shows Nubian and Semitic slaves making bricks.[101] This matches the biblical depiction of Jewish slaves making bricks in Egypt. Look:[102]

Hiromi: That's at least "evidence of [something] like a Jewish captivity in Egypt."[103] But what about the exodus itself? Can we connect the dots between Egypt and Israel?

Astrid (using her tablet): Scholars like James Hoffmeier, Richard Hess, and Benjamin Noonan have documented cultural and linguistic links between late Bronze Age Egypt and the Pentateuch, the first five books of the Old Testament, that point to the authenticity of these stories.[104] According to Noonan: "Given the observation that at least some of the Egyptian loanwords in the exodus and wilderness narratives were borrowed during the Late Bronze Age, it is likely that the events of these narratives took place during the Late Bronze Age, just as one would expect if they represent

---

101. See Littman et al., "With & Without Straw."
102. See "Maler der Grabkammer des Rechmirê."
103. Dawkins, *Outgrowing God*, 50.
104. See Hoffmeier et al., *Did I Not Bring Israel Out of Egypt?*

authentic history."[105] Edwin Yamauchi reports that: "The similarity of the Mosaic covenant to the Hittite suzerainty treaties, which date from the second millennium BC, has convinced many scholars of the antiquity of the Mosaic covenant."[106]

Theologians Scott Hahn and Curtis Mitch note that Exodus displays an accurate knowledge "of local conditions described in the story, such as the Egyptian agricultural calendar . . . and the use of acacia wood [which] is indigenous to parts of Egypt and the Sinai Peninsula but is not found in Palestine."[107] They argue that "it is difficult to believe that authors in postexilic Palestine . . . could have known and accurately portrayed the conditions of second-millennium Egypt (c. 1400–1200 B.C.)."[108]

Stephen O. Moshier and James K. Hoffmeier have used information from geology, archaeology, digital topography, and satellite imagery to produce a map of the eastern Nile Delta and Sinai Peninsula during the Bronze Age. They found that: "The restored geography . . . provides a plausible map of the region that is described in the Exodus texts."[109]

Dating to around 1210 BC, the Merneptah Stela records the existence of a people group called Israel. Set up by Pharaoh Merneptah to commemorate his military victories in Cannan, it proclaims, with obvious exaggeration, that "Ashkelon is carried off, and Gezer is captured. Yeno'am is made into nonexistence; Israel is wasted, his seed is not." The name "Yeno'am" is followed by an Egyptian hieroglyph that designates a town, but "Israel" is followed by a hieroglyph that means a people. Michael G. Hasel comments that "While the Merneptah stela does not give any indication of the actual social structure of the people of Israel, it does indicate that Israel was a significant socioethnic entity that needed to be reckoned with."[110] Here's a photo[111]:

105. Noonan, "Egyptian Loanwords as Evidence," 66–67.

106. Yamauchi, "Current State of Old Testament Historiography," 13.

107. Hahn and Mitch, *Ignatius Catholic Study Bible*, 15.

108. Hahn and Mitch, *Ignatius Catholic Study Bible*, 15.

109. Moshier and Hoffmeier, "Which Way Out of Egypt?," 101.

110. Hasel, "Israel in the Merneptah Stela," 56n12. See also van der Veen et al., "Israel in Canaan (Long) Before Pharaoh Merenptah?"

111. See "Merenptah Israel Stele Cairo."

Recent excavations at Khirbet el-Mastarah, in the Jordan Valley six miles north of Jericho, revealed stone enclosures, rectilinear rooms, and pottery dating to the Late Bronze Age II/Iron Age I. The site appears to have been used by a nomadic or semi-nomadic group at the beginning of the Iron Age, about 1200 BC. Archaeologist David Ben-Shlomo says: "this might fit the biblical story of the Israelites coming from east of the Jordan River, then crossing the Jordan and entering into the hill country of Israel later."[112]

Hiromi: Interesting, but not conclusive.

---

112. Ben-Shlomo, quoted in Pettit, "Do These Ruins Prove the Biblical Story of the Exodus?," para. 12.

Sophie: The next period in Jewish history is the era of the "united monarchy."[113]

Douglas (using his phone): Dawkins says: "King David . . . made no impact either on archaeology or on written history outside the Bible. This suggests that, if he existed at all, he was probably a minor local chieftain rather than the great king of legend and song."[114]

Astrid (using her tablet): Dawkins obviously doesn't know that "The publication of fragments of an Old Aramaic stela from Tel Dan in 1993/1995 bought to light the first recognized nonbiblical mention of the tenth-century king David, in a text that reflected events of the year 841 and would have been set up at no great interval after that date."[115] This Stela famously mentions "the house of David." Eric Cline, a professor of classics, anthropology, and history at George Washington University, explains that: "the finding of this inscription brought an end to the debate and settled the question of whether David was an actual historical person."[116] Here's a photo[117] with the house of David reference highlighted:

---

113. See Williams, "King David"; Williams, "King Solomon"; Gladwell, *David & Goliath*; Kitchen, *On the Reliability of the Old Testament*, chapter 4; Ortiz, "Archaeology of David and Solomon"; Provine et al., *Biblical History of Israel*, chapters 8, 9.

114. Dawkins, *Outgrowing God*, 48.

115. Kitchen, *On the Reliability of the Old Testament*, 92.

116. Cline, *Biblical Archaeology*, 60.

117. See "Tel Dan Stela."

There's another reference to the "house of David" on the ninth-century BC Mesha Stele.[118] Moreover, Kitchen argues that the phrase "[he]ig[hts] (of) David" appears in the Egyptian Topographical List of Shishak/Shoshenq I. This list contextually locates David's heights in the Negev area, and dates to 925 BC, about forty-five years after David, which as Kitchen notes, is "within living memory of the man."[119]

Thomas: Okay, David existed. But perhaps he was "a minor local chieftain rather than the great king of legend and song"?[120]

Astrid (using her tablet): Here's a *Science Daily* report on the discovery of some clay seals, known as "bullae," in southern Israel. Professor Jimmy Hardin says: "these bullae . . . date to the 10th century BC, and [this] lends general support to the historical veracity of David and Solomon as recorded in the Hebrew biblical texts."[121]

Archaeologists investigating several tenth-century BC sites in Israel have argued for an accumulation of evidence pointing to the existence of a large Davidic state. For example, discoveries from Tel 'Eton, on the southeastern edge of ancient Israel's territory, fit the biblical description of an expanding kingdom during the reign of King David. Archaeologists Avraham Faust and Yair Sapir report that carbon dating from Tel 'Eton

> suggest that the site was transformed around the first half of the 10th century BCE. . . . A new edifice, probably serving as a residence of the family of a high ranking official . . . was built on the top of the mound, using impressive building technology. . . . The construction of the building coincided with the expansion of the mound (and probably also with the erection of the city wall), signifying a major change of the entire site. Both historical circumstances and the plan of the building—a classical four-room house—connect the changes with the highland polity, most likely the contested United Monarchy.[122]

Archaeologist Eilat Mazar discovered the remains of a large structure in Jerusalem that was probably a palace built for King David.[123]

---

118. See Borschel-Dan, "High-tech Study of Ancient Stone."

119. Kitchen, *On the Reliability of the Old Testament*, 93.

120. Dawkins, *Outgrowing God*, 48.

121. Hardin, "Discovery of Official Clay Seals," para. 4.

122. Faust and Sapir, "'Governor's Residency' at Tel 'Eton," 816–17.

123. See CBN—The Christian Broadcasting Network, "Perfect for a Palace."

Sophie: After the "united monarchy" era, the Jews split under the "divided monarchy" of Israel and Judah, which led up to conquest by the Babylonian Empire, which took many Jews into "exile" to work as slaves.

Hiromi: Of the captivity in Babylon, Dawkins admits "There's plenty of evidence for that."[124]

Astrid: At last, Dawkins gets something right![125]

Douglas (using his phone): But you don't think Dawkins is right when he says: "It was during or around the time of the Babylonian exile that most of the Old Testament books were written"?[126]

Astrid (using her tablet): I don't. As Kitchen comments: "There is not one scintilla of hard, verifiable, independent evidence that the accounts of David and Solomon's reigns were invented in either the Neo-Babylonian or Achaemenid periods. This view is purely hypothetical."[127]

The later we date the Old Testament's historical narratives, the harder it is to explain their accuracy about the details of the ancient cultures they depict. Here's what archaeologists Yosef Garfinkel, Saar Ganor, and Michael G. Hasel conclude in their recent book, *In the Footsteps of King David: Revelations from a Biblical City*:

> Historical processes and cultural phenomena referred to in the Bible relating to the 10th century BCE thus find concrete expression at Khirbet Qeiyafa at the same time period. Such clear examples of correspondence between archaeological finds and the biblical tradition stand in contrast to the theories of scholars advocating the minimalist approach, and their assertion that the Bible was written during the Hellenistic or Persian period, or at the end of the 7th century BCE, and contains no historical memory, but who have no data or finds to support such views. . . . The Khirbet Qeiyafa excavations have provided archaeological evidence corroborating historical memories from the time of King David. . . . The excavations showed that at the end of the 11th century BCE an urban society and central monarchy began to take shape. . . .

124. Dawkins, *Outgrowing God*, 52.

125. See Kitchen, *On the Reliability of the Old Testament*, chapter 3; John C. Lennox, *Against the Flow*; McDowell, *Daniel in the Critics' Den*; Millard, "Daniel in Babylon: An Accurate Record?"; Provine et al., *Biblical History of Israel*, chapter 11.

126. Dawkins, *Outgrowing God*, 53.

127. Kitchen, "Controlling Role of External Evidence," 127.

The proposal that the Bible was written many hundreds of years after the events is describes, and that it reflects only the period in which it was written, is no longer sustainable.[128]

Sophie: I think we can wrap things up there. As we discussed online, Hiromi has convinced me that we should skip chapter 4 of *Outgrowing God* until we've looked at chapters 5 and 6, and she's volunteered to lead our discussion next week on chapter 5.

As the others were leaving, Hiromi complimented Astrid on her Marillion T-shirt. Astrid explained that *Brave* was one of her favorite albums. She liked the way it told a story that criticized modern society whilst still finding a place for a sense of redemption.

Hiromi asked what "redemption" meant. Astrid said the term originally meant to free something from a bond, such as by paying the ransom cost of a slave's freedom. Christians used the term to describe Jesus' costly obedience to God the Father in going to the cross to establish the process through which God frees people from the bonds of sin.[129] Jesus reportedly used the metaphor when telling his followers that: "whoever would be great among you must be your servant . . . even as the Son of Man came not to be served but to serve, and to give his life as a ransom for many."[130] Astrid explained that "The Son of Man" was an Old Testament phrase Jesus used to refer to himself. Hiromi commented how surprising it was to see a religion centered on something God did for people, rather than on something people must do for God.

Astrid asked Hiromi what music she liked. Hiromi expressed her admiration for several "modern" composers, from Dimitri Shostakovich[131] to Paul Mealor[132] and Yoko Kanno.[133] She explained how she loved playing piano works by Johann Sebastian Bach[134] and Philip Glass,[135] but that she also played electric guitar, and was really into "progressive" music.[136]

128. Garfinkel et al., *In the Footsteps of King David*, 201–2.
129. See "Redeem, Redemption."
130. Matt 20:27–28.
131. Williams, "Shostakovich."
132. See Williams, "'Desert Island Discs' Event with Composer Paul Mealor"; Williams, "Paul Mealor."
133. See Oh No, Anime!, "Yoko Kanno: Musical Mastermind."
134. See Williams, "Johann Sebastian Bach."
135. See Williams, "Philip Glass."
136. See Pinzon, "What is Prog?"

They ended up discussing their favorite "prog" bands. Starting with classic 1970s groups such as Genesis, Yes, and Pink Floyd, they moved on to contemporary bands like Marillion and IQ, swapping listening recommendations along the way.

Hiromi mentioned a Japanese group called Yuka & Chronoship.[137] Astrid suggested a Scandinavian band called Opeth.[138] She also recommended some Christians working in the genre: The Celtic-flavored Iona, whose British keyboard/lead-guitar player Dave Bainbridge was also the driving force behind Celestial Fire; American band Glass Hammer; and American keyboard maestro Neal Morse, of The Neal Morse Band and progressive super-group Transatlantic.[139]

Eventually, Astrid had to leave "for an appointment," so Hiromi headed off to do some piano practice.[140]

137. See Yuka & Chronoship's website at www.omp-company.com/chronoship/. See also CathyduProgSud, "Yuka and the Chronoship 2"; and CathyduProgSud, "Yuka and the Chronoship 3."

138. See Opeth's YouTube channel at www.youtube.com/channel/UCmQSJTFZa XN85gYk6W3XbdQ.

139. See Williams, "Christian Prog Rock."

140. See Williams, "Hiromi's Playlist." An extensive list of chapter-specific recommended resources can be found on this book's webpage at www.peterswilliams.com/publications/books/outgrowing-god/.

Fourth Meeting

Can There Be Good without God?

R eturning from the barista, Thomas set his glass down next to his knitting.

"You realize it's cold out, don't you?" joked Douglas.

"What can I say," replied Thomas, "I like iced coffee."

Hiromi placed a notebook on the table. Before she opened it up, Astrid noticed the cover was adorned with anime artwork and the words "March comes in like a lion."[1] Flicking through the notebook, Hiromi came to a stop and began speaking to the group:

Hiromi: Chapter 4 offers moral objections to the biblical God, Yahweh, with Dawkins declaring: "Whether or not we think God is an entirely fictional character, we can still judge whether he is good or bad."[2] But I thought it was odd to ask readers to make these moral judgements *before* looking at the nature of morality and moral judgements in chapters 5 and 6. Sophie agreed it would make sense to swap things around, and I volunteered to lead today's discussion on chapter 5.

So, in chapter 5, Dawkins looks at the nature of morality and the relationship between morality and religion. I say "religion," because Dawkins shows no interest in the philosophical issue of the relationship between moral values on the one hand and the existence and nature of God on the other. Instead, he stresses that our morality must stem from a source that transcends the Bible, asking "how do we know which statements in the Bible are good, which bad? How do we decide? That decision has to be based

---

1. See "March Comes in Like a Lion."
2. Dawkins, *Outgrowing God*, 72.

on something outside the Bible."[3] Dawkins lays the groundwork for this "revelation" by criticizing some of the Ten Commandments from the Old Testament, as well as some of Jesus' words and actions.

Douglas: Do I detect a hint of sarcasm in that review?

Hiromi (tilting her head to one side): What is this "sarcasm"? I'm sure I don't know the meaning of the word!

Hiromi grinned, and everyone laughed.

Douglas: My mistake! But sarcasm would've been an appropriate way to highlight the banality of Dawkins's argument. Chapter 5 does have an odd focus, and it does rather studiously ignore the key philosophical questions.

Thomas: Isn't Dawkins basically arguing we can't ground morality in the Bible?

Astrid: Indeed; but who is he arguing against? I mean, the author of Psalm 19 doesn't recommend embracing the law simply because it's in the Pentateuch, or even because it was written by Moses acting as the prophet of Yahweh. He says: "the precepts of the LORD are right, rejoicing the heart."[4]

Thomas: But what about people who don't have the Mosaic law?

Astrid: Dawkins *agrees* with the biblical teaching that people without the Mosaic law can and do make accurate moral judgements! In Romans 2:14–15 the apostle Paul says that "when Gentiles, who do not have the law, by nature do what the law requires, they are a law to themselves, even though they do not have the law. They show that the work of the law is written on their hearts."

Thomas: I see.

Astrid: Moreover, the fact that our morality is rooted in a source that transcends the Bible is entirely consistent with the claim that the Bible can play an important role in shaping our moral beliefs.

Thomas: How come?

3. Dawkins, *Outgrowing God*, 115.
4. Ps 19:8.

Astrid: Well, neither the laws of logic, nor my ability to grasp the basic laws of logic depend in any way on the professor who taught me logic; but that professor certainly influenced my grasp of logic.

Thomas: I get the analogy.

Hiromi: It's all very well arguing that morality isn't based on the Bible; but Dawkins ducks questions about whether we have any objective metaphysical basis or foundation for making moral judgements about anything.

Thomas: What do you mean? Everyone has a right to their own opinions.

Hiromi: Yes, but do you think your opinions can put you in touch with moral facts, or are they merely subjective opinions equivalent to your personal preference for iced coffee? If one person says God is good, and another person says God is evil, are they just sharing their preferences? Or are they making contradictory truth-claims about moral facts independent of their opinions?

Astrid: Is your right to hold your own moral opinion something the state objectively shouldn't interfere with, or something the state could try to override without doing anything objectively wrong?

Thomas: I think I see what you're getting at; but could you clarify what it means for moral claims to be "objective" or "subjective"?

Sophie: Good question, Thomas.

Hiromi (referring to her notebook): For a moral fact to be "objective" means that instead of being contingent upon our desires, decisions, or preferences, they provide "standards by which people's own desires, decisions and preferences can themselves be judged."[5] Moral objectivism says there are moral facts that we can discover, so "to say, for example, that the Holocaust was objectively wrong is to say that it was wrong even though the Nazis who carried it out thought that it was right and that it would still have been wrong even if the Nazis had won World War II and succeeded in exterminating or brain-washing everyone who disagreed with them."[6]

By contrast, moral subjectivism claims "that value judgements . . . are matters of personal prejudice or private opinion. Our judgements of

5. Smith, *Atheist Overreach*, 56.
6. Craig, *God? A Debate between a Christian and an Atheist*, 17.

matters of fact are genuine knowledge, but not our value judgements."[7] As Thomas L. Carson and Paul K. Moser write, moral subjectivism "states that moral judgements are not objectively true or false and thus that different individuals or societies can hold conflicting moral judgements without any of them being mistaken."[8]

Sophie: Can you give a concrete illustration of this distinction?

Hiromi: Suppose one person thinks Pythagoras's Theorem is true and another thinks it false.

Sophie: Pythagoras's Theorem states that in any right-angled triangle, the square of the hypotenuse is equal to the sum of the squares of the other two sides.[9]

Hiromi: We know Pythagoras's Theorem is true.[10] Anyone who thinks otherwise, *however sincerely*, is mistaken. Our coming to know the truth of Pythagoras's Theorem was a matter of *discovering* truth, not *inventing* it. Likewise, moral objectivism says ethics is a matter of *discovering* truths that hold even if people sincerely disagree with them. According to objectivism, the fact that people hold opposing moral opinions just means some people are mistaken. By contrast, subjectivism says that opposing moral opinions are *equally valid, because there is no objective fact of the matter to get right or wrong.*

Thomas: Well, I want to be able to object to Yahweh on moral grounds, so I guess that makes me a moral objectivist!

Astrid: But you're not just buying into moral objectivism as a way to argue against Yahweh, are you?

Thomas: I'm not. Actually, I think you've given me the language to express something I've been thinking ever since I watched an ancient Greek play a few weeks back.

Sophie: Which play?

7. Adler, *Adler's Philosophical Dictionary*, 153.

8. Carson and Moser, "Introduction," 2.

9. See www.mathsisfun.com/pythagoras.html.

10. See Woo, "Visual Proof of Pythagoras' Theorem"; Math Antics, "The Pythagorean Theorem"; Bogomolny, "Pythagorean Theorem and Its Many Proofs."

Thomas (using his tablet): *Antigone*, by the fifth-century-BC Greek play-wright Sophocles.[11] As the play opens, Princess Antigone's brother Polynices has been defeated in battle by her other brother, Eteocles, king of Thebes. Unfortunately, both brothers died in the fighting, and their uncle Creon now controls Thebes. Antigone meets with her sister Ismene, saying: "Don't you know that Creon has decided to honor one of our brothers with burial but not the other? They say that he has hidden Eteocles beneath the earth, to have his share of honor with the dead below; but Polynices's corpse . . . must lie unwept, untombed, a heap of treasure to entice the hungry birds."[12] Creon has backed this command with the death penalty. Ismene says that, since she's "under compulsion," she will "obey the authorities" because "Trying to do more than we can makes no sense at all."[13] Antigone declares: "I will bury him myself, and so die nobly. I'll lie beside him in love, guilty of devotion! For I must please the dead a longer time than I must please the living. With them I'll lie forever. But you—go on, dishonor what's honored by the gods."[14] As she later tells Creon, it wasn't "Justice who lives with the gods below" who made "laws like these for men, nor did I think your decrees so formidable that you, mere mortal as you are, could override the laws of the gods, unwritten and unshakable."[15] While "tyranny enjoys many blessings, not least the power to do and say what it pleases,"[16] *might does not make right* and can't make it right to hate what we should love. Antigone concludes: "I can't join in hate, but only in love." Creon seals Antigone into a cave to die. Although he eventually relents, it's too late and events lead his son and wife to commit suicide.

So, *Antigone* is all about whether what's right and wrong is something subjective, something that can be invented at will by the power of the state, or whether there exists a state-transcending moral law by which the state's use of power can be objectively judged. And on the answer to *that* question, leaving aside the ethics of burying the dead, I have to side with Sophocles.[17]

Astrid: Me too. To borrow a moral example from atheist philosopher Peter Cave: "whatever sceptical arguments may be brought against our belief that

---

11. See Animated Books, "Antigone by Sophocles—Animated Play Summary"; Williams, "National Theatre, Antigone"; Sophocles, *Antigone*.

12. Lefkowitz and Romm, *Sophocles, Aeschylus, & Euripides: The Greek Plays*, 282.

13. Lefkowitz and Romm, *Sophocles, Aeschylus, & Euripides: The Greek Plays*, 283.

14. Lefkowitz and Romm, *Sophocles, Aeschylus, & Euripides: The Greek Plays*, 283.

15. Lefkowitz and Romm, *Sophocles, Aeschylus, & Euripides: The Greek Plays*, 294.

16. Lefkowitz and Romm, *Sophocles, Aeschylus, & Euripides: The Greek Plays*, 296.

17. See National Theatre, "Antigone: Religion and Modern Context."

killing the innocent is morally wrong, we are more certain that the killing is morally wrong than that the argument is sound. . . . Torturing an innocent child for the sheer fun of it is morally wrong. Full stop."[18]

Hiromi (using her tablet): *Antigone* reminds me of this quote from philosopher Richard Taylor:

> A duty is something that is owed. . . . But something can be owed only to some person or persons. There can be no such thing as duty in isolation. . . . The idea of political or legal obligation is clear enough. . . . Similarly, the idea of an obligation higher than this, and referred to as moral obligation, is clear enough, provided reference to some lawmaker higher . . . than those of the state is understood. In other words, our moral obligations can . . . be understood as those that are imposed by God. This does give a clear sense to the claim that our moral obligations are more binding upon us than our political obligations. . . . But what if this higher-than-human lawgiver is no longer taken into account? Does the concept of a moral obligation . . . still make sense? . . . the concept of moral obligation [is] unintelligible apart form the idea of God. The words remain, but their meaning is gone.[19]

Douglas (using his phone): I agree with Taylor. I don't like Yahweh any more than Creon, but I reluctantly find myself agreeing with Gilbert Harman when he says: "What is right in relation to one moral framework can be morally evil in relation to a different moral framework. And no moral framework is objectively privileged as the one true morality."[20] As Michael Ruse affirms: "if you stay with naturalism . . . substantive ethics is an illusion."[21]

Hiromi (referring to her notebook): Although Dawkins *seems* to offer an objective moral critique of Yahweh, *Dawkins is a moral subjectivist.* Writing in *Scientific American*, Dawkins says: "The universe that we observe has precisely the properties we should expect if there is, at bottom, no design, no purpose, no evil, no good, nothing but pitiless indifference."[22] Indeed, Dawkins asserts that there's a distinction "between ideas that are false or

---

18. Cave, *Humanism*, 146.
19. Taylor, *Ethics, Faith, and Reason*, 83–84.
20. Harman, "Moral Relativism," 3.
21. Ruse, "Evolution and Ethics," 862.
22. Dawkins, "God's Utility Function," 85.

true about the real world (factual matters, in the broad sense) and ideas about what we ought to do . . . for which the words 'true' and 'false' have no meaning."[23]

Thomas: But how can Dawkins say that *and* make moral objections to religion?

Douglas: He contradicts himself.

Thomas: Oh.

Astrid (using her tablet): I did notice that in *Outgrowing God* Dawkins sometimes avoids this problem by discussing questions about morality in the second person. He asks the key question about accounting for the existence of objective morality *in the second person* when he writes: "But, you may say, it's all very well talking about an independent set of standards. It does seem to be there, but what is it?"[24]

Thomas: I see. But *I'm* a moral objectivist, so *I* can criticize Yahweh! *I* can coherently say I'm entitled to judge, *on what I think are objective moral grounds*, that Yahweh's actions are objectively evil.

Hiromi: Ah, but *if* Dawkins and company are right when they say that an atheistic worldview excludes objective moral values, *then* your judgement about Yahweh being evil would contradict your atheism, and your position would be incoherent after all.

Douglas: That's why I'm a moral subjectivist.

Thomas: *Now* I see why we need to grapple with chapters 5 and 6 before chapter 4! Dawkins agrees with Douglas here, that one has to choose between atheism and moral objectivism. And like Douglas, he chooses the former over the latter. But he encourages his readers to morally condemn Yahweh *before* thinking about the relationship between their ethics and their worldview.

Hiromi: Yes. What if, in order to make objective moral judgements about *anyone's* character, we actually need the existence of a transcendent deity who can ground the objectivity of moral values and obligations? Which

23. Dawkins, "Afterword," in Brockman, *What Is Your Dangerous Idea?*, 307.
24. Dawkins, *Outgrowing God*, 122.

brings me to Dawkins's ambiguous statement in chapter 4 that theists "think it's impossible to be good . . . without God."[25]

Thomas: How is that ambiguous?

Hiromi: On the one hand, it could mean theists think it's impossible to be good, *without a personal belief in God.*

Douglas (using his phone): That seems to be how Dawkins understands the statement. He complains that "lots of people seem to think you need to believe in some sort of god, any kind of 'higher power', in order to have any chance of being moral—of being good. Or that, without belief in a higher power, you'd have no basis for knowing right from wrong, good from bad, moral from immoral."[26]

Astrid: Some people may think that knowing right from wrong or being good depend upon belief in God, but as we've seen, that's an unbiblical view.

Thomas: Okay, but what's on the other hand?

Hiromi: On the other hand, Dawkins's claim might be understood as a statement that *it's impossible to be objectively* good *if there's no God.*

Sophie: Hiromi is drawing a distinction between a claim about belief or knowledge, an "epistemological" claim, and a claim about what exists, an "ontological" claim. The statement that "it's impossible to be good . . . without God"[27] is ambiguous because it can be taken as either an epistemological claim or an ontological claim.

Hiromi (using her tablet): Yes. Dawkins asks: "why should somebody think you need God in order to be good?" He gives two answers, both off the top of his head, both of which are *epistemological* answers concerned with *what people believe.* He says: "I can think of only two reasons, both bad ones. One is that the Bible, the Quran, or some other holy book tells us how to be good, and without a book of rules we wouldn't know what's right and what's wrong. The other possible reason is that people have such a low regard for humans

---

25. Dawkins, *Outgrowing God*, 77.
26. Dawkins, *Outgrowing God*, 95–96.
27. Dawkins, *Outgrowing God*, 77.

that they think we . . . will only be good if [they think that] somebody—God, if nobody else—is watching us: the theory of the Great Policeman in the Sky."[28]

Douglas: Dawkins says "there doesn't seem to be much clear evidence that religion makes people behave either better or worse."[29] However, he also admits: "Some studies suggest that religious people give more generously to charity."[30] And he speculates that: "The tendency to be good when you are being watched may even be quite primitive, built deeply into our brains."[31]

I've been reading sociologist Christian Smith, who argues that: "if anyone thinks 'good without God' means a system in which oversight, control, and punishment are eliminated in favor of widespread voluntary expressions of ethical behavior, she will be waiting forever. The choice between God and (social) god, between one's creator and judge and the myriad social control mechanisms of society, is inescapable."[32]

Astrid (using her tablet): I don't know about that. I recognize God as my judge, but atheist Bruce Sheiman has a good point when he writes: "Religious people do not strive to be good because they want to avoid punishment and earn bonus points in the heavenly sweepstakes; they strive to behave consistent with God's love and grace in much the same way we naturally strive to be good for anyone we love."[33] For me, Christian ethics is a response to God's love expressed in forgiveness through Jesus, but divine forgiveness can only be appreciated against the background recognition that God's love ultimately expresses itself in judgement against unrepentant sinfulness. As the apostle John says: "There is no fear in love, but perfect love casts out fear. For fear has to do with punishment, and whoever fears has not been perfected in love. We love because he first loved us."[34]

Thomas: Dawkins also notes that: "Even if the Great Spy Camera theory has some truth in it, it's certainly not a good reason to believe in the factual existence of God."[35]

28. Dawkins, *Outgrowing God*, 96.

29. Dawkins, *Outgrowing God*, 100.

30. Dawkins, *Outgrowing God*, 100.

31. Dawkins, *Outgrowing God*, 96.

32. Smith, *Atheist Overreach*, 30–31.

33. Sheiman, *Atheist Defends Religion*, 26.

34. 1 John 4:18–19.

35. Dawkins, *Outgrowing God*, 103.

Astrid: I don't know anyone who claims it is! Dawkins is attacking a "straw man."

Thomas: Like a scarecrow?

Sophie: That's right: "In the straw man argument, someone attacks a position the opponent doesn't really hold. Instead of contending with the actual argument, he or she attacks the equivalent of a lifeless bundle of straw, an easily defeated effigy, which the opponent never intended upon defending anyway."[36]

Astrid: Unfortunately, Dawkins tackles the relationship between God and morality by making stuff up off the top of his head rather than teaching himself or his readers about the standard discussion of this topic among philosophers. A flick though an introductory philosophy text or two would have informed him about the centrality of the ontological question he ignores.

Douglas: I agree.

Thomas: But why think moral objectivism says anything positive about God's existence?

Douglas (using his phone)**:** Many atheists have argued that objective morality stands or falls with the existence or nonexistence of God. If that's right, then the only way to coherently include objective morality within our worldview is to include God as well. As Julian Baggini says: "If there is no single moral authority, we have to in some sense 'create' values for ourselves . . . [and] that means that moral claims are not true or false . . . you may disagree with me but you cannot say I have made a factual error."[37]

Astrid: That's right. Given that moral objectivism entails theism, and given that moral objectivism is true, it follows that theism must be true.

Sophie: This outline of a "moral argument" for theism is logically valid, meaning that the conclusion follows from the premises, and must be true if the premises are true. In other words, the real question is, are the premises of this argument both true?

Astrid: I think they are.

---

36. Ferrer, "15 Logical Fallacies," paras. 10–12. See also Pirie, *How To Win Every Argument*, 55–157.

37. Baggini, *Atheism*, 41–51.

Thomas: But doesn't that mean we'd be judging God's morality by God's moral standards. Isn't that suspect?

Douglas: That reminds me of an objection to the moral argument made by Kai Nielsen. He argues that before we can claim that God is good we must already have in mind a standard of goodness by which we judge God. But in that case, it can't be claimed that ethical principles that originate in God provide the ultimate ethical standard. Rather, our own ethical intuitions must be acknowledged to be the ultimate standard.

Astrid (using her tablet): But as Paul Chamberlain writes: "It is true that our *knowledge* of [moral goodness] must come before we can apply it back to God. But as to its *existence*, it could have existed in God before we knew about it."[38]

Hiromi: That seems right. You may need to look at a map before you know where Tokyo is, so the map comes first in your knowledge, in what's called "the order of discovery"; but Tokyo existed prior to the map in "the order of reality." The map depends upon the real Tokyo, even if you can't find the real Tokyo without the map. Likewise, God's goodness could exist in the order of reality prior to our understanding of goodness, even though we have to understand what "goodness" means before we can judge that God is good in the order of discovery.[39]

Sophie: Notice how the distinction between epistemology, or "the order of discovery," and ontology, or "the order of reality," underlies this rebuttal of Nielson's objection.

Douglas (using his phone): According to Bertrand Russell:

> if you are quite sure there is a difference between right and wrong, you are then in this situation: is that difference due to God's [commands] or is it not? If it is due to God's [commands], then for God himself there is no difference between right and wrong, and it is no longer a significant statement to say that God is good. If you are going to say, as theologians do, that God is good, you must then say that right and wrong have some meaning which is independent of God's [commands], because God's [commands] are good and not bad independently of the mere

38. Chamberlain, *Can We Be Good without God?*, 186.

39. See J. P. Moreland's discussion of this point in Moreland and Nielson, *Does God Exist?*, 131.

fact that He made them. If you are going to say that, you will
then have to say that it is not only through God that right and
wrong came into being, but that they are in their essence logically anterior to God.[40]

Sophie: Russell's objection traces back to Plato's *Euthypro* dialogue,
where Socrates asks: "Is what is holy holy because the gods approve it, or
do they approve it because it is holy?"[41] The question poses a dilemma: Are
the god's commands arbitrary, or is there some standard of goodness independent of the god's commands to which their commands must conform
in order to be good?

Hiromi: I think the finite gods of polytheism are caught on the horns of that
dilemma. As contingent inhabitants of the universe, and as beings who are
themselves often immoral, polytheistic gods can't offer an adequate ground
for objective morality. But the necessarily existent, transcendent, morally
perfect God of monotheism can split the horns of the dilemma by having
objective moral goodness be part of God's character. There *is* something
over and above God's *commands*, but that something is God's *character*.
God's commands are necessarily consistent with God's holy character, and
God's holy character *is* "the good."

Astrid (using her tablet): As William Lane Craig says: "Plato himself saw
the solution to this objection: you split the horns of the dilemma by formulating a third alternative, namely, God is the Good . . . God *is* necessarily . . .
loving, kind, just, and so on, and these attributes of God comprise the Good.
God's moral character expresses itself towards us in the form of certain
commandments, which become for us our moral duties. Hence God's commandments are not arbitrary, but necessarily flow from his own nature."[42]

Thomas: Let me go through this step by step. The first premise of the "moral
argument" claims that *if* morality is objective, *then* that's something that's
explained by the existence of God.

Astrid (using her tablet): At the very least, I think the existence of a wholly
good God offers the most plausible account of the existence of objective
moral claims. As H. P. Owen argues, objective moral claims: "transcend

40. Russell, *Why I Am Not a Christian*, 12.
41. Plato, *Euthyphr.* 178.
42. Craig, *God, Are You There?*, 38–39.

every human person [and] it is contradictory to assert that impersonal claims are entitled to the allegiance of our wills. The only solution to this paradox is to suppose that the order of [objective moral] claims . . . is in fact rooted in the personality of God."[43] The moral argument doesn't claim to offer a complete description of "God," but it certainly argues against naturalism and for the existence of some kind of moral God with a capital G.

Thomas: I see. And the other premise is that morality *is* objective.

Astrid: That's right.

Thomas: And given both premises, it follows that a morally perfect, transcendent deity exists. Or probably exists at any rate.

Hiromi: Yes. Astrid accepts this argument. Douglas accepts the first premise and avoids the conclusion by rejecting the second premise. You've accepted the second premise by endorsing moral objectivism, so in order to avoid the conclusion you presumably reject the first premise?

Thomas: I guess I should. But the idea that we could have objective, transcendent moral obligations without a transcendent someone *to whom we are obligated* does seem implausible.

Douglas: Another line of argument worth considering is that we experience moral duties as *commands* that tell us how we ought to behave.

Thomas: I suppose so.

Douglas: Well, *if* these moral commands have an objective validity, *then* it would seem that there must be an objectively existent moral commander, some transcendent personal reality with the absolute moral authority to command our behavior.

Thomas: I can see the sense in that.

Douglas: And that's why I deny any objective validity to moral duties.

Thomas: Hang on, why don't you draw the conclusion that there's a transcendent moral commander?

43. Owen, "Why Morality Implies the Existence of God," Davies, *Philosophy of Religion*, 648.

Douglas (using his phone): Well, as Joel Marks, Professor Emeritus of Philosophy at the University of New Haven, explains:

> the religious fundamentalists are correct: without God, there is no morality. But they are incorrect, I still believe, about there being a God. Hence, I believe, there is no morality. . . . In sum, while theists take the obvious existence of moral commands to be a kind of proof of the existence of a Commander, i.e., God, I now take the non-existence of a Commander as a kind of proof that there are no Commands, i.e., morality.[44]

Thomas: I see. But if I do *that*, I can't make any objective moral criticism of anyone, including religious people and including the biblical character of Yahweh, without contradicting myself! What do you make of this "moral argument," Hiromi?

Hiromi: It doesn't claim to establish everything theists believe about God, though it clearly favors theism over atheism. Personally, I agree with Douglas that objective morality stands or falls with the existence or nonexistence of a transcendent, wholly good, God. And I guess I see the attractions of believing in objective morality backed by the authority of a wholly good deity. But I don't want to accept that worldview just because I'd like it to be true, not without being satisfied that the arguments for moral objectivism are stronger than the arguments for atheism. That's something I'm still thinking about. So I'm currently agnostic.

Astrid: But the very fact that you're concerned about the *integrity* of your beliefs, about treating opposing arguments *fairly* and not being *unduly* influenced by personal preference, shows how deeply committed you are to the existence of objective moral values, obligations, and duties!

Hiromi: You mean that my commitment to reasoning objectively carries an implicit commitment to objective morality?!

Astrid: That's right. If we try to separate talk about thinking from talk about morality, we can't coherently think about *thinking with integrity, fairness, or objectivity.* The same goes for the commitment you just expressed to not contradicting yourself, Thomas.

Douglas: And what about my commitment to moral subjectivism?

44. Marks, "An Amoral Manifesto: Part I," para. 2.

Astrid: I'd say your admirable commitment to philosophical consistency is ultimately moral in nature. I'd say you've got to wrestle with the question posed by the nihilist philosopher Friedrich Nietzsche: "Why should you pay attention to the truth?"

Hiromi: That's a *really* interesting question.

Sophie: I suggest we leave that as a point for private meditation and move on to other matters.

Thomas (using his tablet): Dawkins says: "Christianity and Islam have traditionally taught that sinners after their death will be tormented for all eternity in hell."[45] I'd like to put Dawkins's question to Astrid: "What do you think of people who threaten children with eternal fire after they are dead?"[46] Dawkins says he "can't think of anybody who more richly deserves to go there."[47]

Astrid: By issuing that moral judgment, Dawkins is contradicting his own subjectivism and tacitly endorsing the second premise of the moral argument for theism.

Thomas: Point taken. But what do you think about threatening children with "hideous torture"?[48]

Astrid: I think Dawkins is right to point out that some people misuse the doctrine of hell, especially as he focuses on a picture of "hell" that owes more to medieval imagery than to what the Bible says.

Douglas: But Jesus talks about sinners being "thrown into the hell of fire,"[49] and the Revelation of John talks about sinners being thrown into the "lake of fire."[50]

---

45. Dawkins, *Outgrowing God*, 99.
46. Dawkins, *Outgrowing God*, 100.
47. Dawkins, *Outgrowing God*, 100.
48. Dawkins, *Outgrowing God*, 100.
49. See Matt 18:9.
50. Dawkins, *Outgrowing God*, 100. See Rev 20:15.

Astrid: True; but Jesus also describes sinners being "thrown into the outer darkness."[51] The imagery is mutually contradictory if taken literally; but the symbolic nature of the imagery is clear in a passage like Hebrews 6:7–8, which likens those who follow Jesus to "land that has drunk the rain that often falls on it, and produces a crop," but likens apostates to land that "bears thorns and thistles . . . and its end is to be burned."

Hiromi: So the burning suffered by apostate "land" is no more literal than the "thorns and thistles" they produce, or the "crop" produced by faithful disciples?

Astrid: That's right. The "lake of fire"[52] is explicitly defined by John as a symbol for "the second death,"[53] *the post-judgement destruction of those who culpably reject Jesus.* Jesus advised his disciples: "do not fear those who kill the body but cannot kill the soul. Rather fear him who can destroy both soul and body in hell."[54] This is the same point driven home by Jesus' *parable* in Luke 19, where a king orders rebellious subjects to be executed for treason. In light of texts like these, I think the symbol of fire is best understood as pointing to the eternal destruction of culpably unrepentant sinners.[55]

Thomas: But many Christians believe hell involves unending conscious torment.

Astrid: They do, though some of them say that the fire of hell symbolizes the unrepentant sinner's experience of God's unwanted love. Every worldview accommodates disputed ideas.

Thomas: Fair enough.

Douglas (using his phone): Dawkins complains: "The God character in the Old Testament was morbidly obsessed with rival gods. He hated them with a passion and was consumed by the fear that his people might be tempted to worship them."[56]

---

51. See Matt 8:12.

52. See Rev 20:15.

53. See Rev 20:14.

54. See Matt 10:28.

55. See Williams, "Heaven & Hell"; see the Rethinking Hell website at http://rethinkinghell.com; Fudge, *Fire that Consumes.*

56. Dawkins, *Outgrowing God*, 106.

Astrid (using her tablet): Dawkins's objection to divine "jealousy" is really a complaint against the first commandment and the exclusive, marriage-like covenant between God and Israel. Concerning the significance of the first commandment, American poet and theologian Joy Davidman wrote that:

> belief in one God slew a host of horrors . . . the beast-headed bullies of old time. It laid the ax to sacred trees watered by the blood of virgins, it smashed the child-eating furnaces of Moloch, and toppled the gem-encrusted statues of the peevish divinities halfheartedly served by Greece and Rome. The old gods fought among themselves, loved and hated without reason, demanded unspeakable bribes and meaningless flatteries . . . what pleased one deity would offend another. . . . Then came the knowledge of God . . . a single being, creator of heaven and earth, not to be bribed with golden images or children burned alive; loving only righteousness.[57]

Thomas (using his tablet): But Dawkins quotes Exodus 20:5: "You shall not bow down to them or worship them; for I, the Lord your God, am a jealous God, punishing the children for the sin of the fathers to the third and fourth generation of those who hate me."[58] And he asks: "What do you think about that last sentence? God is so jealous that, if you worship a rival god, he will punish not only you but your children, your grandchildren and your [poor] innocent great-grandchildren."[59]

Astrid (using her tablet): Norman L. Geisler and Thomas Howe comment that "this does not mean that the innocent children are guilty of the sins of their parents . . . they too, like their fathers, had sinned against God. Noteworthy is the fact that God only visits the iniquities of 'those who hate' Him . . . not those who do not."[60]

Hiromi (using her tablet): Dawkins objects to the "Third Commandment: You shall not misuse the name of the Lord your God, for the Lord will not hold anyone guiltless who misuses his name. This means you mustn't use swear words involving God's name. Like 'God damn it!' Or 'Don't be such a

---

57. Davidman, *Smoke on the Mountain*, 21–22.

58. Dawkins, *Outgrowing God*, 106.

59. Dawkins, *Outgrowing God*, 107.

60. Geisler and Howe, "Ezekiel 18:20—Does God Ever Punish One Person," paras. 2–3. See also Cole, *Tyndale Old Testament Commentaries: Exodus*, 156.

god-damn fool!' You can see why God might not like it, but it doesn't seem like a terribly serious crime, does it?"[61]

Astrid (using her tablet): This isn't a commandment against expletives! To "misuse the name of the Lord" is to misrepresent God's character by invoking his approval or authority for something evil. The third commandment defends truth and integrity against the temptation to deliberately misrepresent the ultimate source morality for immoral gain. As Davidman comments, the third commandment affirms that: "The Lord was a Lord of righteousness; he was not to be invoked for evil ends."[62]

Douglas: I can think of some politicians who should heed that command!

Thomas (using his tablet): Dawkins takes a swipe at the sixth commandment: "When Moses came down from the mountain with the stone tablets, can you imagine the people reading them and saying, 'Oh! Thou shalt not kill? Good heavens, we'd never thought of that. Fancy! Thou shalt not kill. Well, well, well. Right, I'll remember that, no more murdering people from now on.'"[63]

Hiromi: How silly! Would Dawkins turn his sarcasm on the American Declaration of Independence for stating truths its authors considered "to be self-evident," including the claim that people have unalienable rights to "Life, Liberty and the pursuit of Happiness"?

Astrid: Look at the historical context! Many ancient Near Eastern cultures practiced human sacrifice.[64] Infanticide was common in pagan cultures.[65] The spread of Christianity helped to end gladiatorial combat as a form of public entertainment.[66]

---

61. Dawkins, *Outgrowing God*, 107.

62. Davidman, *Smoke on the Mountain*, 43.

63. Dawkins, *Outgrowing God*, 109.

64. See Ngo, "Did the Carthaginians Really Practice Infant Sacrifice?"; Pavid, "New Evidence of Ancient Child Sacrifice Found in Turkey"; Recht, "Human Sacrifice in the Ancient Near East"; Schwartz, *Sacred Killing*; Shanks, "First Person."

65. See Evans-Grubbs, "Infant Exposure and Infanticide." See also Craven, "Christian Conquest of Pagan Rome."

66. See Butt, "Gladiators and Christianity Clash."

Thomas: Dawkins says "the Sixth Commandment is violated in war, on a grand scale, and with the blessing of the clergy."[67]

Astrid (using her tablet): The sixth commandment outlaws "murdering people,"[68] as Dawkins himself says. Davidman comments: "the Sixth Commandment meant only to forbid murder . . . both Hebrew and Greek, both Old Testament and New, actually use the word for 'murder' in this context and not the word for 'kill.'"[69]

Thomas: But according to Dawkins: "What the Sixth Commandment originally meant was 'Thou shalt not kill members of thine own tribe.'"[70]

Astrid: That's ridiculous! The biblical prohibition against murder, which precedes the Mosaic law, is rooted in the fact that *all humans* are created in the image of God. Deuteronomy 10:18–19 commands Jews to "show your love for the alien, for you were aliens in the land of Egypt." You can't "show your love" for aliens whilst murdering them!

Thomas (using his tablet): The Old Testament may tell people to love their neighbors, but Dawkins says "there's any number of verses of the Old Testament which preach vengeance. If anyone injures his neighbour, whatever he has done must be done to him: fracture for fracture, eye for eye, tooth for tooth. As he has injured the other, so he is to be injured ([Lev] 24:19)."[71]

Astrid (using her tablet): That's a misreading of the so-called *lex talionis* legal texts. The "eye for an eye" principle is about taking vengeance *out of the hands of the private citizen* and ensuring that punishments mandated *by the law* are *proportionate* to the crime committed. As Copan explains:

> an investigation of the Pentateuch's *lex talionis* texts . . . reveals that, except for capital punishment ('life for life'), these are *not taken literally*. None of the examples illustrating 'an eye for an eye' calls for bodily mutilation, but rather just (monetary) compensation . . . this principle served as useful guide for exacting proportional punishment and compensation; this was designed to prevent blood feuds and disproportionate acts of retaliation.[72]

---

67. Dawkins, *Outgrowing God*, 110.

68. Dawkins, *Outgrowing God*, 109.

69. Davidman, *Smoke on the Mountain*, 73.

70. Dawkins, *Outgrowing God*, 111.

71. Dawkins, *Outgrowing God*, 117.

72. Copan, "Is Yahweh a Moral Monster?"

Thomas (using his tablet): Dawkins notes that the tenth commandment counts the neighbor's wife as being "among his possessions, like his house or his ox."[73] How do you feel about "the idea that a woman is the property of some man: one of his possessions, a 'thing' that he owns?"[74]

Astrid: If I was married, I could refer to "my husband" without implying he was a "thing," or that I "owned" him in the same sense that I own my tablet, and that I could therefore treat him as I wish.[75]

Hiromi: You think Dawkins misunderstands the text?

Astrid: The Mosaic law should be understood in light of Genesis 1, where men and women share together in the "image of God" and Genesis 2, where the archetypal marriage is the "one flesh"[76] union of Adam and Eve. It's true that, like most ancient societies, Jewish culture fell short of this ideal. But a Jewish wife was neither considered a "thing," nor as being among a man's possessions in the way that "his ox" was.[77] The Mosaic law didn't permit a man to divorce his wife at will, but only if she broke her marriage vows. Likewise, a wife could divorce her husband if he broke his marriage vows.[78] So, the tenth commandment wasn't interpreted as implying that a wife was a "thing" a man could treat as he liked! As the biblical Song of Songs says: "My beloved is mine, and I am his. . . . I am my beloved's and my beloved is mine."[79] Likewise, in the New Testament, Paul describes marriage as a form of mutual ownership.[80]

Thomas (using his tablet): Dawkins mentions "the 'Code of Hammurabi' . . . a renowned Babylonian king" whose "rulebook was written down about a thousand years before the Old Testament."[81]

Astrid (using her tablet): That's a really useful comparison. Commenting on the Code of Hammurabi, historian Paul Johnson observes: "These

---

73. Dawkins, *Outgrowing God*, 113–14. See: Exod 20:17 and the different phrasing of the same command in Deut 5:21.

74. Dawkins, *Outgrowing God*, 114.

75. See Wojciechowski, "Marriage as a (Mutual) Ownership."

76. Gen 2:24.

77. See Walton et al., *IVP Bible Background Commentary*, 96.

78. See Instone-Brewer, *Divorce and Remarriage in the Church*, 21–22, 36.

79. Song 2:16; 6:3.

80. See 1 Cor 7:2–5.

81. Dawkins, *Outgrowing God*, 117.

dreadful laws are notable for the ferocity of their physical punishments, in contrast to the restraint of the Mosaic Code."[82]

Thomas: Can you give some examples?

Astrid (using her tablet): For example, the Code of Hammurabi treated crimes against property as more serious than crimes against people, whereas the laws in Exodus 21–23 treat crimes against people as more serious than crimes against property. Copan notes that: "in Babylonian or Hittite law, status or social rank determined the kind of sanctions for a particular crime whereas biblical law holds kings and priests and those of social rank to the same standards as the common person."[83] If you lived in the ancient world, you'd much rather live under the law of Moses than the Code of Hammurabi!

Thomas: Maybe; but you obviously don't live under the law of Moses today.

Astrid (using her tablet): You're right. Christians *don't* live under the law of Moses, especially if by that you mean the whole spiritual "rule of life" set out in the Old Testament for Jews, including rules about purity and the distinction between Jews and gentiles. Christians live under the "new covenant" established by Jesus. As Paul declared: "There is neither Jew nor Greek, there is neither slave nor free, there is no male and female, for you are all one in Christ Jesus."[84]

To be "in Christ Jesus" means to live according to Jesus' spiritual "way," or "rule" of life. This Jesus-centered spirituality is rooted in a response to God's forgiveness and empowers a desire to love God with our whole being, and in that context to love our neighbors.[85]

This Christ-centered spirituality points us back to God's intentions for humanity spelt out in the opening narratives of Genesis, and forward to the promised "new heavens and earth."[86] As Copan comments:

> Mosaic legislation isn't the Bible's moral *pinnacle* but rather a *springboard* anticipating further development or, perhaps more accurately, a *pointer back* to the loftier moral ideals of Genesis 1–2; 12:1–3. These ideals affirm the image of God in each person (regardless of gender, ethnicity or social class), life-long

---

82. Johnson, *Art: A New History*, 33.
83. Copan, *Is Yahweh a Moral Monster?*, 93.
84. Gal 3:28.
85. See Williams, *Understanding Jesus*.
86. See Wright, *Surprised by Hope*.

monogamous marriage and God's concern for the nations. . . . Consequently, the [Christian] need not justify all aspects of the Sinaitic legal code. After all, God begins with an ancient people who have imbibed dehumanizing customs and social structures from their ancient Near Eastern context. Yet Yahweh desires to treat them as morally responsible agents who, it is hoped, *gradually* come to discover a better way; he does this rather than risk their repudiating a loftier ethic—a moral overhaul—that they cannot even understand and for which they are not culturally or morally prepared.[87]

Douglas (using his phone): I'm reminded of sociologist Christian Smith's observation that: "few ancient human cultures appear to have possessed the embryonic metaphysical and moral cultural material from which could have evolved the robust commitment to universal benevolence and human rights that many moderns today embrace."[88] Smith argues that if we ask: "how it is that so many modern people do appear to believe in universal benevolence and human rights . . . the best answer—one that many believers in naturalism recognize—points us in a historical direction, toward the metaphysics and moral teachings of religious traditions, particularly Judaism and Christianity."[89]

Sophie: This returns us to the question of how the Bible can play a role in shaping people's moral convictions without being the foundation of morality as such.

Thomas: What metaphysics and teachings does Smith have in mind?

Douglas (using his phone): Smith says:

the transcendent monotheism of ancient Judaism introduced a set of uncommon ethical sensibilities that were crucial in the eventual development of the culture of benevolence and rights. These included . . . beliefs in all human persons being made 'in the image of God'; in God liberating the Hebrews from oppressive Egyptian slavery; in Yahweh as a God of justice, righteousness, and loving kindness; in Yahweh as the only true God . . . and in the Promised Land as a place of abundance but also social justice, economic equality, and judicial integrity. Yahweh abhorred

87. Copan, "Are Old Testament Laws Evil?," 138.

88. Smith, *Atheist Overreach*, 53.

89. Smith, *Atheist Overreach*, 51.

infanticide and human sacrifice, demanded justice for the poor, and set legal limits on ill treatment of servants and criminals. Over centuries, Judaism developed a keen self-consciousness through recurrent prophetic condemnations of injustice, exploitation, and neglect of the poor, the needy, widows, strangers, aliens, and the unjustly accused. Judaism also evolved a universal vision of God's chosen people on a mission not to conquer the nations but to serve as the people through whom all of the nations might come to know God's love and righteousness.[90]

Thomas: And you agree with Smith?

Douglas (using his phone): I think he makes a strong case for the monotheistic roots of the concept of universal human rights inherited by secular humanists like Dawkins. I also think he makes a strong case that "a belief in universal benevolence and human rights as moral fact and obligation does not fit well with, or naturally flow from, the realities of a naturalistic universe."[91] That's why I, as a naturalist, reluctantly find myself embracing moral subjectivism.

Astrid: Because you think you *ought* to be reasonable and that you *should* try to think coherently about reality rather than having your cake and eating it?

Sophie: Although Dawkins's comments about Jesus do look like escapees from chapter 4's focus on moral issues, I think we'd best discuss them now.

Astrid: Actually, while Dawkins may think he's raising ethical issues about Jesus, I think the real issue is that Dawkins frequently misreads the biblical text.

Hiromi (using her tablet): I was interested to see Dawkins acknowledge that "Jesus was not a bad man,"[92] and affirming that "Jesus said some pretty nice things, in the Sermon on the Mount, for instance. Certainly very different from anything in the Old Testament."[93]

---

90. Smith, *Atheist Overreach*, 51–52.
91. Smith, *Atheist Overreach*, 49.
92. Dawkins, *Outgrowing God*, 121.
93. Dawkins, *Outgrowing God*, 115.

Astrid (using her tablet): I'm glad Dawkins recognizes the goodness of Jesus, but otherwise I'm afraid he's just sharing his ignorance again. As theologian Jonathan Pennington comments:

> Jesus's message in the sermon [on the Mount] is that God is our Father who sees and cares about the heart, not just external righteous deeds and religion.
>
> This teaching is rooted in and resonates with the prophetic tradition, particularly Isaiah and Jeremiah, with a healthy dash of Daniel and the minor prophets thrown in for good measure. There is deep continuity between Jesus's words and the rest of the Bible.[94]

Thomas (using his tablet): What about when Jesus says: "If anyone comes to me and does not hate his father and mother, his wife and children, his brothers and sisters—yes, even his own life—he cannot be my disciple"?[95] Do you really "hate" your Mum for Jesus, Astrid?

Astrid opened her mouth and shut it again as her eyes welled up with tears. She wiped her eyes with the sleeve of her jumper and took a sip of black coffee. Taking a deep breath, she said: "I know that was just a rhetorical question and you didn't mean to hurt me; but my Mum died in a traffic accident."

After a moment's silence, everyone expressed their sympathies, especially Thomas, who apologized profusely. Hiromi hugged her. Astrid looked uncomfortable and turned the conversation back to Jesus.

Astrid: Dawkins fails to realize that Jesus is using a hyperbolic form of expression where "hate" means "love less than,"[96] as is clear from Matthew 10:37.

Sophie: Where Jesus says: "Whoever loves father or mother more than me is not worthy of me, and whoever loves son or daughter more than me is not worthy of me."

Astrid (using her tablet): Theologian Leon Morris comments: "Discipleship means giving one's first loyalty. There is no place in Jesus' teaching for literal

---

94. Pennington, "3 Things You Didn't Know About the Sermon on the Mount," paras. 6–7.

95. Dawkins, *Outgrowing God*, 120. See Luke 14:26.

96. See Pitre, "Hatred in the Bible"; Morris, *Tyndale New Testament Commentaries*, 253; Stein, *New American Bible Commentary*, 397.

hatred. He commanded his followers to love even their enemies . . . so it is impossible to hold that he is here telling them literally to hate their earthly nearest. . . . But hating can mean something like loving less ([Gen] 29:21, 33; [Deut] 25:15)."[97] In context, it's clear that Jesus is actually warning that his disciples must be willing to suffer estrangement and even persecution from those that will reject them for choosing to follow him.

Sophie: A recent British government report noted that "the overwhelming majority (80%) of persecuted religious believers are Christians."[98] The charity *Open Doors* calculates that "1 in 9 Christians experiences high levels of persecution."[99] They state that during 2018: "4,136 Christians were killed for their faith, which means an average of 11 Christians are martyred every day. In addition, 2,625 Christians were imprisoned without trial."[100]

Thomas: That's terrible.

Hiromi (using her tablet): Dawkins complains that Jesus "took petty revenge on . . . a fig tree . . . he was hungry. Seeing a fig tree by the road, he went up to it but found nothing on it except leaves. Then he said to it, 'May you never bear fruit again!' Immediately the tree withered (Matt 21:18). Mark's version (11:13) adds that the reason there were no figs on the tree was that it was too early in the year. . . . Christians are understandably embarrassed by the story of the fig tree. Some say it never happened . . . others say it was 'symbolic'. There never was an actual fig tree. It was some kind of metaphor for the nation of Israel. That's a favourite dodge of theologians, had you noticed? If you don't like something in the Bible, say it's only symbolic, it never really happened, it's a metaphor to convey a message. And of course they get to choose which verses are metaphors and which are to be taken literally."[101]

Astrid: Dawkins poses a false dilemma.[102] Far from being an act of "petty revenge," this was a symbolic event involving a real tree, one that Jesus treated as a metaphor for the spiritual fruitlessness of the temple-authorities.[103] Mark's cryptic comment about it not being the season for figs may be an

---

97. Morris, *Tyndale New Testament Commentaries*, 253.

98. Wintour, "Persecution of Christians," para. 3.

99. Earls, "Christian Persecution Worsens Around The World," para. 3.

100. Earls, "Christian Persecution Worsens Around The World," para. 4.

101. Dawkins, *Outgrowing God*, 118.

102. See Reasons to Believe, "Informal Fallacies: The False Dichotomy Fallacy"; J Gainor, "False Dilemma/either-or Discussion."

103. See Real Truth. Real Quick, "Why Did Jesus Curse the Fig Tree in Mark 11?"; Holding, "Did Jesus Unfairly Kill the Fig Tree?"; Stein, *Baker Exegetical Commentaries On The New Testament: Mark*, 508–15.

allusion to symbolic comments in the Old Testament prophets about the spiritual fruitlessness of Israel.[104]

Douglas: You know, it strikes me that if Dawkins wants to be taken seriously when he accuses theologians of bad faith in their judgements about when to take biblical verses literally and when not to take them literally, he really should engage in some literary analysis and debate, rather than simply advancing unsubstantiated assertions to the contrary. As things stand, it's tempting to accuse *Dawkins* of bad faith when *he* gets "to choose which verses are metaphors and which are to be taken literally"[105] in ways that suit *his* agenda.

Sophie: A point worth pondering, and one with which we'll end today's meeting.

As they prepared to leave, Thomas caught Astrid's attention and said: "I'm sorry about your Mum. I didn't mean to hurt you."

"I know," she replied. "By the way, I think it's cool you knit."

"Uh, thanks," said Thomas. "I took it up to help me quit smoking and discovered I just like making stuff."

"Was it hard to learn?" asked Astrid.

"Not too hard," responded Thomas. "I got started with some YouTube tutorials; but it was helpful to have someone show me in person how to recover when things go wrong."

After a thoughtful pause, Astrid said: "I see a counselor once a week, because on top of everything, I have depression. She's been encouraging me to 'engage in structured activities with people' and to 'set and achieve manageable goals.'"

"Like book club," said Thomas.

"Like book club," she affirmed. "Anyway, I've been watching you knit, and thinking it might be a good hobby for me, if you'd be willing to teach me?"

"Sure, if you want. I can get you some needles and wool and we can go over the basics."

"Can we meet here, in the Café?" Astrid asked.

"Sure thing," replied Thomas. "Thanks for sharing, Astrid."

She managed a brief, nervous smile.[106]

---

104. See Brooks, *New American Commentary: Mark*, 182; Hooker, *Black's New Testament Commentaries*, 262.

105. Dawkins, *Outgrowing God*, 118.

106. An extensive list of chapter-specific recommended resources can be found on this book's webpage at www.peterswilliams.com/publications/books/outgrowing-god/.

Fifth Meeting

How Do We Decide What Is Good?

Pushing through the door of *The Campus Coffee Cup Café*, Astrid stamped the snow off her shoes before buying a black coffee and joining the others. She'd overslept, again, and had only just sat down when Sophie asked Douglas to summarize chapter 6 of *Outgrowing God*.

Douglas (using his phone)**:** Dawkins asks readers to assume that "niceness, of a special limited kind, is part of our evolutionary heritage" that "probably feeds into our sense of right and wrong."[1] He says: "Brains evolve like all other parts of the body. And that means that what we do, what we like doing, what feels right or wrong, also evolve. We inherit from our ancestors a liking for sweet things and a 'yuck' reaction to the smell of decay. . . . We also seem to have inherited a desire to be nice to other people, to be friends with them, spend time with them, cooperate with them, sympathize when they are in distress, help them when they are down."[2] And he says this "probably feeds into our sense of right and wrong. We have evolved moral values, inherited from our remote ancestors."[3]

Now, it's important to bear in mind that when Dawkins talks about "our sense of right and wrong" and our "evolved moral values," he's talking about *our subjective feelings about* right and wrong. Chapter 6 doesn't address the question of whether or not our evolved "sense of right and wrong" accurately reflects any *objective* moral facts. But we know he isn't saying that the evolutionary process was in any way purposefully aimed at or guided

---

1. Dawkins, *Outgrowing God*, 125.
2. Dawkins, *Outgrowing God*, 124.
3. Dawkins, *Outgrowing God*, 125.

towards the goal of producing in humans moral feelings that reflect an independent realm of objective moral facts.

Hiromi (using her tablet): When Dawkins provides examples of how public opinion about various ethical matters has changed over time, he suggests this change has all been in the same direction, and then asks *but doesn't answer* a key question: "It's the same direction, but is it the 'right' direction? Well, I think so and I expect you do too. Is that only because we are twenty-first-century people? I'll leave that for you to decide."[4]

Thomas: And you suspect he leaves that to readers to decide because he rejects the idea that there's as an objectively "right' direction"[5] for the evolution of our moral beliefs or behavior?

Hiromi (using her tablet): Yes. Dawkins says:

> In moderation, sugar is good for us, although too much is not. We now live in a world where too much sugar is readily available. But this was not true of our wild ancestors on the African savanna. Fruit was good for them, and many fruits contain moderate amounts of sugar. It was impossible to get too much sugar, so we evolved an open-ended appetite for it. The smell of decay is associated with dangerous bacteria. It benefited our ancestors to avoid decaying meat, and that included a revulsion to the smell. It's obvious why we evolved a desire for the opposite sex.[6]

The thing is, even assuming evolution explains why we have certain behavioral inclinations, from eating sugar[7] to making babies, it can't show that greed is *morally bad* rather than just *pragmatically* or *functionally bad for us.* Nor can evolutionary biology show that rape is *evil.*

Thomas: But isn't doing something that harms your body, or someone else's, morally bad?

Astrid: Perhaps we should say those things are bad "in the absence of mitigating circumstances."

4. Dawkins, *Outgrowing God*, 130.

5. Dawkins, *Outgrowing God*, 130.

6. Dawkins, *Outgrowing God*, 124.

7. To quote Stephen Jay Gould, such an account: "presents no neurological evidence of a brain module for sweetness and no palaeontological data about ancestral feeding. This 'Just-so story' therefore cannot stand as a 'classic example of an adaptation' in any sense deserving the name of science" (Gould, "More Things in Heaven and Earth," 100.)

Thomas: What do you mean?

Astrid: Well, would it be wrong for a bodyguard to take a bullet to protect the King of Norway, even though that would harm their own body? Is it wrong for a surgeon to harm someone's body, say by removing their appendix, in order to save their life?

Thomas: Point taken.

Hiromi (using her tablet): Leaving aside questions about the circumstances in which doing something that's functionally bad for a body is also morally bad, the point is that the morality of harming your body isn't something *science* can determine. Science can give us data that *informs* our ethical judgements, but science can't *detect* the rightness or wrongness of things. To quote Thomas Huxley, the agnostic known as "Darwin's Bulldog": "evolution may teach us how the good and the evil tendencies of man have come about; but, in itself, it is incompetent to furnish any better reason why what we call good is preferable to what we call evil than we had before."[8]

Astrid (using her tablet): Bertrand Russell came to the same conclusion. He wrote: "We judge . . . that happiness is more desirable than misery . . . goodwill than hatred, and so on. Such judgements . . . may be *elicited* by experience. . . . But it is fairly obvious that they cannot be proved by experience; for the fact that a thing exists or does not exist cannot prove either that it is good that it should exist or that it is bad. The pursuit of this subject belongs to ethics."[9]

Douglas: Forensic science can tell us someone's death was a murder, but it can't justify the claim that murder is wrong.

Thomas: But is that so much the worse for scientism, showing the idea that science is the only way to know anything to be false, or so much the worse for ethics, showing moral objectivism to be false?

Hiromi: I'd say it's so much the worse for scientism. Ethics is just one of several subjects that deals with knowledge that doesn't depend upon science.

Thomas: Along with?

8. Huxley, "Evolution and Ethics," 80.
9. Russell, *Problems of Philosophy*, 42–43.

Hiromi: Along with subjects like logic, mathematics, and aesthetics.

Thomas: I can see why you say logic and mathematics, but aesthetics deals with beauty doesn't it?

Hiromi: That's right.

Thomas: Isn't beauty "in the eye of the beholder"?

Hiromi: I don't think so. People may or may not "get" the beauty of the things they "behold," depending on their personal taste, culture, and so on. But that doesn't mean beauty is subjective. After all, you could say the same thing about *ethical* value.

Douglas (using his phone): Atheist philosopher J. L. Mackie made just that point when he argued his belief that ethical values are subjective must be extended to "non-moral values, notably aesthetic ones, beauty and various kinds of aesthetic merit" on the grounds that "much the same considerations apply to aesthetic and to moral values, and there would be at least some initial implausibility in a view that gave the one a different status from the other."[10]

Thomas: So that argument can go in either direction?

Hiromi: That's right. The question is, which direction is more plausible? Is it more plausible to say that goodness and beauty are *both* objective, or that they are *both* subjective?[11]

Thomas: Then I guess my commitment to the objectivity of ethics should incline me to believe in the objectivity of aesthetics.

Hiromi: I think that's right. But I also think belief in the objectivity of beauty is intuitively plausible in and of itself. As Alvin Plantinga says: "To grasp the beauty of a Mozart D Minor piano concerto is to grasp something that is objectively there; it is to appreciate what is objectively worthy of appreciation."[12]

---

10. Mackie, *Ethics*, 15.

11. See Williams, "Beauty"; Williams, *Faithful Guide to Philosophy*, chapter 14.

12. Plantinga, "Plantinga's Original 'Two Two Dozen (or so) Theistic Arguments,'" 226. See Forye, "Mozart: Concerto for Piano and Orchestra."

Astrid (using her tablet): The apostle Paul wrote of truth, goodness, and beauty as objective realities, recommending: "whatever is true, whatever is honorable, whatever is just, whatever is pure, whatever is lovely, whatever is commendable, if there is any excellence, if there is anything worthy of praise, think about these things."[13]

Douglas: I'd say that scientism and objectivism about moral and aesthetic values are all false.

Hiromi: In any case, we can at least agree that science doesn't tell us about the philosophical study of objective moral values.

Thomas (using his tablet): According to Dawkins, biological evolution *doesn't* explain how the moral views of a society change. He says: "our view of right and wrong changes as the centuries go by . . . on a historical time-scale much too fast to represent evolutionary change. The dominant moral values of the twenty-first century, in which we are now living, are noticeably different from those of even a hundred years ago."[14]

Astrid: I see his point, but I wonder if he isn't exaggerating?

Douglas: In what way? Attitudes to the environment, to race, to sex, gender and gender roles, have obviously changed a lot since the 1950s, wouldn't you say?

Astrid: I guess I'd say that's true, at least for most of the Western world. But do those changes really represent "the dominant moral values of the twenty-first century," *globally speaking*? And even in the West, are those really the "dominant" values? Aren't the "dominant values" the same as they were in 1950, or 950 come to that?

Hiromi: What "dominant values" are you thinking of, Astrid?

Astrid: How about: Being loving and compassionate towards other people, especially those close to you and those worse off than yourself. Displaying appropriate humility rather than being full of yourself.[15] Hav-

13. Phil 4:8.

14. Dawkins, *Outgrowing God*, 125.

15. See Men & Machines, "2019 Men & Machines Men's Breakfast"; Dickson, *Humilitas*.

ing integrity rather than being a hypocrite. Being willing to forgive people who've wronged you.

Thomas: Obviously.

Astrid (using her tablet): In other words, with the notable exception of loving God with one's whole being, the values Jesus taught and modeled. To quote the Russian author Fyodor Dostoyevsky: "Even those who have renounced Christianity and attack it, in their inmost being still follow the Christian ideal, for hitherto neither their subtlety nor the ardour of their hearts has been able to create a higher ideal of man and of virtue than the ideal given by Christ of old."[16]

Thomas (using his tablet): Perhaps the "dominant values" of Western culture haven't changed, but less central values have changed, or the way we apply our values in some situations has changed? Hasn't people's *behavior* changed? Perhaps people today are living out their values more consistently than in the past? Dawkins says: "the psychologist Steven Pinker has written a . . . book called *The Better Angels of our Nature*. . . . He shows how, over the centuries, over the millennia, we humans have been getting nicer, gentler, less violent, less cruel. The change has nothing to do with genetic evolution and nothing to do with religion."[17]

Astrid: On the one hand, I think some aspects of society have improved over time. The nineteenth-century abolition of slavery was an objective improvement, not just a change.

Thomas: Dawkins mentions the Bible's attitude towards slavery. We should come back to that.

Astrid: On the other hand, I think some aspects of society have become worse. I certainly don't think humans have become inherently better over time.

Douglas: I don't think Dawkins is saying that humans have become *innately* nicer. He says the behavioral change documented by Pinker "has nothing to

16. See "Quotes: Jesus' Influence on History," para. 16.
17. Dawkins, *Outgrowing God*, 130.

do with genetic evolution."[18] I think he means that human social structures have undergone a *cultural evolution* that leads them to behave better.

Astrid: But he's excluding religion from the list of social structures that have produced this result! That's hardly tenable in light of the evidence isn't it?

Thomas: What evidence?

Astrid: For example, one has to take into account the Christian faith of Jean Henry Durant, who received the first-ever Nobel Peace Prize for his role in founding the International Red Cross Movement and initiating the Geneva Convention.[19]

Sophie: The Geneva Convention "was a series of international diplomatic meetings that produced a number of agreements, in particular the Humanitarian Law of Armed Conflicts, a group of international laws for the humane treatment of wounded or captured military personnel, medical personnel and non-military civilians during war or armed conflicts."[20]

Astrid (using her tablet): Talking of international law, Eleanor Roosevelt, First Lady of the United States from 1933 to 1945, was the first Chairperson of the UN Human Rights Commission and played an instrumental role in drafting the Universal Declaration of Human Rights. She was a Christian.[21]

Likewise, the Lebanese diplomat and Christian philosopher Charles Habib Malik was the *rapporteur* or secretary for the drafting committee of the Declaration, which bears signs of his Thomistic philosophy.[22]

Another key member of the Commission was the Jewish jurist and judge René Cassin. The declaration opens by affirming the "inherent dignity" of humans, a concept derived from, and arguably most at home within, a theistic worldview.[23] As Cassin stated: "Human rights are an integral part of the faith and tradition of Judaism. The beliefs that man was created in the divine image, that the human family is one, and that every person is obliged

---

18. Dawkins, *Outgrowing God*, 130.

19. See Flick, "Christian Origin of the Red Cross"; Bugnion, "Geneva and the Red Cross".

20. "Geneva Convention," para. 1.

21. See "Faith of a First Lady."

22. See UN Human Rights, "Universal Declaration of Human Rights"; "Universal Declaration of Human Rights."

23. See Liberty University, "ACE Interview Angus Menuge 'Human Rights.'"

to deal justly with every other person are basic sources of the Jewish commitment to human rights."[24]

Douglas: People *don't* have objective moral duties or rights. The notion is
a legal fiction, created and enforced by mutual agreement between states.
"Ethical judgements are social instruments," as Charles L. Stevenson
concluded.[25]

Hiromi (using her tablet): That's ironic. It bears out sociologist Christian
Smith's observation that: "Atheists scorn the idea of a punishing God who
induces fearful obedience, but in the end they must substitute their own
version of the same, a watchful and punishing human society, to secure
moral order."[26]

Astrid (using her tablet): Professor Emanuel Paparella says: "It was the
monk's commitment to reading, writing, and education which ensured
the survival of Western civilization after the fall of the Roman Empire. . . .
They laid the foundations for European universities and became the bridge
between antiquity and modernity."[27] Medieval monasteries gave birth to
hospitals and universities.[28] According to the London Science Museum:
"Between 500 and 1100, monasteries played an important role in European
agricultural communities. Among their many welfare functions, they established early hospitals, which provided hospitality and healing for the
sick. Monasteries were also sites of medical learning, possessing important
libraries."[29] As the Indian philosopher Vishal Mangalwadi observes: "The
scientific perspective flowered in Europe as an outworking of medieval
biblical theology nurtured by the Church . . . the Bible created and under-
pinned the scientific outlook."[30]

Hiromi: Western "scientific" medicine was introduced into Japan in the six-
teenth century by Jesuit missionaries.[31]

---

24. "Making the Jewish Case for Human Rights," para. 7.

25. Stevenson, "Emotive Meaning of Ethical Terms," 279.

26. Smith, *Atheist Overreach*, 30.

27. Paparella, "Medieval Monks as Preservers of Western Civilization," para. 17.

28. See PerHedetun, "Catholic Church—Builder of Civilization."

29. National Archives, "Monasteries," para. 1.

30. Mangalwadi, *Book that Made Your World*, 223–24. See Discovery Science,
"Three Big Ways Christianity Supported the Rise of Modern Science."

31. See "Brief History of Medicine in Japan."

Astrid (using her tablet): Christians have founded many charities like Christian Aid,[32] Oxfam,[33] and The Children's Society[34]; and they support numerous charities by donating their time and money.[35] A 2017 study of US charitable giving conducted by the University of Indiana found that:

> "Someone with a religious affiliation was more than two times more generous than someone without a religious affiliation. And among those with a religious affiliation [people] who attend services were much more likely to give . . ."
>
> Not surprisingly, religiously affiliated households are much more likely than nonreligious households to donate to religious institutions defined in the report as congregations, denominations, missionary societies and religious media.
>
> But religious people also contribute to other types of charity at similar or higher rates than their secular counterparts. . . .
>
> While 62 percent of religious households give to charity, only 46 percent of nonreligious households do.[36]

Thomas: We get it. Christians do lots of nice things. They also do lots of nasty things.

Astrid (using her tablet): I'm not saying they don't! I'm simply saying that insofar as Dawkins has a point when he claims "humans have been getting nicer, gentler, less violent, less cruel," it's implausible for him to say this "has . . . nothing to do with religion."[37]

Thomas: Perhaps Dawkins should have said this change wasn't *only* down to religion. Then he could still point out that you don't need to believe in God in order to do good in the world. After all, the UN includes officially atheistic nations like China, and the Human Rights Commission had members who didn't believe in God.

Astrid: I agree on all counts.

32. See www.christianaid.org.uk.

33. See www.oxfam.org/en.

34. See www.childrenssociety.org.uk.

35. See Craig, "Christians Give MORE to Charity than Atheists"; "Share of Adults Who Volunteered"; Gary James Jason, Review of *Who Really Cares?*

36. Richardson, "Religious People More Likely to Give to Charity," para. 4.

37. Dawkins, *Outgrowing God*, 130.

Hiromi (using her tablet): I discovered that Pinker's statistics about the supposed decrease in murder rates since medieval times have been criticized by agnostic mathematician David Berlinski. He highlights the difficulties associated with estimating population sizes in the thirteenth century, and concludes: "If it is not possible reliably to assess the size of thirteenth-century populations, then neither is it possible reliably to assess the number of thirteenth-century homicides."[38] He also says that: "If mass murders are not included in the homicide rate for the twentieth century, then the homicide rate is no very good measure of violence; and if they are included, then the homicide rate does not indicate a long-term declining trend in violence. It indicates the opposite."[39]

Sophie: Let's turn our attention to what Dawkins has to say about normative ethics.

Thomas: What's "normative ethics"?

Sophie: Philosophers traditionally divide ethics into three sub-disciplines. The first is "applied ethics." This deals with practical decision making in answer to questions like: "Should we let this patient die?" The second is "normative ethics," which deals with the moral norms we use to answer applied ethical questions. The third and most fundamental is "metaethics." This deals with questions about the nature of moral norms and values, whether they are objective or subjective, and the critical assessment of different normative ethics.

For example, why make moral choices using the Utilitarian norm of taking those actions one calculates will maximize overall human happiness? To answer that "By adopting this norm one increases the chances of overall human happiness being maximized" would be question-begging. If a normative ethic offers an approach to the ethical dimension of life that seems to chime with our properly basic intuitions about morality, we might trust it to help us navigate difficult ethical situations where our intuitions are not so clear. However, if we discover a way in which a normative ethic conflicts with our properly basic ethical beliefs, we might begin to doubt it. As moral philosopher Jonathan Glover says: "The hardest questions in ethics are often about finding a middle ground between uncritical acceptance of intuitive

38. Berlinski, *Human Nature*, 54.
39. Berlinski, *Human Nature*, 67.

responses and abandoning all our emotionally rooted human values in the face of some abstract theory."[40]

Thomas: So now we're asking what Dawkins has to say about the question of how to deal with applied ethical questions. Got it.

Astrid: Can a moral subjectivist even engage in normative ethics, if they think there are no moral norms?

Douglas: They can think there are subjective, societal "norms." They can redefine morality as being about empirically measurable things like pain and pleasure, and then argue that there are *pragmatic* "norms" that take the form: "*If* you want to maximize pleasure over pain, *then* you should x."

Astrid: But the subjectivist can't say we *should* aim to maximize pleasure over pain, objectively speaking.

Douglas: They can't coherently say that, no.

Sophie: What does Dawkins have to say about different schools of moral philosophy?

Douglas (using his phone): Dawkins writes: "There are various schools of moral philosophy. I shall talk about only two of them: absolutists and consequentialists."[41] He says: "Absolutists think some things just are right and some things just are wrong. No argument. Rightness or wrongness is just a fact, just plain true, like the statement in geometry that parallel lines never meet."[42] By contrast: "Consequentialists judge right and wrong differently. You'll have guessed from the name that they care about the consequences of an action. For example, who *suffers* as a consequence."[43] Dawkins's sympathies are with the consequentialists.

Hiromi: I don't see the point of Dawkins's narrow focus on moral absolutism and consequentialism, unless he's associating absolutism with religion and consequentialism with secular, atheistic modernism.

---

40. Glover, "Ethics and Humanity," para. 5.
41. Dawkins, *Outgrowing God*, 132.
42. Dawkins, *Outgrowing God*, 132.
43. Dawkins, *Outgrowing God*, 133.

Thomas: But that's right, isn't it? Religious people believe in moral absolutes and modern people believe in acting in light of the practical consequences of our actions.

Astrid: Speaking as a *modern* religious person, I do believe in moral absolutes. I believe it's always right to love God. I believe it's always right to love one's neighbor. I believe one should always choose good over evil, and always choose the lesser of two evils when faced with a forced choice.

Thomas: Well, when you put it like that . . .

Astrid: However, Dawkins seems to confuse the claim of moral absolutism, that certain things are *always* objectively wrong, with the claim of moral objectivism, that certain things are *sometimes* objectively wrong.

Thomas: Can something be *objectively* wrong without *always* being wrong?

Astrid: Wouldn't you agree that a policeman who deliberately shoots an innocent civilian has done something wrong, but a policeman who shoots a rampaging terrorist has done the right thing? Or that lying about your age in order to buy alcohol is wrong, but lying in order to save someone's life is right?

Thomas: I see.

Astrid: "Absolutism" is often used to describe the view that certain actions, such as lying, are *always* wrong. But the objective rightness or wrongness of an action can be judged against an absolute moral standard *as it applies in the circumstances.*

Hiromi (using her tablet): I wonder if Dawkins is confusing normative ethics and metaethics? He describes "absolutism" as the belief that "Rightness or wrongness is just a fact, just plain true."[44] Whether or not rightness and wrongness is factual, such that moral statements can be objectively true or false, is a meta-ethical issue. Consequentialism is a normative ethical theory about how to "judge right and wrong." One could be both a moral objectivist and a consequentialist.

Astrid (using her tablet): I get the impression that Dawkins associates religious people with a moral absolutism that's about applying rules from

44. Dawkins, *Outgrowing God*, 132.

Scripture without regard for context or consequences. But the Bible offers general goals and general rules that set a context for the specific rules. In the words of the Old Testament prophet Micah: "what is good; and what does the LORD require of you but to do justice, and to love kindness, and to walk humbly with your God?"[45] Jesus criticized religious leaders by pointing out that although they made religious offerings of mint and dill and cumin, they had "neglected the weightier matters of the law: justice and mercy and faithfulness."[46] In Mark's Gospel, one of the scribes asks Jesus:

> "Which commandment is the most important of all?" Jesus an-
> swered, "The most important is, 'Hear, O Israel: The Lord our
> God, the Lord is one. And you shall love the Lord your God with
> all your heart and with all your soul and with all your mind and
> with all your strength.' The second is this: 'You shall love your
> neighbor as yourself.' *There is no other commandment greater
> than these.*"[47]

Christian philosopher Norman L. Geisler advocated a Christian ethic of "graded absolutism,"[48] arguing that: "there is a pyramid of value: God at the pinnacle, people next, then things at the bottom. We are to love God more than people and people more than things. And when any two levels unavoidably conflict, we should always take the higher over the lower."[49] Moreover, he said: "There are levels and spheres of love, and one is always higher than another. Each love command is absolute *in its area*. But when that area overlaps with another area, then the lower responsibility of love should be subordinated to the higher."[50]

But biblical ethics isn't just about rules, it's also about character. Actually, I think it's more about character than it is about rules. The rules are like a trellis that helps a plant grow the way the gardener wants, and for the Christian that "way" is defined by the character of God's love expressed in Jesus, who claimed to be "the way, and the truth, and the life."[51] Christian ethics is about developing our character within the pattern of his character as we relate to God through and in communion with him. The biblical rules describe the behavior required by the divine love, a love seen most clearly in Jesus. This is why Augustine of Hippo, commenting on the divine love mentioned in 1

---

45. Mic 6:8.
46. Matt 23:23.
47. Mark 12:28–31, emphasis added.
48. See Geisler, *Options in Contemporary Christian Ethics.*
49. McDowell and Geisler, *Love Is Always Right*, 100.
50. McDowell and Geisler, *Love Is Always Right*, 159.
51. John 14:6.

John 4:8, said: "Once for all, then, a short precept is given thee: Love, and do what you will: whether you hold your peace, through love hold your peace; whether you cry out, through love cry out; whether you correct, through love correct; whether you spare, through love you should spare: let the root of love be within, of this root can nothing spring but what is good."[52]

Sophie: It may be useful at this point to introduce three basic types of normative ethic. "Deontology," from *deon*, the ancient Greek for duty, designates normative ethics that are about following rules "that guide and assess our choices of what we ought to do . . . in contrast to those that guide and assess what kind of person we are and should be."[53] Theories that do the latter fall under the banner of "Virtue Theories," which "addresses the question: What sort of people ought we to become?"[54] You might describe virtue ethics as being concerned with how our actions shape our character, and with how we can develop a character that does the right things for the right reasons as a matter of course.

Consequentialist theories "hold that choices . . . are to be morally assessed solely by the states of affairs they bring about."[55] Most famously, Utilitarians aim to act in such a way as to maximize human "happiness," seeking "the greatest happiness for the greatest numbers."[56]

Utilitarians generally have in mind a "happiness" that has to do with pleasure and enjoyment. However, "happiness" as a translation of the ancient Greek word *eudaimonia*, with which Western ethics was traditionally concerned, has to do with a richer concept of "happiness" that might be described as "flourishing that includes valuable activity."[57] You see, in both ancient and medieval Western thought: "happiness presupposed an objective moral order to which one would conform one's life. For Aristotle, for example, happiness was not the effect of momentary pleasure but the result of cultivation of a life lived virtuously."[58]

One might think of these ethical theories as being action-centered (deontology), agent-centered (virtue theory), and outcome-centered (consequentialist). While they are distinct, these theories can overlap somewhat.

---

52. Augustine, "Seventh Homily on 1 John 4:4–12," para. 8.

53. Alexander and Moore, "Deontological Ethics," para. 1.

54. Keenan, "Moral Theological Reflections," 24.

55. Alexander and Moore, "Deontological Ethics," para. 2.

56. Francis Hutcheson, *Inquiry Concerning Moral Good and Evil*, quoted by Driver, "History of Utilitarianism," para. 19.

57. Hunter and Nedelisky, *Science and the Good*, 159.

58. Hunter and Nedelisky, *Science and the Good*, 159. See BBC Radio 4, "Aristotle on Flourishing."

For example, a virtue theorist might care about the consequences of their actions with respect to the goal of developing a character that fulfills their moral duties.

Thomas: Dawkins doesn't mention "virtue ethics."

Astrid (using her tablet): Aristotle's deeper view of "happiness" reminds me of two things. First, a passage by Martha Nussbaum, professor of law and ethics at the University of Chicago, where she writes: "Pleasure is only as good as the thing one takes pleasure in: if one takes pleasure in harming others, that good-feeling emotion is very negative; even if one takes pleasure in shirking one's duty and lazing around, that is also quite negative. If one feels hope, that emotion is good only if it is based on accurate evaluations of the worth of what one hopes for."[59] Second, it reminds me of the biblical concept of blessedness, where you can have and take comfort in your "happiness" even while you're sad. As Jesus says: "Happy are the mourning," that is, those who mourn their own sinfulness, "because they shall be comforted."[60]

Hiromi: Astrid, it seems to me that you're saying Christian ethics sits in an overlap between the normative ethics outlined by Professor Minerva?

Astrid (using her tablet): I suppose I am. I don't think we can assess moral choices "solely by the states of affairs they bring about,"[61] but I agree with Christian philosopher Garret J. DeWeese that "virtue theory is not exclusive of consequentialist or deontological considerations."[62] Christian virtue theory can see human goodness as an appropriate refection of divine goodness that humans are obligated to pursue, a goodness of character that includes dispositions to fulfill one's moral obligations. The virtuous person will naturally try to act with due regard for the foreseeable consequences of their actions, including how those actions will contribute to the ongoing formation of their character.

Moreover, virtue ethics is the only normative theory that doesn't treat life as just a matter of repeatedly seeking an answer to the question: "What is the right thing to do now?" As the late Ralph McInerny, author of the Father Dowling mystery novels[63] and a professor of philosophy at the University

---

59. Nussbaum, "Who Is the Happy Warrior?"
60. Matt 5:4 (YLT). See https://biblehub.com/commentaries/matthew/5-4.htm.
61. Alexander and Moore, "Deontological Ethics," para. 2.
62. DeWeese, *Doing Philosophy as a Christian*, 210.
63. See McInerny, "Father Roger Dowling."

of Notre Dame, observed: "We cannot assume that knowing the solution is the solution. Nothing, alas, is more familiar to us than that we sometimes act against our best knowledge of what it is that we ought to do."[64] According to McInerny: "What natural law maintains is that there are objective parameters of our moral life . . . virtue is the personal appropriation of the good sketched in the precepts of natural law."[65]

Douglas: But doesn't the Old Testament major on obeying God's revealed "law"?

Astrid (using her tablet): God's "law" is an important part of the covenant between God and Israel in the Old Testament. However, the opening chapters of Genesis set the stage for that revelation, laying out God's intentions for humanity; and the wisdom literature of the Old Testament "provides numerous parallels with virtue ethics."[66] Then the all-embracing new covenant revealed in the New Testament emphasizes faithful discipleship as a response to Christ: "We love because he first loved us."[67] The apostle Paul describes this love in one of his letters, saying: "Love is patient and kind. Love does not envy or boast. It is not arrogant or rude. It does not force itself on others and is not self-seeking. It is not irritable or resentful. It does not rejoice at wrongdoing, but rejoices with the truth. Love patiently endures everything, trusts God always, always looks for the best and never looks back. Love never fails."[68]

Hiromi: That's beautiful.

Astrid: While characteristic actions of the virtuous character may be listed in a set of rules, like the Ten Commandments, it's impossible to write out a set of rules that will cover every ethical situation we might come across. General principles, like loving your neighbor, have to be applied in specific situations with wisdom. And besides, as the apostle Paul recognized, making ethics all about trying to obey lists of do's and don'ts makes it a joyless exercise: "for the letter kills, but the Spirit gives life."[69]

---

64. McInerny, "Natural Law and Virtue," loc. 24.

65. McInerny, "Natural Law and Virtue," loc. 165, 273.

66. Wilkins, "Introduction," 12.

67. 1 John 4:19.

68. 1 Cor 13:5–8 (I have adapted the ESV translation here).

69. 2 Cor 3:6.

Christianity morality isn't about obeying lists of absolute rules out of fear; it's about a relational context for spiritual development and flourishing. It's about a community, centered on relationship with God in and through Jesus; a community that provides an attractive *vision* of the good life, motivates us to adopt the *right intention* to pursue that life, and offers practical *means* for spiritual formation. You might say that in Christianity, deontological ethics and virtue ethics meet in the *ideal personal being who invites us into loving relationship with himself.*

Douglas: You're not keen on consequentialism then?

Astrid (using her tablet): Utilitarianism gains some plausibility from the fact that it gives intuitively correct answers to many applied ethical questions. But it suffers from some severe problems. For example, Christian Smith points out that:

> utilitarianism is oblivious to inalienable human rights. In fact, if feeding members of a minority religion to the lions for the stadium entertainment of the masses would increase the overall, calculated, bottom-line happiness of the collective, then doing so would be moral in utilitarian terms. . . . In the end, since pleasure and happiness are simply on a qualitatively different plane than innate, universal human rights, utilitarianism is unable to get us from the former to the latter. If anything, utilitarianism greatly endangers the latter.[70]

Thomas (using his tablet): Dawkins himself admits "that consequentialist thought experiments sometimes lead in uncomfortable directions."[71] He discusses a classic thought experiment about a trapped coal miner[72] and points out that the money spent on rescuing him "could save a lot more lives and reduce a lot more suffering" if it was spent "on food for starving children around the world."[73] Therefore, it seems that "a true consequentialist" would "abandon the poor miner to his fate, never mind his weeping wife and children."[74] Dawkins's response to the thought experiment is to say: "I couldn't bear to leave him underground. Could you? But it's hard to justify the decision to rescue him on purely

70. Smith, *Atheist Overreach*, 76.
71. Dawkins, *Outgrowing God*, 139.
72. See: Jonathan Glover, *Causing Death and Saving Lives.*
73. Dawkins, *Outgrowing God*, 140.
74. Dawkins, *Outgrowing God*, 140.

consequentialist grounds. Not impossible but hard."[75] He doesn't explain how a consequentialist can justify rescuing the trapped miner.

Hiromi (using her tablet): Sociologist James Davison Hunter and philosopher Paul Nedelisky critique Utilitarianism by arguing that: "there is no way to compare one person's happiness to another's, or even to compare a single person's experience of happiness at one moment to anything she experienced in the past. There are no units by which comparison can be made."[76]

Douglas: Couldn't people just tell you how they felt; for example, whether they were more or less happy than they had been before?

Hiromi: They could, but with no standard unit of measurement, any calculation of happiness based on subjective data like that would lack the sort of rigor to which Utilitarianism traditionally aspires.

Astrid: Again, considering the apparent consequences of our actions is tied to the morality of our intentions. But if you "hold that choices . . . are to be morally assessed solely by the states of affairs they bring about,"[77] haven't you lost any categories for judging people's character? Can you separate character from ethics like that?

Douglas: Couldn't a Utilitarian say that good people are those whose actions increase the sum of human happiness and bad people are those whose actions reduce the sum of human happiness?

Hiromi: They could, but wouldn't that make it a matter of luck whether or not you were a good person?

Thomas: How so?

Hiromi: You might do things with the best of intentions that by chance turn out to decrease the sum of human happiness. Likewise, someone else might do things with evil intentions that, by chance, turn out to increase the sum of human happiness.

Astrid: We're certainly limited in our ability to predict the consequences of our actions, especially in the long term. If a Utilitarian says we should act to

75. Dawkins, *Outgrowing God*, 140.

76. Hunter and Nedelisky, *Science and the Good*, 210.

77. Alexander and Moore, "Deontological Ethics," para. 2.

produce "the greatest happiness for the greatest numbers,"[78] do they mean in the short term or in the long term, and why? As Hiromi says, actions that seem likely to maximize happiness as far as we can see might end up producing greater unhappiness in the long term. The Utilitarian would have to ignore our good intentions and say our actions had been wrong because they didn't turn out to maximize happiness.

Hiromi: Perhaps only an omniscient God could know what the long term effects of different actions would be; and perhaps God would give us rules or goals he knew would maximize happiness in the long term?

Douglas: That's an interesting thought.

Astrid (using her tablet): Here's another significant criticism of utilitarianism: "What justified an act as right or wrong according to utilitarianism . . . is its production of a greater balance of pleasure over pain than any alternative action, but, if we are always motivated to produce such a greater balance, it will be impossible for any of us to care for, or value particular individuals, and the important goods of love and friendship will be denied us."[79]

Hiromi: That does seem to show that utilitarianism is massively counter-intuitive.

Astrid (using her tablet): By contrast, as philosopher Steve Wilkins explains: "virtue theorists argue that, while the outcomes of our choices are not inconsequential, the more significant moral activity occurs at the motivational level. In other words, the main goal of ethics is not to get the right actions but to mold people who possess the right character qualities or virtues."[80]

Sophie: Does anyone want to address Dawkins's comments about abortion?

Douglas: Dawkins's dramatized discussion about abortion between Connie the consequentialist and Abby the absolutist is just a way for him to contrast absolutism with consequentialism, though he probably chose this

---

78. Hutcheson, *Inquiry Concerning Moral Good and Evil*, quoted by Driver, "History of Utilitarianism," para. 19.

79. Crisp and Slote, "Introduction," 7.

80. Wilkins, "Introduction," 6.

topic because it's a hot button issue in the American "Culture War" between liberals and conservatives.[81] We don't want to get into that do we?

Astrid: Whatever you think about abortion, Dawkins does a poor job of exploring the relevant questions. He only looks at the issue from the perspectives of a straw man version of moral absolutism on the one hand and a narrow consequentialism focused entirely on avoiding suffering on the other hand. Dawkins asks: "who suffers as a consequence of an abortion? Or who suffers as a consequence of refusing an abortion."[82] But he doesn't ask who might *gain happiness* as a consequence or an abortion or its refusal!

Thomas: Given our limited ability to predict the consequences of our actions, how reliably can we know how having or refusing an abortion will affect the mental state of the mother,[83] the father, family, and friends, or society as a whole? Not to mention the fetus that's being considered for abortion.

Hiromi (using her tablet): Dawkins says "The argument about when, in the womb, a 'person' begins [to exist]" is "very much a religious argument."[84] But how is that a religious argument, even if it's an argument religious people often use? Assuming it's wrong to kill a person without sufficient cause, I'd think the question of if and when a person begins to exist in the womb is obviously relevant to the question of abortion.

Astrid (using her tablet): As a consequentialist, Connie doesn't attach any particular value to *being a person* as such, only to *being able to suffer*. She says: "my question would not be 'Is this creature human?' but 'Can this creature suffer?'"[85]

Hiromi (using her tablet): Connie also says: "I prefer to ask a different question. Not 'When does it become human?' but 'When does it become capable of feeling pain and emotion?' And there is no sudden moment when that happens. It's gradual."[86] Now, I can see that pain comes in degrees. But surely something either is or is not able to feel pain!

81. See Hunter, *Culture Wars*.

82. Dawkins, *Outgrowing God*, 133.

83. See Franciscan University of Steubenville, "Abortion vs. Childbirth"; Shuping, "Women's Mental Health and Abortion"; Reardon, "Abortion and Mental Health Controversy"; Astbury-Ward, "Emotional and Psychological Impact of Abortion."

84. Dawkins, *Outgrowing God*, 139.

85. Dawkins, *Outgrowing God*, 137.

86. Dawkins, *Outgrowing God*, 137.

Douglas (using his phone): What about Connie's point that: "absolutists want to draw a hard and fast line between human and non-human. Does an embryo become human at the moment of conception, when the sperm first joins the egg? Or at the moment of birth? Or at some point between, in which case precisely when?"[87]

Astrid: One's answer to those questions will depend mainly upon one's philosophy of mind,[88] but what's Dawkins's argument for thinking that there *isn't* "a hard and fast line between human and non-human"[89]?

Thomas: Well, he doesn't give one. But perhaps his point is that there's no hard and fast way for us to *know* when an embryo becomes a human?

Astrid: Even assuming that's the case, it's a "red herring."

Hiromi: What's a "red herring"?

Sophie: A "red herring" is "A form of irrelevance which leads the unwary off on a false trail. A red herring is literally a dried fish which when dragged across a fox's trail leads the hounds off on the wrong scent."[90]

Thomas: And why is our inability to draw "a hard and fast line between human and non-human"[91] a "red herring"?

Astrid: Because it's obvious that in situations where a lack of knowledge might lead us to cause serious harm, we should err on the side of caution. I mean, if you were on a firing range and thought that there may or may not be a person hiding behind your paper target, would you shoot it?

Thomas: I see. So, if we think an embryo may or may not be a person, at a certain stage of its development, we should err on the side of caution and treat it as if it were a person.

Astrid: Right.

87. Dawkins, *Outgrowing God*, 137.
88. See Williams, "Introduction to Ethics."
89. Dawkins, *Outgrowing God*, 137.
90. Warburton, *Thinking from A to Z*, 124.
91. Dawkins, *Outgrowing God*, 137.

Hiromi (using her tablet): Dawkins's consequentialism leads him to views that many people find ethically counterintuitive. For example, he says if a baby would be born with Down's syndrome it should be aborted. As reported by *The Guardian*:

> The British author made the comment in response to [someone] who said she would be faced with "a real ethical dilemma" if she became pregnant and learned that the baby would be born with the disorder. Dawkins tweeted: "Abort it and try again. It would be immoral to bring it into the world if you have the choice." He faced a backlash for his comment, with one mother, who has a child with the genetic condition, saying: "I would fight till my last breath for the life of my son. No dilemma."[92]

The Down's Syndrome Association issued a response to Dawkins, saying: "People with Down's syndrome can and do live full and rewarding lives, they also make a valuable contribution to our society. At the Down's Syndrome Association we do not believe Down's syndrome in itself should be a reason for termination."[93]

Thomas: What about Dawkins's point that "many conceptions abort spontaneously"?[94]

Astrid: They do. And most people die of natural causes after they are born; but that doesn't mean it's all right to kill them!

Hiromi (using her tablet): Abby rightly observes that Connie starts with an absolute moral belief: "by simply saying 'Causing suffering is wrong.' You offer no justification for that."[95] Connie replies: "Yes, I admit that," and all Dawkins can do to soften the admission is to change the subject, pointing to a straw man version of absolutism grounded in the "absolutist belief, 'It says so in my holy book.'"[96] But plenty of nonreligious people believe in objective and even absolute moral values.

And even if someone's moral absolutism were grounded in the content of a holy book, you can't just beg the question against the status of that book!

92. "Richard Dawkins: 'Immoral' Not to Abort," paras. 2–4.

93. "Richard Dawkins: 'Immoral' Not to Abort," paras. 7–8. See TEDx Talks, "I Have One More Chromosome Than You"; This Morning, "Sally Phillips On Challenging Misconceptions Around Down's Syndrome."

94. Dawkins, *Outgrowing God*, 136.

95. Dawkins, *Outgrowing God*, 137.

96. Dawkins, *Outgrowing God*, 138.

I mean, what if the book in question was a genuine revelation from God that spelt out some moral absolutes for us to obey?!

Sophie: Shall we consider Dawkins's comments about slavery?

Douglas (using his phone)**:** Dawkins notes that: "Not surprisingly, since the Bible's morality was of its time, slavery is not condemned there."[97]

Sophie: We shouldn't allow ourselves to feel too superior to the ancient world on this matter. After all, an estimated 40.3 million victims are trapped in modern-day slavery, which is defined by the United Nations as including "debt bondage, serfdom, forced marriage and the delivery of a child for the exploitation of that child."[98]

Astrid: I think what Dawkins says about slavery is misleading.

Douglas: How so?

Astrid (using her tablet)**:** Well, let's begin with the cultural background of the time that makes Dawkins suggest a biblical failure to condemn slavery is unsurprising. Jewish scholar E. E. Urbach suggests that in the economic context of the Roman Empire "it was virtually impossible for anyone to conceive of abolishing slavery as a legal-economic institution. To have turned all the slaves into free day laborers would have been to create an economy in which those at the bottom would have suffered even more insecurity and potential poverty than before."[99]

As Glenn Sunshine summarizes the situation:

> Slavery was ubiquitous in the ancient world. People could become slaves as the result of war, criminal penalties, kidnapping, or poverty . . . faced with severe poverty, parents would sell children or even the entire family as slaves to pay off debts and to get food, since as slaves they would be fed by their owners. In a world with no social safety net, this was sometimes the only option to avoid starvation. Whatever the reasons for being enslaved, throughout the ancient world slaves were legally property, not persons, and their status was permanent unless for

97. Dawkins, *Outgrowing God*, 126.

98. Stop the Traffik, "What is Human Trafficking?" See United Nations, "Trafficking in Persons."

99. Urbach, *Law Regarding Slavery*, 93–94.

some reason the master chose to set the slave free or the conditions that caused the slavery were changed.[100]

Thomas: So the biblical attitude to slavery is acceptable because everyone else was doing it?!

Astrid: Hang on, I haven't finished the quote yet! Having established the cultural background, Sunshine adds: "The crucial exception to this was Israel."[101]

Thomas: But Israel had slavery, didn't it?

Astrid (using her tablet): Professor Thomas Schirrmacher says the Hebrew term "is given to misunderstanding, because it is all too easy to mistakenly read the cruel slavery of the Greeks, Romans, Muslims, Europeans, and Americans into the [Old Testament]."[102] A Hebrew slave was often a *voluntarily bonded servant* who didn't receive a wage but was instead provided for as part of a household for a set period of time, unless *they* chose to make the arrangement permanent. And the fact that they might choose to make their service permanent says a lot. As Schirrmacher observes: "The legal position of a slave/servant in Israel, over against the position of slaves among other peoples, was extraordinarily good. . . . A slave/servant in the Old Testament was not a possession of his or her master without rights as was the case in Greek, Roman, Islamic or the varieties of modern colonial slavery."[103]

Sophie: In the ancient world, slaves were *widely* seen as intrinsically inferior people. In his *Nicomachean Ethics*, Aristotle refers to slaves as "living tools."

Astrid (using her tablet): Which is why it's surprising that even non-voluntary servants in Israel *weren't* treated as possessions, but

> as persons with rights that were unknown in the surrounding countries. Servants who had been injured by their masters were immediately set free . . . and if a servant died soon after being struck by a master, the master was considered guilty of murder. . . . In other countries in the Ancient Near East, by contrast, slaves were commonly mutilated as legal punishment for

---

100. Sunshine, "Christianity and Slavery," 288.
101. Sunshine, "Christianity and Slavery," 288.
102. Schirrmacher, "Slavery in the Old Testament," 43.
103. Schirrmacher, "Slavery in the Old Testament," 44–45.

disobedience . . . and slaves could be killed by their masters with impunity.[104]

Like everyone else in Israel, servants got a day off every week, on the Sabbath. A servant could own possessions.[105] A servant "could become an heir by marrying a daughter who was to receive an inheritance," meaning that "upward mobility was possible for a slave."[106] Uniquely, Israelites were commanded to protect runaway foreign slaves. Moreover, kidnapping someone to sell as a slave was a capital offense in the Law of Moses.

Thomas: Well, I suppose that's not as bad as Dawkins makes it sound.

Astrid (using her tablet): Despite all this, voluntarily bonded service is clearly regarded by the Old Testament as a less-than-ideal social safety-net of last resort. As theologian David L. Baker writes: "the predominant attitude towards slavery in the Old Testament law is negative. One of the primary motivations for obedience in the law on care for the poor and oppressed is the exodus, God's liberation of his people from slavery in Egypt. . . . Slavery did not fit well with the ideals of Israelite society, and laws were designed to reduce the number of people in slavery and protect slaves who were not actually freed."[107] According to the prophet Isaiah, God told Israel: "Is not this the fast that I choose: to loose the bonds of wickedness, to undo the straps of the yoke, to let the oppressed go free, and to break every yoke?"[108]

Hiromi: How did Old Testament law try to reduce slavery?

Astrid (using her tablet): First, Israel had laws to protect the poor and prevent them having to enter into servanthood. The "Law of Gleaning . . . required that fields and fruit trees not be stripped bare during harvest, but

104. Sunshine, "Christianity and Slavery," 289.

105. See Schirrmacher, "Slavery in the Old Testament," 46.

106. Schirrmacher, "Slavery in the Old Testament," 47.

107. Baker, "Humanisation Of Slavery In Old Testament Law," 14. Baker notes that: "Only one law permits chattel slavery (Lev 25:44–46a), and even this does not encourage it, but limits it to those outside the covenant community: residents of other countries and foreign residents in Israel. The law permits buying slaves, not kidnapping, so it concerns acquisition of those who are already slaves, or are offered for sale by their families, not forcible enslaving of free people." Baker, "Humanisation Of Slavery In Old Testament Law," 14. Paul Copan argues that the provision for sheltering runaway slaves in Deuteronomy 23:15–16 "wasn't simply for a foreign slave running *to Israel* but also for a foreign servant *within Israel* who was being mistreated." Copan, *Is God A Moral Monster?*, 147.

108. Isa 58:6.

that some produce be left for the poor to collect to feed themselves. The Israelites were also instructed to lend to the poor without interest and without taking necessities as collateral for the loan. . . . Debts were to be cancelled every seven years."[109]

Second, for those who *did* enter servanthood voluntarily, that condition wasn't permanent: "the 'slave' was to work for six years and be set free without condition on the seventh year . . . in fact, the master was instructed to give generously to the released servant to help him reestablish himself."[110] There was also a "right of redemption" for voluntary servants, "who had to be set free when they either bought their own freedom or when someone else bought their freedom. . . . There even existed a 'redemption duty' upon . . . the closest relatives."[111]

Thomas (using her tablet): But what about the New Testament? Dawkins quotes Paul's instructions from Ephesians 6:5: "Slaves, obey your earthly masters with respect and fear, and with sincerity of heart, just as you would obey Christ. Obey them not only to win their favor when their eye is on you, but like slaves of Christ, doing the will of God from your heart." Here's another, from 1 Timothy 6: "All who are under the yoke of slavery should consider their masters worthy of full respect, so that God's name and our teaching may not be slandered."[112]

Astrid: You have to recognize that if the early Christians had protested against slavery, it would have been taken as the incitement of insurrection and the Roman Empire would have probably slaughtered everyone concerned, as happened to several slave-rebellions in Roman history.

Sophie: The most famous slave rebellion in Roman history, led by Spartacus in 73–71 BC, ended with the crucifixion of six thousand captives.[113] You might like to watch Stanley Kubrick's 1960 epic film *Spartacus*, though I'd also recommend checking out something straightforwardly historical on the man and his revolt.[114]

109. Sunshine, "Christianity and Slavery," 289.
110. Sunshine, "Christianity and Slavery," 288–89.
111. Schirrmacher, "Slavery in the Old Testament," 47.
112. Dawkins, *Outgrowing God*, 126.
113. TED-Ed, "From Slave to Rebel Gladiator."
114. See Spartakirk109, "Real Spartacus."

Astrid (using her tablet): So, while the New Testament doesn't call for the abolition of slavery, that doesn't mean it thinks slavery is a good thing. Slavery was a fact of life imposed by the iron fist of Rome and the New Testament includes advice to Christians on living with this reality. But selling people as slaves is among the sins listed in Revelation 18:13. Paul includes slave traders in a list of lawbreakers in 1 Timothy 1:9–10, and he tells slaves to take their opportunities to become free.[115] In one of his letters, Paul calls upon a Christian called Philemon to treat a runaway slave who'd since become a Christian under Paul's influence: "no more as a servant, but above a servant—a brother beloved, especially to me, and how much more to thee, both in the flesh and in the Lord!"[116]

Building on the Old Testament belief that all humans are made in the image of God, Christianity highlighted moral principles that countered slavery in the ancient world and which led to the abolition of slavery in the nineteenth century under the leadership of Christians like William Wilberforce.[117]

Sophie: For an introduction to William Wilberforce and the abolitionist movement in nineteenth century Britain, you might like to watch Michael Apted's 2007 film, *Amazing Grace*.[118]

Thomas: But Christians were also involved in the colonial slave trade.

Astrid: Setting aside the fact that people can be only *nominally* "Christian," let's just say that any genuine Christians involved in the slave trade were clearly failing to follow biblical teaching.

Hiromi (using her tablet): Dawkins seems to be more charitable towards nineteenth-century racists like Darwin,[119] Huxley, and Lincoln[120] than first-century non-racists like the apostle Paul. I mean, Paul made the famous

---

115. See 1 Cor 7:21.

116. Phil 1:16 (YLT). Peter J. Williams notes: "Christians could not change the legal system. A slave rebellion would have led to the execution of the rebels. There were also legal restrictions concerning the number of slaves who could be freed and freeing them early (before the age of 30) could bar them from becoming Roman citizens." Williams, "Does the Bible Support Slavery?," para. 22.

117. See Bingham, "William Wilberforce: A Force for Change"; Christian Concern, "Faith of William Wilberforce"; Calvary Church with Skip Heitzig, "Amazing Grace."

118. Williams, "Amazing Grace."

119. See Rose, "Darwin, Race and Gender."

120. See Foner, "Was Abraham Lincoln a Racist?"

egalitarian statement "There is neither Jew nor Greek, there is neither slave nor free, there is no male and female, for you are all one in Christ Jesus,"[121] whereas Dawkins admits "it would not have occurred to either Darwin or Lincoln that Africans could be the equal of what they called 'the civilized races.'"[122] Yet Dawkins also says: "It's a poor historian who would condemn Lincoln and Darwin and Huxley as racists. They were as near to being non-racist as men of their time ever got."[123]

Sophie: Perhaps some historical context would be useful here. In 1858, Lincoln said: "I have no purpose to introduce political and social equality between the white and black races . . . the negro . . . is not my equal in many respects, certainly not in color—perhaps not in intellectual and moral endowments."[124] In 1865, after the abolition of slavery, Huxley said:

> no rational man, cognisant of the facts, believes that the average negro is the equal, still less the superior, of the average white man. . . . The highest places in the hierarchy of civilisation will assuredly not be within the reach of our dusky cousins, though it is by no means necessary that they should be restricted to the lowest. . . . But whatever the position of stable equilibrium into which the laws of social gravitation may bring the negro, all responsibility for the result will henceforward lie between nature and him. The white man may wash his hands of it, and the Caucasian conscience be void of reproach for evermore. And this, if we look to the bottom of the matter, is the real justification for the abolition policy.[125]

Thomas: Yikes.

Sophie: Is there anything we haven't covered yet that anyone would like to discuss before we finish?

Hiromi: I just want to highlight the fact that it's one thing to have a moral rule at the level of normative ethics and another to account for that rule having an objective normativity at the level of metaethics.

121. Gal 3:28.
122. Dawkins, *Outgrowing God*, 127.
123. Dawkins, *Outgrowing God*, 128.
124. "Sixth Debate: Quincy, Illinois," para. 10.
125. Huxley, "Emancipation—Black and White," paras. 2–3.

Douglas (using his phone): Dawkins explains how "the great German philosopher Immanuel Kant—"

Astrid: Who was a theist!

Douglas (using his phone): Who was a theist,

> stated a rule called the Categorical Imperative: "Act only according to that maxim whereby you can, at the same time, will that it should become a universal law." The key word here is "universal." A rule encouraging stealing is ruled out, for example, because if it were universally adopted, that is, if everybody stole, no one would benefit: thieves prosper only in a society dominated by honest victims. If everybody told lies all the time, lying would cease to have meaning because there wouldn't be any reliable truth to compare it with.[126]

Hiromi: Showing that a behavior is self-defeating if everyone does it all the time is not the same as showing that it's morally wrong. All that's saying is that ethical rules need to be coherent! Nor does it explain why we have a *duty* to refrain from lying without sufficient mitigating circumstances, like lying to save a life.

Douglas (using his phone): Dawkins mentions how another "modern deontological theory proposes that we should devise our moral rules behind a 'veil of ignorance'. Pretend you don't know whether you are rich or poor, gifted or untalented, beautiful or ugly. Those facts lie concealed behind the imagined 'veil of ignorance'. Now devise the system of values you'd like to live under, given that you can't know whether you will be at the top of the heap or the bottom. Deontology is interesting, but I'll say no more about it here in a book about religion."[127]

Astrid: As if there haven't been any religious deontologists!

Hiromi: Isn't the "veil of ignorance" just a self-interested way of saying we should treat everyone fairly, in light of their common humanity?

Astrid: I'm struck by how keen Dawkins is to impress on us the thought that, while belief in God might make people behave better: "the Great Spy

---

126. Dawkins, *Outgrowing God*, 138.
127. Dawkins, *Outgrowing God*, 139.

Camera in the Sky is surely not a praiseworthy reason to be good."[128] I think he's right about that; but it's odd he seems to think theists are principally concerned with goodness out of fear, rather than out of love.

Hiromi: Right. And Dawkins goes from there to the conclusion that: "perhaps we should all give up the idea that we 'need God in order to be good.'"[129] It's as if he's never heard of the moral argument for God and thinks fear of punishment is the only possible connection between God and morality!

Astrid (using her tablet): Dawkins says he hopes "Chapters 4, 5 and 6 might have led you away from believing that religion is necessary for us to be good,"[130] but he also sets these issues aside as *irrelevant to his principle theme*, writing: "Would that mean we should all give up believing in God? No. Not for that reason alone. He might still exist even if we don't need him"—that is, *belief* in God—"in order to be good."[131]

Hiromi: Yeah, I can't wait to get stuck into Dawkins's discussion about whether there is "any good evidence anywhere, for any kind of god."[132]

As the meeting broke up Astrid drew Hiromi aside and handed her a gift-wrapped package, saying: "I wanted to thank you for coming over the other evening. I saw this and thought of you." Carefully stripping back the wrapping-paper, Hiromi uncovered a book entitled *A Gift of Music: Great Composers and Their Influence*, by Jane Stuart Smith and Betty Carlson. Astrid found herself being hugged by Hiromi, who asked: "Does this mean I can visit again?!"

"Of course. I'd like that," replied Astrid. "Can we watch more Japanese anime on Crunchyroll?"

"Yes," said Hiromi, "I'd like to introduce you a series called *March Comes in Like a Lion*. I think it will resonate with you."

"Okay, sure, let's do that. Same time?"

"Yes, same time."[133]

---

128. Dawkins, *Outgrowing God*, 141.

129. Dawkins, *Outgrowing God*, 141.

130. Dawkins, *Outgrowing God*, 141.

131. Dawkins, *Outgrowing God*, 141.

132. Dawkins, *Outgrowing God*, 141.

133. An extensive list of chapter-specific recommended resources can be found on this book's webpage at www.peterswilliams.com/publications/books/outgrowing-god/.

Sixth Meeting

The Good God of "the Good Book"?

Outside *The Campus Coffee Cup Café*, a fresh fall of snow was settling. Inside, the conversation was drifting towards deeper things.

Astrid: I meant to bring Norwegian biscuits, but I forgot.

Sophie: That's alright, Astrid. There's no expectation concerning provisions, only for providing a summary of chapter 4.

Astrid: I have that. I think we should start with an overview we can unpack as we discuss each topic in turn.

Sophie: Sounds like a plan.

Astrid (using her tablet): Dawkins repeats his assertions that "the biblical books were written long after the events they claim to describe,"[1] and that "modern archaeology and scholarship can find no evidence that any of these Old Testament stories are historically true"[2]; but most of chapter 4 tries to make a *moral* critique of the biblical God, who we can call "Yahweh."

I'd like to point out that even if it works, Dawkins's argument here only amounts to an argument against biblical inerrancy. It's not an argument against Christianity as such, or against theism.

So, Dawkins cherry-picks episodes from the Bible he thinks will provoke a negative moral reaction from readers towards Yahweh *as a character in the narrative*. He declares: "Whether or not we think God is an entirely

---

1. Dawkins, *Outgrowing God*, 92.
2. Dawkins, *Outgrowing God*, 84.

141

fictional character, we can still judge whether he is good or bad."[3] Hiromi has already helped us to see the problematical nature of this claim, and how Dawkins dodges some significant issues by making this claim before his discussion of morality in the following chapters, which we've covered over the last two weeks.

Now, we agreed to postpone discussion of Dawkins's moral criticism of the exodus plagues, because it was a thematic fit with chapter 4. The key episodes Dawkins adds in chapter 4 itself are: Abraham's near sacrifice of Isaac, the Jewish invasion of Canaan, Jephthah's sacrificial oath and Jesus' interpretation of his crucifixion as a sacrifice of atonement. In light of his descriptions of these episodes, Dawkins challenges readers to: "decide for yourself whether you think it's still possible to love God in spite of everything."[4]

Thomas: Can I ask what "cherry-picking" means?

Sophie: Of course. It's an informal name for the fallacy of suppressed evidence, which occurs: "When only select evidence is presented in order to persuade the audience to accept a position, and evidence that would go against the position is withheld. The stronger the withheld evidence, the more fallacious the argument."[5]

Thomas: I see. But if there's another side to Yahweh, perhaps the biblical picture of God is contradictory?

Astrid: I don't see a contradiction. You have to bear in mind that God is against sin *because* he's good and loving. If you love someone you want the best for them, and within the biblical worldview sin is by definition something that's bad for people.

Douglas: As an atheist who thinks atheism entails moral subjectivism, I'm in no position to pass any moral judgments on Yahweh considered as a literary character. But I can join Dawkins in challenging moral objectivists to decide if *they* can love the biblical God.

Hiromi: I can see that, but why spend so much time making arguments consistent with theism? I could decide not to love Yahweh, while still thinking

3. Dawkins, *Outgrowing God*, 72.
4. Dawkins, *Outgrowing God*, 72.
5. "Cherry Picking."

he exists. I could conclude there's a real God, loveable or not, who didn't do the things the Bible says Yahweh did.

Douglas: But while those conclusions are consistent with theism or a liberal form of Christianity, they'd be a big shift for someone like Astrid.

Hiromi (using her tablet): I would like to raise a historical point. Dawkins mentions how Moses supposedly went up a mountain to talk with God, and how the Israelites "persuaded Moses's brother Aaron to collect a lot of gold from everybody, melt it down and make them a new god while Moses wasn't looking: a golden calf. They bowed down and worshipped the golden calf."[6] And Dawkins comments: "That may seem odd, but worshipping statues of animals, including bulls, was quite common among local tribes at the time."[7]

Douglas: Worshipping a golden calf seems odd to me. Where are you going with this?

Hiromi: Well, Dawkins is saying that the exodus narrative accurately depicts the specific religious culture at the time when the exodus story is set. But he also says the exodus narrative is unreliable because it was written hundreds of years after the time it is set. So, was the inclusion of a golden calf in the story a lucky guess?! Did an exilic author have reliable information about religious practices from hundreds of years before they lived? Or was the exodus narrative written earlier than Dawkins thinks?

Thomas: In any case, we've already noted that Dawkins focuses too much on the gap between historical events and the biblical text, as if the time since the events described is the primary indicator of reliability.

Douglas: Didn't Astrid say earlier sources are preferable to later sources?

Astrid: As a general rule.

Thomas: General rules can have exceptions. Historians prefer the second-century-AD account of Alexander the Great's life written by Arrian over earlier sources, like second-century-BC comments of Polybius, because other historical rules of thumb tell us that Arrian is the better historian.[8]

---

6. Dawkins, *Outgrowing God*, 78.
7. Dawkins, *Outgrowing God*, 78.
8. See Dickson, *Is Jesus History?*, 69–74.

Sophie: I think we'd best turn our attention to Dawkins's moral concerns, starting with Abraham and the story Jews refer to as the "*Akedah*," or "binding of Isaac."

Thomas (using his tablet): According to Genesis 22:2, God tells Abraham to take Isaac to the land of Moriah: "and offer him there as a burnt offering on one of the mountains of which I shall tell you."

Astrid (using her tablet): Yes, but the Hebrew translated as "and offer him there as a burnt offering" *literally* means "and cause him to ascend there as a thing that ascends." The Hebrew here can literally refer to a stairway. According to the famous medieval Jewish exegete Rashi, God gave Abraham an ambiguous command, omitting any explicit instruction to "slaughter" Isaac (which would've required the Hebrew word *shachtehu*[9]): "because the Holy One . . . did not desire that he should slay him, but he told him to bring him up to the mountain to prepare him as a burnt offering. So when he had taken him up, God said to him, 'Bring him down.'"[10] In other words, God told Abraham to take Isaac up the mountain as an offering, but he didn't actually tell Abraham to kill Isaac. And in the end, of course, God provided an alternative sacrifice, one that Christians read as foreshadowing God's self-sacrificial provision in the crucifixion of Christ.

Thomas (using his tablet): But Abraham did try to kill Isaac. Dawkins says: "If anything like this happened in modern times, Abraham would be locked up for terrible cruelty to his child. Can you imagine what the judge would say if a man pleaded, 'But I was only following orders.' 'Orders from whom?' 'Well, Your Honour, I heard this voice in my head'. . . . What would you think, if you were on the jury? Would you think it was a good enough excuse? Or would you send Abraham to prison?"[11]

Hiromi (using her tablet): In chapter 5, Dawkins says: "Judging people of an earlier time by the standards of your own time is one of the things good historians just don't do."[12] By his own standard, Dawkins is asking us to behave as bad historians when he asks us to judge characters like Abraham by the standards of "modern times."[13]

---

9. Freedman, "Portion of Vayera," esp. paras. 30–36.
10. Rashi, "Genesis Rabbah 56:8."
11. Dawkins, *Outgrowing God*, 76.
12. Dawkins, *Outgrowing God*, 121.
13. Dawkins, *Outgrowing God*, 76.

Douglas: Not to mention the fact that, as a moral subjectivist, Dawkins is in no position to issue moral condemnations of anyone.

Thomas: Well, I'm a moral objectivist, and I think we *can* make moral judgements about historical figures, if we take steps to understand their historical and cultural context.

Astrid (using her tablet): I agree with you on that; but Dawkins is asking us to judge Abraham's actions on the question-begging assumption that Abraham *didn't* receive a divine revelation. In the biblical narrative, Abraham's obedience takes place in the context of God's proven faithfulness, most especially seen in his miraculous provision of Isaac as the child of promise. As Paul Copan points out: "Abraham had confidence that even if the child of promise died, God would somehow accomplish his purposes through that very child. . . . That's why Abraham told his servants before he headed to Mount Moriah with Isaac: '*We* will worship and then *we* will come back to you.' (Genesis 22:5[14]). No wonder the author of Hebrews observed that since Abraham 'had received the promises' he 'considered that God is able to raise people even from the dead' [Heb 11:17, 19]. In *some* way, God would fulfill his promises. Abraham was confident of that—and commended for it. After all, Abraham confidently affirmed a few chapters earlier, 'Shall not the judge of the whole earth deal justly?' [Gen 18:25]."[15]

Thomas (using his tablet): Yeah, but as Dawkins suggests, try imagining that: "God had ordered your father to kill you and offer you up as a burnt sacrifice. But it turned out to be just a tease—a test of your father's loyalty to God. If you were Isaac (Ishmael), could you ever forgive your father? If you were Abraham, could you ever forgive God?"[16]

Astrid: Dawkins's emotive retelling of this story is the strongest rhetorical move in this chapter, but it lacks cultural and literary sensitivity. Reading further in Genesis, we see Abraham arranging a marriage for Isaac in Genesis 24 and Isaac burying his father after he dies in Genesis 25, so they don't seem to have been estranged by the events of chapter 22!

Hiromi: I wonder why not?

---

14. NIV, emphasis added.
15. Copan, *Is God a Moral Monster?*, 48.
16. Dawkins, *Outgrowing God*, 75–76.

Astrid (using her tablet): We need to take seriously the fact that God's request wouldn't have been shocking in its original cultural context. Ironically, it's the story of the *Aqedah* that led to an ethic that's opposed to child sacrifice. Jean E. Jones points out that:

> In Abraham's birthplace Ur, religious rituals included human sacrifice. One of the most startling excavations from Ur is the so-called 'Royal Cemetery' with its pits containing human sacrifices, most of them adults. . . . Abraham moved to Haran, not far from other sites where human sacrifices have been uncovered from the same age. . . . Although there were also infant sacrifices in the regions, these are mostly adult sacrifices. This is significant because at the time God tested Abraham by asking him to sacrifice Isaac, Isaac was not a child.[17]

Genesis 22:5 uses the same term to describe Isaac as Genesis 14:24 uses to describe a young man of military age. Isaac Kalimi explains that:

> Some rabbis consider the *Aqedah* not only a test of Abraham but also of Isaac . . . he was aware that his father was leading him to death, yet willingly followed and obeyed him. This is the intention of the repeated phrase, 'and they went both of them together' (Gen. 22:6b, 8b). . . . The willingness of Isaac to be sacrificed is stated already by Josephus [*Antiquities* 1.232], Pseudo-Philo (*Liber Antiquitatum Biblicarum* 32:1–3), and 4 [*Maccabees*] 7:13–14.[18]

Thomas: But isn't that reading between the lines?

Astrid (using her tablet): Sure; but Dawkins is *also* reading between the lines! I'd argue that Josephus sticks closer to "the lines" than Dawkins. There are textual clues pointing in that direction, like the repeated "and they went both of them together," and the fact that Isaac was big enough to carry the firewood for the sacrifice.[19] So it seems to me that Abraham and Isaac *both* thought God was asking for a *customary* ritual:

> The people of Abraham's day would not have thought there was anything immoral about human sacrifices. In fact, they considered it an act of great piety . . . in cultures that believed in gods

17. Jones, "Abraham and Human Sacrifice?," para. 12.

18. Kalimi, "Go, I Beg You," 8–9. See also Keren, "What Can We Learn from the Akeidah?"

19. See Horn, *Hard Sayings*, 322.

that give blessings in return for sacrifices, sacrificing offspring would be considered a moral good. . . . It was a test and proof to all that Abraham's devotion to his God was as high as all others' devotion to their gods. Then the Lord God provided a ram to show that this God was different: This God did not want humans sacrificing humans.[20]

Douglas (using his phone): Dawkins asks: "Why doesn't God seem to speak to people any more, as he did to Abraham? In parts of the Old Testament he seemingly couldn't keep his mouth shut. He seemed to speak to Moses almost every day. But nobody hears a peep from him today—or if they do, we think they need psychiatric help."[21]

Astrid: Hearing the voice of God is a rare event, even in the Bible. But notice how Dawkins's criticism is question-begging! He says that God doesn't seem to speak to anyone today, but he also says that anyone who claims God spoke to them needs psychiatric help!

Hiromi: Dawkins is like a man with his eyes shut complaining he can't see anything.

Sophie: Well put, Hiromi. Let's turn to the Exodus plagues.

Thomas (using his tablet): Dawkins says: "God wanted the Egyptian king, the Pharaoh, to set the Israelite slaves free. You might have thought it would be within God's power to change Pharaoh's mind miraculously. He deliberately did the exact reverse. . . . But first he put pressure on Pharaoh by sending a series of ten plagues to Egypt."[22]

Astrid: If God had changed the Pharaoh's mind miraculously, wouldn't Dawkins complain about God trampling over Pharaoh's free will?

Douglas: Dawkins doesn't believe in free will.

Astrid: Okay, but if we're tempted to say God should have miraculously changed Pharaoh's mind, wouldn't it make more sense to say God should have miraculously *prevented* Pharaoh from taking slaves in the first place?

20. Jones, "Abraham and Human Sacrifice?"
21. Dawkins, *Outgrowing God*, 81.
22. Dawkins, *Outgrowing God*, 51.

Thomas: I guess so.

Astrid: But in that case, wouldn't it make sense to say God should eliminate *all* sin by miraculously preventing people from choosing to do anything wrong?

Thomas: Well, maybe he should!

Hiromi: But there are things I do that God supposedly dislikes, and I'm not sure I'd want God to stop me doing *all* of them.

Thomas: You may have a point there.

Douglas (using his phone)**:** I rather like what psychiatrist Norman Doidge writes about this: "my first reaction to a command might just be that nobody, not even God, tells me what to do, even if it's good for me. But the story of the golden calf also reminds us that without rules we quickly become slaves to our passions—and there's nothing freeing about that."[23]

Astrid: That's right, and the quintessential sin, on the biblical worldview, is the willful rejection of a faithful relationship with God. So, to demand that God prevent all sin is to demand that humans lack the freedom that allows them to reject God. It's basically to demand that God treats us as puppets rather than people. It's to demand that God forces himself on us, as it were. I think God values human freedom, despite the sin it permits, because our freedom is necessary for genuine relationships, whether with him, or each-another.

Sophie: Astrid is articulating what philosophers call a free will "greater good" theodicy: free will facilitates moral evil, but it also facilitates greater goods that justify God in creating creatures with free will.

Hiromi: Greater goods like love?

Astrid: Yes.

Thomas (using his tablet)**:** Well, Dawkins says: "The final plague was the clincher. . . . God killed the eldest child in every Egyptian household. . . . The Israelites were to paint their doorposts with lamb's blood, so the angel of death could tell which houses to avoid on the child-slaughtering spree.

23. Doidge, "Foreword," viii.

You'd think that God, being all-wise and all-knowing, might have been able to tell which house was which. But perhaps the author thought the lambs' blood would add a nice splash of colour to the story."[24]

Astrid: The blood obviously isn't a signpost to help God know who lives where! It's a ritualistic expression of the Israelites' trust that God will figuratively "pass over" the doorway to their homes when "the destroyer" falls upon their Egyptian captors.

Thomas (using his tablet): Okay, but as Dawkins points out: "Pharaoh had been on the point of giving up and letting the Israelites go earlier, and this would have been nice because all those innocent children would have been saved. But God deliberately used his magic powers to make Pharaoh obstinate, so that God could send some more plagues, as 'signs' to show the Egyptians who was boss."[25] Dawkins quotes Exodus 7:2–3: "But I will harden Pharaoh's heart, and though I multiply my miraculous signs and wonders in Egypt, he will not listen to you. Then I will lay my hand on Egypt and with mighty acts of judgment I will bring out . . . my people the Israelites. And the Egyptians will know that I am the Lord when I stretch out my hand against Egypt and bring the Israelites out of it."[26]

Astrid (using her tablet): That's misleading, and not just because that's actually verses 3–5 of chapter 7! According to theologian Junia Pokrifka: "The text does not present Yahweh as hardening Pharaoh apart from or in contradiction to Pharaoh's own will and character. . . . In the beginning of the plague narrative, the text simply describes Pharaoh's heart as being hardened, resolute, and unyielding, without saying who hardened it. . . . Pharaoh's character is portrayed . . . as already set in stone. . . . In the middle . . . Pharaoh is said to willfully harden his own heart . . . making it increasingly calloused against severer plagues. In the last phase. . . . If there is any danger of Pharaoh's will weakening due to the severest of punishments, Yahweh hardens Pharaoh's heart to ensure his continued resistance until the complete fulfillment of God's divine purposes."[27]

Thomas: All so God could "show the Egyptians who was boss"!

24. Dawkins, *Outgrowing God*, 51.

25. Dawkins, *Outgrowing God*, 51.

26. Dawkins, *Outgrowing God*, 52.

27. Pokrifka, *Exodus*, 103–4.

Astrid (using her tablet): But God's aim wasn't self-aggrandizement. God wanted to free the Israelite slaves from the Egyptians, and to undermine the Egyptians' false religion. As Exodus 7:5 says: "The Egyptians shall know that I am the LORD, when I stretch out my hand against Egypt and bring out the people of Israel from among them." Kenneth Kitchen observes that: "the impact of various plagues can be understood as devaluing or denying Egyptian beliefs . . . the deep darkness eclipsed the supreme sun god, Re or Amen-Re. . . . Death of so many throughout the land . . . would probably seem to Egyptians to have negated the power of the gods completely, and the king's personal and official key role of ensuring their favor."[28]

Since Egypt was the dominant military power at this time, its gods were presumed to be the strongest. The plagues thereby served notice on the polytheism of Canaanite culture, as part of God's strategy to drive false religion out of Canaan before the Israelites, and to bless the whole world through Israel. The Gibeonites speak of "the fame of the Lord your God; for we have heard the report of Him and all He did in Egypt."[29] Rahab the Canaanite woman who hid the Jewish spies in Jericho, and who later married into the Jewish tribe of Judah,[30] says: "I know that the LORD has given you this land. . . . For we have heard how the LORD dried up the waters of the Red Sea before you when you came out of Egypt."[31]

Thomas: I see your point, but why "harden Pharaoh's heart" *at all?*

Astrid (using her tablet): Notice what happens when Pharaoh *seems to be* on the point of giving up and letting the Israelites go after the seventh plague:

> Pharaoh summoned Moses and Aaron. "This time I have sinned," he said. "The LORD is righteous, and I and my people are wicked. Pray to the LORD, for there has been enough of God's thunder and hail. I will let you go; you do not need to stay any longer." Moses said to him, "When I have left the city, I will spread out my hands to the LORD. The thunder will cease, and there will be no more hail, so that you may know that the earth is the LORD's. But as for you and your officials, I know that you still do not [respect] the LORD our God." Then Moses departed from Pharaoh, went out of the city, and spread out his hands to the LORD. The thunder and hail ceased, and the rain no longer poured down on the land. When Pharaoh saw that the rain and

---

28. Kitchen, *On the Reliability of the Old Testament,* 253.
29. Josh 9:9 (NIV).
30. See Matt 1:5.
31. Josh 2:9–10.

hail and thunder had ceased, he sinned again and hardened his heart—he and his officials. So Pharaoh's heart was hardened, and he would not let the Israelites go.[32]

So you see how, although Pharaoh and his officials were *temporarily over-awed by Yahweh's power*, they quickly went back on their word to let their Israelite slaves go free, because they were still treating Yahweh as just another polytheistic god with whom the Egyptian gods could contend. In the last few plagues, God permits Pharaoh's stubbornness and even strengthens his resolve against any similarly temporary changes of heart until he's finally willing to give Israel permission to leave for long enough that they actually get to leave.[33] And even then, Pharaoh eventually changes his mind once again and tries to recapture his former slaves!

Thomas (using his tablet): Hang on, Exodus 14:8 says: "the LORD hardened the heart of Pharaoh king of Egypt so that he pursued the Israelites."

Astrid (using her tablet): But "The text does not present Yahweh as hardening Pharaoh apart from or in contradiction to Pharaoh's own will and character."[34] Paul Marston and Roger Forster note that: "'strengthened his resolve' would perhaps be a nearer English equivalent than 'hardened his heart'"[35] for the relevant Hebrew word in Exodus 14:8.

Hiromi: Did God undermine the Egyptians' polytheism?

Astrid: When Pharaoh's magicians couldn't mimic the third plague's production of gnats, they admitted: "This is the finger of God."[36] When Israel left Egypt, the text adds that "a mixed multitude also went up with them."[37] At least some of them may have been Egyptian.

Hiromi: I have been thinking. If God exists, he's responsible for a world where *everyone* dies of something, despite the fact that he could miraculously prevent anyone from dying at all. Now, we *might* think creating such a world probably isn't the sort of thing God would do, and treat the fact that people die as evidence against his existence. But even if we *do* argue that

32. Exod 9:27–30, 33–35.
33. See Marston and Forster, *God's Strategy in Human History*, 63–69, 260–74.
34. Pokrifka, *Exodus*, 103.
35. Marston and Forster, *God's Strategy in Human History*, 270.
36. Exod 8:19.
37. Exod 12:38.

death is evidence against God's existence, that isn't actually the same thing as arguing that God doesn't exist, or that, whether or not God exists, he doesn't have a loveable character.

Thomas: Why not?

Hiromi: Well, that depends on what positive warrant or evidence there might be to believe in God's existence and good character. And here's the thing: I don't see much difference between the issues that arise from God making a world where everyone dies, and the issues that arise from God arranging for some specific people to die a certain way at a certain time.

Thomas (using his tablet): Talking of making specific people die, what about the Israelite invasion of the so-called "promised land"? Dawkins says: "Adolf Hitler in the Second World War justified his invasion of Poland, Russia and other lands to the east by saying that the superior German master race needed Lebensraum, or 'living space'. And that is exactly what God was urging his own 'chosen people' to claim by war."[38]

Astrid: Having fled enslavement in Egypt, the Jews were refugees attempting to resettle in the land of their ancestors, a land that was still dominated by the Egyptian Empire.[39] Remember, "Canaanite" is a geographical rather than an ethnic or linguistic designation.

God says he'll accomplish several purposes by driving the Canaanites out of Canaan and giving the land to Israel. First, God will *bless Israel*, and through them *bless and call all nations to himself*.[40] Second, God will *express judgement on systemic cultural "abominations"* that included *child sacrifice*.[41] As Deuteronomy 12:31 says: "You shall not worship the LORD your God in that way, for every abominable thing that the LORD hates they have done for their gods, for they even burn their sons and their daughters in the fire to their gods."

Hiromi: If there was a nation in the world today that was sacrificing children to their gods, I think many people would demand a humanitarian intervention.

---

38. Dawkins, *Outgrowing God*, 83.

39. See Gen 17:8 and Gichon, *Battles of the Bible*, 49.

40. See Ps 67:2; Isa 2:1–5.

41. See Deut 18:9–12. See also *Watson's Biblical & Theological Dictionary's* entry for "Abomination."

Thomas: What's that?

Sophie: According to the Danish Institute of International Affairs: "humanitarian intervention is defined as coercive action by States involving the use of armed force in another State without the consent of its government, with or without authorisation from the United Nations Security Council, for the purpose of preventing or putting to a halt gross and massive violations of human rights or international humanitarian law."[42] The International Committee of the Red Cross says: "armed intervention in response to grave violations of human rights and international humanitarian law may be unavoidable in certain extreme situations."[43]

Thomas (using his tablet): But according to Dawkins: "the God of the Old Testament was continually urging his chosen people to slaughter other tribes."[44]

Astrid (using her tablet): That's untrue. Israel avoided confronting the Edomites, Moabites, and Ammonites. The Gibeonites welcomed and fed their new Israelite neighbors, initiating a peace treaty with them. And as Paul Copan points out:

> a number of battles that Israel fought on the way to and within Canaan were defensive: the Amalekites attacked the traveling Israelites . . . the Canaanite king of Arad attacked and captured some Israelites . . . the Amorite king Sihon refused Israel's peaceful overtures and attacked instead. . . . Bashan's king Og came out to meet Israel in battle. . . . Israel responded to Midian's calculated attempts to lead Israel astray through idolatry and immorality . . . five kings attacked Gibeon, which Joshua defended because of Israel's peace pact with the Gibeonites (Josh. 10:4). Furthermore, God *prohibited* Israel from conquering other neighboring nations. . . . Third, all sanctioned 'Yahweh battles' *beyond* the time of Joshua were *defensive* ones.[45]

Thomas: But God *did* command the Israelites to attack cities like Jericho and Ai.

---

42. *Humanitarian Intervention, Legal and Political Aspects*, 11.
43. Ryniker, "ICRC's Position on 'Humanitarian Intervention,'" 532
44. Dawkins, *Outgrowing God*, 79.
45. Copan, "Yahweh Wars and the Canaanites."

Astrid (using her tablet): He did; but these "cities" weren't population centers filled with civilians. Copan explains that "Jericho, Ai, and many other Canaanite cities were mainly used for government buildings and operations, while the rest of the people (including women and children) lived in the surrounding countryside."[46] He comments: "There is no archaeological evidence of civilian populations at Jericho or Ai. Given what we know about Canaanite life in the Bronze Age, Jericho and Ai were military strongholds. In fact, Jericho guarded the travel routes from the Jordan valley up to the population centres in the hill country. . . . That means that Israel's wars here were directed toward government and military installments."[47] The mound on which Jericho stood covers an area of about an acre. Copan says that: "According to the best calculations from Canaanite inscriptions and other archaeological evidence . . . Jericho was a small settlement of probably one hundred or fewer soldiers. . . . Rahab and her family would have been the exceptional noncombatants dwelling within this military outpost."[48]

Thomas (using his tablet): But what about the comprehensive nature of God's commands to attack these cities? In Deuteronomy 7, Moses commands: "when the LORD your God gives them over to you, and you defeat them, then you must devote them to complete destruction. You shall make no covenant with them and show no mercy to them." Joshua 6:21 says: "they devoted all in the city to destruction, both men and women, young and old, oxen, sheep, and donkeys, with the edge of the sword." That sounds like wholesale slaughter!

Astrid (using her tablet): According to Matthew Flannagan: "histories of this sort are highly stylized and often use . . . exaggeration for what could be called hagiographic purposes to commend the kings as faithful servants of the gods, rather than for giving literal descriptions of what occurred . . . Near Eastern conquest accounts . . . Are highly hyperbolic, hagiographic, and figurative."[49] Kitchen agrees that:

> The type of rhetoric in question was a regular feature of military reports in the second and first millennia. . . . In the later fifteenth century Tuthmosis III could boast 'the numerous army of Mitanni was overthrown within the hour, annihilated totally, like those (now) non-existent.'—whereas, in fact, the

46. Copan, *Is God a Moral Monster?*, 175–76.
47. Copan, *Is God a Moral Monster?*, 175–76.
48. Copan, *Is God a Moral Monster?*, 176.
49. Flannagan, "Did God Command the Genocide of the Canaanites?," 239–40.

forces of Mitanni lived to fight many another day . . . about 840/830, Mesha king of Moab could boast that "Israel has utterly perished for always"—a rather premature judgment at that date. . . . It is in this frame of reference that the Joshua rhetoric must also be understood.[50]

Likewise, theologian John Walton argues that in biblical warfare narratives: "the actual details of the totality of the destruction or the quantity of victims is likely couched in rhetorical hyperbole, in accordance with the expectations of the genre."[51] For example, Copan argues that: "The use of 'women' and 'young and old' were merely stock ancient Near Eastern language that could be used even if women and young or old weren't living there. The language of 'all' ('men and women') at Jericho and Ai is a 'stereotypical expression for the destruction of all human life in the fort, presumably composed entirely of combatants.'"[52]

Thomas: Aren't you just resorting to a non-literal reading of these texts because they are uncomfortable?

Astrid (using her tablet): Not at all. As David Baggett and Jerry L. Walls write: "Taking scripture seriously requires thoughtful, sensitive interpretation, and it may well be that the troublesome text itself gives us significant clues that it should not be read literally. If so, it does not represent a high view of scripture to insist on a literal reading nonetheless."[53]

Sophie: The question is, are there indications *within the relevant biblical texts* that point to rhetorical hyperbole?

Astrid (using her tablet): Plenty! The very fact that "Rahab, her father and mother, her brothers and sisters and all who belonged to her"[54] were spared proves that Moses' command wasn't universal in scope. Moreover, a literal reading of Deuteronomy 7:2's "devote them to complete destruction," that is to ḥǎ-rîm, pronounced *herem*, would make Deuteronomy 7:3's "Do not intermarry with them" redundant![55]

---

50. Kitchen, *On the Reliability of the Old Testament*, 174.

51. Walton and Walton, *Lost World of the Israelite Conquest*, 178.

52. Copan, *Is God a Moral Monster?*, 175–76.

53. Baggett and Walls, *Good God*, 139.

54. Josh 6:23.

55. As the *Benson Commentary* observes: "on the supposition that nothing that breathed was to be saved alive . . . there could be no occasion for this injunction. What end could it answer to forbid all intermarriages with a people supposed not to

Theologian David T. Lamb argues that: "The hyperbolic nature of the
. . . Joshua [conquest] texts can be seen when they are examined alongside
other texts. While Joshua 10:40 and Joshua 11:12–15 speak of everyone
being destroyed, elsewhere in Joshua and Judges a different perspective is
given. These other texts repeatedly state that the Israelites did not kill all the
Canaanites; they couldn't even drive all of them from out of the land."[56] For
example, Joshua 10:20 says the Israelite army "completely destroyed" their
enemies, *immediately before observing*: "the remnant that remained of them
had entered into the fortified cities." As Flannagan says: "In this context, the
language of total destruction is clearly hyperbolic."[57]

In fact, the Hebrew verbs for "annihilate/perish" and "destroy" can be
used figuratively, as shown by their use in Deuteronomy 28:63 to describe
God *removing Israel from the promised land* in the exile: "the LORD will . . .
make you perish and destroy you; and you will be torn from the land." The
conquest accounts likewise equate the destruction of the Canaanites with
the idea of their being driven from Cana.

Douglas: Doesn't the idea of making something *herem* entail its literal
destruction?

Astrid (using her tablet): Actually, Walton points out that: "When *herem*
objects are destroyed, the purpose of the destruction is to make sure that nobody can use it, but not all *herem* objects are destroyed. . . . Joshua 11:12–13
reports that all the northern cites were *herem*, yet Joshua destroys only one
of them (Hazor)."[58] Walton argues that Israel was principally commanded to
put *Canaanite religious culture* to *herem*.

By analogy, consider how the Allies dealt with Germany after WWII:
They rounded up Nazi leaders, put them on trial and executed them; but the
rank and file of German soldiers were told to go home, rebuild their lives,
never wear the Nazi uniform again, and never again display anything "Nazi."
What the Allies effectively did was *destroy Nazi identity and culture in Germany.* That meant killing German soldiers and destroying Nazi strongholds

---

exist?" (see https://biblehub.com/commentaries/deuteronomy/7-3.htm). This isn't a
forbidding of inter-*racial* marriage, but of inter-*religious* marriage: "Moses married
interracially, and there would be many interracial marriages among the Israelites who
included the 'mixed multitude' among them. It was inter-religious marriage that was in
mind, for such could draw a person away from the true God" (see www.studylight.org/
commentaries/pet/deuteronomy-7.html).

56. Lamb, *God Behaving Badly*. See Josh 13:1–6; 15:63; 17:12; Judg 1:19–34.

57. Flannagan, "Did God Command the Genocide of the Canaanites?," 239.

58. Walton and Walton, *Lost World of the Israelite Conquest*, 170.

to get to the Nazi leadership, but it didn't mean killing every last German. Likewise, says Walton: "The Canaanite tribal kingdoms which occupied the land were to be destroyed as nation states, not as individuals. The judgment of God upon these tribal groups, which had become so incredibly debauched by that time, is that they were being divested of their land."[59]

Thomas: Coming back to the issue of child sacrifice, what about Jephthah offering his daughter as a burnt sacrifice because of his vow to God?

Astrid: If Jephthah offered his daughter as a burnt sacrifice, it was something clearly against Abrahamic precedent and Mosaic law.[60] Dawkins assumes, without argument, that such an event would be presented as a positive example to follow rather than a negative example *not* to follow.[61]

Douglas (using his phone): What do you mean, "If Jephthah offered his daughter . . ."? In Judges 11:31, Jephthah says: "whatever comes out of the door of my house to greet me on my triumphant return from the Ammonites will belong to the LORD, and I will offer it up as a burnt offering."

Astrid (using her tablet): Professor Rabbi Jonathan Magonet, Emeritus Professor of Bible at Leo Baeck College, points out that the Hebrew *vav* conjunctive translated as "and" can also be read as "or," so that whatever or whoever came out to greet Jephthah "would be dedicated to God, and, only should it prove appropriate, would be sacrificed."[62] So Young's Literal Translation of Judges 11:31 has: "that which at all cometh out from the doors of my house to meet me in my turning back in peace from the Bene-Ammon—it hath been to Jehovah, or I have offered up for it—a burnt-offering."

Alternatively, one could take Jephthah's vow as a pledge to *figuratively* "offer up" or "sacrifice" a member of his household *to permanent religious service.*[63] After all, contextually, literal "burnt offerings" were associated with the forgiveness of sin, *not* with vows or thanksgiving. Nor would the

---

59. Craig, "Slaughter of the Canaanites Revisited," para. 6.

60. See Lev 18:21; 20:2–5; Deut 12:31; 18:10.

61. The "negative example" interpretation is adopted by Kaiser et al., *Hard Sayings of the Bible*, 193–95; Laney, *Answers to Tough Questions*; and Dell, *Who Needs the Old Testament?*, 103–8. Paul Copan considers this interpretation as a "worst-case scenario" in *Is God a Mortal Monster?*

62. Magonet, "Did Jephthah Actually Kill His Daughter?," para. 17.

63. See Holding, "Jephthah's Daughter: Answers to Objections"; "Jephthah's Daughter: Examining an Old Testament Story"; Archer, *Encyclopedia Of Bible Difficulties*, 164–65; Geisler and Howe, *Big Book of Bible Difficulties*, 148–49; Sailhamer, *NIV Compact Bible Commentary*, 211.

Jews at this time have gone along with a human sacrifice. Plus, literal burnt offerings *had to be male*.

Douglas: Okay, those sound like good *contextual* points, but what about *the actual text* itself?

Astrid (using her tablet): There are several *textual* signs that literal human sacrifice isn't the point of this story. For one thing, the period of mourning that Jephthah granted his daughter wasn't for grieving impending death, but for grieving the fact that *she'd never marry*. For another thing, the text goes out of its way to state that Jephthah *had no other children*: "she was his only child. Besides her he had neither son nor daughter" (11:34). Given Jephthah's age, his lack of other heirs and the infant mortality rate, for his daughter to be consigned to perpetual celibacy probably meant *the extinction of his family line*, which was looked upon as a tragedy in that culture. After stating that Jephthah "did with her according to his vow which he had vowed," the text immediately adds that she "knew no man" (11:39), that is, *she didn't marry or have children*. Finally, the declaration of Jephthah's sorrow in 11:35 comes right after we're informed he had no other children in 11:34. He wasn't sad because his daughter would *die*. He was sad because she'd *live as a virgin*.[64]

Douglas: But how does that fit with the fact that Judges 11:40 says: "the daughters of Israel went year by year to lament the daughter of Jephthah"? That sounds like they're *mourning* her death.

Astrid (using her tablet): Actually, the word translated as "lament" literally means to recount or rehearse, and can also mean "to ascribe praise to or celebrate,"[65] as is reflected in many translations of this verse. For example, the American Standard Version reads: "the daughters of Israel went yearly to celebrate the daughter of Jephthah." I think they're celebrating how she sacrificed marriage and motherhood for religious service.

Sophie: Let's end with Dawkins's comments about the atonement.

---

64. I owe these points to Miller, "Jephthah's Daughter."
65. Holding, "Jephthah's Daughter: Answers to Objections," para. 77.

Thomas (using his tablet): According to Dawkins: "The doctrine of atonement, which Christians take very seriously indeed, is so deeply, deeply nasty that it deserves to be savagely ridiculed."[66]

Hiromi: I don't know; the very fact that millions of Christians like Astrid take the atonement "very seriously" makes me question if it can really be as "nasty" as Dawkins says. Perhaps he misunderstands it?

Thomas (using his tablet): Here's Dawkins's description of the doctrine. First of all: "Paul and the other early Christians believed that we all inherit the sin of Adam, the first man, who was tempted by Eve, the first woman, after she in turn was tempted by a talking snake."[67] Now, as Dawkins observes: "we know that Adam never existed. Everybody who ever lived had two parents, and the line of great-great-great-grandparents goes on back through various apes and early monkeys to fish, worms and bacteria. There never was a first couple—never an Adam or Eve."[68]

Douglas: Didn't we touch on Adam and Eve before?

Astrid: I think I mentioned that some Christians don't believe in a historical Adam and Eve, while others believe in a historical Adam and Eve without thinking of them as the "first couple."

Hiromi: In other words, Dawkins's argument is only relevant to Christians who think there *was* a historical Adam and Eve *who were also the first couple.*

Douglas: There *are* Christians like that though.

Astrid (using her tablet): Sure. In any case, Dawkins is confusing Paul with the fourth-century theologian Augustine of Hippo. He even says, on the same page, that: "According to St Augustine, one of Christianity's most revered theologians, 'Original Sin' is inherited from Adam down the male line."[69] As theologian Katherine Dell says, the idea of inherited sin is actually "a somewhat later interpretation (going back to the early Church Father Augustine)."[70]

---

66. Dawkins, *Outgrowing God*, 89.
67. Dawkins, *Outgrowing God*, 85.
68. Dawkins, *Outgrowing God*, 86.
69. Dawkins, *Outgrowing God*, 85.
70. Dell, *Who Needs the Old Testament?*, 9.

Thomas (using his tablet): Dawkins depicts God the Father as telling God the Son: "I'm going to put you in a woman's womb and you'll have to be born, brought up and educated, teenage angst and all that stuff. Otherwise you wouldn't be fully human, so I wouldn't feel you were truly representing humanity when I eventually have you crucified to save them. Don't forget, by the way, it's me myself being crucified too, because I am you and you are me."[71]

Astrid: Dawkins is ridiculing what he doesn't understand; but yes, as C. Stephen Evans observes: "When Jesus gives his life for us, it is not God punishing an innocent victim, but God giving himself for us."[72] And as Thomas Aquinas argued, while Jesus didn't *have* to be crucified in order for God to forgive us, it was highly *appropriate* that God should save us through the suffering of Jesus.

Sophie: Aquinas discusses this question in the *Summa Theologiae* Part I, question 46.[73]

Thomas (using his tablet): But according to Dawkins: "Jesus's death was a sacrifice, like an Old Testament burnt offering, to appease God and ask him to forgive all human sin."[74] *That's* right, isn't it?

Astrid (using her tablet): Actually, that's *not* right. As theologians Joel B. Green and Mark D. Baker write: "Whatever meaning atonement might have, it would be a grave error to imagine that it focused on assuaging God's anger or winning God's merciful attention."[75]

Douglas: But wasn't that the Old Testament idea of sacrifice?

Astrid (using her tablet): Actually, in his commentary on Exodus, theologian Alan Cole argues that while pagan religions had the idea of appeasing the wrath of gods through sacrifices: "Israel's concept was basically different. To Israel all sacrifice originated with God in any case [Lev 7:11]. It was He who ordained and accepted the sin-offering that made possible the atonement, just as He had provided the lamb for Abraham [Gen 22:8]." Cole argues that Jewish religious sacrifice: "was no extortion of forgiveness from

---

71. Dawkins, *Outgrowing God*, 88.
72. Evans, *Why Believe?*, 131.
73. See Thomas Aquinas, *Summa Theologiae*, I.46.
74. Dawkins, *Outgrowing God*, 86.
75. Green and Baker, *Recovering the Scandal of the Cross*, 51.

an unwilling God: it was a way of approach to Him that He had graciously granted."[76] Moreover, he notes that: "Even within the Old Testament . . . it was not the sacrifice itself that averted God's wrath, but the broken contrite heart that it should ideally represent [Ps 51:16–17]."[77]

In the same way, Jesus' death *doesn't* "appease God" in the sense of making or allowing God to love us. Nor is it accurate to describe Jesus' death as his way to "ask [God] to forgive all human sin."[78] Jesus died for us *because* God loved us, in order *to ask us* to engage with the way of reconciliation he designed. As 1 John 4:10 observes: "God . . . loved us and sent his Son as an atoning sacrifice for our sins." Again, Romans 5:8 notes that: "God demonstrates his own love for us in this: While we were still sinners, Christ died for us." In other words, God's love for us *preceded* and *motivated* Jesus' death as a sacrifice that facilitates our forgiveness, if and when we respond to this "good news" through repentant faith in Jesus.

Thomas: But Dawkins says he's "just reporting the official Christian belief."[79]

Astrid: Well, that *can't* be true!

Thomas: Why not?

Astrid: Because there is no "official" Christian doctrine of the atonement for him to report!

Douglas: Isn't it mentioned in one of those ancient church creeds?

Sophie: The so-called "Apostle's Creed" mentions belief that Jesus "suffered under Pontius Pilate, was crucified, died, and was buried" and later mentions belief in "the forgiveness of sins"; but it makes no theological connection between these beliefs. The fourth-century "Nicene Creed" makes a broad connection, saying that "Jesus Christ . . . for our salvation . . . was incarnate by the power of the Holy Spirit of the Virgin Mary, and was made man, and was crucified for us under Pontius Pilate." Later on, the creed also speaks of acknowledging "one baptism for the remission of

---

76. Cole, *Tyndale Old Testament Commentaries: Exodus*, 34.

77. Cole, *Tyndale Old Testament Commentaries: Exodus*, 34.

78. Dawkins, *Outgrowing God*, 86.

79. Dawkins, *Outgrowing God*, 87.

sins." So, neither of the earliest and most widely adopted church creeds lays out a theology of atonement.

Astrid (using her tablet): Theologian Alister E. McGrath writes: "the New Testament is not . . . concerned with the detailed and intricate mechanics of redemption. The New Testament actually presents us with a series of images of what Christ achieved for us through his death and resurrection. It is dominated by proclamation of the *fact* that the cross and resurrection have the power to change us, along with a number of superb illustrations of the ways in which we can visualize this potential."[80] Christian philosopher C. Stephen Evans agrees, writing: "it is the *fact* of atonement that Christians are asked to believe, not any particular *theory* as to how this is achieved by Christ's death and resurrection. Indeed, Christians have over the centuries held a variety of theories about how this occurred."[81]

Thomas: But some Christians do embrace theories of atonement along the lines Dawkins describes.

Astrid (using her tablet): Sure, but the Christian worldview, like all worldviews, accommodates disputed ideas. With Catholic philosopher Richard Purtill: "I think that [the theory of] strict retribution . . . leads to the mistaken view that Christ was *punished* for our sins, a view quite different from the view that Christ *suffered* for our sins."[82] But whatever you think about *how* a medicine works, the important thing is to demonstrate trust the doctor who testifies *that* it works *by taking your medicine*.

Hiromi: But if someone were to push you on the "mechanics of redemption," what would you say?

Astrid (using her tablet): I like how philosopher Keith Ward describes the atonement:

> Sin . . . causes a change in the divine nature—the realization of anger, even when transformed by compassion, the frustration of divine purpose, and the frustration of joy. These are costs that God [freely] bears whenever sin impairs a possible divine-creaturely relationship. The crucifixion of Jesus, in so far as it is an act of God as well as the self-offering of a human life, is the particular

80. McGrath, *Making Sense of the Cross*, 43.
81. Evans, *Why Believe?*, 130–31.
82. Purtill, *Reason to Believe*, 196.

and definitive historical expression of the universal sacrifice of God in bearing the cost of sin. Sin is a harm done to God, inasmuch as it causes God to know, and to share, the suffering and reality of evil. The 'ransom' God pays is to accept this cost, to bear with evil, in order that it should be redeemed, transfigured, in God. . . . The patience of God, bearing the cost of sin, takes the life and death and resurrection of Jesus as its own self-manifestation, and makes it the means by which the liberating life of God is made available in its essential form to the world.[83]

Hiromi: That's interesting. We know from experience, don't we, that to reach out in forgiveness means to suffer by shouldering or absorbing the wrong someone has done to us.

Astrid: I think Jesus *exhibited* the fact of divine sin-bearing through his crucifixion *and* his subsequent resurrection. More than that, Jesus' repurposing of the Passover meal[84] means that his crucifixion, when understood in light of his resurrection, was a performative act that *inaugurated* the availability of a new covenantal relationship between God and humans.

Thomas: What's "a performative act"?

Astrid (using her tablet)**:** Just as a person with the appropriate authority breaking a bottle of champagne on the side of a ship while saying "I name this ship X" *brings about the naming of a ship*, so Jesus' repurposing of the Passover meal and his death on the cross *brings about the existence of the new covenant*, in light of the fact that his resurrection shows him to be an appropriate authority. As theologian Mark L. Strauss explains, Jesus' "Last Supper" with his disciples was a Jewish Passover celebration with a twist:

> The original Passover represented God's greatest act of deliverance in the Hebrew scriptures and the creation of Israel as a nation . . . Yahweh . . . delivered his people . . . and brought them out of slavery in Egypt. Giving them his law at Mount Sinai, he established a covenant relationship with them. When Israel was later oppressed and defeated by her enemies, the prophets would predict the day when Yahweh would return to Zion to accomplish a new and greater exodus. . . . Drawing symbolism from the Passover meal, the covenant at Sinai, and the new exodus and new covenant imagery in the prophets, Jesus inaugurates a new

83. Ward, *What the Bible Really Teaches*, 109–10.

84. See: 1 Cor 10:16; 11:23–26; Mark 14:22–24; Matt 26:26–29; Luke 22:19–20; John 6:54–56.

Passover meal celebrating the new covenant and the arrival of the kingdom of God. While the first covenant was instituted with the blood of sacrificial animals, this new covenant will be established through his own blood . . . as a sacrifice of atonement, leading his people in a new exodus from bondage to sin and death.[85]

Hiromi: But how does someone become a part of this "new exodus"?

Astrid (using her tablet): The apostle Paul describes "the way" of Christian spirituality as an ongoing act of *communion* in, or *identification* with, Jesus' sacrificial death and resurrection life:

> Don't you know that all of us who were baptized into Christ Jesus were baptized into his death? We were therefore buried with him through baptism into death in order that, just as Christ was raised from the dead through the glory of the Father, we too may live a new life. . . . The death he died, he died to sin once for all; but the life he lives, he lives to God. In the same way, count yourselves dead to sin but alive to God in Christ Jesus . . . offer yourselves to God as those who have been brought from death to life; and offer every part of yourself to him as an instrument of righteousness. . . . For the wages of sin is death, but the gift of God is eternal life in Christ Jesus our Lord.[86]

Hiromi: You know, perhaps it's not so much the narratives highlighted by Dawkins that make people uncomfortable as the fundamental assumption made by these narratives.

Douglas: What assumption is that?

Hiromi (using her tablet): That we were created by an almighty, perfectly wise, perfectly good God with rights over us that transcend the rights we have over one another. I was reading a paper recently in which philosophers Nick Trakakis and Yujin Nagasawa point out that "Parents . . . have certain rights over their children which strangers do not. . . . Similarly, God—in virtue of his role as our creator . . . may have rights over us that we do not have over each other."[87] Whether or not we're treating God as a fictional character, we have to treat him as a character with unique rights, and that might affect how we judge his actions.

85. Strauss, *Four Portraits, One Jesus*, 504–5.

86. Rom 6:3–4, 10–11, 13, 23.

87. Trakakis and Nagasawa, "Skeptical Theism and Moral Skepticism: A Reply to Almeida and Oppy."

Thomas: How come?

Hiromi: Well, if God exists, he can plausibly command people to do some things they wouldn't have the right to do unless God had commanded it. And God's rights plausibly include the right to either forgive our sins or, whether directly or indirectly, bring judgement upon us. And if that makes us uncomfortable with the concept of God, perhaps that says more about us than about God.

Douglas: Does that mean God can do *anything*, and it would be consistent with his existence and character?

Hiromi (using her tablet): Philosophers David Baggett and Jerry L. Walls discuss this issue. They argue that while God's goodness "must be recognizable for our ascriptions of goodness to him to remain meaningful . . . there could still arise occasions when it isn't easy to see the goodness of what he commands."[88] Because choosing to do something that's bad can be morally right if it's the lesser of two evils, we can't simply assume that everything God commands is something he commands because of its goodness. What we *can* say is that everything God commands is something he has the moral right to command.

Thomas: But can we draw a line between bad things God may be right to command and bad things God couldn't and wouldn't command?

Astrid: God could never do anything with an evil motive. He could never do anything, or command that anything be done, for the sake of evil. That's why the Bible says God never tempts anyone to sin.[89] The Bible also insists God never lies, and never breaks an unconditional promise.[90]

Hiromi (using her tablet): Baggett and Walls propose that

> when confronted with . . . some alleged or hypothetical command by God or state of affairs allowed by God, we should

---

88. Baggett and Walls, *Good God*, 134.

89. See Jas 1:13: "God is not tempted by evil and He Himself doesn't tempt anyone." God could *allow* or even arrange for someone to experience a "testing" situation in which he knows they will be tempted to sin, for example, because he also knows that their being tempted is a necessary condition of some compensatory good, or of avoiding some greater evil. This wouldn't count as God "tempting" someone, if we define "tempting" as "leading or allowing someone to be tempted *for evil's sake*" (i.e. because one has oneself been "tempted by evil"). I take it that such divine maliciousness is what James refutes.

90. See Copan, *When God Goes To Starbucks*, chapter 3.

ask it we can identify a possibly true proposition, consistent with God's moral perfection . . . that would potentially entail such a command or state of affairs. If we can identify such a proposition, then the command or state of affairs in question can be said to be reconcilable with our nonnegotiable moral commitments.[91]

Astrid: I suppose failing to identify such a proposition in cases that didn't obviously contradict our nonnegotiable moral intuitions might only prove our lack of imagination; but even then, the harder we find it to think of such a proposition, the more certain we can be that God couldn't command or permit the state of affairs in question.

Hiromi (using her tablet): That's right. While it's probably impossible for us to draw the line between commands God can and cannot issue with absolute certainty, we can give examples of commands that probably fall on either side of the line. Baggett and Walls suggest that while God couldn't command anyone to torture children just for fun, "he may well be acting in accord with moral perfection when he . . . allows death to take place."[92] They note: "God is the author of life, and it's his prerogative to take it away, and presumably his prerogative to use human agency to do so, so long as he has morally sufficient reasons."[93] As philosopher Charles Taliaferro argues:

> If there is a robust sense in which the cosmos belongs to God, then God's moral standing from the outset is radically unequal to ours. . . . Arguably our rights are at least hedged if the ownership of God is taken seriously. Being thus beholden to God would not seem to entitle God to create beings solely to torment them, but if life is indeed a gift from God . . . then certain complaints about the created order may be checked.[94]

And what applies to complaints about the created order must also apply to complaints about God's actions, whether you're treating God as a literary character or as real being.

Sophie: An interesting point on which to close.[95]

---

91. Baggett and Walls, *Good God*, 136.

92. Baggett and Walls, *Good God*, 135.

93. Baggett and Walls, *Good God*, 139.

94. Taliaferro, *Contemporary Philosophy of Religion*, 317.

95. An extensive list of chapter-specific recommended resources can be found on this book's webpage at www.peterswilliams.com/publications/books/outgrowing-god/.

Seventh Meeting

Evolution and Beyond

Sophie: Astrid says she hasn't been doing so well this week with her depression, and sends her apologies.

Thomas: I'm sorry to hear that. We were knitting together only last Saturday.

Hiromi: I'll message her to see if there's anything I can do.

Sophie: Let's press on, as agreed, to chapters 7–10 of *Outgrowing God*. This meeting might run slightly long, but I think we can cover all four today.

Thomas (using his tablet)**:** At the end of chapter 6, Dawkins admitted readers: "might still cling to belief in . . . some sort of creative intelligence who made the world and the universe and—perhaps above all—made living creatures, including us."[1] He confessed: "I clung to such a belief myself until I was about 15, because I was so deeply impressed by the beauty and complexity of living things. Especially by the fact that living things look as though they must have been 'designed.'"[2] However, he reports: "I finally gave up on the very idea of any gods when I learned about evolution and the true explanation for why living things look designed."[3] Part 2 of *Outgrowing God* is mainly dedicated to arguing that evolution is a better explanation for living things than divine design.

1. Dawkins, *Outgrowing God*, 141.
2. Dawkins, *Outgrowing God*, 141.
3. Dawkins, *Outgrowing God*, 141.

Hiromi: We've been studying the design argument in my philosophy course. I think it adds something to the theistic side of the scale in the God debate, so I'm happy to advocate design in Astrid's absence.

Sophie: Excellent.

Thomas (using his tablet): Dawkins observes that: "Everything about an animal or plant, every detail of every one, looks overwhelmingly as though somebody designed and created it."[4]

Douglas: Sorry to interrupt, but he's being so sloppy!

Thomas: How come?

Douglas (using his phone): Well, although he praises "The glowing beauty of a peacock's tail"[5] and so on, Dawkins contradicts himself by claiming there are "flaws" in living things that are "very much not what you'd expect to see if the animals had been intelligently designed."[6]

Thomas: So, Dawkins *doesn't* think "every detail" of life "looks overwhelmingly as though somebody designed and created it"?[7]

Douglas: He doesn't. I don't think anyone does.

Hiromi: But he *does* think, in more general terms, that "Biology is the study of complicated things that give the appearance of having been designed for a purpose,"[8] as he said in *The Blind Watchmaker*.

Douglas: He does.

Hiromi: So, he concedes an important point.

Thomas: What point?

---

4. Dawkins, *Outgrowing God*, 160.

5. Dawkins, *Outgrowing God*, 163. On beauty in biology, see Williams, "Intelligent Design, Aesthetics and Design Arguments."

6. Dawkins, *Outgrowing God*, 164.

7. Dawkins, *Outgrowing God*, 160.

8. Dawkins, *Blind Watchmaker*, 1.

Hiromi: That *organic life gives the overall appearance of being designed*. Do you remember my discussion with Astrid, in our first meeting, about "properly basic" beliefs?

Thomas: I remember the basics.

Douglas: Pun intended?

Thomas: A "basic" belief isn't based on other things you believe. A "properly basic" belief is a basic belief *grounded in your experience of how things appear to be*. Astrid gave the example of it being rational to think you are in a café right now, even if you didn't *argue* your way to this conclusion from other things you believe, *simply because it appears to you that you're in a café*.

Hiromi (using her tablet): That's right. This lines up with philosopher Richard Swinburne's discussion of a fundamental principle of rationality that he calls "the principle of credulity," namely: "that we ought to believe that things are as they seem to be . . . unless and until we have evidence that we are mistaken."[9] He points out that: "If you say the contrary—never trust appearances until it is proved that they are reliable—you will never have any beliefs at all. For what would show that appearances are reliable, except more appearances? And, if you cannot trust appearances as such, you cannot trust these new ones either."[10]

Douglas: Does Swinburne restrict this principle to physical senses?

Hiromi (using her tablet): No. He says it applies to appearances besides those gathered via "your ordinary senses (e.g. your sense of sight)."[11] He says it applies to "how we are inclined to believe that things are."[12]

Thomas: So, if it *seems to me* I'm in a café, the rational thing to do is to believe I *am* in a café, unless and until I receive what seems to me to be evidence strong enough to show that previous appearance of reality to have been deceptive.

---

9. Swinburne, *Does God Exist?*, 115.

10. Swinburne, *Does God Exist?*, 115.

11. Swinburne, *Does God Exist?*, 115.

12. Swinburne, *Does God Exist?*, 114.

Hiromi: Yes. And we should apply the same approach to the appearance of design in living things. That means we should believe they are designed unless and until we have what seems to be contrary evidence strong enough to show otherwise.

Sophie: In other words, Dawkins accepts he bears "the burden of proof"; that it's his task to provide sufficient reason to think that living things aren't the product of design they appear to be.

Hiromi (using her tablet): Charles Darwin dodged this burden of proof, writing:

> If then we have under nature variability and a powerful agent always ready to act and select, why should we doubt that variations in any way useful to beings . . . would be preserved, accumulated, and inherited? . . . What limit can be put to this power, acting during long ages . . . favouring the good and rejecting the bad? I can see no limit to this power, in slowly and beautifully adapting each form.[13]

Just like that, Darwin awarded the presumption of truth to his theoretical extrapolation from small-scale evolution to large-scale evolution.[14] He went from saying he *saw* no limit to evolution by natural selection, to saying there *was* no limit. In other words, Darwin made a question-begging "argument from ignorance,"[15] and Dawkins follows in his footsteps.

Thomas: But Dawkins doesn't seek to counter the appearance of design *simply* by pointing to the theory of evolution. He *also* points to "flaws" in "living things" that are "very much not what you'd expect to see if the animals had been intelligently designed."[16]

Douglas: Let's call this "the argument from bad design."

Hiromi: But two invalid arguments don't make a valid argument, let alone a sound one! Yes, Dawkins points to details of certain organisms that he thinks aren't designed, or to have been badly designed, or to have been designed by someone evil. I'm not really sure what he's arguing. But in any

13. Darwin, *Origin of Species*, 353.
14. See Swift, "What is the difference between Microevolution and Macroevolution?"
15. See All Grey Matters, "'Argument from Ignorance' Fallacy."
16. Dawkins, *Outgrowing God*, 164.

case, the *specific* examples in Dawkins's "argument from bad design" can't undermine the *general* appearance of design *that he concedes.*

Thomas: Why not?

Hiromi: Well, arguing against the *general* appearance of design this way is like saying that a landscaped garden isn't the result of design because it includes a small bed of wild flowers; or because there are some weeds on the lawn.

Thomas: I see.

Douglas: If we take the "bad design" argument in a moral sense, isn't it like arguing that: "Since jail limits people's freedom, and since having one's freedom limited is a bad thing, therefore no jail was designed by a morally good architect?" Not only does the argument fail to rule out the existence of immoral architects, but it depends on a questionable moral judgement. I mean, even if limiting a criminal's freedom by putting them in jail is a bad thing, it might be a better choice than letting them go free!

Thomas: But we might agree with the specific moral judgement made by a "bad design" argument.

Douglas: Maybe; but that would mean rejecting the moral subjectivism to which Dawkins subscribes!

Thomas: True.

Sophie: We've already discussed the moral argument for God.

Hiromi (using her tablet): Most people have thought the world was designed, despite the existence of death, sickness, and so on. It's obvious that good engineering often involves trade-offs between competing design goals. Indeed, as mathematician and philosopher William A. Dembski points out: "higher-order designs of entire eco-systems might require lower-order designs of individual organisms to fall short of maximal function."[17]

Thomas: I guess.

17. Dembski, *Design Revolution*, 61.

Hiromi: Not that I'd trust Dawkins's examples.[18]

Thomas: Why not? Biology is his turf.

Hiromi (using her tablet): I did some research on his claim that vertebrate eyes are wired "back to front."[19] The supposed flaw here is that: "unlike the otherwise similar eyes of the invertebrate octopus, the vertebrate retina is wired 'backwards'—its light-sensitive cells are situated in back of the nerve cells that carry the image to the brain."[20] This arrangement creates the eye's "blind-spot," and has been taken to mean that "light entering the eye has to pass through layers of cells before it hits the retina, which could cause the light to scatter, blurring vision."[21]

Thomas (using his tablet): As Dawkins comments in *The Blind Watchmaker*: "Each photocell is, in effect, wired in backwards, with its wires sticking out on the side nearest to the light. This means that the light, instead of being granted an unrestricted passage to the photocells, has to pass through a forest of connecting wires, presumably suffering at least some attenuation and distortion."[22]

Hiromi (using her tablet): Agnostic biologist Michael J. Denton argues that "consideration of the very high energy demands of the photoreceptor cells in the vertebrate retina suggests that . . . the curious inverted design of the vertebrate retina may in fact represent a unique solution to the problem of providing the highly active photoreceptor cells of higher vertebrates with copious quantities of oxygen and nutrients."[23] Biologist George Ayob argues that trying to eliminate the blind-spot in the vertebrate eye results in "a host of new and more severe functional problems."[24]

Thomas: But what about the "attenuation and distortion"[25] of light?

18. See Bergman, "The Left Recurrent Laryngeal Nerve Design"; Luskin, "'Biomimetics' Exposes Attacks on ID as Poorly Designed"; Bergman, *Poor Design*.
19. Dawkins, *Outgrowing God*, 165.
20. Behe, *Darwin Devolves*, 49.
21. Behe, *Darwin Devolves*, 49.
22. Dawkins, *Blind Watchmaker*, 94.
23. Denton, "Inverted Retina: Maladaptation or Pre-adaptation?," para. 6.
24. Ayoub, "On the Design of the Vertebrate Retina," para. 36.
25. Dawkins, *Blind Watchmaker*, 94.

Hiromi (using her tablet): According to Dawkins: "The layer of nerve cells running over the surface of the retina is thin, and they are transparent enough to let light through."[26] But that's *not* the point I want to make! You see, in 2007 a team of physicists and biologists discovered that "light actually doesn't pass through layers of cells to get to the retina. Instead, some cells act as *living fiber-optic cables* to directly channel light from the surface of the structure straight to the rods and cones of the retina."[27] Moreover, further research on these fiber-optic "glia" cells showed they channel specific light wavelengths in such a way that they "actually improve daytime vision without sacrificing the quality of night-time vision."[28] So, as an article on the science news site Phys.org explained: "Having the photoreceptors at the back of the retina is not a design constraint, it is a design feature. The idea that the vertebrate eye . . . might have been improved somehow if it had only been able to orient its wiring behind the photoreceptor layer . . . is folly."[29]

Douglas: Dawkins's argument is scientifically out of date![30]

Hiromi (using her tablet): Yes. In the end, as molecular biologist Michael J. Behe points out:

> the whole reverse wiring criticism is a shining example of the classic logical fallacy called the 'argument from ignorance.' In a nutshell, the argument goes like this: 'We can't think of any good reason for this arrangement; therefore there is no good reason for it. So no intelligent designer would have done it that way.' But ignorance of the workings of sophisticated biological machinery is no argument for Darwinism.[31]

---

26. Dawkins, *Outgrowing God*, 166.

27. Behe, *Darwin Devolves*, 49.

28. Behe, *Darwin Devolves*, 49–50.

29. Hewitt, "Fiber Optic Light Pipes in the Retina," para. 1.

30. See Discovery Science, "Be Grateful for the Intelligent Design of Your Eyes"; Ayoub, "On the Design of the Vertebrate Retina"; Bergman, "Inverted Human Eye a Poor Design?"; Denton, "Inverted Retina: Maladaptation or Pre-adaptation?"; Franze et al., "Müller Cells Are Living Optical Fibers in the Vertebrate Retina"; Labin and Ribak, "Retinal Glial Cells Enhance Human Vision Acuity"; Labin et al., "Müller Cells Separate between Wavelengths to Improve Day Vision with Minimal Effect upon Night Vision"; Luskin, "*Phys.org*: Specialized Retinal Cells Are a 'Design Feature'"; Wells, *Zombie Science*, chapter 7.

31. Behe, *Darwin Devolves*, 50. See All Grey Matters, "'Argument from Ignorance' Fallacy."

Thomas: Isn't Behe a Christian advocate of "Intelligent Design Theory"?

Sophie: He is, but take care not to make an invalid "*ad hominin*" or "against the person" attack that fails to address Behe's arguments.[32]

Hiromi: Behe is a Catholic who has no theological problem with evolution and who used to believe the theory before being prompted to question it when he read a critique by Michael Denton.[33]

Douglas: Besides, we can't use the "bad design" argument as an excuse to avoid the real issue.

Thomas: Which is?

Douglas: Which is whether organic systems, including those Dawkins thinks are examples of "bad design," can be plausibly accounted for by a "Blind Watchmaker."[34]

Thomas: Okay, so the argument from bad-design is badly designed.[35] But what about the argument that evolution explains organic systems, including the appearance of biological design?

Hiromi: Of course, even if evolution is the best explanation, that doesn't mean theism is false. At most, it would conflict with some interpretations of the Bible.

Sophie: I think it's worth noting that what one might call "the Grand Evolutionary Story," the official creation story of "Western" culture, contains several distinct claims:

- The Ancient Earth Thesis says the earth is about 4.5 billion years old.
- The Progress Thesis says that living things increased in complexity over time.
- The Common Ancestry Thesis says that contemporary organisms are all descended from simpler ancestral organisms.

---

32. See Wireless Philosophy, "Introduction to Ad Hominem Fallacies."

33. See Denton, *Evolution: A Theory in Crisis.*

34. A point made by David W. Swift in personal correspondence.

35. See Craig, "Viability of Intelligent Design 3/3"; Nelson, "Jettison the Arguments, or the Rule?"

- According to the Universal Common Ancestry Thesis, as referenced by Darwin's famous "tree of life" metaphor, "all living things are descended from one original primordial organism."[36]

- According to the "Blind Watchmaker" Thesis, evolution must occur "through natural processes requiring no divine guidance or non-material orienting force."[37] Now, this philosophical thesis motivates the scientific theory that: "mutation and selection—and perhaps other similarly undirected mechanisms—are fully sufficient to explain the appearance of design in biology."[38] The neo-Darwinian "Modern Evolutionary Synthesis" combined Darwin's theory of adaptation by natural selection with the science of genetics.[39] There is currently a discussion between adherents to the "Modern Synthesis" and advocates of an "Extended Evolutionary Synthesis."[40] To quote comments by Professor Kevin Laland and colleagues in *Nature*, the Modern Synthesis has a

> gene-centric' focus [that] fails to capture the full gamut of processes that direct evolution. Missing pieces include how physical development influences the generation of variation (developmental bias); how the environment directly shapes organisms' traits (plasticity); how organisms modify environments (niche construction); and how organisms transmit more than genes across generations (extra-genetic inheritance).[41]

In the same article, defenders of the Modern Synthesis say they "do not think that these processes deserve such special attention as to merit a new name such as 'extended evolutionary synthesis',"[42] because they are "'add-ons' to the basic processes that produce evolutionary change. . . . None of these additions is essential for evolution, but they can alter the process under certain circumstances."[43] Despite their different emphases, both schools of thought typically share a commitment to

36. West, "Debating Common Ancestry," para. 3.

37. Johnson, "Religion of the Blind Watchmaker," para. 4.

38. Meyer et al., "Origin of Biological Information and the Higher Taxonomic Categories," para. 73.

39. See Nature League, "Gregor Mendel: The Father of Modern Genetics."

40. Dierker, "Why One-Third of Biologists Now Question Darwinism." See also Zimmer, "Biologists Who Want to Overhaul Evolution."

41. Laland et al., "Does Evolutionary Theory Need a Rethink?," para. 13.

42. Laland et al., "Does Evolutionary Theory Need a Rethink?," para. 32.

43. Laland et al., "Does Evolutionary Theory Need a Rethink?," para. 45. See also Grant, "Should Evolutionary Theory Evolve?"

explanations of evolution that avoid genuine purpose or design[44] and which are ultimately framed in terms of "an unguided, unplanned process"[45] of physical "Chance and Necessity."[46] In other words, they are both typically committed to the "Blind Watchmaker" thesis.

- According to the Darwinian Naturalistic Origins Thesis, life arose from nonliving matter by virtue of an unguided, unplanned physical process.

It's also worth noting that it's possible to doubt parts of "the Grand Evolutionary Story" without thereby doubting the whole story. For example, atheist philosopher Jerry Fodor points out that common descent "could be true even if the adaptationism [evolution by natural selection] isn't."[47]

Thomas: Dawkins is a neo-Darwinian, right?

Sophie: Yes. Commenting on calls for an extended evolutionary synthesis, Dawkins said: "we have already expanded the Modern Synthesis. The Modern Synthesis was never monolithic. I don't think that we need to talk about it as a major movement that's happening now. It's happening all the time."[48]

Hiromi (using her tablet): I think the evidence for the first few theses in "the Grand Evolutionary Story" is better than it is for the last few. For example, Behe argues that, while the "Blind Watchmaker" has the resources to account for evolution at the levels of species and genus, it can't explain the evolution of higher taxonomic levels. He observes that "other than Eugene Koonin (who relies on an infinity of universes),"[49] proponents of the Extended Synthesis "all still leave the heavy lifting to orthodox neo-Darwinism, either explicitly or implicitly . . . neo-Darwinism is still the keystone of modern evolutionary thought, and the credibility of both are inextricably linked."[50] He argues that:

---

44. Gauger, "Teleonomy and Evolution."

45. Letter from Nobel Laureates to Kansas State Board of Education, September 9, 2005.

46. See Monod, *Chance and Necessity.*

47. Fodor, "Why Pigs Don't Have Wings," para. 7.

48. Dawkins quoted by Grant, "Should Evolutionary Theory Evolve?," para. 43.

49. Behe, *Darwin Devolves*, 137.

50. Behe, *Darwin Devolves*, 137. See Behe, *Darwin Devolves*, Part 2; Behe, *Edge of Evolution*, 159–62; Meyer, *Darwin's Doubt*, 291–335.

random mutation and natural selection are in fact fiercely *devo-lutionary*. It turns out that mutation easily *breaks* or *degrades* genes, which, counterintuitively, can sometimes help an organism to survive, so the damaged genes are hastily spread by natural selection . . . recent non-Darwinian accounts of evolution . . . are severely limited in scope . . . studies indicate that not only is the Darwinian mechanism *de*volutionary; it is also self-limiting—that is, it actively prevents evolutionary changes at the biological classification level of family and above.[51]

Thomas: How can breaking genes help something survive?

Hiromi: It's like throwing things off a hot air balloon to keep it aloft.[52]

Douglas (using his phone): To quote atheist philosopher Michel Ruse: "we have today a vocal anti-Darwinian party, consisting somewhat surprisingly not only of the evangelical Christians of the American South but of some of today's most eminent atheist philosophers."[53] Thomas Nagel argues that: "the reductive account of life . . . faces problems of probability that I believe are not taken seriously enough, both with respect to the evolution of life forms through accidental mutation and natural selection and with respect to the formation from dead matter of physical systems capable of such evolution. The more we learn about the intricacy of the genetic code and its control of the chemical processes of life, the harder those problems seem."[54] Likewise, Jerry Fodor says: "the classical Darwinist account of evolution as primarily driven by natural selection is in trouble on both conceptual and empirical grounds . . . an appreciable number of perfectly reasonable biologists [by which he means nonreligious biologists] are coming to think that the theory of natural selection can no longer be taken for granted."[55]

Fodor and cognitive scientist Massimo Piatelli-Palmarini jointly affirm that "Darwin's theory of natural selection is fatally flawed," and that "As far as we can make out, nobody knows exactly how phenotypes [different types of organism] evolve."[56] Günter Theißen, who holds the chair of genetics at Fried-

51. Behe, *Darwin Devolves*, 10–11. See Behe, "Experimental Evolution, Loss-of-Function Mutations, and 'the First Rule of Adaptive Evolution.'"

52. See Discovery Channel, "Michael Behe Exposes How Mutations Fail To Invent (Science Uprising EP6)."

53. Ruse, "Darwinism as Religion," para. 5.

54. Nagel, *Mind & Cosmos*, 9–10.

55. Fodor, "Why Pigs Don't Have Wings," para. 8.

56. Fodor and Piatelli-Palmarini, *What Darwin Got Wrong*, xvi, 153.

rich Schiller University of Jena, says that although we know a lot about how organisms adapt to the environment: "much less is known about the mechanisms behind the origin of evolutionary novelties, a process that is arguably different from adaptation. Despite Darwin's undeniable merits, explaining how the enormous complexity and diversity of living beings on our planet originated remains one of the greatest challenges of biology."[57]

Thomas: But if those guys are right, why is Dawkins so confident that neo-Darwinism is "the true explanation for why living things look designed"?[58]

Sophie: That question might tempt us into trying to psychoanalyze Dawkins's *motives*, so let's stick to examining the *arguments* Dawkins gives in *Outgrowing God*.

Hiromi: Well, he starts by moving on from intuitive appearances, defining a widely accepted criterion of design detection that can be used to make design inferences. He admits this criterion *appears* to apply to life, but claims the theory of evolution shows that living things don't satisfy this design criterion after all.

Sophie: And what criterion of design detection does Dawkins discuss?

Thomas: Improbability?

Hiromi: Actually, it's *not* improbability *as such*. It's *a specific type of improbability*.

Thomas (using his tablet): Hang on, Dawkins says: "When we say something is improbable we mean it's very unlikely to just happen by random chance. If you shake ten pennies and toss them on the table, you'd be surprised if all ten came up heads. It could happen but it's very unlikely."[59]

Hiromi (using her tablet): Yes, and then he observes: "If somebody did the same thing with a hundred pennies it's still just possible they'd all come up heads. But it's so very very very improbable that you'd suspect a trick, and you'd be right. I'd bet everything I have that it was a trick."[60]

57. Theißen, "Saltational Evolution," 44.

58. Dawkins, *Outgrowing God*, 141–42.

59. Dawkins, *Outgrowing God*, 172.

60. Dawkins, *Outgrowing God*, 172.

Sophie: What is it about the hundred-pennies event that points to design?

Thomas: It's much more improbable than the ten-pennies event.

Sophie: It is. But improbability on its own doesn't point to design. After all, *any* pattern of heads and tails exhibited by a hundred coins tossed onto the table is just as improbable as any other. Each possible outcome is one possible outcome out of all the possible outcomes.

Thomas: I see what you're getting at! It's not just that a hundred tossed coins displayed an unlikely pattern, but that they displayed the pattern "All heads"!

Hiromi (using her tablet): Yes. The coins exhibited what information theorists call "specified complexity" or "complex specified information,"[61] and *that's* why Dawkins would be right to bet "that it was a trick."[62] As William Lane Craig explains:

> as a basis for a design inference . . . in addition to high improbability there also needs to be conformity to an independently given pattern. When these two elements are present, we have . . . 'specified complexity,' which is the tip-off to intelligent design. Thus, for example, in a poker game any deal of cards is equally and highly improbable, but if you find that every time a certain player deals he gets all four aces, you can bet this is not the result of chance but of design.[63]

Thomas (using his tablet): That reminds me of something Marcus Tullius Cicero said in the first century BC! He said: "If a countless number of copies of the one-and-twenty letters of the [Greek] alphabet . . . were thrown together into some receptacle and then shaken out onto the ground, [would it] be possible that they should produce the *Annals of Ennius*? I doubt whether chance could possibly succeed in producing a single verse."[64]

---

61. See Williams, "Specified Complexity." Dembski, "Specification: The Pattern That Signifies Intelligence"; Meyer, "Evidence of Intelligent Design in the Origin of Life," 424–28; Dembski, *No Free Lunch*; Dembski and Witt, *Intelligent Design*, chapter 4; Dembski and Wells, *Design of Life*, chapter 7.

62. Dawkins, *Outgrowing God*, 172.

63. Craig, "Fine Tuned Universe," para. 2.

64. Cicero, *Nat. d.*, 2.37.

Hiromi: That's interesting. Imagine randomly drawing Scrabble tiles out of a bag. A long string of random letters is *complex* but it's not *specified*. It doesn't conform to any independently given pattern we haven't simply read off the event in question. A short string of letters could easily be specified—like "this"—but wouldn't be complex enough to outstrip the ability of chance to plausibly explain the match. So, neither complexity without specificity, nor specificity without complexity entail design. However, if we saw a poem written out in Scrabble tiles, we'd infer design. A poem is specified, because it conforms to rules of spelling and grammar. And a poem is a sufficiently complex arrangement of contingent parts to make it unreasonable to attribute this match to luck. It's this combination of specificity with sufficient complexity that justifies making an inference to a poet, on the grounds that: "in all cases where we know the causal origin of . . . specified complexity, experience has shown that intelligent design played a causal role."[65]

Thomas: And Dawkins accepts that specified complexity signals design?

Douglas (using his phone): He doesn't use the technical terminology in *Outgrowing God*, but he's clearly talking about specified complexity.[66] He says:

> If you scramble the parts of [a] watch a thousand times, you'll get a thousand random messes. But not one of them will tell the time or do anything useful. That's the key difference between watch and stone. Both are equally improbable in that they are a unique combination of parts which won't just 'happen' by sheer luck. But the watch is unique in another, and more interesting way which separates it from all the random scramblings: it does something useful; it tells the time. . . . Of all the thousands of ways the bits of a watch could come together, only one [or very few] of those ways . . . will tell the time.[67]

Indeed, a watch is a specifically complex arrangement of specifically complex parts, just like many biological systems.[68]

---

65. Meyer, "Teleological Evolution," para. 4.

66. In *Free Inquiry*, Richard Dawkins writes: "'specified complexity' takes care of the sensible point that . . . in the unique disposition of its parts a pile of detached watch parts tossed in a box is . . . as improbable as a fully functioning, genuinely complicated watch. What is specified about a watch is that it is improbable in the specific direction of telling the time." Dawkins, "Who Owns the Argument from Improbability?," 11–12.

67. Dawkins, *Outgrowing God*, 190–91.

68. A point made by David W. Swift in personal correspondence.

Hiromi (using her tablet): According to origin-of-life researcher Leslie Orgel: "Living organisms are distinguished by their specified complexity. Crystals such as granite fail to qualify as living because they lack complexity; mixtures of random polymers fail to qualify because they lack specificity."[69] Agnostic astrobiologist Paul Davies says: "Living organisms are mysterious not for their complexity per se, but for their tightly specified complexity."[70] Bernard-Olaf Kuppers discusses specified complexity under the rubric of biological "information"[71] when he observes: "The problem of the origin of life is clearly basically equivalent to the problem of the origin of biological information."[72]

Thomas: I'm happy to agree with Dawkins that although *any* arrangement of watch parts is *equally improbable*, it's nevertheless *highly improbable* that they should be arranged so as to tell the time *in the absence of design*. But isn't Dawkins's main argument that specified complexity can be explained by evolution?

Hiromi: Actually, that's *not* his argument. Remember, for something to exhibit specified complexity is for it to combine specificity with *sufficient* complexity or unlikeliness. Dawkins takes the *explaining away* approach, claiming that although living things *appear* to be full of specified complexity, their specificity *isn't sufficiently unlikely*.

Douglas: If you think about it, organic life has to exhibit functional specificity in order to live; so, the relevant question is *just how unlikely*, or complex, that specificity is.

Sophie: Of course, the likelihood of any given contingent event *is relative to the resources available to produce it*. William A. Dembski explains:

> A seemingly improbable event can become quite probable when placed against the appropriate reference class of probabilistic resources. On the other hand, it may remain improbable even after all the relevant probabilistic resources have been factored in. If it remains improbable (and therefore complex) and

69. Orgel, *Origins of Life*, 189.

70. Davies, *Fifth Miracle*, 112.

71. See Meyer, "Evidence of Intelligent Design in the Origin of Life," 424–28.

72. Kuppers, *Information and the Origin of Life*, 170.

if the event is also specified, then the complexity-specification criterion is satisfied.[73]

Douglas (using his phone): That's useful. As I understand it, then, Dawkins's argument is that neo-Darwinian evolution offers a preferable third option to the false dilemma of assuming living things are either the product of design, or of *chance forces that have to act all in one go*. Dawkins admits: "a human eye cannot spring spontaneously into existence. That would be too improbable, like throwing a hundred pennies down and getting all heads."[74] The spontaneous appearance of such functional specificity *would* be improbable enough to suggest design. But: "an excellent eye can come from a random change to a slightly less excellent eye. And that slightly less good eye can come from an even less good eye. And so on back to a really rather poor eye [as long as it's] better than no eye at all. . . . Improbability dissolves away when you see it as arriving gradually . . . step by tiny step, where each step brings about only a really small change."[75] In other words, organisms can *gradually accumulate* specified functionally *in a way that doesn't outstrip the naturally available explanatory resources*. If that's true, it means organisms *don't* exhibit specified complexity.

Hiromi: I think that's accurate. Dawkins believes the appearance of organic design is a delusion based on a failure to take into account "the appropriate reference class of probabilistic resources." He thinks that reference class is revealed by the Modern Synthesis. In other words, his argument depends upon the claim that *the relevant functional specificities can gradually accumulate in a way that doesn't outstrip the relevant, naturally available explanatory resources*. However, Dawkins doesn't offer any evidence for this claim! For example, he offers no detailed evolutionary explanation for the existence of the multi-protein molecular machines he mentions.

Douglas (using his phone): Dawkins says: "Some of these knotted molecules are tiny machines, miniature 'pumps', or tiny 'walkers' which literally stride about on two legs inside the cell, busily doing chemical errands! Look on YouTube for 'Your body's molecular machines' and be utterly amazed."[76]

73. Dembski, *No Free Lunch*, 21.

74. Dawkins, *Outgrowing God*, 186.

75. Dawkins, *Outgrowing God*, 186.

76. Dawkins, *Outgrowing God*, 222.

Hiromi (using her tablet): I did, and the appearance of design is impressive.[77] Behe explains that cells contain many multi-protein machines that exhibit an "irreducible complexity." That basically means these machines can't work without all their essential parts.[78] Behe argues that not only is the co-ordination of many parts to achieve a function, as seen in irreducibly complex cellular machinery, an obvious sign of design, but that evolution can't plausibly explain these systems:

> An irreducibly complex system cannot be produced directly by numerous, successive, slight modifications of a precursor system, because any precursor . . . that is missing a part is by definition nonfunctional. . . . Although an irreducibly complex system can't be produced directly, one can't definitively rule out the possibility of an indirect, circuitous route. However, as the complexity of an interacting system increases, the likelihood of such an indirect route drops precipitously.[79]

It seems that some, if not all of these "irreducibly complex" machines are complex enough to count as examples of "specified complexity."

Douglas: It's interesting to note that, in *The God Delusion*, Dawkins concedes: "genuine irreducible complexity would wreck Darwin's theory if it were ever found."[80]

Sophie: Could you give us some examples, Hiromi?

Hiromi (using her tablet): Here's two. First, Dawkins's account of vertebrate eye evolution presupposes the existence of "a cell sensitive to light and able to react in a specific way to visible radiation."[81] But a light sensitive cell turns out to be an "irreducibly complex" system.[82] Second, some bacteria swim using a self-assembling outboard motor, spinning their whip-like 'flagella' at up to 100,000 rpm: "The flagellum includes an acid powered rotary engine, a stator, O-rings, bushings and a drive shaft. The intricate machinery of this

77. See Williams, "Inside the Cell."

78. See Williams, "Irreducible Complexity"; Behe, "Irreducible Complexity: Obstacle to Darwinian Evolution"; Dembski, "Irreducible Complexity Revisited"; Behe, *Darwin's Black Box*; Behe, *Darwin Devolves*, esp. "Appendix: Clarifying Perspective"; Behe, *Edge of Evolution*, esp. "Appendix C: Assembling the Bacterial Flagellum"; Dembski, *No Free Lunch*; Dembski and Wells, *Design of Life*.

79. Behe, "Evidence for Intelligent Design from Biochemistry," para. 16.

80. Dawkins, *God Delusion*, 125.

81. Wolf, "Two Kinds of Causality."

82. See Behe, *Darwin's Black Box*, 15–22.

molecular motor requires approximately fifty proteins. Yet the absence of any one of these proteins results in the complete loss of motor function."[83] Japanese scientists have studied the flagellum with the aim of making energy saving nanotechnology,[84] because "The rotary motor, with a diameter of only 30 to 40 nm [nanometers], drives the rotation of the flagellum at around 300 Hz, at a power level of 10–16 W with energy conversion efficiency close to 100%."[85] Here's a simplified conceptual diagram:[86]

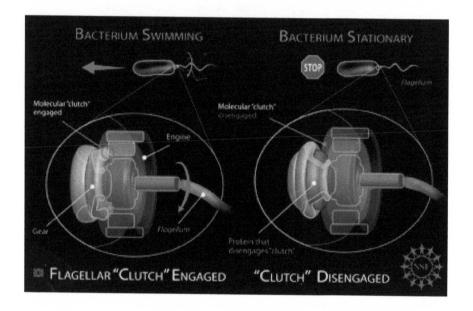

Thomas (using his tablet): That certainly *looks* designed. But as Dawkins explains, starting from the fact that humans engineer biological change by selectively breeding animals: "What Darwin brilliantly realized is that you don't need the human selector. Nature does the job all by itself. . . . Some mutant genes help animals to survive and reproduce. Those genes become more frequent in the population. Other mutant genes make it harder for them to survive and reproduce, and so become less frequent in the population until they disappear altogether. It only takes a few centuries to turn a

83. Dembski, "Reinstating Design Within Science," 253.

84. See Phad Pyakurel, "Rotary Nonomachine."

85. Namba, "Self-Assembly of Bacterial Flagella."

86. "Insights into the Workings of a Bacterium's Flagellum."

wolf into a whippet or a Weimaraner. Just think how much change could be achieved in a million centuries."[87]

Hiromi (using her tablet): But that's just a weak analogy combined with a rhetorical question. Dawkins *assumes* that the answer to his question is "enough change to mean living things don't exhibit specified complexity," *and that makes his argument question-begging*. As atheist philosopher Daniel Dennett observes: "This is a purely theory-driven explanation, argued a-priori from the assumption that natural selection tells the true story—some true story or other—about every curious feature of the biosphere . . . it assumes that Darwinism is basically on the right track."[88]

Douglas (using his phone): To quote atheist and Nobel-Prize-winning physicist Brian Josephson:

> In books such as *The Blind Watchmaker* [by Richard Dawkins], a crucial part of the argument concerns whether there exists a continuous path, leading from the origins of life to man, each step of which is both favoured by natural selection, and small enough to have happened by chance. It appears to be presented as a matter of logical necessity that such a path exists, but actually there is no such logical necessity; rather, commonly made assumptions in evolution require the existence of such a path.[89]

Hiromi (using her tablet): Dawkins asserts that: "Since our ancestors were fish crawling out of the sea, three million centuries have gone by. That's an awful lot of time—a huge opportunity for change—step by step down the generations."[90] But he never quantifies how much change one can reasonably expect, "step by step down the generations." And without a principled way to distinguish between what the neo-Darwinian process can and can't plausibly accomplish, even in rough-and-ready terms, all Dawkins has to offer is a vague just-so story that begs the question against the proper burden of proof.

Thomas: Has *anyone* quantified how much change one can reasonably expect evolution to produce?

---

87. Dawkins, *Outgrowing God*, 179.
88. Dennett, "Leibnizian Paradigm," 49.
89. Josephson, "Letter to the Editor."
90. Dawkins, *Outgrowing God*, 179.

Hiromi (using her tablet): Actually, modern physics and molecular biology have enabled numerical answers to your question that strongly disconfirm the "Blind Watchmaker" thesis. To start with an educated estimate of the available probabilistic resources: there are a limited number of elementary particles in the observable universe (about 10^{80}), and elementary particles can only interact with each other so many times per second (at most 10^{43} times), and there has been a limited amount of time since the Big Bang (about 10^{17} seconds). We can calculate the total number of events that could have taken place in the observable universe since the Big Bang by multiplying these factors together. The product, which is 10^{140}, provides a measure of the probabilistic resources of the entire observable universe.[91] William A. Dembski rounds up somewhat to set a "Universal Probability Bound" of 10^{150} events.[92]

Thomas: Are you sure you want to be that generous? I mean, it's obvious that most of the universe *isn't* dedicated to rearranging amino acids or mutating genetic information!

Hiromi (using her tablet): You have a point. Robert Shapiro estimates that the early Earth could have provided for around 10^{51} trials for the origin of life.[93] But using a generous estimate of the available probabilistic resources isn't a problem for the design argument, because we need to account for specified biological structures that are *very* unlikely.

Thomas: What level of complexity are we talking about?

Hiromi (using her tablet): New life-forms require new protein molecules. And as David Gelernter, Professor of computer science at Yale University, explains:

> A protein molecule is based on a chain of amino acids; 150 elements is a 'modest-sized' chain.... The total count of *possible* 150-link chains, where each link is chosen separately from 20 amino acids, is 20^{150} [which] roughly equals 10^{195}.... What proportion of these many polypeptides are useful proteins? Douglas Axe did a series of experiments to estimate how many 150-long chains are capable of stable folds—of reaching the final step in the protein-creation process (the folding) and of holding their shapes long

91. See Abel, "Universal Plausibility Metric (UPM) & Principle (UPP)."

92. See Dembski and Witt, *Intelligent Design Uncensored*, 68–69.

93. See Monton, *Seeking God in Science*, 99.

enough to be useful. . . . He estimated that . . . 1 in 10^{74} will be capable of folding into a stable protein . . . your chances of hitting a stable protein that performs some useful *function*, and might therefore play a part in evolution, are even smaller.[94]

Thomas: So, only a *very* small proportion of these "modest-sized" amino acid sequences form stable proteins.

Hiromi (using her tablet): What's more, Axe and biologist Ann Guager took two bacterial proteins with different functions but very similar structures. They experimentally determined that shifting the function of one enzyme to the function of the other would take at least seven mutations, which is "too many mutations to have occurred by an unguided neo-Darwinian process. . . . The waiting time for seven coordinated neutral mutations to arise in a bacterial population is on the order of 10^{27} years."[95] The universe is only about 13.8×10^{10}—13.8 billion—years old![96]

Thomas: What about starting with shorter proteins and evolving longer ones?

Hiromi: Because the forces between amino acids are very weak, the need for enough overall force to hold a protein in its folded state generally requires functional proteins to have a minimum of about seventy amino acids.[97] Plus, "Most biological functions require many mutually dependent proteins . . . and the improbability of evolving such systems increases exponentially with each additional protein required."[98]

Douglas: Whichever way you look at it, molecular biology is so complex that the probabilistic resources of the observable universe are quickly swamped.[99]

94. Gelernter, "Giving Up Darwin," paras. 25, 33–34. See Discovery Institute, "Biologist Douglas Axe on Evolution's Ability to Produce New Functions"; Axe, "Estimating the Prevalence of Protein Sequences Adopting Functional Enzyme Folds"; Axe, *Undeniable.*

95. Guager, "Science and Human Origins," 20. See Guager and Axe, "Evolutionary Accessibility of New Enzyme Function."

96. See "How Old Is Our Universe?"

97. See Swift, "Biochemical Reasons against Genes Evolving." See also Swift, *Evolution under the Microscope*, chapter 7.

98. Swift, "Biochemical Reasons against Genes Evolving," para. 29.

99. See Discovery Institute, "Biologist Douglas Axe on Evolution's Ability to

188 OUTGROWING GOD?

Hiromi (using her tablet): Gelernter concludes that, while Darwin's theory of evolution is

> perfectly reasonable in the abstract . . . he is overwhelmed by numbers he couldn't possibly have foreseen. . . . The obvious fact is that genes . . . encode an awe-inspiring amount of information. . . . Where on earth did it all come from? Neo-Darwinism says that nature simply rolls the dice, and if something useful emerges, great. Otherwise, try again. But useful sequences are so gigantically rare that this answer simply won't work.[100]

Gelernter writes: "Darwin successfully explained the small adjustments by which an organism adapts to local circumstances. . . . Yet there are many reasons to doubt whether he can answer the hard questions and explain the big picture."[101] In short, the evidence says living things are brimming with specified complexity at the molecular level.

Thomas: That all sounds very impressive. But when I was reading Dawkins's descriptions of how things "spontaneously form themselves into particular shapes"[102] in a process of natural "self-assembly,"[103] it really seemed like he'd explained the appearance of design in purely material, naturalistic terms.

Sophie: Perhaps we should interrogate Dawkins's claims about "self-assembly."[104]

Thomas (using his tablet): Dawkins says that: "When 'design' emerges from the obeying of simple rules, where there is no overall plan in existence, anywhere, it is called 'bottom-up', as opposed to 'top-down', design."[105] As

---

Produce New Functions"; Zentrum für BioKomplexität & NaturTeleologie, "Thermodynamic Analysis of the Rarity of Protein Folds"; Axe, "Extreme Functional Sensitivity to Conservative Amino Acid Changes on Enzyme Exteriors"; Axe, "Estimating the Prevalence of Protein Sequences Adopting Functional Enzyme Folds"; "Case Against a Darwinian Origin of Protein Folds"; Axe and Guager, "Model and Laboratory Demonstrations That Evolutionary Optimization Works Well Only if Preceded by Invention"; Behe, "Waiting Longer for Two Mutations"; Guager and Axe, "Evolutionary Accessibility of New Enzyme Functions: A Case Study from the Biotin Pathway"; Reeves et al., "Enzyme Families—Shared Evolutionary History of Shared Design?"; Axe, *Undeniable*.

100. Gelernter, "Giving Up Darwin."
101. Gelernter, "Giving Up Darwin."
102. Dawkins, *Outgrowing God*, 196.
103. Dawkins, *Outgrowing God*, 196.
104. Dawkins, *Outgrowing God*, 196.
105. Dawkins, *Outgrowing God*, 213.

examples of the 'bottom-up' emergence of *apparent* design, he describes the mound-building behavior of termites[106] and the flocking behavior of starlings. He has a picture of a termite "castle" that looks like a church in Barcelona, and he points out that when starlings flock together in flight: "There's no director, no conductor, no architect, no boss bird . . . all the individual birds, each one following bottom-up rules, together produce an effect which looks top-down."[107]

Hiromi: See how Dawkins claims apparent design can emerge "from the obeying of simple rules," and that in all such cases "there is no overall plan in existence, anywhere"[108]?

Thomas: What's the problem with that?

Hiromi: The problem is that evidence for the first claim isn't evidence for the second! Showing that apparent design can emerge "from the obeying of simple rules" doesn't show that "there is no overall plan in existence, anywhere,"[109] because genuine design can be implemented in a "bottom-up" way through the use of "simple rules."[110] When Dawkins says "Nobody and nothing . . . designed the termite mound,"[111] that's an evidence-free assumption.

Thomas (using his tablet): But you accept that "Each individual termite just follows a set of simple rules, on its own, with no idea of what the other termites are doing, and no idea of what the finished building will be like"[112]?

Hiromi: Yes. But the fact that termites blindly follow rules with no idea of the outcome doesn't mean there *isn't* a designer who deliberately programed those rules into the termites. The same point applies to the flocking behavior of starlings. In fact, Dawkins's own examples give the lie to his confusion of the claim that *the parts of a biological system* don't have a plan in mind with the claim that *no one* has a plan in mind.

Thomas: How come?

106. See Margonelli, "Collective Mind of the Mound"; Wilson, "Why Termites Build Such Enormous Skyscrapers."

107. Dawkins, *Outgrowing God*, 214.

108. Dawkins, *Outgrowing God*, 213.

109. Dawkins, *Outgrowing God*, 213.

110. Dawkins, *Outgrowing God*, 213.

111. Dawkins, *Outgrowing God*, 213.

112. Dawkins, *Outgrowing God*, 213.

Hiromi (using her tablet): Dawkins describes how

> a clever computer programmer called Craig Reynolds . . . wrote
> a program called Boids to simulate flocking birds. . . . He put a
> lot of effort into programming just one bird, with rules such as:
> 'Keep an eye on your neighbouring birds. If a neighbour does so
> and so, you must do such and such.' Having perfected the rules
> for his one bird, he . . . made dozens of copies of the one bird
> and 'released' them all into the computer. . . . The boids flocked
> very much like real birds. Reynolds didn't program at the flock
> level. He programmed at the level of the individual bird. Flock
> behaviour emerged as a consequence.[113]

In this example, the "bottom-up" emergence of flocking was the product of
"clever"[114] programming intended to produce this result!

Thomas: True.

Hiromi (using her tablet): Dawkins describes how "George Oster did the
same kind of thing, but with cells in an embryo. . . . To do this he used lots of
details that biologists already knew about single cells. Really quite complicated details, because cells are complicated things."[115] If Oster[116] had enough
information about single cells, it's unsurprising his virtual cells behaved like
real cells when they were put together.

Thomas: I suppose not.

Hiromi (using her tablet): Dawkins says he's "trying to . . . show you the
power of bottom-up 'design' where there is no architect/choreographer,
only low-level local rules."[117] But all he succeeds in showing is that program-
mers can implement designs using a bottom-up approach!

Thomas: But that doesn't mean the termite's hill or the starling's flocking
were designed, only that they *could be* designed.

---

113. Dawkins, *Outgrowing God*, 215.
114. Dawkins, *Outgrowing God*, 215.
115. Dawkins, *Outgrowing God*, 219.
116. See Nuzzo, "Profile of George Oster."
117. Dawkins, *Outgrowing God*, 220.

Hiromi: I agree. In fact, I think Dawkins exaggerates how designed these things appear to be, setting them up as straw man targets he can easily explain away.

Sophie: A "straw man" fallacy occurs when an opponent's argument or question is distorted in a way that makes it easier to deal with. Of course, this distortion may be either intentional or unintentional.[118]

Thomas: Why do you say Dawkins is setting up straw men?

Hiromi: The termite hill he shows looks *a bit* like the Basílica de la Sagrada Família in Barcelona, but the resemblance is quite general. In fact, the termite hill more closely resembles a bunch of stalagmites, which is just the sort of structure one expects the repeated action of natural processes following simple rules to produce.

Thomas: I guess.

Sophie: The Basílica de la Sagrada Família, by the famous Spanish architect Antoni Gaudí,[119] combines "natural forms and Christian symbolism."[120] Architecture critic Jonathan Glancey explains that: "Gaudí based his designs on . . . forms abstracted from nature and then translated into the design of the columns, vaults and intersecting geometric elements of the structure of the Sagrada Família. . . . Everything he designed, he said, 'comes from the Great Book of Nature.'"[121]

Douglas (showing his phone around): Here's a photo from Wikimedia Commons:[122]

---

118. See Wireless Philosophy, "CRITICAL THINKING—Fallacies: Straw Man Fallacy [HD]"; Pirie, *How To Win Every Argument*, 155–57.

119. See Williams, "Antoni Gaudí's Basílica de la Sagrada Família."

120. Abend, "Inside Barcelona's Unfinished Masterpiece," para. 6.

121. Glancey, "Gaudí's la Sagrada Família: Genius or folly?," para. 7.

122. "Sagrada Família."

Hiromi: As for the flocking behavior of starlings, it's not very tightly specified. The starlings stay together within certain parameters as they fly about, but it's not as if they fly about forming Shakespearean sonnets in the sky.

Douglas: Did anyone else just think of that scene at the end of the 1980 *Flash Gordon* movie, where the Hawk Men form words in the sky?[123]

Hiromi: I love the music for that film by Queen![124]

123. See "Flash Gordon."
124. See Long Live Queen, "Queen: Flash."

Thomas (using his tablet): Dawkins points out that: "Crystals just grow, spontaneously. And some grow into precise geometric shapes which look, overwhelmingly, as though an artist had made them."[125]

Hiromi (using her tablet): Again, do they? I mean, it's not as if crystals grow into statues of animals. Crystals *don't* exhibit specified complexity because they have simple, repetitive structures produced by physical laws. As Dawkins says, the geometrically precise shapes of snow crystals: "comes straight from the arrangement of their atoms. When water is cold enough it crystallizes into ice [and] the natural shape of each tiny ice crystal is six-sided. . . . Crystals—pyrites or diamonds or snowflakes—grow their pretty shapes by local bottom-up rules. In those cases the rules are the rules of chemical bonds."[126] Besides, when Dawkins says, "The important point is that nobody designed the shape of the crystal. The shape emerged through the obeying of local rules,"[127] he's *assuming* that those "local rules" of physics and chemistry are not themselves the product of design.

Sophie: A relevant point, but one that I suggest we "put a pin in" for now because it takes us to the cosmic design argument that Dawkins responds to in his last chapter.

Thomas (using his tablet): Dawkins says his "champion example of living self-assembly is . . . a virus, the lambda bacteriophage."[128]

Hiromi: Dawkins likens the self-assembly of the simple, repetitive order in crystals to the replication of the complex information in a viral parasite, even though the former process can be explained by the "local bottom-up rules" of chemistry acting within particular environmental conditions, whereas the latter process requires a virus to inject its genetic code into the pre-existing, highly complex information processing machinery of its host!

Douglas: Dawkins admits that "snowflakes and other beautiful crystals are . . . not like [a] watch."[129] That's a key admission, because it shows while explaining how crystals self-assemble is analogous to explaining how *some*

---

125. Dawkins, *Outgrowing God*, 192.
126. Dawkins, *Outgrowing God*, 192, 194, 221.
127. Dawkins, *Outgrowing God*, 221.
128. Dawkins, *Outgrowing God*, 196.
129. Dawkins, *Outgrowing God*, 196.

polypeptides[130] *fold into proteins* by chemical "self-jigsawing,"[131] it's irrelevant to explaining *how amino acids get arranged into the right sequences* to form the stable folds that perform selectable functions.[132] It's a "red-herring."[133]

Thomas (using his tablet): But Dawkins says: "we saw how the laws of chemical bonds—by a process that resembles jigsaw pieces slotting into each other—produced more elaborate things than ordinary crystals: protein molecules."[134]

Hiromi (using her tablet): The "laws of chemical bonds" explain how a protein molecule folds *given its sequence of amino acids*. As Dawkins says: "the sequence of amino acids in the 'necklace' is responsible—through 'self-assembly jigsawing'—for the lumpy crevicy shape of the protein."[135] But chemical laws *don't explain the sequence of those amino acids*. The sequence of amino acids isn't determined by *any* physical laws, which is why amino acids can be arranged in many different sequences. Indeed, a relatively short chain of amino acids can be arranged in so many different sequences that the subset of sequences that can perform a biological function is vanishingly small and therefore *highly unlikely to form by chance*. That's why we have to ask, with Dawkins: "what determines the sequence of amino acids in the necklace of any particular enzyme, and therefore the lumpy shape into which the chain folds itself?"[136]

Thomas (using his tablet): I see; but Dawkins answers his own question, saying: "That's obviously a hugely important question because so much else depends on it. And the answer is: the genetic molecule, DNA."[137] He explains that: "Like a protein molecule, DNA is a chain, a necklace of jigsaw

130. Dawkins states that: "any chain of amino acids has a tendency to fold itself into a particular three-dimensional shape." Dawkins, *Outgrowing God*, 202. This is misleading, in that only a minority of amino-acid chains (polypeptides) make stable protein folds, and as David W. Swift notes: "The forces (between the packed amino acids) holding a folded protein in place are so weak that there need to be many amino acids involved to give overall stability, generally at least 70." Finlay et al., *Debating Darwin*, 107. See also Swift, "Proteins Need to Fold."

131. Dawkins, *Outgrowing God*, 202.

132. See Meyer, "Can Chemistry Explain Information in DNA?"

133. See Wireless Philosophy, "Red Herring"; Pirie, *How To Win Every Argument*, 136–38.

134. Dawkins, *Outgrowing God*, 196.

135. Dawkins, *Outgrowing God*, 204.

136. Dawkins, *Outgrowing God*, 204.

137. Dawkins, *Outgrowing God*, 204.

pieces. But here the beads are not amino acids, they are chemical units called nucleotide bases. And there aren't 20 different kinds, only four. Their names are shortened to A, T, C and G. T jigsaws only with A (and A only with T). C jigsaws only with G (and G only with C)."[138]

Hiromi (using her tablet): Which explains linking *between* DNA strands, but *not* the sequencing of the four nucleotide base types *within* DNA strands. As with the sequence of amino acids in a protein, the sequence of nucleotide bases in DNA isn't determined by any physical laws. That's why they can form many different sequences. As Meyer writes:

> Just as magnetic letters can be combined and recombined in any way to form various sequences on a metal surface, so, too, can each of the four bases . . . attach to any site on the DNA back-bone with equal facility, making all sequences equally probable (or improbable). . . . Thus, "self-organizing" bonding affinities cannot explain the sequentially specific arrangement of nucleo-tide bases in DNA because (1) there are no bonds between bases along the information-bearing axis of the molecule, and (2) there are no differential affinities between the backbone and the specific bases that could account for variations in sequence. And because the same holds for RNA molecules, researchers who speculate that life began in an RNA world have also failed to solve . . . the problem of explaining how information in func-tioning RNA molecules could have arisen in the first place.[139]

Or, we can add, the origin of the large amounts of new information needed to specify new biological functions.

Dawkins explains that, as it is transcribed and translated by the ma-chinery of protein synthesis:[140] "the sequence of the four types of bases in a stretch of DNA, when read in threes, determines the sequence of the 20 types of amino acids in a protein chain."[141] He says the sequence of nucleo-tide bases "carries information, in the same way . . . as a computer disc."[142] DNA, like RNA, encodes information that exhibits specified complexity. These molecules embody "a digital code, just like computer code."[143] The

138. Dawkins, *Outgrowing God*, 204–5.

139. Meyer, "Evidence of Intelligent Design in the Origin of Life," 441–42. See: Meyer, "Can Chemistry Explain Information in DNA?"

140. See Williams, "Protein Synthesis."

141. Dawkins, *Outgrowing God*, 204.

142. Dawkins, *Outgrowing God*, 205.

143. Dawkins, *Outgrowing God*, 211.

only known cause of this sort of coded information, and the systems that process it, is intelligence.

Thomas (using his tablet): But isn't this exactly where evolution by natural selection undermines the design argument? As Dawkins says: "What was happening during all the billions of years of evolution was that *the DNA instructions for how to make babies were being gradually built up . . . by natural selection.*"[144]

Douglas (using his phone): Natural selection can compile useful instructions *if* they arise, though Dawkins ignores the problem of how beneficial traits get fixed within a population;[145] but the job of originating useful instructions falls to chance. As Dawkins says: "differences in DNA in different individuals—*ultimately caused by random mutations*—cause differences in the proteins."[146]

Hiromi (using her tablet): And Dawkins is simply *assuming* that random mutations are a probabilistic resource sufficient to prevent the information in living things being complex enough to warrant a design inference. We're back to the question of how much evolution can plausibly explain. Dawkins never addresses this question, but the scientific evidence indicates that the explanatory reach of the "Blind Watchmaker" is pretty limited. As Behe explains:

> Mutation supplies the variation upon which natural selection acts, but the greatest amount of that variation comes from damaging or outright breaking previously working genes. In the case of an already functioning complex systems, natural selection shapes it more and more tightly to its current role, making it less and less adaptable to other complex roles. . . . The need for multiple coordinated mutations [multiplies] the troubles for Darwinism [and] irreducible complexity effectively prohibits the development of intricate molecular machinery by mutation and selection.[147]

144. Dawkins, *Outgrowing God*, 208, emphasis added.

145. See Williams, "Evolution & the Waiting Time Problem"; LeMaster, "Evolution's Waiting-Time Problem and Suggested Ways to Overcome It"; Tsholofelo Pooe, "Evolution's Time Problem"; Sanford et al., "Waiting Time Problem in a Model Hominin Population"; Swift, "Blind Watchmaker"; Guager, "Science and Human Origins."

146. Dawkins, *Outgrowing God*, 222, emphasis added.

147. Behe, *Darwin Devolves*, 246–47.

Although the Extended Synthesis expands the Blind Watchmaker's toolkit somewhat, Behe says: "each of the proffered alternatives points to one or a few classes of phenomena that it has a reasonable shot of accounting for, at least in part. But none of them have the resources to explain the basic, functional, sophisticated molecular machinery of life. In fact, none of them even try to do so."[148]

Besides, even setting aside the problems faced by the Blind Watchmaker thesis, isn't Dawkins's whole discussion of evolution something of a distraction, given his admission that he can't explain the origin of organisms able to undergo evolution in the first place?

Thomas: Where does he say that?

Douglas (using his phone)**:** Just about all Dawkins says about the origin of life is his comment in chapter 12 that: "we still don't know—yet—exactly how the process of evolution got started."[149]

Thomas: I thought life emerged in a process of "chemical evolution."

Sophie: Of course, "chemical evolution" doesn't refer to a process of evolution by natural selection, but to the transition, however it occurred, from the relative simplicity of nonorganic chemistry to the relative complexity of the first life. As Monton notes: "Darwinian evolution only comes into play once life already exists. . . . Darwinian evolution doesn't explain (or even purport to explain) how life came to arise in the first place."[150]

Hiromi (using her tablet)**:** William Lane Craig says: "Most of us were probably taught . . . that life originated in the so-called primordial soup by chance chemical reactions, perhaps fuelled by lightning strikes. All of these old, chemical origin-of-life scenarios have broken down and are now rejected by the scientific community. Today there are a plethora of competing, speculative theories with no consensus on the horizon."[151]

Thomas: Really?

148. Dawkins, *Outgrowing God*, 251.

149. Dawkins, *Outgrowing God*, 268.

150. Monton, *Seeking God in Science*, 29.

151. Craig in Caruso, *Science & Religion*, 36. See Williams, "Origin of Life"; Meyer, "DNA and the Origin of Life"; Abel, *Primordial Prescription*; Abel, *First Gene*; Meyer, *Signature in the Cell*; Pullen, *Intelligent Design or Evolution?*; Thaxton et al., *Mystery Of Life's Origin*.

Douglas (using his phone): Monton states: "We do not know how life originated from non-life, and in fact it seems like the sort of process that would be very unlikely to happen naturalistically."[152] Nagel writes: "the origin of life remains, in light of what is known about the huge size, the extreme specificity, and the exquisite functional precision of the genetic material, a mystery—an event . . . to which no significant probability can be assigned on the basis of what we know of the laws of physics and chemistry."[153] He notes: "the coming into existence of the genetic code . . . together with mechanisms that can read the code and carry out its instructions—seems particularly resistant to being revealed as probable given physical law alone."[154]

Hiromi (using her tablet): Stephen C. Meyer calculates: "The odds of getting even one functional protein of modest length (150 amino acids) by chance from a prebiotic soup is no better than 1 chance in 10^{164}."[155] That's not the odds of getting a *particular* protein by chance, but the odds of getting *any functional protein at all* of that length. He concludes: "it is extremely unlikely that a random search through all the possible amino acid sequences could generate even a single relatively short functional protein in the time available since the beginning of the universe."[156] Even the simplest conceivable non-parasitical organism would require *hundreds* of different stable, functional proteins.

Thomas: That many?!

Hiromi (using her tablet): Meyer reports: "some scientists speculate (but have not demonstrated) that a simple one-celled organism might have been able to survive with as few as 250–400 genes."[157]

Douglas: Atheist molecular biologist Eugene Koonin estimates[158] the probability of just a coupled replication-translation system arising within the observable universe at 1 in $10^{1,018}$.

---

152. Monton, *Seeking God in Science*, 99.

153. Nagel, "Dawkins and Atheism," 25.

154. Nagel, *Mind & Cosmos*, 10.

155. Meyer, *Signature in the Cell*, 212.

156. Meyer, "Evidence for Design in Physics and Biology," 75.

157. Meyer, *Signature in the Cell*, 201.

158. Koonin, *Logic of Chance*, referenced by Behe, *Darwin Devolves*, 105.

Thomas: Those are *long* odds! But maybe the explanation *has* to be naturalistic, even if we don't understand it. Doesn't Dawkins have a philosophical argument against explaining anything with reference to any designer *that isn't itself the product of evolution*? Perhaps life on earth was designed by aliens!

Douglas: Dawkins does argue against un-evolved designers, using the same argument he made in *The God Delusion*. It's an argument atheist philosopher Erik J. Wielenberg concludes is "unconvincing."[159]

Thomas (using his tablet): Dawkins says: "The improbability remains, whether we are talking about the improbability of an eye or the improbability of a creator capable of designing an eye."[160]

Douglas: He seems to be advancing an explanatory principle to the effect that we don't make any explanatory advance if we explain something complex by reference to the actions of something else that isn't less complex.

Thomas: That seem to be what he's saying.

Douglas: But aren't we right to explain this statement from Dawkins *by reference to Dawkins*?

Thomas: Of course. Oh, I see your point. Dawkins is more complex than the statement, but Dawkins is the true explanation for the existence of the statement.

Hiromi: Right. Or suppose the first humans to land on Mars were to discover hieroglyphic texts carved into a mountainside. Wouldn't that indicate that alien life had been on Mars, even if we lacked an explanation for the existence of alien life?

Thomas (using his tablet): I suppose it would. Still, Dawkins says: "God seems to be a good explanation for the existence of improbable things. . . . But if we think about it more carefully, we can see that . . . Anything clever enough—complicated enough—to design things has to arrive late in the

---

159. Wielenberg, "Dawkins's Gambit, Hume's Aroma, and God's Simplicity." See also FOCLOnline, "How Does Dawkins Fail to Refute the Evidence for Design?"; FOCLOnline, "Deconstructing Dawkins' Defence."

160. Dawkins, *Outgrowing God*, 173.

universe."[161] So arguing for alien design is fine, because they could have evolved, but arguing for divine design isn't allowed.

Douglas: Says who?! Dawkins simply *asserts* that anything clever enough to design things must be "complicated," by which he obviously means it must exhibit "specified complexity." He offers no argument for thinking God has to be "complex" *in the relevant sense*, which would require God to be *a contingent arrangement of separable parts*. In other words, Dawkins begs the question against the possibility that God could be a non-contingent, necessary being who therefore isn't "complex" *in the relevant, design-indicating sense*.

Hiromi: That's right. And don't forget that Dawkins simultaneously begs the question in favor of the viability of the "Blind Watchmaker" thesis! Plus, Dawkins's anti-design argument applies to aliens, but not to God! Alien designers presumably *would* exhibit and depend upon the same, *specified type of* complexity that points us to a designing intelligence in the case of life on Earth. The existence of aliens would only *increase* the evidence for design! Only a transcendent designer that doesn't exhibit or depend upon specified complexity can explain the existence of specified complexity without itself pointing to a transcendent source of design; so if we aren't willing to join Dawkins in begging the question, the design of life on Earth by something that's at least God-like does seem to be where the biological evidence points us.

Thomas: Does this mean you believe in God now?

Hiromi: It means I have to take this evidence seriously as I try to figure out what to believe.

Thomas: And Douglas, what do you make of the biological design argument?

Douglas (using his phone): I think the design argument from biology is pretty persuasive, *if* you only take into account the probabilistic resources of the observable universe. But maybe there are other resources that offset the improbabilities we've noted. In other words, I'm happy to admit with Eugene Koonin that: "in a finite universe . . . the emergence of a coupled replication-translation system is unlikely to the extent of being, effectively,

---

161. Dawkins, *Outgrowing God*, 187.

impossible."[162] And I'm happy to admit *that* because I'm also happy to join Koonin in postulating additional probabilistic resources. As Koonin says, for a design-free origin of life: "a vast number of [spatial regions like the visible universe] is, indeed, a must."[163] To quote Monton, the biological design arguments we've discussed "make me less certain of my atheism than I would be had I never heard the arguments. The evidence isn't enough to make me stop being an atheist, though."[164]

Sophie: Inflating our probabilistic resources is something we can discuss further when we get to chapter 12 and Dawkins's discussion of cosmic fine-tuning. In the meantime, let's hope Astrid will join us next week for chapter 11.[165]

162. Koonin, "Cosmological Model of Eternal Inflation," para. 23.

163. Koonin, "Cosmological Model of Eternal Inflation," para. 23. William Lane Craig critiques the cosmological model that Koonin's paper relies upon in "Vilenkin's Cosmic Vision."

164. Monton, *Seeking God in Science*, 39.

165. An extensive list of chapter-specific recommended resources can be found on this book's webpage at www.peterswilliams.com/publications/books/outgrowing-god/.

Eighth Meeting

Did We Evolve to Be Religious and Nice?

" **W**elcome back Astrid," said Sophie with a warm smile. "Thanks," she replied. "I finally remembered to bring some Norwegian biscuits!"

Astrid placed a box of "serinakaker" cookies on the table.[1]

"They look good," said Thomas, helping himself to a sample. "But we're just glad to have you back with us. Mm, vanilla!"

"That's right," said Astrid, "They're a traditional Norwegian Christmas biscuit."

"We had a *monster* session last week, discussing biological design and evolution," said Douglas. Taking a biscuit in turn, he asked Astrid what she'd made of chapters 7–10?

"I don't have any theological problem with evolution as a scientific theory," responded Astrid. "As Thomas H. Huxley said: 'the doctrine of Evolution is neither Anti-theistic nor Theistic.'[2] However, I found Dawkins's argument for thinking evolution is a complete explanation of the relevant facts, quite underwhelming."

"Yeah, we basically concluded that Dawkins spent four chapters playing a 'shell game' with readers," said Hiromi, dunking a serinakaker into her hot chocolate.

"What's a 'shell game'?" asked Thomas.

"A 'shell game,'" interjected Sophie, "is 'a game, typically a swindle, in which spectators are challenged to bet on the location of a small object ostensibly concealed under one of three cups or nutshells manipulated by

---

1. See Manning, "Norwegian Almond Butter Biscuits (Serinakaker)"; Food52, "Norwegian Butter Cookies (Serinakaker)."

2. Huxley, quoted by McGrath, *Dawkins' God*, 115.

sleight of hand.' The term is used to describe 'any scheme for tricking and cheating people.'"[3]

"I'm not saying Dawkins was *deliberately* tricking his readers," added Hiromi. "Perhaps he's just passing on an intellectual trick he's fallen for himself."

"So, how were Dawkins's chapters on evolution a 'shell game'?" asked Thomas.

Hiromi responded: "Dawkins sets out to explain how living things that look designed are made by unintelligent, natural processes, right?"

"Right," affirmed Thomas.

"Well, it was like reading a scientist who says 'novels can be explained by material processes.' He explains how the different parts of a laptop work according to natural laws. For example, he traces how the letters that appear on the screen are determined by electrical currents that flow through the system as various keys on the keyboard are depressed. That's all fine, in its own way. But not only doesn't it explain where the laptop came from in the first place, it doesn't explain where the information that gets typed into the laptop came from."

"That's a succinct analogy for our discussion last week," observed Sophie. "But perhaps we should discuss chapter 11 of *Outgrowing God*: 'Did we evolve to be religious? Did we evolve to be nice?'"

At that, Hiromi produced a Babymetal[4] branded notebook from her backpack, opened it up, and began her prepared remarks:

Hiromi (referring to her notebook): Dawkins focuses on answering two questions in chapter 11: whether there's "a Darwinian explanation of belief in gods,"[5] and how "natural selection favours . . . a limited form of niceness, which might serve as a kind of evolutionary basis for morality."[6]

In answering these questions, Dawkins assumes a reductive account of humans as purely material creatures built by neo-Darwinian evolution. He believes we don't have minds or souls that transcend our brains, and that everything about human nature has an evolutionary explanation. He states: "Everything about a living creature is the way it is because its ancestors evolved that way over many generations. That includes humans and it includes human brains. The tendency to be religious is a property of human

3. "Shell Game," www.collinsdictionary.com/dictionary/english/shell-game. See Vanishing Inc. Magic, "Three Shell Game."

4. See Babymetal, "One"; Goodman, "Babymetal: A New Dawn for the Kawaii-metal Pioneers."

5. Dawkins, *Outgrowing God*, 226.

6. Dawkins, *Outgrowing God*, 238.

brains, as is the tendency to like music."[7] Again, he says: "the tendency towards religious belief has an evolutionary explanation, like everything else about us. And the same goes for our tendencies, such as they are, to be moral, or to be nice."[8] Of course, by hypothesis, the same goes for the human tendency to try to understand ourselves and the world we live in, a tendency that leads to science and to the theory of evolution.

Dawkins goes on to set out various, admittedly speculative evolutionary explanations for religion and belief in gods, but they all amount to the claim that humans are either directly or indirectly disposed towards certain religious beliefs by events in our natural history.

Thomas: Having a chapter with the title "Did we evolve to be religious? Did we evolve to be nice?" is kind of ironic given how many awful things religious people do, isn't it?

Douglas: I'm not overly impressed with evolutionary accounts of religion, though the evidence suggests there are genetic *influences* upon general personality factors that indirectly *affect*, but don't *determine*, people's responsiveness to "spirituality" and "religion" very broadly defined.

Thomas: What evidence?

Douglas (using his phone): For example, Laura Koenig led a study of 169 identical twin brothers and 104 fraternal twin brothers.[9] She concluded that genetic factors accounted for *almost half* the variability seen in this population's "religiosity." The thing is, these genetic factors don't determine whether one becomes a Christian or a Buddhist. In other words, they don't determine whether or not one believes in God.

All we can say on the basis of the evidence is that "religious interest and commitment to certain practices . . . partly reflect genetically based personality traits such as traditionalism and conformance to authority."[10] As atheist Michael Shermer writes: "50 percent heritability of religious tendencies may sound like a lot, but that still leaves the other half. . . . Virtually all studies implemented over the past century have found strong environmental factors in religiosity, including everything from family to class to culture. In other words, even with a genetic component to religiosity we still

---

7. Dawkins, *Outgrowing God*, 224.

8. Dawkins, *Outgrowing God*, 224.

9. See Mckee, "Genes Contribute to Religious Inclination."

10. Segal, *Entwined Lives* (1999), quoted by Shermer, *How We Believe*, 64.

must examine other variables."[11] To quote evolutionary biologist Stephen Jay Gould: "Once reason is admitted as a characteristic of human nature . . . it can be shown to do the work imputed to phantom genes in almost any examples that sociobiologists want to bring up."[12]

Thomas: You think belief in God should actually be attributed to humans *thinking* about reality?!

Douglas: I mean it *could* be. After all, lots of other false theories are the product of rational reflection! As we saw last week, even Dawkins admits the natural world looks like the product of design, and that the design argument was plausible before Darwinism.

Hiromi: Of course, this whole chapter assumes that Dawkins's naturalistic account of human nature and human origins is true. Given our discussion last week, I'm not so sure about that.

Astrid: Dawkins ignores the possibility that people believe in God due to genuinely revelatory events within human history that give them good reason to believe. He says belief in Yahweh "evolved"[13] from animistic roots, but ask a Jew from the twelfth century BC why they believe in Yahweh and they'd tell you Yahweh miraculously set his people free from slavery in Egypt and had given them the promised land of Israel. Ask a first-century gentile convert to Christianity why they believe in one God instead of the many gods of Greco-Roman polytheism and they might well reply that: "Christ died for our sins in accordance with the Scriptures, that he was buried, that he was raised on the third day in accordance with the Scriptures, and that he appeared to Cephas, then to the twelve. Then he appeared to more than five hundred brothers at one time. . . . Then he appeared to James, then to all the apostles."[14]

Hiromi (referring to her notebook): Dawkins says: "Often we think we notice a pattern when there really isn't one. Often we fail to notice a pattern when there really is one."[15] It has to be worth asking if Dawkins has failed to notice a pattern of divine revelation that's open to historical investigation.

11. Shermer, *How We Believe*, 64–65.

12. Gould, quoted by Menuge, "Reductionism, Bane of Christianity and Science," 142.

13. Dawkins, *Outgrowing God*, 234.

14. 1 Cor 15:3–7.

15. Dawkins, *Outgrowing God*, 230.

Douglas: But perhaps it's Jews and Christians who are seeing a pattern that's not there.

Astrid: Either way, it's worth trying to answer the question by seriously investigating the relevant evidence.[16]

Sophie: What do you think is at stake in chapter 11?

Astrid (using her tablet): I don't think Dawkins is attacking belief in God so much as trying to shore up his own worldview by drawing upon the reductive research program of "Evolutionary Psychology."[17] But as philosopher Stephen M. Downes reports: "There is a broad consensus among philosophers of science that evolutionary psychology is a deeply flawed enterprise."[18]

Thomas: Why think evolutionary psychology is a "flawed" research program?

Douglas (using his phone): Well, atheist and evolutionary biologist Jerry Coyne complains that: "evolutionary psychologists routinely confuse theory and speculation. Unlike bones, behavior does not fossilize, and understanding its evolution often involves concocting stories that sound plausible but are hard to test."[19]

Philosopher R. C. Richardson observes that "the relevant social environment in ancestral hominids, which surely did much to shape our cognitive capacities and our emotional profiles, is not something we have much access to from the available record. Even the details of, say, the cognitive capacities of our ancestors is in many ways obscure, though we can see some

---

16. See Kitchen, *On the Reliability of the Old Testament*; Williams, *Getting at Jesus*; Williams, *Understanding Jesus*.

17. See Buller, "Evolutionary Psychology"; StepDownes, "Evolutionary Psychology"; see the special edition of the *Journal of Theology and Psychology*, on the topic of Christianity and evolutionary psychology (Biola University, Winter 2001), https://journals.sagepub.com/toc/ptja/29/4; Holcomb, "Buller Does to Evolutionary Psychology What Kitcher Did to Sociobiology," 392–401; Evolution News, "Biology Journal: Evolutionary Psychology Is 'Impossible'"; Buller, *Adapting Minds*; Moreland, "Intelligent Design and Evolutionary Psychology as Research Programs"; Menuge, *Agents Under Fire*; Richardson, *Evolutionary Psychology as Maladapted Psychology*; Rose and Rose, *Alas Poor Darwin*; Stove, *Darwinian Fairytales*; Tallis, *Aping Mankind*.

18. Downes, "Evolutionary Psychology," para. 1.

19. "Evolutionist's Devastating Critique of *Evolutionary Psychology*," para. 3.

things in broad outline. The outline is not enough to support any detailed evolutionary explanation for human psychological capacities."[20]

According to psychologist Dr. Christopher Ryan:

> many of the most prominent voices in the field [of evolutionary psychology] are less scientists than political philosophers. They choose some aspect of modern life and construct elaborate justifications located in an inaccessible ancient environment. Often, the fact that their story *seems* to make sense is the only evidence they offer. For them, it may be enough, but it isn't enough if you're aspiring to be taken seriously as a science.[21]

Hiromi (referring to her notebook): I thought the most interesting stuff in this chapter was what Dawkins said about the human "tendency to believe in agency,"[22] which psychologist Justin Barrett labels the "Hypersensitive Agency Detection Device" or "HADD."

Douglas (using his phone): Dawkins writes:

> You see a movement in the grass which just might be a lion. It could instead be the wind. You are making good progress in digging out a really big tuber and don't want to stop. But that noise just could be a lion . . . a general policy of believing that mysterious movements or sounds spell danger could save your life. Because sometimes it really will be a lion. If you take it too far and run scared from every rustle in the grass, you'll miss out on the yams and the other business of living. But an individual who gets the balance right will still, on some occasions, find himself believing it's a lion when it actually isn't.[23]

Dawkins applies this to religious beliefs by noting that "The fear of agents, even if irrational, even if inappropriate on this particular occasion, may lurk within us from our ancestral past. . . . And religion is all about seeing agency all around us."[24]

Astrid (using her tablet): But a general policy of retreat in the presence of mysterious movements that *might* indicate the presence of a dangerous

---

20. Richardson, *Evolutionary Psychology as Maladapted Psychology*, 174.
21. Ryan, "Evolutionary Psychology Deserves Criticism," para. 8.
22. Dawkins, *Outgrowing God*, 227
23. Dawkins, *Outgrowing God*, 227.
24. Dawkins, *Outgrowing God*, 228.

agent could have the same survival value without involving any false beliefs. To turn to Dawkins's other illustration: "Alone in bed at night, you hear a noise. . . . As far as you are concerned, you fear an unnamed agent, as opposed to a non-agent like the wind. . . . The fear of agents, even if irrational, even if inappropriate on this particular occasion, may lurk within us from our ancestral past."[25] But *fearing* an unnamed agent made that noise isn't the same as believing there *is* an unnamed agent who made that noise. Plus, you'd probably investigate and conclude it was only the wind after all.

Hiromi: Intuitive belief in God might be based on multiple factors, including multiple appearances of design in the natural world and apparently direct experiences of God.[26] It doesn't seem fair to compare that to a quickly corrected snap judgement that there *might* be a burglar in the house.

Thomas: Dawkins's application of all this to religion is a bit vague.

Hiromi (referring to her notebook): I agree. To quote a critique from philosophers of science Russell Powell and Steve Clarke, we might say that Dawkins

> makes a plausible case for the conclusion that having a HADD would be evolutionarily advantageous for us. But establishing that it would have been evolutionarily advantageous for us to have a HADD is a far cry from establishing that a HADD has actually evolved and that it is disposed to cause religious by-products, even if we are able to establish that the human mind is suited to containing modular structures like the HADD. One cannot reliably infer from a particular adaptive pattern of behaviour . . . that there is a specific organ or cognitive mechanism 'designed' by natural selection to produce that behaviour. . . . We know that people are disposed to believe in supernatural agents, and it might seem simple enough to attribute such beliefs to the activity of the HADD; but without making a credible case for the conclusion that the operation of the HADD actually causes people to believe in supernatural agents, we are not entitled to this inference. Indeed, the lack of evidence for the role of a specialized HADD in generating religious phenotypes is acknowledged by Barrett and some of his recent collaborators. . . . To establish that the HADD causes belief in supernatural agents, we need an

25. Dawkins, *Outgrowing God*, 228.

26. See Williams, "Religious Experience"; Swinburne, "Justification of Theism"; Gellman, *Experience of God and the Rationality of Theistic Belief*; Swinburne, *Existence of God*; Williams, *Faithful Guide to Philosophy*.

explanation of how and why we come to attribute supernatural rather than natural agency. We also need an explanation of how and why people continue to believe in the existence of supernatural agents. The HADD hypothesis may explain why we tend to infer agency when we hear rustling in the grass, but it does not account for belief in the ongoing existence of the agents that we (mis)attribute. In cases of ordinary agency, we are able to correct our initial attributions: we hear rustling in the grass and turn around expecting to be met by an agent, but when we fail to see an agent and instead observe wind moving the grass around, we typically correct our initial overattribution. . . . In contrast, it seems that attributions of supernatural agents are highly resilient and rarely corrected for.[27]

Thomas: So, basically, the theory and its application to religious beliefs are both a stretch.

Astrid (using her tablet): Philosopher Helen De Cruz notes that:

Under experimental conditions people are pretty good at detecting and identifying agency-like movements on computer animations . . . sometimes agency detection does go awry, as when we hear wooden planks creak in an old house and form the belief that there's a burglar in the house. But many more times, we form the belief that there is an agent, when there actually *is* an agent. . . . When debunkers of religious belief appeal to hyperactive agency detection, they are already assuming that the agent that is being detected (e.g., God) is of the false-positive kind. . . . . But I don't see how they can assume this in a non-question begging sense.[28]

Hiromi (referring to her notebook): Alvin Plantinga makes a related point, observing:

the fact that belief in supernatural agents arises from HADD (if indeed that is a fact) doesn't even tend to show that such belief is among the false positives; that same device is [by hypothesis] also responsible for many true beliefs, for example, the belief that there are other minds, other people. Presumably no one would argue that belief in other minds is dubious or irrational

27. Powell and Clarke, "Religion As an Evolutionary Byproduct," 469–70.
28. De Cruz, "Thoughts on Evolutionary Debunking Arguments," paras. 13–14.

or intellectually second rate on the grounds that it has been produced by an agent detection device that sometimes produces false positives.[29]

Thomas: I suppose not. So, even if religious beliefs did turn out to be rooted in a "Hypersensitive Agency Detection Device," the burden of proof would still lie with the skeptic to show that this or that belief is a false positive.

Hiromi: That's right. Appealing to a HADD doesn't get around the "principle of credulity" that we've discussed in past meetings.

Astrid (using her tablet): Philosopher Keith Ward notes that although "there is virtually no extant evidence for what the origins of religion were . . . this has not stopped scholars making definitive claims about what really happened. This is an instance in which claims to certainty are in inverse proportion to the amount of evidence available."[30] Likewise, Richard Swinburne says he's "inclined to think that since we have so little historical evidence about the early stages of religious practice, any theories about this are pretty speculative."[31]

Douglas: Dawkins admits he's only "speculating"[32] and offering "possible"[33] explanations that "may"[34] be true, or that he thinks are "plausible."[35]

Astrid (using her tablet): But he makes confident assertions such as: "Our ancestor's religions were 'animistic'. . . . Yahweh evolved in people's minds to become the one God of the Jews. . . . Bronze Age animism came to be pared down to Iron Age monotheism."[36] The notion that animism was an earlier stage in an evolutionary progression of religious beliefs that advanced on through polytheism and finally arrived at monotheism, was popularized in the nineteenth century by the "armchair anthropology"[37]

29. Plantinga, *Where the Conflict Really Lies*, 141.

30. Ward, *Is Religion Dangerous?*, 10–11.

31. Swinburne in Dennett and Swinburne, "How Should We Study Religion?," para. 19.

32. Dawkins, *Outgrowing God*, 234.

33. Dawkins, *Outgrowing God*, 238.

34. Dawkins, *Outgrowing God*, 239.

35. Dawkins, *Outgrowing God*, 234.

36. Dawkins, *Outgrowing God*, 226–27.

37. Anthropology 101.

of classicist James Frazer's *The Golden Bough*. But according to Ward: "that the earliest form of religious belief was animism [is] pure speculation without any evidence at all."[38]

Thomas: Interesting.

Astrid (using her tablet): Addressing theories of belief formation that are supposed to call religious beliefs into question, Peter S. Williams points out that: "the mere fact that a theory, *if true*, can explain why theists believe in God . . . does nothing to establish either the truth of the theory of belief-formation concerned, or the truth of atheism."[39] Moreover, he notes that: "it's hard to construct such hypotheses *so that that the hypotheses don't undermine themselves*."[40]

Thomas: How so?

Astrid (using her tablet): For example, take Dawkins's concept of theistic belief as a "meme," the hypothetical cultural analogue of a gene. Biochemist and theologian Alister McGrath argues that:

> The problem with this approach is immediately obvious. If all ideas are memes, or the effects of memes, Dawkins is left in the decidedly uncomfortable position of having to accept that his own ideas must also be recognized as the effects of memes. Scientific ideas would then become yet another example of memes replicating within the human mind. This would not suit Dawkins' purpose at all, and he excludes the notion [in] a case of special pleading.[41]

Thomas: I see. So, all in all, Dawkins's explanations leave some room for doubt.

Astrid (using her tablet): At the very least; but I'm happy to accept the conclusion of Oxford psychologist Justin Barrett, who says: "Belief in gods and God particularly arises through the natural, ordinary operation of human

---

38. Ward, *Is Religion Dangerous?*, 12–13. See Wartick, "Book Review: 'In the Beginning God'"; Corduan, *In the Beginning God*.

39. Williams, *Sceptic's Guide to Atheism*, loc. 2000.

40. Williams, *Sceptic's Guide to Atheism*, loc. 2013.

41. McGrath, *Dawkins' God*, 124.

minds in natural ordinary environments."[42] In other words, generally speaking, *belief in God is the result of psychologically normal mental processes.* This conclusion hardly poses a problem for theism! And I don't think that changes if these "natural, ordinary operations of human minds" have an evolutionary explanation.

Thomas: Why not?

Astrid: On the one hand, if the evolutionary explanations Dawkins offers are false, that diminishes the plausibility of his naturalistic worldview.

Thomas: Why?

Astrid: Because it would leave him without a naturalistically acceptable explanation for belief in God.

Thomas: Okay.

Astrid: On the other hand, even supposing the evolutionary explanations Dawkins offers are true, they don't contradict belief in God.

Hiromi (referring to her notebook): I agree. To use an example from last week, theists could view the evolutionary processes Dawkins suggests as examples of "bottom-up" design that stem from a divine programmer. Dawkins says that if "belief in some kind of god or gods [helped] our ancestors to survive and pass on their genes for religious belief . . . that doesn't mean that the gods people believe in . . . are really there. That's a completely different question."[43] But if the truth of theism is "a completely different question," then the truth of atheism must also be "a completely different question"!

Psychologists have shown that "from birth, human beings have certain beliefs about both mathematics and physics. Babies know, for example, that one plus one is not three, and they know that solid objects fall to the floor, unless something or someone holds them up."[44] Dawkins says that everything about us has an evolutionary explanation, and he'd probably be able to offer some speculative evolutionary explanation for babies' beliefs about basic arithmetic and the behavior of unsupported objects. But, obviously,

42. Barrett, *Why Would Anyone Believe in God?*

43 Dawkins, *Outgrowing God*, 262.

44. Murray, "Belief in God: A Trick of our Brain?," para. 2.

none of that would do anything to show that one plus one *doesn't* equal two, or that unsupported objects *don't* fall to the ground! Nor would it show that babies' belief about these things are unreasonable.

Astrid (using her tablet): Right. Theists could accept Dawkins's evolutionary speculations whilst viewing them as describing secondary causes through which God arranged for humans to have certain innate tendencies. As Paul Copan says, natural processes that contribute to the formation of religious belief "are not at odds with God's existence; indeed, such processes may indicate that our minds are properly functioning—according to the way they've been designed."[45] And that's why I think it's the plausibility of Dawkins's brand of naturalism that's at stake here, rather than the plausibility of theism. It's Dawkins who writes: "Shouldn't there be a Darwinian explanation of belief in gods? . . . I suspect the answer is probably yes."[46]

Hiromi (referring to her notebook): Philosopher Michael J. Murray writes: "There is a great deal of [evidence] which makes it seem that religion is a natural product of the mental tools of a properly functioning human mind. But doesn't this show that religion is just a trick that our minds play on us?"[47]

Thomas: What does Murray think?

Hiromi (referring to her notebook): He says:

> It looks as if someone drawing this conclusion must be arguing as follows:
>
> 1. The development of the human mind through natural history has provided those minds with a number of special properties.
>
> 2. When considering the natural and social world, these properties encourage humans to believe in gods.
>
> 3. Therefore, the development of human minds has produced belief in gods . . .
>
> 4. Therefore, belief in gods is false.
>
> However, this argument commits a well known logical fallacy called the 'genetic fallacy.' Genetically fallacious reasoning aims to argue for the truth or falsity of a belief simply from

45. Copan, "Does Religion Originate in the Brain?," para. 38.
46. Dawkins, *Outgrowing God*, 226.
47. Murray, "God and Neuro-Science," para. 29.

considerations of the origin of belief. But, of course, perfectly true beliefs can emerge even from crazy sources. I might think there are 449 people in the library because my watch reads 4:49. Can we conclude that this belief is false as a result of my strange reasoning? Of course not. It may be true, despite the strange origin.[48]

Astrid (using her tablet): Alistair McGrath discusses a distinction philosophers of science draw

between a "logic of discovery" and a "logic of confirmation." To simplify . . . a logic of discovery is about how someone arrives at a scientific hypothesis, and a logic of confirmation about how that hypothesis is shown to be reliable and realistic. Sometimes hypotheses arise from a long period of reflection on observation; sometimes they come about in a flash of inspiration. Yet if the logic of discovery can often be more inspirational than rational, the same is clearly not true of the logic of justification. Here, any hypothesis—however it is derived—is rigorously and thoroughly checked against what may be observed, to determine the degree of empirical fit between theory and observation.[49]

A famous example that illustrates this distinction

is August Kekulé's hypothesis that the chemical benzene possessed a cyclical structure. Kekulé (1829–96) first set out this idea in a French article of 1865. . . . Kekulé did not explain the "logic of discovery" which led to the formulation of this innovative idea at that time, although his subsequent work provided an extensive "logic of justification" for the ring structure of benzene. But in 1890, at a celebration marking the twenty-fifth anniversary of this suggestion—by then widely accepted—Kekulé spoke of how this idea came to him. . . . He had a dream of a snake chasing its own tail. But while the origins of this idea might indeed be somewhat speculative, even mystical, the fact remains that, when it was checked out against the evidence, it seemed to work. The manner of its derivation might be opaque; the manner of its verification, however, was perfectly clear—and ultimately persuasive.[50]

48. Murray, "God and Neuro-Science," paras. 29–30. See also Drcraigvideos, "Genetic Fallacy"; Dowden, "Fallacies: Genetic."

49. McGrath, *Dawkins' God*, 10.

50. McGrath, *Dawkins' God*, 159.

So, knowing the origin of a hypothesis isn't the same as knowing whether or not it is true, or whether or not there's a good case for its truth.

Douglas: I agree. As atheist philosopher Kai Nielson writes: "naturalistic explanations [of theistic belief] will become of paramount interest only when the critique of theism has been thought to have done its work."[51] However, can't we modify the argument Hiromi just gave to focus on the *rationality* or *warrant* of belief in God, rather than the truth of belief in God?

Thomas: How would we do that?

Douglas: Well, why not argue like this:

1. The development of the human mind through natural history has provided those minds with a number of special properties.

2. When considering the natural and social world, these properties encourage humans to believe in gods.

3. Therefore, the development of human minds has produced belief in gods.

4a. Therefore, belief in gods is *unwarranted*.[52]

Hiromi: But that conclusion doesn't follow from those premises. Look what happens to that argument if we remove the word "gods" and replace it with "teapots," "other human minds," "the basic principles of logic," or "the past"! Humans naturally form beliefs about all sorts of things besides God, and we generally think these beliefs are right. So, why not think people get things right when it comes to belief in God? One could say, "Because theism is false." But, as Murray notes, "that . . . just begs the question."[53]

Thomas: But if belief in God arises from natural mental processes, doesn't that mean people would believe in God even if there were no God?[54]

Hiromi (referring to her notebook): Murray considers and responds to just this point, writing:

---

51. Nielson, "Naturalistic Explanations of Theistic Belief," 403.
52. Adapted from Murray, "God and Neuro-Science," para. 32.
53. Murray, "God and Neuro-Science," para. 34.
54. Adapted from Murray, "God and Neuro-Science."

it is not clear that what the critic is saying is true. Is it true that
... Human minds would exist and believe in God, even if there
were no God? I don't think so. I don't think there would be a
universe if there were no God. I don't think the universe would
be fine-tuned for life if there were no God. . . . Am I wrong? If
I am, nothing about evolutionary or cognitive psychology indicates that I am.[55]

Astrid: Alvin Plantinga observes that, for many people, God's existence is a
properly basic belief. Remember them?

Thomas: Sure. In our first meeting you introduced the idea of beliefs it's
reasonable to hold without their being based on other beliefs, where the
burden of proof is on the person who tells us things aren't as they seem to
us to be.

Astrid (using her tablet): So, Plantinga develops theologian John Calvin's
belief that

> there is a kind of faculty or cognitive mechanism, what Calvin
> calls a *sensus divinitatis* or sense of divinity, which . . . is a disposi-
> tion or set of dispositions to form theistic beliefs in various cir-
> cumstances. . . . The deliverances of the *sensus divinitatis* are not
> . . . inferences from the circumstances that trigger its operation.
> It isn't that one beholds the night sky, notes that it is grand, and
> concludes that there must be such a person as God. . . . It is rather
> that, upon the perception of the night sky . . . these beliefs just
> arise within us. They are *occasioned* by the circumstances; they are
> not conclusions drawn from them. . . . In this regard, the *sensus
> divinitatis* resembles perception, memory, and *a priori* belief.[56]

Thomas: In other words, Plantinga is filling out the idea that intuitive beliefs carry the presumption of truth and applying that to basic belief in God?

Astrid (using her tablet): Right. Plantinga offers a philosophically sophisticated account of "warranted" beliefs as basic beliefs produced by properly functioning cognitive faculties, reliably aimed at truth, working in an

---

55. Murray, "God and Neuro-Science," paras. 36–38.
56. Plantinga, *Warranted Christian Belief,* 175.

appropriate environment.[57] He applies this account of warrant to basic belief in God, explaining:

> You may think humankind is created by God . . . with a natural tendency to see God's hand in the world about us. . . . Then of course you will not think of belief in God as in the typical case a manifestation of . . . a belief-producing power or mechanism that is not aimed at truth. . . . On the other hand . . . you may think there is no God. . . . Then perhaps you will be inclined to accept the sort of view according to which belief in God is . . . properly traced to wishful thinking or some other cognitive mechanism not aimed at truth. . . . And this dependence of the question of warrant . . . on the truth or falsehood of theism leads to a very interesting conclusion. If the *warrant* enjoyed by belief in God is related in this way to the *truth* of that belief, then the question whether theistic belief has *warrant* is not after all independent of the question whether theistic belief is *true*.[58]

In other words, we can't show that a cognitive mechanism that produces basic belief in God is unreliable without showing that it wasn't intended by God; and the only way to do *that* would seem to be to disprove God's existence. In sum, you can't attack the warranted nature of a basic belief in God without demonstrating that atheism is true. As Plantinga concludes: "a successful atheological objection will have to be to the truth of theism, not to its rationality, or justification, or intellectual respectability."[59]

Hiromi (referring to her notebook): I think Plantinga offers a plausible rebuttal to arguments against the rationality of basic belief in God. As Michael J. Murray says: "it seems perfectly acceptable for the Christian to hold that God created the world, human beings, and human minds in such a way that when they are functioning properly, they form beliefs in the existence of rocks, rainbows, human minds, and . . . God."[60] But to defend the *rationality* of theism isn't to demonstrate the *truth* of theism.

Sophie: What do you make of Dawkins's comments about the evolution of "niceness"?

---

57. See Plantinga, *Warrant and Proper Function*; Plantinga, *Warranted Christian Belief*.

58. Plantinga, *Warranted Christian Belief*, 151.

59. Plantinga, *Warranted Christian Belief*, 151.

60. Murray, "God and Neuro-Science," para. 39.

Astrid (using her tablet): We covered this when we discussed chapter 6. Although his chapter title only mentions the evolution of niceness, Dawkins says: "Natural selection may have built into our brains the basis for a limited amount of niceness. But it builds in the basis for nastiness too."[61] Plus, he says that while "there does indeed seem to be some Darwinian pressure to be nice, which could serve as the original basis for our sense of right and wrong . . . I think it's swamped by later learned morals."[62]

Hiromi (referring to her notebook): According to Michael J. Murray: "There is indeed a good deal of evidence that lots of human behaviour that we would describe as 'moral' arises from innate or hard-wired dispositions . . . [various] moral beliefs and desires appear to be part of our built-in 'operating system'."[63] For example: "Across times and cultures human beings display firm beliefs and feel strong desires pulling them in the direction of punishing those who do wrong. When we learn that someone has abused a child . . . we feel strongly that the wrongdoer deserves to be penalised."[64]

Douglas: And perhaps these innate tendencies have an evolutionary explanation. But so what if they do? As with religious beliefs, so with moral beliefs. In either case, evolutionary explanations don't show these beliefs to be either true or false, rational or irrational. Scientific *explanations* aren't philosophical *evaluations*.

Sophie: It would certainly seem that the two subjects are parallel, and that similar arguments as apply to one would apply to the other. In which case, we may as well draw our meeting to an end. Thank you everyone. I look forward to seeing you all next week.[65]

61. Dawkins, *Outgrowing God*, 239.
62. Dawkins, *Outgrowing God*, 248.
63. Murray, "Belief in God: A Trick of our Brain?"
64. Murray, "Belief in God: A Trick of our Brain?"
65. An extensive list of chapter-specific recommended resources can be found on this book's webpage at www.peterswilliams.com/publications/books/outgrowing-god/.

Ninth Meeting

From Science to Atheism?

O utside *The Campus Coffee Cup Café*, the world reminded Hiromi of the poem by Christina Rossetti that began:

> In the bleak midwinter, frosty wind made moan,
> Earth stood hard as iron, water like a stone;
> Snow had fallen, snow on snow, snow on snow,
> In the bleak midwinter, long ago.[1]

Inside Astrid was addressing the book club:

Astrid (using her tablet): Dawkins opens chapter 9 by conceding that it's "apparent common sense" to say "there must be a God to explain the universes' origin and other so-far unsolved problems."[2] Then he tries to undermine our confidence in common sense.

Dawkins accuses theists of believing in and arguing for God's existence based on "unsolved problems in science—gaps in what we so far understand."[3] He complains that "some people are tempted" to argue: "'We don't yet understand how the evolutionary process began in the first place, so God must have started it.' 'Nobody knows how the universe began, so God must have made it.' 'We don't know where the laws of physics come from, so God must have made them up.'"[4]

Dawkins isn't just warning readers to avoid fallacious arguments from ignorance. He's trying to defend having faith in naturalism despite the lack

---

1. Rossetti, "In the Bleak Midwinter." See Corrinne May, "In The Bleak Midwinter."
2. Dawkins, *Outgrowing God*, 251.
3. Dawkins, *Outgrowing God*, 250.
4. Dawkins, *Outgrowing God*, 250.

of plausible naturalistic explanations for many important aspects of reality, aspects of reality that seem to point to God. He says: "Whenever there is a gap in our understanding, people try to plug the gap with God. But the trouble with gaps is that science has the annoying habit of coming along and filling them."[5] To illustrate this alleged pattern, having admitted that "It used to be simple common sense that living things had to be created by God,"[6] Dawkins says: "Darwin exploded that particular piece of common sense."[7] He goes on to offer a series of additional examples that are supposed to bear out his claim that "science regularly upsets common sense."[8] This claim is made in support of his plea for faith in naturalism rather than common sense. So, he ends *Outgrowing God* by stating: "the bold step into the frightening void of what seems improbable has turned out right so often in the history of science. I think we should take our courage in both hands, grow up and give up on all gods. Don't you?"[9]

Douglas: In principle, there's nothing wrong with defending the rationality of faith in one's worldview despite problems, such as arguments from data one's worldview currently fails to explain. However, this should be done by carefully weighing the warrant for one's worldview against the warrant for the alternatives. One shouldn't resort to rhetorical tricks to purchase victory on the cheap.

Sophie: I take it you think Dawkins does the latter rather than the former?

Douglas (using his phone): Well, I agree that moving from a premise about the need to explain this or that aspect of reality, to the conclusion that God exists, without a second premise defending a link between the two, is to make an invalid "God of the gaps" argument from ignorance. And I expect some people believe in a God-of-the-gaps. But there are obviously theistic arguments, including arguments that start from the data Dawkins reviews here, that *don't* take this fallacious form. Dawkins seems to be more interested in setting up "straw men" to blow away than he is in seriously engaging the issues. It's no wonder Professor Antony Flew chided Dawkins for "his

---

5. Dawkins, *Outgrowing God*, 250.
6. Dawkins, *Outgrowing God*, 250.
7. Dawkins, *Outgrowing God*, 250.
8. Dawkins, *Outgrowing God*, 260.
9. Dawkins, *Outgrowing God*, 278.

scandalous and apparently deliberate refusal to present the doctrine which he appears to think he has refuted in its *strongest* form."[10]

Astrid (using her tablet): I agree. As Malissa Cain Travis comments:

> the God-of-the-gaps label is often misused; it is not uncommon for materialists to unfairly apply it to philosophical conclusions that are based upon the existing evidence, not missing scientific information. For example, suggesting that a designing intelligence is responsible for the elegant mathematical order of the cosmos or the exquisite complexity of life is not a gaps argument; it is a philosophical conclusion drawn from mounds of data, not a lack thereof.[11]

Hiromi (using her tablet): Dawkins rests much on the assumption that "the main mystery of life—how did it come to be so complex, so diverse and so beautifully 'designed'—is solved"[12] by Darwin's theory of evolution. But there's good reason to doubt this claim, as we discussed a couple of weeks ago. Indeed, although Dawkins asserts that "where life is concerned, Darwinian evolution provides a full explanation,"[13] he also admits "we still don't know . . . exactly how the process of evolution got started."[14] But that means Darwin *didn't* provide "a full explanation."[15] So, for me, there's a question mark over everything Dawkins argues here from the start.

Astrid: Of course, it's debatable whether the theory of evolution undermines the common-sense belief that God exists, or even the belief that he created living things. There's an important asymmetry here.

Thomas: How do you mean?

Astrid (using her tablet): If there's evidence for a theistic explanation of something—the origin of life, for example—that's simultaneously evidence against naturalism. But if there's evidence for a natural explanation of the same data, that isn't evidence against theism. Explanation isn't a zero-sum game for theists, because we hold God responsible for the existence and

10. Flew, "Professor Antony Flew Reviews *The God Delusion*," para. 4.
11. Travis, *Science and the Mind of the Maker*, 271.
12. Dawkins, *Outgrowing God*, 268.
13. Dawkins, *Outgrowing God*, 269.
14. Dawkins, *Outgrowing God*, 268.
15. Dawkins, *Outgrowing God*, 269.

normal workings of the natural world.[16] As philosopher of science John Lennox writes: "understanding the mechanism by which a Ford car works is not in itself an argument for regarding Mr Ford himself as nonexistent. The existence of a mechanism is not in itself an argument for the non-existence of an agent who designed the mechanism."[17]

Hiromi: There's a gap between the observation that scientific explanations have often been discovered for previously unexplained phenomena and the conclusion that faith in naturalism is reasonable despite the lack of plausible naturalistic explanations for important aspects of reality that seem to point to God. To bridge this gap, Dawkins *defines* "unsolved problems in science" as "gaps" in an understanding of reality *that's naturalistic by default*. In other words, he assumes that gaps in the naturalistic account of reality are merely gaps *in our knowledge of a naturalistic reality*, rather than gaps *in the ability of naturalism to explain reality*. But that's to *assume* that naturalism is true and that every argument for theism is unsound. In other words, Dawkins confuses "science" with "naturalism" and then *begs the question* against God being the best explanation for any data the naturalistic worldview finds hard to explain. The whole chapter is an exercise in what philosopher of science Karl Popper called "promissory materialism."[18] It's a sermon commending "faith" in naturalism!

Thomas: But Dawkins *infers* that, although God is a common-sense answer to some puzzles posed by the natural world, because science regularly upsets common sense, science will probably upset this common sense as well.

Astrid: How regularly does science upset common sense, though? What percentage of common-sense beliefs get upset? The fact that Dawkins doesn't even try to answer these questions suggests he's cherry-picking his data.

Sophie: Remember, as a figurative expression, "cherry-picking" refers to the fallacy of "suppressed evidence," where "only select evidence is presented in order to persuade the audience to accept a position, and evidence that would go against the position is withheld."[19]

---

16. A point made by Travis, *Science and the Mind of the Maker*, 283.

17. Lennox, *God's Undertaker*, 89.

18. See Sheldrake, "What Will Change Everything?"

19. "Cherry Picking," para. 1.

Astrid: Dawkins's argument is like saying "no one should ever be convicted of murder because some people in the past have been wrongly convicted."[20]

Hiromi (using her tablet): I doubt science upsets the majority of our common-sense beliefs. But even if it does, it clearly has to do so *on a case by case basis*, by *meeting the burden of proof common-sense imposes*. As J. P. Moreland and William Lane Craig explain: "if one carefully reflects on something, and a certain viewpoint intuitively seems to be true, then one is justified in believing that viewpoint in the absence of overriding counterarguments (which will ultimately rely on alternative intuitions)."[21] Indeed, in the end, science can only upset common-sense beliefs *on the basis of other common-sense beliefs*, beliefs the very practice of science depends upon and therefore *cannot* "upset."

Thomas: Such as?

Hiromi (using her tablet): Moreland lists the following presuppositions of science, which science itself cannot justify:

1. A world exists "out there," independent of [human minds], language, or theory.

2. The nature of the world is orderly, especially its "deep structure" that lies under and beyond the manifest world of ordinary perception.

3. Objective Truth Exists.

4. Our sensory and cognitive faculties are reliable for gaining truth and knowledge of the world, and they are able to grasp the world's deep structure that lies beyond the sense-perceptible world.

5. Various types of values and "oughts" exist (e.g., moral and aesthetic values).

6. The laws of logic and mathematics exist.[22]

Thomas: So, I guess *these* beliefs are safe from scientific critique.

---

20. Glass, *Atheism's New Clothes*, 127.
21. Moreland and Craig, *Philosophical Foundations for a Christian Worldview*, 422.
22. Moreland, "How Scientism Rules Out the Presuppositions," paras. 3–4.

Hiromi: Indeed, because science depends upon them, science can't be used to undermine them, *or to explain them.*

Sophie: That's a nice point, Hiromi. Trying to give a scientific explanation of such assumptions of science would be an example of circular reasoning.

Hiromi: Yes. And that means there *cannot* be scientific explanations for *everything.*

Thomas: Come again?

Douglas: It means the "science only" worldview of *scientism* is false, because every coherent worldview requires a *metaphysical* foundation.[23]

Astrid: Arguably, these science-justifying beliefs all fit comfortably within a theistic worldview but go against the grain of a naturalistic worldview.

Douglas: That's debatable. What's clear to me is that Dawkins can't be allowed to get away with arguing that because science sometimes gives us cause to abandon common-sense beliefs, and because belief in God is common-sense for many people, therefore everyone should abandon belief in God! He might as well argue that because science sometimes gives us cause to abandon common-sense beliefs, and because belief in science is common-sense for many people, therefore everyone should stop believing in science!

Sophie: Well put, Douglas. Let's turn our attention to the data highlighted by Dawkins.

Hiromi (using her tablet): Dawkins says: "A pretty big step concerns the origin of the entire universe."[24] He tries to downplay the importance of this step by suggesting that "an even bigger step was to understand the evolution of life";[25] but even if we assume we can explain the origin and evolution of life, explaining the origin of the universe seems like a big "step"!

Thomas: People used to think God explained where everything came from, but now we know about the "Big Bang."

---

23. See Trigg, *Beyond Matter.*
24. Dawkins, *Outgrowing God,* 265.
25. Dawkins, *Outgrowing God,* 265.

Astrid (using her tablet): But this isn't an either/or choice. "Big Bang" cosmology offers a *description* of the universe where "there was in the past an event occupying a nonzero, finite temporal interval that was absolutely first, not proceeded by any equal interval."[26] It doesn't offer an *explanation* of why a cosmos with that finite past exists.

Hiromi (using her tablet): There are philosophical arguments for the impossibility of the universe having an infinite past,[27] and we have scientific evidence that the universe has a finite past. Indeed, at the "State of the Universe" conference honoring Stephen Hawking's seventieth birthday,[28] atheist cosmologist Alexander Vilenkin said that "all the evidence we have says that the universe had a beginning."[29] A *New Scientist* editorial on the conference commented:

> The big bang is now part of the furniture of modern cosmology.
> ... Many physicists have been fighting a rearguard action against
> it for decades, largely because of its theological overtones. If you
> have an instant of creation, don't you need a creator? Cosmologists ... have tried on several different models of the universe
> that dodge the need for a beginning while still requiring a big
> bang. But recent research has shot them full of holes. It now
> seems certain that the universe did have a beginning. Without
> an escape clause, physicists and philosophers must finally answer a problem that has been nagging at them for the best part
> of 50 years: how do you get a universe, complete with the laws of
> physics, out of nothing.[30]

Astrid: The "theological overtones" of the Big Bang are brought out by an ancient form of cosmological argument, called the *kalam* argument, that underwent a renaissance in the twentieth century after the discovery of the "Big Bang."

Sophie: How would you express the *kalam* argument, Astrid?

---

26. Copan and Craig, *Creation Out of Nothing*, 199.

27. See Copan with Craig, *Kalam Cosmological Argument*; Moreland, *Scaling the Secular City*; Williams, *Faithful Guide to Philosophy*.

28. See www.ctc.cam.ac.uk/hawking70/multimedia.html.

29. Vilenkin quoted by Grossman, "Death of the Eternal Cosmos." See Vilenkin, "Did the Universe Have a Beginning?"

30. "In the Beginning," 3.

Astrid (using her tablet): I'd focus on the fact that Big Bang cosmology entails the existence of a first physical event, and that when it comes to explaining that first event, our options are very limited. As Paul Davies writes: "One might consider some supernatural force . . . as being responsible for the big bang, or one might prefer to regard the big bang as an event without a cause. It seems to me that we don't have too much choice. Either . . . something outside of the physical world [or] an event without a cause."[31] I think it's more reasonable to believe in a supernatural creator than in a physical event without a cause. As philosopher Dallas Willard argues: "the dependent character of all physical states, together with the completeness of the series of dependencies underlying the existence of any given physical state, logically implies at least one self-existent, and therefore nonphysical, state of being."[32] To lay the argument out in formal terms:

1. Since the universe had a finite past, there was a first physical event.

2. All physical events have at least one cause outside and independent of themselves.

3. Therefore, the first physical event had at least one cause outside and independent of itself.

4. The cause of the *first* physical event can't have been anything physical.

5. Therefore, the first physical event had a *non-physical* cause.

6. The non-physical cause of the first physical event was most probably a personal cause.

7. Therefore, the first physical event had a non-physical cause that was probably personal (i.e., "God").

Thomas: Doesn't quantum mechanics show you *can* get a universe out of nothing?

Astrid (using her tablet): According to physicist David Hutchings and astronomer David Wilkinson: "Physics . . . emphatically does *not* allow for a universe from nothing and—because its models are *always* dependent on an already-present law, principle or the like—*it never will.*"[33]

---

31. Davies, "Birth of the Cosmos," 8–9.
32. Willard, "Three-Stage Argument for the Existence of God," para. 3.
33. Hutchings and Wilkinson, *God, Stephen Hawking and the Multiverse*, 193.

Douglas (using his phone): That's right. As atheist philosopher Quentin Smith explains, considerations to do with quantum mechanics: "at most tend to show that acausal laws govern the *change of condition* of particles. . . . They state nothing about the causality or acausality of absolute beginnings, of beginnings of the existence of particles."[34] To quote philosopher of science and theoretical physicist David Albert:

> Relativistic-quantum-field-theoretical vacuum states . . . are particular arrangements of *elementary physical stuff*. . . . The fact that some arrangements of fields happen to correspond to the existence of particles and some don't is not a whit more mysterious than the fact that some of the possible arrangements of my fingers happen to correspond to the existence of a fist and some don't. And the fact that particles can pop in and out of existence, over time, as those fields rearrange themselves, is not a whit more mysterious than the fact that fists can pop in and out of existence, over time, as my fingers rearrange themselves. And none of these poppings . . . amount to anything even remotely in the neighbourhood of a creation from nothing.[35]

Thomas: But don't many theists believe in creation *"ex nihilo"* or "out of nothing"?

Astrid: In the theological context, the doctrine of creation *"ex nihilo"* refers to the belief that, unlike the gods of polytheism, God didn't create using preexisting stuff that he didn't create. It means that God's creation of the universe was not out of independently existing material, but that God created everything apart from himself. So, for the Judeo-Christian tradition, creation is about an uncreated, necessarily existent God creating a contingent universe.

Thomas: Oh.

Hiromi (using her tablet): In light of the Big Bang, neo-atheist chemist Peter Atkins reckons that: "The task before science . . . will be to show how something can come from nothing without intervention. . . . The unfolding of absolutely nothing . . . into something is a problem of the profoundest difficulty and currently far beyond the reach of science."[36] But this task will

34. Smith, "Uncaused Beginning of the Universe," 50.
35. Alberts, "On the Origin of Everything."
36. Atkins, *On Being*, 11–12.

always be beyond the reach of science, or any other discipline! "Nothing" *can't* unfold "into something" for the simple reason that "Nothing" *isn't anything*. "Nothing" isn't a thing that exists, so "Nothing" can't *do* anything, because *only things that exist can do things*!

Thomas: But if "nothing" can't explain the universe, does that mean it must have been created by God?

Douglas: Only if you accept that "All physical events have at least one cause outside and independent of themselves." The alternative is to accept the universe is a "brute" fact that has no explanation. To quote Quentin Smith: "the most reasonable belief is that we came from nothing, by nothing, and for nothing."[37]

Astrid (using her tablet): Atheist philosopher Kai Nielson wrote: "Suppose you suddenly hear a loud bang . . . and you ask me, 'What made that bang?' and I reply, 'Nothing, it just happened.' You would not accept that."[38] Why accept the "Nothing, it just happened" response when it comes to the first physical event?

Hiromi: Sounds like a leap of faith to me.[39]

Sophie: What about Dawkins's discussion of the life-permitting structure of laws and conditions that characterize our universe from its birth?

Hiromi (using her tablet): The so-called "Fine Tuning" of the universe is a discovery about what Dawkins calls "the fundamental laws and constants of physics."[40] Theoretical physicist Lee Smolin describes it as the discovery of "the fact that life can arise only in an extremely narrow range of all possible physical parameters and yet, oddly enough, here we are, as though the universe had been designed to accommodate us."[41] Dawkins illustrates this "Fine Tuning" by discussing "the gravitational constant, symbolized by the

---

37. Smith in Craig and Smith, *Theism, Atheism and Big Bang Cosmology*, 135.

38. Nielson, *Reason and Practice*, 48.

39. See "Sean Carroll and Brute Facts"; Williams, *Faithful Guide to Philosophy*.

40. Dawkins, *Outgrowing God*, 271.

41. Smolin, *Trouble with Physics*, 161–62.

letter G."[42] He explains that "if G were even slightly different, the universe would be very, very different."[43] In what way, I hear you ask?

Thomas: In what way?

Hiromi (using her tablet): Well, "If G were smaller than it is, gravity would have been too weak to gather matter into clumps. There'd be no galaxies, no stars, no chemistry. . . . If G had been just a little bit bigger than it is, stars couldn't exist as we know them. . . . They'd all collapse under their own gravity. . . . No stars, no planets, no evolution, no life."[44] As Dawkins points out: "There are more than a dozen of these constants. . . . And in all cases you can say that, if their value were different, the universe as we know it could not exist."[45] In fact, the force of gravity is fine-tuning to one part in 10^{40}.[46] So, tweaking G doesn't describe possible universes where different forms of life might exist, but where no material systems of any kind could exist!

Astrid (using her tablet): William Lane Craig explains that, in addition to the existence of the different physical laws themselves,

> fine-tuning is of two sorts. First, when the laws of nature are expressed as mathematical equations, you find appearing in them certain constants, like the constant that represents the force of gravity. . . . The laws of nature are consistent with a wide range of values for these constants. Second . . . there are . . . initial conditions on which the laws of nature operate, for example, the amount of entropy or the balance between matter and antimatter in the universe . . . these constants and quantities fall into an extraordinarily narrow range of life-permitting values.

For example:

> a change in the strength of the atomic weak force by only one part in 10^{100} would have prevented a life-permitting universe. The cosmological constant which drives the inflation of the universe [is] fine-tuned to around one part in 10^{120} . . . the odds of the Big Bang's low entropy condition existing by chance are on the order of one out of $10^{10(123)}$.

42. Dawkins, *Outgrowing God*, 271.
43. Dawkins, *Outgrowing God*, 272.
44. Dawkins, *Outgrowing God*, 272.
45. Dawkins, *Outgrowing God*, 272.
46. See Meyer, "Evidence for Design in Physics and Biology," 60.

Douglas: Multiplying together the *joint* improbability of these constants and quantities *all* falling within the narrow life-permitting range of values, gives an improbability to the "Fine Tuning" that's literally beyond "astronomical"!

Sophie: That's the evidence under consideration. But why think this evidence supports theism?

Hiromi: We can articulate the cosmic design argument using the same two forms of argument we applied to organic design.

Astrid: What were they?

Hiromi: First, by using the "principle of credulity" applied to the appearance of cosmic design. Second, by applying the criterion of "specified complexity" to the data of fine-tuning.

Sophie: I think some of us would value a summary of those two starting points.

Hiromi (using her tablet): The "principle of credulity" says "we ought to believe that things are as they seem to be . . . unless and until we have evidence that we are mistaken."[47] The specified complexity criterion says that the combination of "high improbability [and] conformity to an independently given pattern"[48] or "specification," is a reliable sign of intelligent design. For example: "in a poker game any deal of cards is equally and highly improbable, but if you find that every time a certain player deals he gets all four aces, you can bet this is not the result of chance but of design."[49]

Sophie: How do these principles apply to the fine-tuning data?

Hiromi (using her tablet): The first argument would go like this:

> Premise One) "we ought to believe that things are as they seem to be . . . unless and until we have evidence that we are mistaken."[50]
>
> Premise Two) It seems that cosmic fine-tuning is the product of design.

47. Swinburne, *Does God Exist?*, 115.
48. Craig, "Fine Tuned Universe," para. 2.
49. Craig, "Fine Tuned Universe," para. 2.
50. Swinburne, *Does God Exist?*, 115.

Conclusion) Therefore, we ought to believe that cosmic fine-tuning is the product of design, "unless and until we have evidence that we are mistaken."[51]

Douglas: As Paul Davies writes concerning the fine-tuning of the cosmos: "the impression of design is overwhelming."[52] I accept that, since the universe *seems* designed, the burden of proof lies with those of us who think this appearance is misleading.

Hiromi (using her tablet): The second argument would go like this:

Premise One) If something exhibits specified complexity, it's probably the product of design.

Premise Two) The fine-tuning of the universe exhibits specified complexity.

Conclusion) Therefore, the fine-tuning of the universe is probably the product of design.

Douglas: Plenty of atheists would accept the first premise whilst rejecting the second premise, by invoking the existence of multiple universes.

Hiromi: Right; so the key question is whether the appeal to the existence of multiple universes is more reasonable than the appeal to the existence of a single designer.

Thomas: Actually, Dawkins seems to have *three* responses to the fine-tuning argument: the anthropic principle, multiple universes, and the improbability of any universe designer.

Sophie: Let's consider Dawkins's responses one by one.

Hiromi: As far as I can see, the "anthropic principle" is just a way of saying that, because we exist in this universe, we can deduce that it has properties consistent with our existence. But, of course, that's *not* to say that a universe with these life permitting qualities *must* exist.

Astrid: In *The God Delusion*, Dawkins himself rejects the idea that the anthropic principle is an "explanation" of fine-tuning, referencing philosopher

51. Swinburne, *Does God Exist?*, 115.
52. Davies, *Cosmic Blueprint*, 203.

John Leslie's analogy of a man who survives a firing squad and muses: "Well, obviously they all missed, or I wouldn't be here thinking about it."[53] Dawkins admits the man "could still, forgivably, wonder why they'd all missed, and toy with the hypothesis that they were bribed."[54]

Douglas (using his phone): For once, I agree with Dawkins! *The fact that an event is a pre-condition of its being observed doesn't explain the occurrence of the event.* The prisoner's observation that his existence depends on a very unlikely set of preconditions (the firing squad missing) does nothing to *explain* his existence. Noting that the sentenced man wouldn't exist if the firing squad hadn't missed doesn't explain *why* they missed. As atheist philosopher Peter Cave argues: "conscious beings, exist. So, of course, the universe is such a place that conscious beings exist; but it may still be surprising that the universe *is* such a place."[55]

Hiromi: Likewise, noting that life wouldn't exist if the laws of nature weren't fine-tuned doesn't explain *why* the laws of nature are fine-tuned. Indeed, the fact that the universe appears to be fine-tuned suggests it was designed.

Thomas (using his tablet): Ah, but the life-permitting structure of our universe might not be unlikely after all, if there are multiple universes. According to Dawkins: "it is likely that even our expanding universe of 100 billion galaxies is not the only universe. Many scientists think—with good reason—that there are billions of universes like ours. On this view, our universe is just one universe in a *multiverse* of billions of universes."[56]

Hiromi: It's a pity Dawkins can't be bothered to provide the "good reason" that leads "many scientists" to think this way. He's asking readers to take things on authority again. His case for atheism repeatedly boils down to "Trust me, I'm a scientist"!

Astrid: I suppose, if "many" means "the majority" here, this would at least be an argument from appropriate authority. But physicist David Hutchings and astronomer David Wilkinson reckon the existence of multiple universes "is, by no means, the consensus."[57]

---

53. Dawkins, *God Delusion*, 144–45.

54. Dawkins, *God Delusion*, 145.

55. Cave, *Humanism*, 31.

56. Dawkins, *Outgrowing God*, 269.

57. Hutchings and Wilkinson, *God, Stephen Hawking and the Multiverse*, 176.

Hiromi: I've come across several reasons to doubt the Many Universes hypothesis.

Sophie: Let's take them one at a time.

Hiromi (using her tablet): First, as astrophysicist Rodney Holder comments: "the physics associated with multiverses is speculative, to say the least, especially when it comes to string theory."[58]

Douglas: That's fair; but it doesn't mean the multiverse is an *unreasonable* hypothesis.

Hiromi (using her tablet): Second, the multiverse hypothesis is highly complex. On the one hand, you'd need lots of *differently tuned* universes to improve the odds of having a life permitting universe. On the other hand, you'd also need lots of universes tuned *like ours* to improve the odds of life emerging from non-life and then evolving by blind material processes into the variety of complex forms we see around us today. In both cases, the multiverse hypothesis has to posit some sort of universe-generating mechanism. Altogether, that's a *lot* of complexity to posit just to avoid common sense. As Richard Swinburne says: "To postulate a trillion-trillion other universes, rather than one God, in order to explain the orderliness of our universe, seems the height of irrationality."[59]

Douglas: You've got to balance simplicity in terms of the *number* of things you posit with the complexity of positing more than one *type* of thing. Positing multiple universes only invokes material things. Appealing to God introduces something supernatural.

Hiromi: But material things seem unable to bring the regress of explanations to a close in the way that a necessarily existent God can. Postulating more and more material things just gives you more and more things that need to be explained! Besides, not only does the God hypothesis carry the presumption of truth by the principle of credulity, but it's supported by other arguments, like the moral and cosmological arguments. In other words, the God hypothesis seems to economically explain a wider range of data than the multiverse hypothesis.

---

58. Holder, *Big Bang, Big God*, 130. See Smolin, *Trouble with Physics*.
59. Swinburne, *Is There a God?*, 68.

Astrid: And what if you already had reason to believe in immaterial entities, like minds that aren't reducible to brains? That would make belief in a transcendent Mind less of a stretch.[60]

Douglas: God would still be an unusual type of immaterial reality.

Astrid: And a universe-generating mechanism would be an unusual type of physical reality.

Hiromi (using her tablet): Third, the multiverse hypothesis is empirically *unverifiable*. Cosmologist George Ellis says the "existence of multiverses is neither established nor scientifically establishable."[61] Rodney Holder points out that this "ought to undermine its credentials with scientific naturalists like Dawkins who [mistakenly] make this complaint about religion!"[62]

Douglas: Holder's point is more a dig at Dawkins than the multiverse theory. Empirical verifiability is an important scientific value, but it isn't "make or break."

Hiromi: Fourth, the multiverse hypothesis is an "ad hoc" hypothesis that's adopted purely for the purpose of saving naturalism from the difficulty posed by the fine-tuning evidence, without any independent rationale.[63]

Thomas: What do you mean?

Hiromi: Think about it this way: When you read a book, you naturally assume it has an explanation for its existence that ultimately tracks back to an author. How would you respond to someone who claimed that there might not be an author after all, because *if* there were to exist enough monkeys with enough typewriters and enough time, they could in theory produce the same book?

Thomas: I'd be skeptical.

Hiromi (using her tablet): Right, because in the absence of independent evidence for the existence of enough monkeys and so on, the "many monkeys" hypothesis is "ad hoc" and the "author" hypothesis is clearly preferable.

60. See Williams, *Faithful Guide to Philosophy*.

61. Ellis, "Multiverses: Description, Uniqueness, Testing."

62. Holder, *God, the Multiverse, and Everything*, 158.

63. See Dowden, "Ad Hoc Rescue."

Likewise, even granting that a multiverse *could* produce the fine-tuning of our universe by chance, in the absence of independent evidence for the existence of other universes, the "God" hypothesis is clearly preferable. But as philosopher Chad Meister reports: "there is currently no experimental evidence in support of the many-universes hypothesis."[64]

Astrid (using her tablet): Theoretical physicist and philosopher David H. Glass makes the same point with a nice analogy of his own. He says:

> suppose Joe stands accused of robbing a bank on grounds that include an eyewitness having seen him at the scene of a crime. Detectives are not likely to be impressed at the suggestion that it was really Joe's identical twin brother if they have no good reason to believe that he has a twin brother. The mere possibility that there might be an alternative explanation would not be good enough.[65]

Likewise, since everyone agrees the fine-tuning *looks* designed, "if the fine-tuning evidence is to be explained by the existence of a multiverse rather than design, there must be some good reason to think the proposed multiverse actually exists or is likely to exist."[66] So, as Columbia University physicist and mathematician Brian Greene concludes: "people should be skeptical of multiverse theories because there is no evidence supporting their existence."[67]

Douglas: The existence of a multiverse is part-and-parcel of many versions of "inflation," a popular addition to Big Bang cosmology designed to explain the uniformity of the universe by positing a brief phase of super-fast growth at a very early stage of its expansion.[68]

Astrid (using her tablet): True; but cosmic "inflation" has itself been criticized as a speculative and "ad hoc" attempt to explain away one aspect of cosmic fine-tuning![69] Neo-atheist cosmologist Lawrence M. Krauss cautions that "inflation . . . relies on the existence of a new and completely

---

64. Meister, *Introducing Philosophy of Religion*, 98.

65. Glass, *Atheism's New Clothes*, 132.

66. Glass, *Atheism's New Clothes*, 132.

67. Greene, quoted by Ghose, "Stranger Things: How Realistic are Parallel Worlds?"

68. See Penrose, *Faith, Fashion & Fantasy in the New Physics of the Universe*, 294–310.

69. See William Lane in Strobel, *Case for a Creator*, 130; Gordon, "Balloons on a String," 569–70; Holder, *God, the Multiverse, and Everything*, 141.

ad hoc scalar field—invented solely to help produce inflation and fine-tuned to initiate it as the early universe first began to cool down after the Big Bang."[70] So, as Rodney Holder explains, while "inflation may explain some of the parameter values" of the big bang, "it too needs fine-tuning" so that "the specialness of the initial conditions in the standard Big Bang is merely replaced by the, arguably equally special, propensity of a region to inflate."[71] In fact, Roger Penrose argues that the theory of inflation actually "makes the problem of how the very special initial conditions of the universe came about even worse!"[72] Finally, David Glass notes that "While inflation theory is widely accepted as part of big bang cosmology, the idea that inflation can give rise to separate universes with different laws of physics is much more controversial."[73]

Hiromi: Plus, several of these other objections to the multiverse hypothesis obviously count as objections to versions of "inflation" that include a multiverse.

Thomas: Noted.

Hiromi (using her tablet): Fifth, cosmic fine-tuning is *so* complex that a multiverse isn't automatically big enough to explain it away. Stephen Hawking said that the overarching multiverse model within string-theory, "M-theory . . . allows for 10^{500} different universes, each with its own laws."[74] But as Bruce L. Gordon observes: "there are so many independent constants and factors that are fine-tuned to a high degree of precision that the cumulative effect of all these fine tunings significantly erodes the probabilistic resources of the [string theory] landscape."[75]

Douglas: That's an interesting point.

Hiromi (using her tablet): Sixth, the multiverse hypothesis is *question begging*, in that it assumes a universe generating mechanism *that would itself require fine-tuning*! Theoretical physicist Sabine Hossenfelder writes that: "Ever

70. Krauss, *Greatest Story Ever Told... So Far*, chapter 23.

71. Holder, *God, the Multiverse, and Everything*, 156–57. See Gordon, "Balloons on a String," 570.

72. Penrose, *Faith, Fashion & Fantasy in the New Physics of the Universe*, 305.

73. Glass, *Atheism's New Clothes*, 135.

74. Hawking and Mlodinow, *Grand Design*, 118. See Smolin, *Trouble with Physics*, xiv, 158.

75. Gordon, "Balloons on a String," 581.

since the results of the Planck [space telescope] in 2013 it hasn't looked good for inflation. After the results appeared, Anna Ijjas, Paul Steinhardt, and Avi Loeb argued . . . that the models of inflation which are compatible with the data themselves require fine tuning, and therefore bring back the problem they were meant to solve."[76] As philosopher Robin Collins points out:

> even if an inflationary/superstring many-universes generator exists, it along with the background laws and principles could be said to be an *irreducibly complex* system . . . with just the right combination of laws and fields for the production of life-permitting universes: if one of the components were missing or different, such as Einstein's equation or the Pauli-exclusion principle, it is unlikely that any life-permitting universes could be produced . . . the existence of such a system suggests design since it seems very unlikely that such a system would have just the right components by chance. It does not seem, therefore, that one can escape the conclusion of design merely by hypothesizing some sort of many-universes generator.[77]

Astrid (using her tablet)**:** Paul Davies concurs that to postulate a multiverse is to "merely shift the problem [of 'fine-tuning'] up a level from universe to multiverse."[78]

Hiromi (using her tablet)**:** Seventh, the multiverse hypothesis *undermines the practice of science.* The more universes you posit to lessen the improbability of our own, the more you undermine the basis of scientific explanation for things within our universe, by making increasingly bizarre possibilities unexceptional features of the cosmos.

Brian Green cautions:

> The danger, if the multiverse idea takes root, is that researchers may too quickly give up the search for underlying explanations. When faced with seemingly inexplicable observations, researchers may invoke the framework of the multiverse prematurely—proclaiming some phenomenon or other to merely reflect conditions in our own bubble universe and thereby failing to discover the deeper understanding that awaits us.[79]

76. Hossenfelder, "Inflation: Status Update," para. 9.
77. Collins, "Design and the Many Worlds Hypothesis," 20.
78. Davies, *Goldilocks Enigma*, 231–32, 237.
79. Greene, "Multiverse," 120–21.

Bruce L. Gordon comments: "if it is a consequence of the [eternal inflation] theory that endless copies of ourselves exist holding every conceivable opinion and involved in every conceivable activity . . . it has successfully reduced itself to absurdity. A fundamental implication of the theory is that every possible event, no matter how improbable . . . will happen countlessly many times . . . *destroying science altogether* as a rational enterprise."[80]

Astrid (using her tablet): I came across a similar criticism from David Hutchings and David Wilkinson, who warn that, if we assume the existence of a multiverse, "we can have no idea whether (a) we have found genuine laws of nature that will predict our futures or (b) we just happen to have observed a freakish run of very unlikely outcomes for a very long time that will suddenly cease without warning and revert to another principle altogether. . . . Anyone seeking to call on the multiverse and the anthropic principle to get rid of God, then, had better be careful—for they might end up throwing out the scientific baby with the (holy) bathwater."[81]

Thomas: It's pretty ironic for a scientist like Dawkins to defend his atheism by appealing to a theory that undermines science!

Hiromi (using her tablet): Eighth and finally, the multiverse hypothesis appears to be *falsified* by observation. For one thing, according to Anna Ijjas, Paul J. Steinhardt, and Abraham Loeb, on the simpler theories of inflation, "if inflation took place the [Cosmic Microwave Background] should contain evidence of cosmic gravitational waves—ripples in spacetime caused by the early stretching—yet it does not."[82] In other words: "the simplest inflationary models, including those described in the standard textbooks, are strongly disfavored by observations. Of course, theorists rapidly rushed to patch the inflationary picture but at the cost of making arcane models of inflationary energy and revealing yet further problems."[83]

For another thing, atheist Roger Penrose points out "how ridiculously cheaper (in the sense of improbabilities) it would be simply to produce, by mere random collisions of particles, the entire solar system with all its life ready-made, or even just a few conscious [so-called Boltzmann] brains . . . So the problem is: why did we not come about *this* way, rather than from an

80. Greene, "Multiverse," 120–21.

81. Hutchings and Wilkinson, *God, Stephen Hawking and the Multiverse*, 180.

82. Ijjas et al., "Pop Goes the Universe," 35.

83. Ijjas et al., "Pop Goes the Universe," 36.

absurdly less probable . . . 1.4 x 10^{10} tedious years of [cosmic] evolution?"[84] Penrose concludes: "It seems to me that this conundrum simply points to . . . the incorrectness of the bubble-universe idea."[85]

Thomas: What's a "Boltzmann brain"?

Sophie: Named after the famous German physicist Ludwig Boltzmann, "Boltzmann brains" are hypothetical observers, consisting of just a brain (and maybe some sense organs), that randomly fluctuate into existence out of the quantum vacuum. Boltzmann brains are very unlikely, but they're much less unlikely than the finely tuned universe we inhabit. The Boltzmann brain concept suggests that *if* there is a multiverse, *then* Boltzmann brains probably dominate the proportion of observable universes within the multiverse.[86]

Hiromi (using her tablet): Theoretical astrophysicist Luke Barnes explains that Boltzmann brains "do not need [cosmic] fine-tuning, because they form by means of freak [quantum] fluctuations."[87] He argues that, if there is a multiverse, it's probable that observable universes consisting of Boltzmann brains "are vastly more common than observers in large, low entropy universes like ours."[88] He adds that: "If only very special [that is, ad hoc] multiverses avoid this problem, then the multiverse itself is fine-tuned."[89] In either case, *positing a multiverse doesn't explain away the evidence for design.*

I think I agree with Barnes's comment that the real problem here "is not that we might be Boltzmann brains, the problem is that we aren't."[90] Indeed, as Holder argues, there are various observational factors which show the multiverse hypothesis "is inconsistent with the amount of order found in this universe, and with the persistence of order. Our universe is far more special than we would expect it to be, even if it were merely a random member of the subset of universes compatible with our existence."[91]

Astrid: While some of those arguments seem less than conclusive on their own, all eight taken together offer a *formidable* response to the multiverse

84. Penrose, *Faith, Fashion & Fantasy in the New Physics of the Universe*, 327–28.

85. Penrose, *Faith, Fashion & Fantasy in the New Physics of the Universe*, 328.

86. See Craig, "What Is a Boltzmann Brain?"; Craig "Fabric of the Cosmos (part 3)."

87. Barnes, "Good God!," para. 31. That is, they require relatively little fine-tuning. They obviously require the laws of quantum mechanics.

88. Barnes, "Good God!," para. 31.

89. Barnes, "Good God!," para. 31.

90. Lewis and Barnes, *Fortunate Universe*, 317.

91. Holder, *God, the Multiverse, and Everything*, 158.

hypothesis. Of course, even if the multiverse hypothesis *did* undermine the design argument, it wouldn't contradict theism or prove atheism.

Hiromi: As for Dawkins third objection to design, this is just a repeat of the simplistic "Who made God?" argument we dismantled a few weeks ago as question-begging.[92]

Douglas (using his phone)**:** That's accurate. I think Bradley Monton's right to admit that arguments for God from the probably finite past existence and apparent fine-tuning of the one universe we know "do have *some* force—they make me less certain of my atheism than I would be had I not heard the arguments."[93]

Sophie: A conclusion worth pondering as we look towards our final meeting next week, when we will review our findings.[94]

92. Williams, "Who Designed the Designer/Caused God?"; Craig, "Dawkins' Delusion"; Craig, *Reasonable Faith*, 170–72.

93. Monton, *Seeking God in Science*, 7–8.

94. An extensive list of chapter-specific recommended resources can be found on this book's webpage at www.peterswilliams.com/publications/books/outgrowing-god/.

Outgrowing God or Dawkins?

A s Hiromi headed towards *The Campus Coffee Cup Café*, the last remnants of ice were melting in the rain. Arriving at her destination, she saw the rest of the club in their usual corner. Collapsing her "Hello Kitty" umbrella, she pushed through the door and wiped her combat boots on the welcome mat. Then she bought a hot chocolate and joined her friends.

Sophie: This meeting, which will be our last of the academic year, is about looking at the big picture. I want to give each of you a chance to reflect on your experience of reading and discussing *Outgrowing God* over the past nine weeks. Let's start with Astrid, who we should thank for contributing a well-informed and articulate Christian perspective to our investigation.

Astrid: I'd like to thank you all for being patient with me when I zoned out, or couldn't face getting out of bed. This club has been really good for me. I've even taken up knitting, thanks to Thomas!

When I settled in to read *Outgrowing God*, I was anticipating a serious challenge to my faith. After all, Dawkins is a scientist with a doctorate from Oxford University, and he's a Fellow of the Royal Society, so I was expecting some intellectual heft. And I'd seen some glowing reviews of *Outgrowing God*, like the one in *Aero* magazine.[1] But I was shocked to see how badly researched it was, how avoidably ignorant Dawkins was on the subjects he addressed. It really seems like he didn't bother to do even the most basic research on the topics he addressed. As we noted, even some of his science is out of date. As Rebecca McLaughlin comments in her

---

1. See Sharp, "An Argument Worth Having." See also Carty, "Book Review: Richard Dawkins, *Outgrowing God.*"

review: "Dawkins's book consistently fails to engage opposing arguments and frequently falls short of the research standards we should expect of an academic author—whatever his beliefs."[2]

I was surprised to realize that, while Dawkins spends many pages criticizing particular interpretations of particular theistic revelation claims, and many pages trying (and, I think, failing) to undermine theistic arguments, especially the design argument, he really only briefly offers *one* positive argument for atheism! And that's his question-begging "Who made God then?" argument! Indeed, I was shocked by how many fallacies Dawkins managed to commit. Still, I enjoyed thinking through the wide range of topics the book raises, and I enjoyed meeting with you guys.

Sophie: Thank you, Astrid. Who'd like to go next?

Thomas (using his tablet): I think reading and discussing *Outgrowing God* has forced my atheism to mature and become less dogmatic. Dawkins says "some intelligent children, when they grow up, look at the evidence and succeed in breaking away from the bad or useless advice from previous generations—grow out of it. Think about the title of this book. But that doesn't always happen, and I believe this partly explains how religions get started and why they persist."[3] I think that if we apply this comment to "worldviews" in general, then Dawkins has a point. But the point should be applied evenhandedly, to his worldview as much as to any other.

Sophie: Failing to apply such counsel impartially would make one guilty of a "double standard."[4]

Thomas: Here's what I think. I'm intelligent. I'm growing up. I've been looking at the evidence. And I think it's *Dawkins* who's offering "bad or useless advice from previous generations"!

Astrid: How come?

Thomas: I applaud Dawkins's desire "to encourage people to think for themselves."[5] It was that call for people to think about the big questions that

---

2. McLaughlin, "Richard Dawkins's Latest Case for Outgrowing God," para. 35.

3. Dawkins, *Outgrowing God*, 236.

4. See "Double Standard."

5. Dawkins, "Features Interview," 38. See video of this interview at New Scientist, "Richard Dawkins Outgrows God."

first drew me to his work. But I've found myself increasingly disillusioned by the way he actually *discourages* independent thought.

Sophie: How does Dawkins discourage independent thought?

Thomas: He constantly *asserts* things on his own authority, without evidence.

Hiromi: Or footnotes.

Thomas: Or footnotes. And he resorts to begging the question in favor of his own beliefs while issuing "abusive assurances" against dissent. Plus, we came across so many assertions made by Dawkins that were flat out, demonstrably *wrong*. I noted over a dozen false statements in *Outgrowing God*, on points like the supposed lack of archaeological evidence for the existence of King David, or camels supposedly being an anachronism in the Old Testament. He gets his facts wrong about Josephus's references to Jesus and about the design of the human eye, and so on. *Outgrowing God* is basically riddled with misinformation. So, I came to *Outgrowing God* expecting a rational, scientific argument for atheism grounded in evidence; I found a bunch of unreliable assertions and faulty philosophical arguments. I don't know that I'll be outgrowing atheism; but I do know I've outgrown Dawkins's *kind* of atheism. And that means learning more about how to think well and learning more about the God debate from some more reliable sources. I guess I've realized the importance of what Sophie said at the start of our first meeting, about speaking and listening *in love* for both people and truth.

Sophie: That warms my heart to hear. What about you, Douglas?

Douglas (using his phone)**:** I've enjoyed our discussions, but they haven't resulted in any changes to my worldview. Unlike Thomas, I didn't start out with a high opinion of Dawkins. American philosopher of science Michael Ruse wrote that "*The God Delusion* made me ashamed to be an atheist,"[6] and he criticized Dawkins for making "condesending" arguments "from ignorance," and for making "unsubstantiated arguments that science refutes religion."[7] Reading *Outgrowing God* would only deepen his embarrassment!

---

6. Ruse, "Dawkins et al Bring Us into Disrepute," para. 3.

7. Ruse, "Dawkins et al Bring Us into Disrepute," paras. 4, 5.

That said, at the end of the day, my sympathies remain with atheists like Eugene Koonin and Bradley Monton. I'm happy to say with Monton that arguments

> from the fine-tuning of the fundamental constants . . . the fact that the universe began to exist, and . . . the improbability of the naturalistic origin of life from non-life . . . are somewhat plausible . . . there is some evidence for an intelligent designer, and . . . some evidence that that intelligent designer is God. The arguments . . . make me less certain of my atheism that I would be had I never heard the arguments. The evidence isn't enough to make me stop being an atheist though.[8]

I suppose the main thing I'm taking away with me from our discussion, is Astrid's defense of the idea that there are serious arguments, grounded in historical evidence, for a specifically Jewish or Christian God. That's something I hadn't come across before, and plan to investigate further.

Sophie: And what did you make of *Outgrowing God*, Hiromi?

Hiromi: Dawkins's emphasis on physical origins frustrated me, because he leaves so many arguments for God unexplored, even when he raises issues that call out for discussion.

Thomas: Such as?

Hiromi (using her tablet): Such as consciousness. He says: "Your brain . . . contains about 100 billion nerve cells . . . wired up to each other in such a way that you can think, hear, see, love, hate, plan a barbecue, imagine a giant green hippopotamus or dream of the future."[9] But that's just an assertion of the philosophical position that people are wholly physical beings. He completely ignores the significant problems faced by purely physical accounts of the mind,[10] and he pays no attention to those who argue that explaining the existence and nature of consciousness points to God.[11]

---

8. Monton, *Seeking God in Science*, 39.

9. Dawkins, *Outgrowing God*, 161.

10. See Williams, "Mind-Body Dualism, Free Will & Related Issues"; Goetz and Taliaffero, *Naturalism*; Moreland, *Recalcitrant Imago Dei*; Williams, *Faithful Guide to Philosophy*.

11. See Moreland, *Consciousness and the Existence of God*; Williams, *A Faithful Guide to Philosophy*.

Astrid: Hiromi has a point. In Part 1, Dawkins rejects historical revelation claims and ignores the key moral argument discussed by philosophers. In Part 2, he argues that evolution can explain away the appearance of design in biology, before briefly touching upon the origin of life, the life-permitting "fine-tuning" of the cosmos and the question of cosmic origins. And that's it!

Douglas (using his phone): To be fair, Dawkins is upfront about being less than comprehensive. In chapter 1 he says: "plenty of people have offered what they thought were reasons for believing in one god or another. . . . We'll see *some* of them in the course of this book."[12]

Hiromi: He may be upfront about being less than comprehensive, but he doesn't give his readers any sense of how little he covers.

Thomas: How much else is there to cover?

Hiromi: I bought *A Faithful Guide to Philosophy* by Peter S. Williams, the philosopher Astrid mentioned.[13] It's an introductory text, but it covers around three times as many theistic arguments as Dawkins! Alvin Plantinga once famously gave a talk on "Two Dozen (Or So) Theistic Arguments."[14]

Thomas: Okay, so Dawkins is only paddling in the metaphysical sea.

Hiromi (using her tablet): Back in our first meeting, Douglas quoted Dawkins, saying: "The universe we observe has precisely the properties we should expect if there is, at bottom, no design, no purpose, no evil, and no good, nothing but blind pitiless indifference. . . . DNA neither knows nor cares. DNA just is. And we dance to its music."[15] I've been thinking about that all term, and telling myself: "*If* atheism is true, Dawkins is probably right about that, and love is a meaningless delusion after all." The thing is, the universe sure looks to me like it *was* designed for a purpose, like there *is* objective good or evil, and like love *does* have a meaning beyond the survival of our genes or our species. And Dawkins doesn't offer any good reasons to think this impression is mistaken. Not only that, but the more I research the relevant evidence from ethics, biology, and cosmology, the more it seems to point to a Creator God in the Judeo-Christian tradition. So I'm thinking, maybe

12. Dawkins, *Outgrowing God*, 14, emphasis added.
13. See Williams, *Faithful Guide to Philosophy*.
14. See Plantinga, "Two Dozen (or so) Theistic Arguments."
15. Dawkins, *River Out of Eden*, 133.

life *isn't* a meaningless dance forced on us by DNA; maybe it's an invitation to harmonize with a tune written by the composer of life.

Sophie: As we draw our meeting to a close, I'd just like to say how encouraging I've found it to see students eager to pursue a true education, willing to question authority, each other, and even themselves, in a community of friendly disagreement. Whether or not this group has led you to change your mind on any of the issues we've discussed, I hope the process of discussion itself has shown you that, through dialogue with those with whom we disagree, we can and should "learn modesty (or not claiming to possess the whole truth), graciousness (including conceding opponent's good points), patience (in waiting for [people] to think through our points), and forgiveness (when an opponent refuses to concede our own good points)."[16] Furthermore: "When we need to deliberate with opponents, we are forced to present arguments for our positions, and thereby gain a better understanding of our own positions and the reasons for them. . . . Encounters with opponents help us in many ways."[17] And thus we can all be thankful to Professor Dawkins and to each other.

As the meeting broke up and goodbyes were said, Hiromi drew Astrid aside and asked how she was doing. They talked for a while—about love, depression, and grief—before deciding to visit the barista for supplies. They returned with black coffee, hot chocolate, and an iced bun to share. Astrid said it reminded her of the iced buns in the café at Nidaros Cathedral in Trondheim.[18]

"Your book recommendations fitted with my philosophy course," said Hiromi, "so I've been doing lots of reading about God and Jesus. And it's not just that I think there's probably a divine 'composer' that gives us existence and purpose and meaning. The more I've read about Jesus, the more I've wondered if he might really be God's invitation into the heart of things. I'm not sure, but maybe God is that three-way harmony of love you described when we discussed the Trinity."

"You don't have to be *sure*," said Astrid. "You just need to think it's *not unreasonable* to reach out to God. It's like the start of any relationship."

---

16. Sinnott-Armstrong, *Think Again*, 10.

17. Sinnott-Armstrong, *Think Again*, 61.

18. See Dogan, "Nidaros Cathedral 4K"; 2L, "MAGNIFICAT—Nidarosdomens jentekor & Trondheim Solistene"; "Nidaros Cathedral."

"Yes; I see," said Hiromi. "I listened to that album you recommended by Transatlantic: 'The Whirlwind.'[19] The song at the end, 'Dancing with Eternal Glory,'[20] moved me deeply. I cried tears of joy *and* sadness, like I'd found something I had wanted all my life and realized I didn't have, all in the same moment."

"I know what you mean," responded Astrid. "I think our in-built longings are signposts pointing to realities beyond us. And I think many of our in-built longings point to God."[21]

Hiromi considered this for a moment as she drank some chocolate. Then she declared: "I think Dawkins is wrong about humans dancing to the meaningless music of a Blind Watchmaker. And I'd like to know if what that song says, about God inviting us to dance with him through Jesus, is true. So, I wanted to ask if we could keep meeting in this time-slot now book club's over, because I'd like to read through one of those 'Gospels' with you, if that wouldn't be too much trouble?"

"I'd like that," replied Astrid.

Once they'd firmed up plans, and their mugs were empty, Astrid left to attend her weekly counseling session. Stepping out into the snow-free university concourse, Hiromi slipped on her facemask and earphones, before striding away with Transatlantic in her ears and a sense of hope in her heart.[22]

19. See Progressive Vinyl, "Transatlantic, *The Whirlwind*"; Dávid Simon, "Transatlantic—The Whirlwind Full."

20. See Pregilenis, "Transatlantic—The Whirlwind: XII"; "Transatlantic—Dancing With Eternal Glory Lyrics."

21. See Williams, "Argument from Desire"; Kreeft, "Desire"; Boethius, *Consolation of Philosophy*; Horner, "Pursuit of Happiness"; Williams, "C. S. Lewis as a Central Figure in Formulating the Theistic Argument from Desire"; Williams, "In Defence of Arguments from Desire"; Bassham, *C. S. Lewis's Christian Apologetics*; Buras and Cantrell, "C.S. Lewis's Argument from Nostalgia"; Kreeft, *Heaven: The Heart's Deepest Desire*; Puckett, *Apologetics of Joy*; Williams, *C. S. Lewis vs. the New Atheists*; Williams, *Case for God*.

22. An extensive list of chapter-specific recommended resources can be found on this book's webpage at www.peterswilliams.com/publications/books/outgrowing-god/.

Selected Resources

NOTE that an extensive list of chapter-specific recommended resources can be found on this book's webpage at www.peterswilliams.com/publications/books/outgrowing-god/.

Peter S. Williams

Outgrowing God? www.peterswilliams.com/publications/books/outgrowing-god/
Website: www.peterswilliams.com
Podcast: http://peterswilliams.podbean.com/?source=pb
YouTube Channel Playlists: www.youtube.com/user/peterswilliamsvid/playlists?view=
    1&flow=grid
Twitter: @Williams_PeterS

Reviews of *Outgrowing God: A Beginner's Guide* by Richard Dawkins

Flynn, Pat. "Richard Dawkins' Philosophical Offences: A Review of 'Outgrowing God.'"
    Word on Fire (blog), December 4, 2019. www.wordonfire.org/resources/blog/
    richard-dawkins-philosophical-offenses-a-review-of-outgrowing-god/25899/.
Hart, David Bentley. "Richard Dawkins Discovers His Ideal Idiom and Audience."
    Church Life Journal, December 19, 2019. https://churchlifejournal.nd.edu/articles/
    richard-dawkins-discovers-his-ideal-idiom-and-audience/#.Xf3PRr4oZ5o.
    twitter.
McLaughlin, Rebecca. "Richard Dawkins's Latest Case for Outgrowing God." *The
    Gospel Coalition*, December 4, 2019. www.thegospelcoalition.org/reviews/
    richard-dawkins-case-outgrowing-god/.
Robertson, David. "Outgrowing Atheism: It's Time for Richard Dawkins to Grow
    Up." *Christianity Today*, September 20, 2019. www.christiantoday.com/article/
    outgrowing-atheism-its-time-for-richard-dawkins-to-grow-up/133263.htm.

Shortt, Rupert. "Idle Components: An Argument against Richard Dawkins." *Times Literary Supplement*, December 13, 2019. www.the-tls.co.uk/articles/idle-components/.

Thompson, Damian. "If Richard Dawkins Loves Facts So Much, Why Can't He Get Them Right?" *The Spectator*, September 21, 2019. https://blogs.spectator.co.uk/2019/09/if-richard-dawkins-loves-facts-so-much-why-cant-he-get-them-right/.

Watch

Williams, Peter S. "Hiromi's Playlist." *YouTube* playlist, n.d., www.youtube.com/playlist?list=PLQhh3qcwVEWgldnKNgFFB3N4OFA-EZ3G5.

———. "Outgrowing God?" *YouTube* playlist, n.d., www.youtube.com/playlist?list=PLQhh3qcwVEWg5ExdpGFj2IRJpBbKvLEXQ.

Websites

BeThinking: www.bethinking.org
Centre for Public Christianity: www.publicchristianity.org
Paul Copan: www.paulcopan.com
Discovery Institute Centre for Science & Culture: www.discovery.org/csc/
William Lane Craig: Reasonable Faith: www.reasonablefaith.org
Centre for Intelligent Design: www.c4id.org.uk/
Gary R. Habermas: www.garyhabermas.com/
Evolutionary Informatics: www.evoinfo.org/
Last Seminary: www.lastseminary.com
Stephen C. Meyer: www.stephencmeyer.org/
Evolution Under the Microscope: https://evolutionunderthemicroscope.com/home.html
Access Research Network: www.arn.org
Evolution News & Views: https://evolutionnews.org
Illustra Media Website: www.youtube.com/user/IllustraMedia

Introductory Books

Bauckham, Richard. *Jesus: A Very Short Introduction*. Oxford: Oxford University Press, 2011.

Campbell, Charlie H. *Archaeological Evidence for the Bible*. Carlsbad, CA: AlwaysBeReady, 2012.

Copan, Paul. *A Little Book for New Philosophers: Why And How To Study Philosophy*. Downers Grove: IVP Academic, 2016.

Craig, William Lane. *On Guard for Students: Defending Your Faith with Reason and Precision*. Colorado Springs: Cook, 2015.

Dickson, John. *Is Jesus History?* Stanmore, NSW: Good Book, 2019.

Edwards, Brian, and Clive Anderson. *Through The British Museum: With the Bible*. Leominster: DayOne, 2015.

Evans, C. Stephen. *Why Believe? Reason and Mystery as Pointers to God.* Grand Rapids: Eerdmans, 1996.

Johnson, Philip E. *Darwin on Trial.* 3rd ed. Downers Grove: InterVarsity, 2010.

Kreeft, Peter. *Between Heaven & Hell: A Dialog Somewhere Beyond Death with John F. Kennedy, C. S. Lewis & Aldous Huxley.* 2nd ed. Downers Grove: InterVarsity, 2008.

May, Peter. *The Search for God and the Path to Persuasion.* United Kingdom: Malcolm Down, 2016.

Moreland, J. P. *The God Question: An Invitation to a Life of Meaning.* Eugene, OR: Harvest, 2009.

Morrow, Jonathan. *Questioning the Bible: 11 Major Challenges to the Bible's Authority.* Chicago: Moody, 2014.

Orr-Ewing, Amy. *Why Trust The Bible? Answers To 10 Tough Questions.* Downers Grove: InterVarsity, 2005.

Pritchard, John. *Why Go to Church? A Little Book of Guidance.* London: SPCK, 2015.

Strobel, Lee. *The Case for Christ.* 2nd ed. Grand Rapids: Zondervan, 2016.

———. *The Case for Miracles.* Grand Rapids: Zondervan, 2018.

———. *In Defence of Jesus.* Grand Rapids: Zondervan, 2016.

Wallace, J. Warner. *Cold Case Christianity: A Homicide Detective Investigates The Claims Of The Gospels.* Colorado Springs: Cook, 2013.

———. *God's Crime Scene: A Cold-Case Detective Examines the Evidence for a Divinely Created Universe.* Colorado Springs: Cook, 2015.

Wright, Tom. *Why Read the Bible?* London: SPCK, 2015.

Zacharias, Ravi. *Can Man Live Without God?* Dallas: Word, 1994.

Intermediate Books

Barnett, Paul. *Messiah: Jesus: The Evidence of History.* Downers Grove: InterVarsity, 2009.

Barrett, Matthew, et al. *Four Views on the Historical Adam.* Grand Rapids: Zondervan, 2013.

Beale, C. K. *The Erosion of Inerrancy in Evangelicalism: Responding to New Challenges to Biblical Authority.* Wheaton, IL: Crossway, 2008.

Beckwith, Francis J., ed. *To Everyone an Answer: A Case for the Christian Worldview.* Downers Grove: InterVarsity, 2004.

Behe, Michael J. *Darwin Devolves: The New Science About DNA That Challenges Evolution.* New York: HarperOne, 2020.

———. *The Edge of Evolution: The Search for the Limits of Darwinism.* New York: Free Press, 2007.

———. *Darwin's Black Box: The Biochemical Challenge to Evolution.* 10th Anniversary Edition. New York: Free Press, 2006.

Beverley, James A., and Craig A. Evans. *Getting Jesus Right: How Muslims Get Jesus and Islam Wrong.* Lagoon City, ON: Castle Quay, 2015.

Bird, Michael F., et al. *How God Became Jesus: The Real Origins of Belief in Jesus' Divine Nature: A Response to Bart D. Ehrman.* Grand Rapids: Zondervan, 2014.

Blomberg, Craig, et al. *Resurrection: Faith or Fact? A Scholars' Debate Between a Skeptic and a Christian.* Durham: Pitchstone, 2019.

Blomberg, Craig L. *The Historical Reliability of the Gospels* 2nd ed. Downers Grove: InterVarsity, 2008.

Bock, Darrell L., and Daniel B. Wallace. *Dethroning Jesus: Exposing Popular Culture's Quest to Unseat the Biblical Christ.* Nashville: Nelson, 2007.

Chapman, Allan. *Slaying The Dragons: Destroying Myths in the History of Science and Faith.* Oxford: Lion, 2013.

Charles, J. Daryl, ed. *Reading Genesis 1–2: An Evangelical Conversation.* Peabody: Hendrickson, 2013.

Copan, Paul. *Contending with Christianity's Critics: Answering New Atheists and Other Objectors.* Edited by Paul Copan and William Lane Craig. Nashville: B. & H. Academic, 2009.

———. *True for You But Not for Me: Overcoming Objections to Christian Faith.* Rev. ed. Minneapolis: Bethany, 2009.

Copan, Paul, ed. *Will the Real Jesus Please Stand Up? A Debate between William Lane Craig and John Dominic Crossan.* Grand Rapids: Baker, 1998.

Copan, Paul, and Paul K. Moser, eds. *The Rationality of Theism.* London: Routledge, 2003.

Cottingham, John. *Why Believe?* New York: Continuum, 2009.

Davis, Craig. *Dating the Old Testament.* New York: RJ Communications, 2007.

Dembski, William A., and Jonathan Wells. *The Design of Life.* Dallas: Foundation for Thought and Ethics, 2008.

Evans, Craig A. *Fabricating Jesus: How Modern Scholars Distort the Gospels.* Downers Grove: InterVarsity, 2007.

———. *Jesus and His World: The Archaeological Evidence.* London: SPCK, 2012.

———. "What Should We Think About the Gospel of Judas?" In *Evidence for God: 50 Arguments for Faith from the Bible, History, Philosophy, and Science,* edited by William A. Dembski and Michael R. Licona, 247–52. Grand Rapids: Baker, 2010.

Geisler, Norman L. *Christian Apologetics.* 2nd ed. Grand Rapids: Baker Academic, 2013.

Geisler, Norman L., and William D. Watkins. *Worlds Apart: A Handbook on World Views.* 2nd ed. Grand Rapids: Baker, 1989.

Geivett, R. Douglas, and Gary R. Habermas, eds. *In Defence of Miracles: A Comprehensive Case for God's Action in History.* Leicester: Apollos, 1997.

Gilson, Tom, and Carson Weitnauer, eds. *True Reason: Confronting the Irrationality of the New Atheism.* Grand Rapids: Kregel, 2013.

Glass, David H. *Atheism's New Clothes: Exploring and Exposing the Claims of the New Atheists.* Nottingham: Apollos, 2012.

Groothuis, Douglas. *Truth Decay: Defending Christianity Against The Challenges Of Postmodernism.* Downers Grove: InterVarsity, 2000.

Halton, Charles, ed. *Genesis: History, Fiction, or Neither? Three Views on the Bible's Earliest Chapters.* Grand Rapids: Zondervan, 2015.

Hannam, James. *The Genesis of Science: How The Christian Middle Ages Launched The Scientific Revolution.* Washington, DC: Regnery, 2011.

Holder, Rodney. *Big Bang, Big God: A Universe Designed for Life?* Oxford: Lion, 2013.

Holmes, Arthur F. *All Truth Is God's Truth.* Downers Grove: InterVarsity, 1979.

Horner, David A. *Mind Your Faith: A Student's Guide to Thinking & Living Well.* Downers Grove: IVP Academic, 2011.

Howard, David M., Jr., and Michael A. Grisanti, eds. *Giving the Sense: Understanding and Using Old Testament Historical Texts.* Nottingham: Apollos, 2003.

Howard, Jeremy Royal, ed. *The Gospels and Acts*. The Holman Apologetics Commentary on the Bible 1. Nashville: Holman, 2013.

Humphreys, Colin. *The Miracles of Exodus*. London: Continuum, 2003.

Hutchinson, Robert J. *Searching for Jesus: New Discoveries in the Quest for Jesus of Nazareth: And How They Confirm the Gospel Accounts*. Nashville: Nelson, 2015.

Kostenberger, Andreas J., and Justin Taylor. *The Final Days of Jesus*. Wheaton: Crossway, 2014.

Kostenberger, Andreas J., et al. *Truth Matters: Confident Faith in a Confusing World*. Nashville: B. & H. Academic, 2014.

Lennox, John C. *God's Undertaker: Has Science Buried God?* 2nd ed. Oxford: Lion, 2009.

Long, V. Philips, et al. *Windows into Old Testament History: Evidence, Argument, and the Crisis of "Biblical Israel."* Grand Rapids: Eerdmans, 2002.

Millard, A. R., and D. J. Wiseman, eds. *Essays On The Patriarchal Narratives*. Downers Grove: InterVarsity, 1980.

Millard, A. R., et al. *Faith, Tradition & History: Old Testament Historiography in Near Eastern Context*. Winona Lake: Eisenbrauns, 1994.

McGrew, Lydia. *Hidden In Plain View: Undesigned Coincidences in the Gospels and Acts*. DeWard, 2017.

Meister, Chad, and James K. Drew Jr., eds. *God and Evil: The Case for God in a World Filled with Pain*. Downers Grove: InterVarsity, 2013.

Meyer, Stephen C. *Darwin's Doubt: The Explosive Origin of Animal Life and the Case for Intelligent Design*. New York: HarperOne, 2013.

———. *Signature in the Cell: DNA and the Evidence for Intelligent Design*. New York: HarperOne, 2009.

Midgley, Mary. *Are You an Illusion?* Durham: Acumen, 2014.

Miller, Troy A., ed. *Jesus: The Final Days*. London: SPCK, 2008.

Moreland, J. P. *The Recalcitrant Imago Dei: Human Persons and the Failure of Naturalism*. London: SCM, 2009.

Moreland, J. P., and Kai Nielsen. *Does God Exist? The Debate Between Theists & Atheists*. Amherst: Prometheus, 1993.

Moreland, J. P., and William Lane Craig. *Philosophical Foundations for a Christian Worldview*. 2nd ed. Downers Grove: InterVarsity, 2017.

Morris, Thomas V. *The Logic of God Incarnate*. Eugene, OR: Wipf & Stock, 2001.

———. *Our Idea of God: An Introduction to Philosophical Theology*. Notre Dame: University of Notre Dame Press, 1991.

Pitre, Brant. *The Case for Jesus: The Biblical and Historical Evidence for Christ*. New York: Image, 2016.

Price, Randall, with H. Wayne House. *Zondervan Handbook of Biblical Archaeology*. Grand Rapids: Zondervan, 2017.

Provine, Iain, et al. *A Biblical History of Israel*. 2nd ed. Louisville: Westminster John Knox, 2015.

Qureshi, Nabeel. *No God but One: Allah or Jesus? A Former Muslim Investigates the Evidence for Islam & Christianity*. Grand Rapids: Zondervan, 2016.

Reynolds, John Mark. *When Athens Met Jerusalem: An Introduction to Classical and Christian Thought*. Downers Grove: IVP Academic, 2009.

Richelle, Matthieu. *The Bible & Archaeology*. Peabody: Hendrickson, 2018.

Swinburne, Richard. *The Resurrection of God Incarnate*. Oxford: Clarendon, 2003.

———. *Was Jesus God?* Oxford: Oxford University Press, 2008.

Ward, Keith. *The Big Questions in Science and Religion*. West Conshohocken, PA: Templeton, 2008.

———. *Is Religion Dangerous?* Oxford: Lion, 2006.

Wilkins, Michael J., and J. P. Moreland, eds. *Jesus Under Fire: Modern Scholarship Reinvents the Historical Jesus*. Grand Rapids: Zondervan, 1995.

Williams, Peter S. *C. S. Lewis vs. the New Atheists*. Milton Keynes: Paternoster, 2013.

———. *A Faithful Guide to Philosophy: A Christian Introduction to the Love of Wisdom*. Eugene, OR: Wipf & Stock, 2019.

———. *Getting at Jesus: A Comprehensive Critique of Neo-Atheist Nonsense About the Jesus of History*. Eugene, OR: Wipf & Stock, 2019.

———. *I Wish I Could Believe in Meaning: A Response to Nihilism*. Southampton: Damaris, 2004.

———. *A Sceptic's Guide to Atheism*. Milton Keynes: Paternoster, 2009.

———. *Understanding Jesus: Five Ways to Spiritual Enlightenment*. Milton Keynes: Paternoster, 2011.

Wright, Tom. *Simply Christian*. London: SPCK, 2006.

Advanced Books

Bauckham, Richard. *Jesus and the Eyewitnesses: The Gospels as Eyewitness Testimony*. 2nd ed. Grand Rapids: Eerdmans, 2017.

Beckwith, Francis J. *David Hume's Argument against Miracles: A Critical Analysis*. Lanham: University Press of America, 1989.

Bock, Darrell L., and Robert L. Webb, eds. *Key Events in the Life of the Historical Jesus: A Collaborative Exploration of Context and Coherence*. Grand Rapids: Eerdmans, 2010.

Burridge, Richard A. *What Are the Gospels? A Comparison with Graeco-Roman Biography*. 2nd ed. Cambridge: Cambridge University Press, 2004.

Charlesworth, James H., ed. *Jesus Research: New Methodologies and Perceptions*. Grand Rapids: Eerdmans, 2014.

Corduan, Winfried. *In The Beginning God: A Fresh Look at the Case for Original Monotheism*. Nashville: B. & H. Academic, 2013.

Craig, William Lane, and J. P. Moreland, eds. *The Blackwell Companion To Natural Theology*. Wiley-Blackwell, 2009.

———. *Naturalism: A Critical Analysis*. London: Routledge, 2001.

Davis, Stephen T. *Christian Philosophical Theology*. Oxford: Oxford University Press, 2016.

———. *Rational Faith: A Philosopher's Defence of Christianity*. Oxford: Lion, 2001.

———. *Risen Indeed: Making Sense of the Resurrection*. London: SPCK, 1993.

Eddy, Paul Rhodes, and Gregory A. Boyd. *The Jesus Legend: A Case for the Reliability of the Synoptic Jesus Tradition*. Grand Rapids: Baker Academic, 2007.

Evans, C. Stephen. *The Historical Christ and the Jesus of Faith: The Incarnational Narrative as History*. Oxford: Clarendon, 2004.

Gordon, Bruce L., and William A. Dembski, eds. *The Nature of Nature: Examining the Role of Naturalism in Science*. Wilmington: ISI, 2011.

Hoffmeier, James K., and Dennis R. Magary, eds. *Do Historical Matters Matter to Faith? A Critical Appraisal of Modern and Postmodern Approaches to Scripture*. Wheaton, IL: Crossway, 2012.

Hoffmeier, James K., et al. *Did I Not Bring Israel Out of Egypt? Biblical, Archaeological, and Egyptological Perspectives on the Exodus Narratives*. Winona Lake: Eisenbrauns, 2016.

Hoffmeier, James K. *Ancient Israel in Sinai: The Evidence of the Authenticity of the Wilderness Tradition*. Oxford: Oxford University Press, 2005.

———. *Israel in Egypt: The Evidence for the Authenticity of the Exodus Tradition*. Oxford: Oxford University Press, 1996.

Kitchen, Kenneth A. *On the Reliability of the Old Testament*. Cambridge: Eerdmans, 2003.

Klinghoffer, David A., ed. *Debating Darwin's Doubt*. Seattle: Discovery Institute, 2015.

———. *Signature Of Controversy: Responses to Critics of Signature in the Cell*. Seattle: Discovery Institute, 2010.

Larmer, Robert A. *The Legitimacy of Miracle*. Lanham: Lexington, 2014.

Licona, Michael R. *The Resurrection of Jesus: A New Historiographical Approach*. Downers Grove: InterVarsity, 2010.

Menuge, Angus. *Agents Under Fire: Materialism and the Rationality of Science*. Lanham: Rowman & Littlefield, 2004.

Miller, Corey, and Paul Gould, eds. *Is Faith in God Reasonable? Debates in Philosophy, Science, and Rhetoric*. London: Routledge, 2014.

Monton, Bradley. *Seeking God in Science: An Atheist Defends Intelligent Design*. Toronto: Broadview, 2009.

Moreland, J. P. *Consciousness and the Existence of God: A Theistic Argument*. London: Routledge, 2009.

———. *Scaling the Secular City: A Defense of Christianity*. Grand Rapids: Baker, 1987.

Murray, Michael J., ed. *Reason for the Hope Within*. Eerdmans, 1999.

Nash, Ronald H. *The Gospel and the Greeks: Did the New Testament Borrow from Pagan Thought?* 2nd ed. Phillipsburg: P. & R., 2003.

Owen, H. P. *Christian Theism: A Study in its Basic Principles*. Edinburgh: T. & T. Clark, 1984.

Plantinga, Alvin. *Warranted Christian Belief*. Oxford: Oxford University Press, 2000.

———. *Where the Conflict Really Lies: Science, Religion, & Naturalism*. Oxford: Oxford University Press, 2011.

Provan, Iain, et al. *A Biblical History of Israel*. 2nd ed. Louisville: Westminster John Knox, 2015.

Sennett, James F., and Douglas Groothuis, eds. *In Defence of Natural Theology: A Post-Humean Assessment*. Downers Grove: InterVarsity, 2005.

Senor, Thomas D. "The Incarnation and the Trinity." In *Reason for the Hope Within*, edited by Michael J. Murray, 238–60. Grand Rapids: Eerdmans, 1999.

Smart, J. J. C., and J. J. Haldane. *Atheism & Theism*. 2nd ed. Cambridge: Blackwell, 2003.

Smith, Mark D. *The Final Days of Jesus: The Thrill of Defeat, the Agony of Victory: A Classical Historian Explores Jesus's Arrest, Trial, and Execution*. Cambridge: Lutterworth, 2018.

Wright, N. T. *The Resurrection of the Son of God*. London: SPCK, 2003.

Bibliography of Referenced Works

2L. "MAGNIFICAT—Nidarosdomens jentekor & TrondheimSolistene." *YouTube*, August 4, 2014. https://youtu.be/Ym4sH9VaHbU.

Abel, David L. *Primordial Prescription: The Most Plaguing Problem of Life Origin Science.* New York: Long View Press—Academic, 2015.

———. "The Universal Plausibility Metric (UPM) & Principle (UPP)." *Theoretical Biology and Medical Modelling* 6.27 (2009). https://tbiomed.biomedcentral.com/articles/10.1186/1742-4682-6-27.

Abel, David L., ed. *The First Gene: The Birth of Programming, Messaging and Formal Control.* New York: Long View Press—Academic, 2011.

Abend, Lisa. "Inside Barcelona's Unfinished Masterpiece" *TIME Magazine*, July 8, 2019. https://time.com/sagrada-familia-barcelona/.

"Abomination." www.studylight.org/dictionaries/wtd/a/abomination.html.

Adler, Mortimer J. *Adler's Philosophical Dictionary.* New York: Scribner's, 1995.

———. *Great Books of the Western World.* Chicago: Encyclopedia Britannica, 1952.

———. "The Technique of Philosophy." http://radicalacademy.org/adler_the philosopher2.html.

Akin, Jimmy. "Who Wrote the Books of Moses?" www.catholic.com/magazine/print-edition/who-wrote-the-books-of-moses.

Alberts, David. "On the Origin of Everything." *The New York Times*, March 23, 2012.

Alexander, Larry, and Michael Moore. "Deontological Ethics." https://plato.stanford.edu/entries/ethics-deontological/.

All Grey Matters. "'Argument from Ignorance' Fallacy—Quick Explanation." *YouTube*, February 25, 2019. https://youtu.be/XaGEjZDgFJo.

"An Evolutionist's Devastating Critique of *Evolutionary Psychology*." www.ukapologetics.net/3evolpsych.html.

Animated Books. "Antigone by Sophocles—Animated Play Summary." *YouTube*, October 22, 2017. https://youtu.be/gnoZmoZbjwg.

Anthropology 101. http://anthrointro.blogspot.com/2008/05/sir-james-frazer-golden-bough.html.

Aquinas, Thomas. *Summa Contra Gentiles, Book One: God.* Translated by Anton C. Pegis. Notre Dame: University of Notre Dame Press, 2005.

Archer, Gleason L., Jr. *Encyclopedia of Bible Difficulties.* Grand Rapids: Zondervan, 1982.

Aristotle. "Aristotle on Non-contradiction." https://plato.stanford.edu/entries/aristotle-noncontradiction/.

Astbury-Ward, Edna. "Emotional and Psychological Impact of Abortion: A Critique of the Literature." *Journal of Family Planning & Reproductive Health Care* 34.3 (2008) 181–84. https://srh.bmj.com/content/familyplanning/34/3/181.full.pdf.

Atkins, Peter. *On Being*. Oxford: Oxford University Press, 2011.

Augustine. "Seventh Homily on 1 John 4:4–12." www.ccel.org/ccel/schaff/npnf107.iv.x.html.

Axe, Douglas. "The Case against a Darwinian Origin of Protein Folds." *BIO-Complexity* 1 (2010) 1–12. https://bio-complexity.org/ojs/index.php/main/article/view/BIO-C.2010.1.

———. "Estimating the Prevalence of Protein Sequences Adopting Functional Enzyme Folds." *Journal Of Molecular Biology* 341.5 (2004) 1295–315.

———. "Extreme Functional Sensitivity to Conservative Amino Acid Changes on Enzyme Exteriors." *Journal of Molecular Biology* 301.3 (2000) 585–95. www.semanticscholar.org/paper/Extreme-functional-sensitivity-to-conservative-acid-Axe/baf1b57fcf6555a5a3feef3d610ae8333471e094.

———. *Undeniable: How Biology Confirms Our Intuition that Life Is Designed*. San Francisco: HarperOne, 2017.

Axe, Douglas D., and Ann K. Guager. "Model and Laboratory Demonstrations that Evolutionary Optimization Works Well Only if Preceded by Invention—Selection Itself Is Not Inventive." *BIO-Complexity* 2 (2015) 1–13. https://bio-complexity.org/ojs/index.php/main/article/viewArticle/BIO-C.2015.2.

Ayoub, George. "On the Design of the Vertebrate Retina." *Origins & Design* 17.1 (1996) www.arn.org/docs/odesign/od171/retina171.htm.

Babymetal. "Babymetal—The One (Official)." *YouTube*, March 26, 2016. https://youtu.be/TZRvOoS-TLU/.

Baggett, David, and Jerry L. Walls. *Good God: The Theistic Foundations Of Morality*. Oxford: Oxford University Press, 2011.

Baggini, Julian. *Atheism: A Very Short Introduction*. Oxford: Oxford University Press, 2003.

Baker, David L. "The Humanisation Of Slavery In Old Testament Law." In *The Humanisation of Slavery in the Old Testament*, edited by Thomas Schirrmacher, 13–20. Eugene, OR: Wipf & Stock, 2018.

Barnes, Luke. "Good God!" https://inference-review.com/article/good-god.

Barnett, Paul. *Paul: Missionary of Jesus*. Vol. 2, *After Jesus*. Grand Rapids: Eerdmans, 2008.

Barrett, Justin. *Why Would Anyone Believe in God?* Lanham: Alta Mira, 2004.

Bassham, Gregory, ed. *C. S. Lewis's Christian Apologetics: Pro and Con*. London: Rodolpi-Brill, 2015.

Bauckham, Richard. *Jesus and the Eyewitnesses: The Gospels as Eyewitness Testimony*. Grand Rapids: Eerdmans, 2017.

Baxster, Gary. "The James Ossuary." www.adefenceofthebible.com/2016/08/01/the-james-ossuary/.

BBC Radio 4. "Aristotle on 'Flourishing.'" *YouTube*, March 30, 2015. www.youtube.com/watch?v=j_7deRoidvs.

Beckwith, Francis J., et al., eds. *The New Mormon Challenge: Responding to the Latest Defenses of a Fast-Growing Movement*. Grand Rapids: Zondervan, 2002.

Begbie, Jeremy. "Hearing God in C Major." *Stillpoint*, Summer 2005. https://www.yumpu.com/en/document/read/22045248/99-10237-sum05-stillpointindd-gordon-college.

Begbie, Jeremy, ed. *Beholding the Glory: Incarnation through the Arts*. Grand Rapids: Baker, 2000.

Behe, Michael J. *Darwin Devolves: The New Science About DNA that Challenges Evolution*. HarperOne, 2019.

———. "Evidence for Intelligent Design from Biochemistry." www.arn.org/docs/behe/mb_idfrombiochemistry.htm.

———. "Experimental Evolution, Loss-of-Function Mutations, And 'The First Rule of Adaptive Evolution,'" *The Quarterly Review of Biology* 85.4 (2010). www.lehigh.edu/~inbios/Faculty/Behe/PDF/QRB_paper.pdf.

———. "Irreducible Complexity: Obstacle to Darwinian Evolution." www.lehigh.edu/~inbios/Faculty/Behe/PDF/Behe_chapter.pdf.

———. "Waiting Longer for Two Mutations." *Genetics* 181.2 (2009) 819–20. www.ncbi.nlm.nih.gov/pmc/articles/PMC2644969/.

Bergen, Peter L. "September 11th Attacks." www.britannica.com/event/September-11-attacks.

Bergman, Jerry. "Inverted Human Eye a Poor Design?" *Perspectives on Science and Christian Faith* 52 (2000). www.asa3.org/ASA/PSCF/2000/PSCF3–00Bergman.html.

———. "The Left Recurrent Laryngeal Nerve Design in Mammals Is Not Poor Design." https://creation.com/recurrent-laryngeal-nerve-design.

———. *Poor Design: An Invalid Argument against Intelligent Design*. Tulsa, OK: BP Books, 2019.

Berlinski, David. *Human Nature*. Discovery Institute, 2019.

Beverley, James A. *Mormon Crisis: Anatomy of a Failing Religion*. N.p.: Castle Quay, 2013.

Beverley, James, and Craig A. Evans. *Getting Jesus Right*. N.p.: Castle Quay, 2015.

Bingham, Molly. "William Wilberforce: A Force for Change." *YouTube*, August 4, 2015. https://youtu.be/ItJrNuzH9i4.

The Biologos Forum. "Did a Global Flood Really Happen? If Not, Why Does the Bible Describe One?" https://discourse.biologos.org/t/did-a-global-flood-really-happen-if-not-why-does-the-bible-describe-one/4835.

Biologos. "Origins Sessions 6: Human Origins and Adam and Eve." *YouTube*, January 22, 2018. www.youtube.com/watch?v=nfNAjohOy9Y.

Bird, Michael F. "Of Gods, Angels and Men." In *How God Became Jesus: The Real Origins of Belief in Jesus' Divine Nature: A Response to Bart Ehrman*, edited by Michael F. Bird et al., 22–40. Zondervan Academic, 2014.

Bird, Michael F., et al. *How God Became Jesus: The Real Origins of Belief in Jesus' Divine Nature: A Response to Bart Ehrman*. Grand Rapids: Zondervan, 2014.

Birdieupon. "Probability & Resurrection 4: Tim McGrew on 'Extraordinary Claims Require Extraordinary Evidence.'" *YouTube*, Feb 24, 2016. https://youtu.be/H7Gv8Fw_fFE.

Bock, Daniel L. "Recovering the Voice of Moses: The Genesis of Deuteronomy." *JETS* 44.3 (September 2001). https://www.etsjets.org/files/JETS-PDFs/44/44-3/44-3-PP385-408_JETS.pdf.

Boethius, Anicius Manlius Severinus. *The Consolation of Philosophy*. Translated by David R. Slavitt. Harvard: Harvard University Press, 2008.

Bogomolny, Alexander. "Pythagorean Theorem and Its Many Proofs." www.cut-the-knot.org/pythagoras.

Borschel-Dan, Amanda. "High-tech Study of Ancient Stone Suggests New Proof of King David's Dynasty." *The Times of Israel*, May 3, 2019. www.timesofisrael.com/high-tech-study-of-ancient-stone-keeps-davidic-dynasty-in-disputed-inscription/.

"Brief History of Medicine in Japan." https://www.thepharmaletter.com/article/brief-history-of-medicine-in-japan.

Brockman, John, ed. *What Is Your Dangerous Idea? Today's Leading Thinkers on the Unthinkable*. London: Pocket, 2006.

Brooks, James A. *The New American Commentary: Mark*. Nashville: Broadman, 1991.

Bugnion, François. "Geneva and the Red Cross." www.icrc.org/en/doc/assets/files/other/geneve_et_croix_rouge_anglais.pdf.

Buller, David J. *Adapting Minds: Evolutionary Psychology and the Persistent Quest for Human Nature*. Cambridge: MIT Press, 2005.

———. "Evolutionary Psychology." http://host.uniroma3.it/progetti/kant/field/ep.htm.

Buras, Todd, and Michael Cantrell. "C.S. Lewis's Argument from Nostalgia: A New Argument from Desire." In *Two Dozen (Or So) Arguments for God: The Plantinga Project*, edited by Jerry L. Walls and Trent Dougherty, 356–71. Oxford: Oxford University Press, 2018.

Butt, Kyle. "Gladiators and Christianity Clash." *Discovery Magazine*, October 1, 2010. www.apologeticspress.org/apPubPage.aspx?pub=2&issue=946&article=1428.

Calvary Church with Skip Heitzig. "Amazing Grace: Lessons from the Life of William Wilberforce—Eric Metaxas." YouTube, January 20, 2020. https://www.youtube.com/watch?v=njLUCmtLQpY&feature=youtu.be.

Calvin, Melvin. *Chemical Evolution*. Oxford: Clarendon, 1969.

Carr, Bernard, ed. *Universe or Multiverse?* Cambridge: Cambridge University Press, 2007.

Carrier, Richard. *Sense and Goodness without God*. Bloomington, IN: Author House, 2005.

Carson, Thomas L., and Paul K. Moser. "Introduction." In *Moral Relativism: A Reader*, 1–24. Oxford University Press, 2001.

Carty, Pat. "Book Review: Richard Dawkins, *Outgrowing God*." *Hot Press*, October 14, 2019. www.hotpress.com/culture/book-review-richard-dawkins-outgrowing-god-22791775.

Caruso, Gregg D., ed. *Science & Religion: 5 Questions*. N.p.: Automatic, 2014.

Cassin, René. "Making the Jewish Case for Human Rights—Monsieur René Cassin." www.renecassin.org/making-the-jewish-case-monsieur-rene-cassin/.

Cataphatism. "Law of Non-Contradiction." *YouTube*, March 28, 2018. https://youtu.be/JWVzHOhGSCo.

CathyduProgSud. "Yuke and the Chronoship 2." *YouTube*, May 18, 2013. https://www.youtube.com/watch?v=_qAipFEnhTw.

———. "Yuke and the Chronoship 3." *YouTube*, May 19, 2013. https://www.youtube.com/watch?v=3I-b7K-p7aE

Cave, Peter. *Humanism*. Oxford: OneWorld, 2009.

CBN—The Christian Broadcasting Network. "Perfect for a Palace: Find Testifies to David's Royalty." *YouTube*, Jun 7, 2013. www.youtube.com/watch?v=pN6Tl8ea_IQ.

Chamberlain, Paul. *Can We Be Good without God? A Conversation about Truth, Morality, Culture & a Few Other Things that Matter.* Downers Grove: InterVarsity, 1996.

Channel 4 News. "Richard Dawkins on Scientific Truth, Outgrowing God and Life beyond Earth." *YouTube*, August 28, 2019. https://youtu.be/RKjiSu4zD5Y.

Charles, J. Daryl, ed. *Reading Genesis 1–2: An Evangelical Conversation.* Peabody: Hendrickson, 2013.

"Cherry Picking." www.logicallyfallacious.com/logicalfallacies/Cherry-Picking.

Chown, Marcus. "In The Beginning." *New Scientist*, December 1, 2012.

Christian Concern. "The Faith of William Wilberforce | Dr Joe Boot." *YouTube*, February 23, 2017. https://www.youtube.com/watch?v=lHJ55xly5pI&feature=youtu.be.

Cicero. *Cicero in Twenty-Eight Volumes.* Vol. 19, *De Natura Deorum Academica, With An English Translation By H. Rackham.* Cambridge: Harvard University Press, 1967. https://ryanfb.github.io/loebolus-data/L268.pdf.

Cline, Eric. *Biblical Archaeology: A Very Short Introduction.* Oxford University Press, 2009.

Cole, Alan. *Tyndale Old Testament Commentaries: Exodus.* Downers Grove: InterVarsity, 1973.

Coleson, Joseph. *Genesis: A Commentary in the Wesleyan Tradition.* Kansas City: Beacon Hill, 2012.

Collins, Robin. "God, Design, and Fine-Tuning." http://citeseerx.ist.psu.edu/viewdoc/download?doi=10.1.1.470.7166&rep=rep1&type=pdf.

Cooper, David E., ed. *Ethics: The Classic Readings.* Oxford: Blackwell, 1998.

Copan, Paul. "Are Old Testament Laws Evil?" In *God Is Great, God Is Good: Why Believing in God Is Reasonable and Responsible*, edited by William Lane Craig and Chad Meister, 134–54. Downers Grove: InterVarsity, 2009.

———. "Does Religion Originate in the Brain?" www.equip.org/article/does-religion-originate-in-the-brain/.

———. *Is God a Moral Monster? Making Sense of the Old Testament God.* Grand Rapids: Baker, 2011.

———. "Is the Trinity a Logical Blunder? God as Three-in-One." www.paulcopan.com/articles/pdf/is-the-Trinity-a-logical-blunder_God-as-three-and-one.pdf.

———. "Is Yahweh a Moral Monster? The New Atheists and Old Testament Ethics." www.epsociety.org/library/articles.asp?pid=45.

———. "Learn How (Not) To Doubt." www.thegospelcoalition.org/article/learn-how-not-to-doubt/.

———. *True for You, But Not for Me: Overcoming Objections To Christian Faith.* Rev. ed. Minneapolis: Bethany, 2009.

———. *When God Goes To Starbucks: A Guide to Everyday Apologetics.* Grand Rapids: Baker, 2008.

———. "Yahweh Wars and the Canaanites: Divinely-Mandated Genocide or Corporate Capital Punishment?" www.epsociety.org/library/articles.asp?pid=63.

Copan, Paul, and Douglas Jacoby. *Origins: The Ancient Impact and Modern Implications of Genesis 1–11.* Nashville: Morgan James, 2019.

Copan, Paul, and William Lane Craig. *Creation Out of Nothing.* Grand Rapids: Baker, 2004.

Copan, Paul, with William Lane Craig, eds. *The Kalam Cosmological Argument.* Vol. 1, *Philosophical Arguments for the Finitude of the Past.* New York: Bloomsbury Academic, 2017.

Corduan, Winfried. *In the Beginning God: A Fresh Look at the Case for Original Monotheism.* Nashville: B&H, 2013.

Corrinne May. "In the Bleak Midwinter—Performed by Corrinne May." *YouTube,* December 25, 2007. https://youtu.be/ZC9C5kHL884.

Couch, Steve. *Matrix Revelations.* Southampton: Damaris, 2003.

Coyne, Jerry A. *Faith versus Fact: Why Science and Religion Are Incompatible.* New York: Penguin, 2015.

Craig, William Lane. "Christians Give MORE to Charity than Atheists." *YouTube,* August 23, 2009. www.youtube.com/watch?v=imuaiRO5mSQ.

———. "The Concept of God in Islam and Christianity." www.reasonablefaith.org/concept-of-god-in-islam-and-christianity.

———. "Contemporary Scholarship and the Historical Resurrection of Jesus Christ." *Truth* 1 (1985) 89–95. https://appearedtoblogly.files.wordpress.com/2011/05/craig-william-lane-22contemporary-scholarship-and-the-historical-evidence-for-the-resurrection-of-jesus-christ22.pdf.

———. "Dawkins' Delusion." In *True Reason: Confronting the Irrationality of the New Atheism,* edited by Tom Gilson and Carson Weitnauer, 37–41. Grand Rapids: Kregel, 2013.

———. "Fabric of the Cosmos (Part 3)." www.reasonablefaith.org/media/reasonable-faith-podcast/fabric-of-the-cosmos-part-3/.

———. "Fine Tuned Universe." www.reasonablefaith.org/writings/question-answer/fine-tuned-universe/.

———. "A Formulation and Defence of the Doctrine of the Trinity." www.reasonablefaith.org/writings/scholarly-writings/christian-doctrines/a-formulation-and-defense-of-the-doctrine-of-the-trinity/.

———. *God? A Debate between a Christian and an Atheist.* Oxford: Oxford University Press, 2004.

———. *God, Are You There? Five Reasons God Exists and Three Reasons It Makes a Difference.* Norcross: RZIM, 1999.

———. "Is the Oral Tradition Comparable to the Telephone Game?" *YouTube,* November 20, 2015. https://youtu.be/VKudgsPT6No.

———. *Reasonable Faith.* 3rd ed. Wheaton, IL: Crossway, 2008.

———. "The Slaughter of the Canaanites Revisited." www.reasonablefaith.org/writings/question-answer/the-slaughter-of-the-canaanites-re-visited/.

———. "The Viability of Intelligent Design 3/3." *YouTube,* Nov 6, 2009. https://youtu.be/uIzdieauxZg.

———. "Vilenkin's Cosmic Vision: A Review Essay of Many Worlds in One: The Search for Other Universes, by Alex Vilenkin." *Philosophia Christi* 11 (2009) 231–38.

———. "Who Is the Real Jesus: The Jesus of the Bible or the Jesus of the Qur'an?" www.reasonablefaith.org/who-is-the-real-jesus-the-jesus-of-the-bible-or-the-jesus-of-the-quran.

Craig, William Lane, and Quentin Smith. *Theism, Atheism and Big Bang Cosmology.* Oxford: Clarendon, 1993.

Craven, Michael. "The Christian Conquest of Pagan Rome." *Crosswalk* (blog), November 8, 2010. www.crosswalk.com/blogs/michael-craven/the-christian-conquest-of-pagan-rome-11640691.html

Crisp, Oliver, ed. *A Reader in Contemporary Philosophical Theology*. London: T. & T. Clark, 2009.

Crisp, Roger, and Michael Slote. "Introduction." In *Virtue Ethics*, edited by Roger Crisp and Michael Slote, 1–25. Oxford University Press, 1997.

Crofton, Ian. *Big Ideas in Brief: 200 World-Changing Concepts Explained in an Instant.* London: Quercus, 2011.

Crossley, James. "Against the Historical Plausibility of the Empty Tomb Story and the Bodily Resurrection of Jesus: A Response to N.T. Wright." *Journal for the Study of the Historical Jesus* 3.2 (2005) 171–86.

———. *The Date of Mark's Gospel: Insight from the Law in Earliest Christianity*. London: T. & T. Clark, 2004.

Croucher, Tom. *Adam: The First Human? A Fresh Interpretation of Human Origins from Biblical and Ex-biblical Sources—and Why It Still Matters*. Menangle: Albatross, 2019.

Darwin, Charles. "Recapitulation and Conclusion." In *The Origin of Species*, 346–69. Ware, Hertfordshire: Wordsworth Editions, 1998.

Davidman, Joy. *Smoke on the Mountain: An Interpretation of the Ten Commandments*. Philadelphia: Westminster, 1954.

Dávid Simon. "Transatlantic—The Whirlwind Full (Live From Shepherd's Bush Empire, London)." *YouTube*, September 4, 2011. https://youtu.be/TWC2I9TNuco.

Davies, Paul. "The Birth of the Cosmos." In *God, Cosmos, Nature and Creativity*, edited by P. C. W. Davies and Jill Gready, 1–28. Edinburgh: Scottish Academic Press, 1995.

———. *The Cosmic Blueprint: New Discoveries In Natures Ability To Order Universe*. New York: Simon & Schuster, 1988.

Davies, Peter. *The Fifth Miracle: The Search for the Origin of Life*. London: Penguin, 1999.

Davies, Brian, ed. *Philosophy of Religion: A Guide and Anthology*. Oxford: Oxford University Press, 2000.

Davis, Stephen T. *Christian Philosophical Theology*. New York: Oxford, 2006.

———. *The Fifth Miracle: The Search for the Origin of Life*. London: Penguin, 1999.

———. *The Goldilocks Enigma: Why Is the Universe Just Right for Life?* London: Penguin, 2007.

———. *Risen Indeed*. Grand Rapids: Eerdmans, 1993.

———. "Should We Believe the Jesus Seminar?" In *Disputed Issues: Contending for Christian Faith in Today's Academic Setting*, 7–16. Waco, TX: Baylor University Press, 2009.

Davis, Thomas W. "Exodus on the Ground: The Elusive Signature of Nomads in Sinai." In *Did I Not Bring Israel Out of Egypt? Biblical, Archaeological, and Egyptological Perspectives on the Exodus Narratives*, edited by James Hoffmeier et al., 223–39. Winona Lake: Eisenbrauns, 2016.

Dawkins, Richard. *The Blind Watchmaker*. London: Penguin, 1986.

———. "Features Interview: I Want to Break the Cycle, not Indoctrinate." *New Scientist*, September 21, 2019.

———. "God's Utility Function." *Scientific American*, November 1995.

————. *The Magic of Reality: How We Know What's Really True.* London: Bantam, 2011.

————. *Outgrowing God.* London: Bantam, 2019.

————. *River Out of Eden.* New York: Basic, 1995.

————. "Who Owns the Argument from Improbability?" *Free Inquiry* 24.6 (2004) 11–12.

De Cruz, Helen. "Thoughts on Evolutionary Debunking Arguments Against Religious Belief." *New APPS* (blog), September 25, 2012. www.newappsblog.com/2012/09/thoughts-on-evolutionary-debunking-arguments-against-religious-belief.html.

Deem, Rich. "Why the Bible Says Noah's Flood Must Be Local." www.hope-of-israel.org/localflood.html.

Dell, Katherine. *Who Needs the Old Testament? Its Enduring Appeal and Why the New Atheists Don't Get It.* London: SPCK, 2017.

Dembski, William A. *The Design Revolution.* Downers Grove: InterVarsity, 2004.

————. "Irreducible Complexity Revisited." www.designinference.com/documents/2004.01.Irred_Compl_Revisited.pdf.

————. *No Free Lunch: Why Specified Complexity Cannot Be Purchased without Intelligence.* Lanham: Rowman & Littlefield, 2002.

————. "Reinstating Design within Science." In *Unapologetic Apologetics*, edited by William A. Dembski and Jay Wesley Richards, 239–73. Downers Grove: InterVarsity, 2001.

————. "Specification: The Pattern That Signifies Intelligence." https://billdembski.com/documents/2005.06.Specification.pdf.

Dembski, William A., and Jonathan Wells. *The Design of Life: Discovering Signs of Intelligence in Biological Systems.* Dallas: Foundation for Thought and Ethics, 2008.

Dembski, William A., and Jonathan Witt. *Intelligent Design Uncensored: An Easy-to-Understand Guide to the Controversy.* Downers Grove: InterVarsity, 2010.

Dembski, William A., and Michael R. Licona, eds. *Evidence for God: 50 Arguments for Faith from the Bible, History, Philosophy, and Science.* Grand Rapids: Baker, 2010.

Dennett, Daniel C. "The Leibnizian Paradigm." In *The Philosophy of Biology*, edited by David L. Hull and Michael Ruse, 38–51. Oxford: Oxford University Press, 1998.

Dennett, Daniel, and Richard Swinburne. "How Should We Study Religion?" *Prospect Magazine*, March 22, 2006. www.prospectmagazine.co.uk/magazine/howshouldwestudyreligion.

Denton, Michael J. *Evolution: A Theory in Crisis.* Bethesda, MD: Adler & Adler, 1985.

————. "The Inverted Retina: Maladaptation or Pre-adaptation?" *Origins & Design* 19.2 (1999). www.arn.org/docs/odesign/od192/invertedretina192.htm.

"Deucalion." www.britannica.com/topic/Deucalion.

DeWeese, Garret J. *Doing Philosophy as a Christian.* Downers Grove: InterVarsity, 2011.

Dickson, John. *Is Jesus History?* Stanmore, NSW: Good Book, 2019.

Dierker, Benjamin R. "Why One-Third Of Biologists Now Question Darwinism." *The Federalist*, April 16, 2019. https://thefederalist.com/2019/04/16/one-third-biologists-now-question-darwinism/.

Discovery Institute. "Biologist Douglas Axe on Evolution's Ability to Produce New Functions." *YouTube*, Oct 15, 2012. https://youtu.be/8ZiLsXO-dYo.

Discovery Science. "Be Grateful for the Intelligent Design of Your Eyes." *YouTube*, November 20, 2017. https://youtu.be/kboUBQnMP8w.

———. "Michael Behe Exposes How Mutations Fail To Invent (Science Uprising EP6)." *YouTube*, Jul 8, 2019. https://www.youtube.com/watch?v=_ivgQFIST1g&feature=youtu.be.

———. "Three Big Ways Christianity Supported the Rise of Modern Science Explained by Historian Michael Keas." *YouTube*, March 13, 2020. https://www.youtube.com/watch?v=HHcF-ffKkeg.

Doidge, Norman. "Foreword." In *12 Rules for Life: An Antidote to Chaos*, by Jordan B. Peterson, vii–xxiv. London: Penguin, 2018.

Dogan, Lena. "Nidaros Cathedral 4K." YouTube, September 18, 2015. https://youtu.be/YlstH8wgQkY.

"Double Standard." www.logicallyfallacious.com/logicalfallacies/Double-Standard.

Dowden, Bradley. "Fallacies: Ad Hoc Rescue." www.iep.utm.edu/fallacy/#AdHocRescue.

———. "Fallacies: Appeal to Authority." www.iep.utm.edu/fallacy/#AppealtoAuthority.

———. "Fallacies: Equivocation." https://www.iep.utm.edu/fallacy/#Equivocation.

———. "Fallacies: Genetic." www.iep.utm.edu/fallacy/#Genetic.

Downes, Stephen M. "Evolutionary Psychology." http://plato.stanford.edu/archives/sum2014/entries/evolutionary-psychology/.

Drcraigvideos. "The Genetic Fallacy (William Lane Craig)." *YouTube*, October 29, 2011. www.youtube.com/watch?v=yv8L57GAVQo.

———. "The Ontological Argument." *YouTube*, August 16, 2016. https://youtu.be/xBmAKCvWl74.

———. "What Is a Boltzmann Brain?" *YouTube*, May 24, 2014. https://youtu.be/xkLWhrXDuXo.

Driver, Julia. "The History of Utilitarianism." https://plato.stanford.edu/entries/utilitarianism-history/.

Duan, Noël. "Dudes, Why Aren't You Knitting?" https://qz.com/quartzy/1154260/dudes-why-arent-you-knitting/.

Dunn, James D. G. "Social Memory and the Oral Jesus Tradition." In *Memory in the Bible and Antiquity*, edited by Stephen C. Barton et al., 179–94. Tübingen, Germany: Mohr Siebeck, 2007.

Earls, Aaron. "Christian Persecution Worsens Around The World." *Facts & Trends*, January 17, 2019. https://factsandtrends.net/2019/01/17/christian-persecution-worsens-around-the-globe/.

"The Elie Wiesel Foundation for Humanity: Nobel Laureates Initiative." https://web.archive.org/web/20061209120655/http://media.ljworld.com/pdf/2005/09/15/nobel_letter.pdf.

Ellis, George. "Multiverses: Description, Uniqueness, Testing." In *Universe or Multiverse?*, edited by Bernard Carr, 387–409. Cambridge: Cambridge University Press, 2007.

Evans, C. Stephen. *Pocket Dictionary of Apologetics & Philosophy of Religion.* Leicester: InterVarsity, 2002.

———. *Why Believe? Reason and Mystery as Pointers to God.* Rev. ed. Leicester: InterVarsity, 1996.

Evans-Grubbs, Judith. "Infant Exposure and Infanticide." In *Oxford Handbook of Childhood and Education in the Classical World*, edited by Judith Evans Grubbs et al., 83–109. Oxford: Oxford University Press, 2013.

Evelyn-White, Hugh G., trans. "The Theogany of Hesiod." www.sacred-texts.com/cla/hesiod/theogony.htm.

Evolution News. "Biology Journal: Evolutionary Psychology Is 'Impossible.'" https://evolutionnews.org/2020/05/biology-journal-evolutionary-psychology-is-impossible/.

"The Faith of a First Lady." *TruBlog*, December 6, 2017. www.trumanlibraryinstitute.org/faith-first-lady-eleanor-roosevelts-spirituality/.

Faust, Avraham, and Yair Sapir. "The 'Governor's Residency' at Tel 'Eton, The United Monarchy, and the Impact of the Old-House Effect on Large-Scale Archaeological Reconstructions." *Radiocarbon* 60.3 (June 2018) 801–20. https://www.cambridge.org/core/services/aop-cambridge-core/content/view/5CE54AE6CEE838CC0D076186A2FBACE5/S0033822218000103a.pdf/governors_residency_at_tel_eton_the_united_monarchy_and_the_impact_of_the_oldhouse_effect_on_largescale_archaeological_reconstructions.pdf.

Ferrer, David. "15 Logical Fallacies You Should Know before Getting into a Debate." *The Best Schools Magazine*, June 9, 2020. https://thebestschools.org/magazine/15-logical-fallacies-know/.

Finlay, Graeme, et al. *Debating Darwin: Two Debates: Is Darwinism True & Does it Matter?* Milton Keynes: Paternoster, 2009.

Fischer, Richard James. *Historical Genesis: From Adam To Abraham.* Lanham: University Press of America, 2008.

Flannagan, Matthew. "Did God Command the Genocide of the Canaanites?" In *True Reason: Confronting the Irrationality of the New Atheism*, edited by Tom Gilson and Carson Weitnauer, 255–86. Grand Rapids: Kregel, 2013.

"Flash Gordon." https://en.wikipedia.org/wiki/Flash_Gordon_(film).

Flew, Antony. "Professor Antony Flew Reviews *The God Delusion*." www.bethinking.org/atheism/professor-antony-flew-reviews-the-god-delusion.

Flick, Stephen. "The Christian Origin of the Red Cross." https://christianheritagefellowship.com/the-christian-origin-of-the-red-cross.

FOCLOnline. "Deconstructing Dawkins' Defense—Peter S Williams." *YouTube*, July 19, 2018. https://youtu.be/92v-mQjq9FY.

———. "How Does Dawkins Fail to Refute the Evidence for Design?" *YouTube*, July 19, 2018. https://youtu.be/LJuYT1jFIBc.

Fodor, Jerry. "Why Pigs Don't Have Wings." *London Review of Books* 29.20 (2007) 19–22. https://www.lrb.co.uk/the-paper/v29/n20/jerry-fodor/why-pigs-don-t-have-wings#:~:text=But%20it%20would%20be%20difficult,just%20not%20built%20that%20way.

Fodor, Jerry, and Massimo Piatelli-Palmarini. *What Darwin Got Wrong.* London: Profile, 2011.

Foner, Eric. "Was Abraham Lincoln a Racist." *Los Angeles Times*, April 9, 2000. www.latimes.com/archives/la-xpm-2000-apr-09-bk-17473-story.html.

Food52. "Norwegian Butter Cookies (Serinakaker)." *YouTube*, December 23, 2017. https://www.youtube.com/watch?v=gOtCfoxxNh4&feature=youtu.be.

Forster, Roger, and Paul Marston. *Reason, Science & Faith.* Crowborough: Monarch, 1999.

Forye. "Mozart: Concerto for Piano and Orchestra (D-minor) K.466, Uchida." *YouTube*, November 11, 2012. https://www.youtube.com/watch?v=yM8CFR01KwQ.

Franciscan University of Steubenville. "Dr. Martha Shuping: Women's Mental Health and Abortion." *YouTube*, Jul 10, 2014. www.youtube.com/watch?v=Co7Cdo_budg.

————. "Priscilla Coleman, PhD, MA: Abortion vs. Childbirth: Psychological Morbidity and Mortality." *YouTube*, June 19, 2015. https://www.youtube.com/watch?v=tHVSJvpg7oc.

Franze, K., et al. "Müller Cells Are Living Optical Fibers in the Vertebrate Retina." *Proceedings of the National Academy of Sciences USA* 104 (2007) 4319.

Freedman, Binny. "Portion of Vayera." *Small Tastings of Torah, Spirituality, and Judaism from Rabbi Binny Freedman* (blog), October 25, 2018. http://www.isralight.org/small-tastings-torah-judaism-spirituality-rav-binny-freedman-portion-vayera-3/.

Fudge, Edward William. *The Fire that Consumes: A Biblical and Historical Study of the Doctrine of Final Punishment.* 3rd ed. Eugene, OR: Cascade, 2011.

Gainor, J. "False Dilemma/either-or Discussion." *YouTube*, September 19, 2013. www.youtube.com/watch?v=dDT8oPvLWgY.

Ganssle, Gregory E. *A Reasonable God: Engaging the New Face of Atheism.* Waco: Baylor University Press, 2009.

Garfinkel, Yosef, et al. *In the Footsteps of King David: Revelations from a Biblical City.* London: Thames & Hudson, 2018.

Garrett, Duane A. "Type, Typology." www.biblestudytools.com/dictionaries/bakers-evangelical-dictionary/type-typology.html.

Gauger, Ann. "Teleonomy and Evolution." *Evolutionary News and Science Today*, December 1, 2017. https://evolutionnews.org/2017/12/teleonomy-and-evolution/.

Gauger, Ann, et al. *Science & Human Origins.* N.p.: Discovery Institute, 2012.

Geisler, Norman L. *Christian Apologetics.* 2nd ed. Grand Rapids: Baker Academic, 2013.

————. *Options in Contemporary Christian Ethics.* Grand Rapids: Baker, 1981.

Geisler, Norman L., and Thomas Howe. *The Big Book of Bible Difficulties: Clear and Concise Answers from Genesis to Revelation.* Grand Rapids: Baker, 2008.

————. "Ezekiel 18:20—Does God Ever Punish One Person for Another's Sin?" https://defendinginerrancy.com/bible-solutions/Ezekiel_18.20.php.

Geisler, Norman L., and William D. Watkins. *Worlds Apart: A Handbook On Worldviews.* 2nd ed. Grand Rapids: Baker, 1989.

Geivett, Douglas, and Brendan Sweetman, eds. *Contemporary Perspectives on Religious Epistemology.* Oxford: Oxford University Press, 1992.

Gelernter, David. "Giving Up Darwin: A Fond Farewell to a Brilliant and Beautiful Theory." https://claremontreviewofbooks.com/giving-up-darwin/.

Gellman, Jerome I. *Experience of God and the Rationality of Theistic Belief.* Ithaca: Cornell University Press, 1997.

"Geneva Convention." www.history.com/topics/world-war-ii/geneva-convention.

Ghose, Tia. "Stranger Things: How Realistic Are Parallel Worlds?" *LiveScience*, August 2016.

Gichon, Mordechai. *Battles of the Bible.* London: Amber, 2008.

Gladwell, Malcolm. *David & Goliath: Underdogs, Misfits and the Art of Battling Giants.* London: Lane, 2013.

Glancey, Jonathan. "Gaudi's la Sagrada Família: Genius or Folly?" *BBC*, October 21, 2014. www.bbc.com/culture/story/20141014-gaudi-unfinished-business.

Glass, David H. *Atheism's New Clothes: Exploring and Exposing the Claims of the New Atheists.* Nottingham: Apollos, 2012.

Glover, Jonathan. "Ethics and Humanity." www.jonathanglover.org/ethics-and-humanity/ethics-and-humanity.

Godnewevidence. "Jesus, the Gospels, and the Telephone Game." *YouTube*, May 30, 2013. https://youtu.be/-PZEYfLxtsM.

Goetz, Stewart, and Charles Taliaferro. *Naturalism*. Grand Rapids: Eerdmans, 2008.

Goldberg, Gary J. "The Coincidences of the Emmaus Narrative of Luke and the Testimonium of Josephus." *The Journal for the Study of the Pseudepigrapha* 13 (1995) 59–77. www.josephus.org/GoldbergJosephusLuke1995.pdf.

Gooblar, David. "What Is 'Indoctrination'? And How Do We Avoid It in Class?" *The Chronicle of Higher Education*, February 19, 2019. www.chronicle.com/article/What-Is-Indoctrination-/245729.

Goodman, Eleanor. "Babymetal: A New Dawn for the Kawaii-metal Pioneers." *Metal Hammer*, December 18, 2019. www.loudersound.com/features/babymetal-a-new-dawn-for-the-kawaii-metal-pioneers.

Gordan, Mike, and Chris Wilkinson, eds. *Conversations on Religion*. London: Continuum, 2008.

Gordon, Bruce L. "Balloons on a String: A Critique of Multiverse Cosmology." In *The Nature of Nature: Examining the Role of Naturalism in Science*, edited by Bruce L. Gordon and William A. Dembski, 569–70. Wilmington, DE: ISI, 2011.

Gordon, Bruce L., and William A. Dembski, eds. *The Nature of Nature: Examining the Role of Naturalism in Science*. Wilmington, DE: ISI, 2011.

Gould, Paul M., and Courtney McLean. *A Primer on Cultural Apologetics: Conversations on Faith and Flourishing in a Disenchanted World*. N.p.: Two Tasks, 2019.

Gould, Stephen Jay. "More Things in Heaven and Earth." In *Alas Poor Darwin*, edited by Hilary Rose and Steve Rose, 85–105. London: Vintage, 2001.

Grant, Bob. "Should Evolutionary Theory Evolve?" *The Scientist Magazine*, December 31, 2009. www.the-scientist.com/uncategorized/should-evolutionary-theory-evolve-43651.

Grant, Edward. *A History Of Natural Philosophy: From the Ancient World to the Nineteenth Century*. Cambridge: Cambridge University Press, 2007.

Gready, Jill, ed. *God, Cosmos, Nature, and Creativity*. Edinburgh: Scottish Academic, 1995.

Greene, Brian. "The Multiverse." In *What's Your Dangerous Idea?: Today's Leading Thinkers on the Unthinkable*, edited by John Brockman, 120–21. London: Pocket Books, 2006.

Green, Joel B., and Mark D. Baker. *Recovering the Scandal of the Cross: Atonement In New Testament and Contemporary Contexts*. Carlisle: Paternoster, 2000.

Green, Michael. *The Books the Church Suppressed: What the Da Vinci Code Doesn't Tell You*. Oxford: Monarch, 2005.

Grossman, Lisa. "Death of the Eternal Cosmos." *New Scientist*, January 14, 2012.

Guager, Ann. "Science and Human Origins." In *Science & Human Origins*, by Ann Guager et al., 15–30. Seattle: Discovery Institute, 2012.

Guager, Ann K., and Douglas D. Axe. "The Evolutionary Accessibility of New Enzyme Functions: A Case Study from the Biotin Pathway." *BIO-Complexity* 1 (2011) 1–17. www.researchgate.net/publication/272177811_The_Evolutionary_Accessibility_of_New_Enzymes_Functions_A_Case_Study_from_the_Biotin_Pathway.

Guinness, Os. *Time for Truth: Living Free In a World Of Lies, Hype & Spin*. Downers Grove: InterVarsity, 2000

Habermas, Gary R. "Did Jesus Exist?" www.bethinking.org/jesus/did-jesus-exist.

————. "Tracing Jesus' Resurrection to Its Earliest Eyewitness Accounts." In *God is Great, God is Good: Why Believing in God is Reasonable and Responsible*, edited by William Lane Craig and Chad Meister, 202–16. Downers Grove: InterVarsity, 2009.

Hahn, Scott, and Curtis Mitch. *Ignatius Catholic Study Bible: Exodus*. San Francisco: Ignatius, 2012.

Halton, Charles, ed. *Genesis: History, Fiction, or Neither? Three Views On The Bible's Earliest Chapters*. Grand Rapids: Zondervan, 2015.

Hamilton, Jim. "The Virgin Will Conceive: Typology in Isaiah and Fulfilment in Matthew, the Use of Isaiah 7:14 in Mathew 1:18–23." http://beginningwithmoses. org/oldsite/articles/thevirginwillconceive.pdf.

Hannam, James. "A Historical Introduction to the Christ Myth," http://jameshannam. com/christmyth.htm.

Hansen, Hans. "Fallacies." https://plato.stanford.edu/entries/fallacies.

Hardin, Jimmy. "Discovery of Official Clay Seals Support Existence of Biblical Kings David and Solomon, Archaeologists Say." *Science Daily*, December 16, 2014. www. sciencedaily.com/releases/2014/12/141216100433.htm.

Harding, Tim. "Argument from Authority." https://yandoo.wordpress.com/2013/06/23/ argument-from-authority/.

Harman, Gilbert. "Moral Relativism." In *Moral Relativism and Moral Objectivity*, Gilbert Harman and Mel Thomson, 3–64. Oxford: Blackwell, 1995.

Hasel, Manfred Görg. "Israel in the Merneptah Stela." *Bulletin of the American Schools of Oriental Research* 296 (1994) 45–61.

Hasker, William. "Deception and Trinity: A Rejoinder to Tuggy." *Religious Studies* 47.1 (2011) 117–20. www.researchgate.net/publication/231928302_Deception_and_ the_Trinity_A_rejoinder_to_Tuggy.

Hawking, Stephen, and Leonard Mlodinow. *The Grand Design: New Answers to the Ultimate Questions of Life*. London: Bantam, 2010.

Hebblethwaite, Brian. *The Essence of Christianity: A Fresh Look at the Nicene Creed*. London: SPCK, 1996.

————. *Philosophical Theology and Christian Doctrine*. Oxford: Blackwell, 2005.

Heide, Martin. "The Domestication of the Camel: Biological, Archaeological and Inscriptional Evidence from Mesopotamia, Egypt, Israel and Arabia, and Literary Evidence from the Hebrew Bible." *Ugarit-Forschungen* 42 (2010) 331–84. www. academia.edu/2065314/_The_Domestication_of_the_Camel_Biological_ Archaeological_and_Inscriptional_Evidence_from_Mesopotamia_Egypt_Israel_ and_Arabia_and_Literary_Evidence_from_the_Hebrew_Bible_in_Ugarit_ Forschungen_42_2010_Münster_Ugarit-Verlag_2011_331_384.

Heiser, Michael S. "The Almah of Isaiah 7:14." https://drmsh.com/the-almah-of-isaiah-714/.

————. "Archaeology and the Old Testament: Minimalism and Maximalism." http:// drmsh.com/archaeology-and-the-old-testament-minimalism-and-maximalism/.

Hewitt, John. "Fiber Optic Light Pipes in the Retina do Much More than Simple Image Transfer." https://phys.org/news/2014-07-fiber-optic-pipes-retina-simple. html#:~:text=21%2C%202014%20report-,Fiber%20optic%20light%20pipes% 20in%20the%20retina,more%20than%20simple%20image%20 transfer&text=These%20high%20refractive%20index%20cells,through%20a%20 change%20sorting%20machine.

Hill, Carol A. "Making Sense of the Numbers of Genesis." *Perspectives on Science and Christian Faith* 55.4 (2003) 239–51. https://asa3.org/ASA/PSCF/2003/PSCF12-03Hill.pdf.

———. "The Noachian Flood: Universal or Local?" www.csun.edu/~vcgeo0005/Carol%201.pdf.

———. *A Worldview Approach to Science and Scripture.* Grand Rapids: Kregel, 2020.

Hitchens, Christopher. *God Is Not Great.* London: Atlantic, 2007.

Hoffmeier, James F. *The Archaeology of the Bible.* Oxford: Lion, 2008.

Hoffmeier, James K., et al., eds. *Did I Not Bring Israel Out of Egypt? Biblical, Archaeological, and Egyptological Perspectives on the Exodus Narratives.* Winona Lake: Eisenbrauns, 2016.

Holcomb, Harmon R., III. "Buller Does to Evolutionary Psychology What Kitcher Did to Sociobiology: A Review of *Adapting Minds: Evolutionary Psychology and the Persistent Quest for Human Nature* by David J. Buller, Cambridge, MA: MIT Press, 2005." *Evolutionary Psychology* 3 (2005) 392–401.

Holder, Rodney. *Big Bang, Big God.* Oxford: Lion, 2013.

———. *God, the Multiverse, and Everything.* London: Routledge, 2004.

Holding, J. P. "Did Jesus Unfairly Kill the Fig Tree?" www.tektonics.org/uz/zapfigtree.php.

———. "Jephthah's Daughter: Answers to Objections." www.tektonics.org/gk/jepthah.php.

Hooker, Morna D. *Black's New Testament Commentaries: The Gospel According to Mark.* London: A. & C. Black, 1993.

Horn, Trent. *Hard Sayings: A Catholic Approach to Answering Bible Difficulties.* El Cajon, CA: Catholic Answers, 2016.

Hornblower, Simon. *The Greek World 479–323 BC.* 4th ed. London: Routledge, 2011.

Horner, David. "The Pursuit of Happiness: C. S. Lewis's Eudaimonistic Understanding of Ethics." *In Pursuit of Truth*, April 21, 2009. http://www.cslewis.org/journal/the-pursuit-of-happiness-c-s-lewis%E2%80%99s-eudaimonistic-understanding-of-ethics/view-all/.

Hossenfelder, Sabine. "Inflation: Status Update." http://backreaction.blogspot.com/2019/03/inflation-status-update.html.

House, H. Wayne. "James Ossuary." www.christianperspectiveinternational.com/images/7.JAMES_OSSUARY.pdf.

Howard, David M., Jr. *The New American Commentary: Joshua.* Nashville: B. & H., 1998.

"How Old Is Our Universe?" https://astronomy.com/magazine/greatest-mysteries/2019/07/1-how-old-is-the-universe.

Hull, David L., and Michael Ruse, eds. *The Philosophy of Biology.* Oxford: Oxford University Press, 1998.

Humanitarian Intervention, Legal and Political Aspects. Copenhagen: Danish Institute of International Affairs, 1999.

Hunter, James Davison. *Culture Wars: The Struggle to Define America.* New York: Basic, 1992.

Hunter, James Davison, and Paul Nedelisky. *Science and the Good: The Tragic Quest for the Foundations of Morality.* West Conshohocken, PA: Templeton, 2018.

Huston, J. *Reported Miracles: A Critique of Hume.* Cambridge: Cambridge University Press, 1994.

Hutchings, David, and David Wilkinson. *God, Stephen Hawking and the Multiverse*. London: SPCK, 2020.

Huxley, Thomas Henry. "Emancipation–Black and White (1865)." https://mathcs. clarku.edu/huxley/CE3/B&W.html.

———. "Evolution and Ethics." In *Evolution and Ethics and Other Essays*, 30–47. Golden ed. Independently published, 2017.

Ijjas, Anna, et al. "Pop Goes the Universe." *Scientific American* (2017) 32–39. www.cfa. harvard.edu/~loeb/sciam3.pdf.

"IMJ view 20130115 191732." https://commons.wikimedia.org/wiki/File:IMJ_view _20130115_191732.jpg.

"In the Beginning." *New Scientist*, January 14, 2012.

"Insights into the Workings of a Bacterium's Flagellum." https://commons.wikimedia. org/wiki/File:Insights_into_the_workings_of_a_bacterium%27s_flagellum_ (12291548414).jpg.

Instone-Brewer, David. *Divorce and Remarriage in the Church: Biblical Solutions for Pastoral Realities*. Milton Keynes: Paternoster, 2017.

Isaac, Benjamin. *The Invention of Racism in Classical Antiquity*. New ed. Princeton: Princeton University Press, 2006.

"JamesOssuary-1." http://commons.wikimedia.org/wiki/File:JamesOssuary-1-.jpg.

Jason, Gary James. Review of *Who Really Cares? The Surprising Truth about Compassionate Conservatism*, by Arthur C. Brooks. www.researchgate.net/ publication/298970301_Review_of_A_Brooks_Who_Really_Cares_The_ Surprising_Truth_of_Compassionate_Conseervativism.

"Jephthah's Daughter: Examining an Old Testament story." www.biblefellowshipunion. co.uk/2002/Nov_Dec/Jephthan.htm.

Johnson, Paul. *Art: A New History*. New York: HarperCollins, 2003.

Johnson, Phillip. "The Religion of the Blind Watchmaker." www.arn.org/docs/johnson/ watchmkr.htm.

Jones, Jean E. "Abraham and Human Sacrifice? Answering Rachel Held Evans, Part 2." www.jeanejones.net/2015/11/was-abraham-wrong-answering-rachel-held-evans -part-2/.

Josephson, Brian. "Letter to the Editor." *The Independent*, January 12, 1997.

Josephus. *Antiquities of the Jews*: Book 1. https://www.gutenberg.org/files/2848/2848- h/2848-h.htm#link2H_4_0001.

Kaiser, Walter C., Jr., et al. *Hard Sayings of the Bible*. Downers Grove: InterVarsity, 1996.

Kakutani, Michiko. *The Death Of Truth: Notes on Falsehood in the Age of Trump*. Glasgow: Collins, 2018.

Kalimi, Isaac. "Go, I Beg You, Take Your Beloved Son and Slay Him! The Binding of Isaac in Rabbinic Literature and Thought." *Review of Rabbinic Judaism* 13.1 (2010) 1–29. https://pdfs.semanticscholar.org/9797/851dbbf829cfc44e254556350591c1c b201f.pdf.

Keenan, J. F. "Moral Theological Reflections: Virtue Ethics as a Method for Building Bridges between Scripture and Moral Theology." In *Jesus And Virtue Ethics: Building Bridges between New Testament Studies And Moral Theology*, edited by Daniel J. Harrington and James F. Keenan, 24–25. Lanham: Rowman & Littlefield, 2005.

Keller, Timothy. *Genesis: What Were We Put in the World To Do?* New York: Redeemer Presbyterian Church, 2006.

Kendall, Jonathan. "Hallucinations and the Risen Jesus." In *Defending the Resurrection: Did Jesus Rise from the Dead?*, edited by James Patrick Holding, 207–371. Maitland, FL: Xulon, 2010.

Keren, Yuval. "What Can We Learn from the Akeidah?" www.liberaljudaism. org/2018/09/what-can-we-learn-from-the-akeidah/.

Kitchen, K. A. *The Ancient Orient and Old Testament*. Downers Grove: InterVarsity, 1975.

———. "The Controlling Role of External Evidence in Assessing the Historical Status of the Israelite United Monarchy." In *Windows into Old Testament History*, edited by V. Philips Long et al., 111–30. Grand Rapids: Eerdmans, 2002.

———. *On the Reliability of the Old Testament*. Cambridge: Eerdmans, 2003.

Konnikova, Maria. "On Writing, Memory, and Forgetting: Socrates and Hemingway take on Zeigarnik." *Scientific American* (blog), April 30, 2012. https://blogs. scientificamerican.com/literally-psyched/on-writing-memory-and-forgetting-socrates-and-hemingway-take-on-zeigarnik/.

Koonin, E. V. "The Cosmological Model of Eternal Inflation and the Transition from Chance to Biological Evolution in the History of Life." *Biology Direct* 2.15 (2007). https://biologydirect.biomedcentral.com/articles/10.1186/1745-6150-2-15.

———. *The Logic of Chance: The Nature and Origin of Biological Evolution*. Upper Saddle River, NJ: Pearson Education, 2012.

Krauss, Lawrence M. *The Greatest Story Ever Told—So Far*. New York: Atira, 2017. Kindle ed.

Kreeft, Peter. *Because God Is Real: Sixteen Questions, One Answer*. San Francisco: Ignatius, 2008.

———. "Desire." www.peterkreeft.com/audio/23_desire.htm.

———. *Heaven: The Heart's Deepest Desire*. Expanded edition. San Francisco: Ignatius, 1989.

Kuppers, Bernard-Olaf. *Information and the Origin of Life*. Cambridge: MIT Press, 1990.

Kurkjian, Vahan M. *A History of Armenia*. New York: Armenian General Benevolent Union, 1959.

Labin, A. M., and E. N. Ribak. "Retinal Glial Cells Enhance Human Vision Acuity." *Physical Review Letters* 104.158102 (2010). http://phweb.technion.ac.il/~eribak/LabinRibakGlialCells.pdf.

Labin, Amichai M., et al. "Müller Cells Separate between Wavelengths to Improve Day Vision with Minimal Effect upon Night Vision." *Nature Communications* 5 (July 8, 2014) 4319. www.nature.com/articles/ncomms5319.

Laland, Kevin, et al. "Does Evolutionary Theory Need a Rethink?" *Nature* 514 (2014) 161–64. www.nature.com/news/does-evolutionary-theory-need-a-rethink-1.16080.

Lamb, David T. *God Behaving Badly*. Downers Grove: InterVarsity, 2011.

Laney, J. Carl. *Answers to Tough Questions: A Survey of Problem Passages and Issues from Every Book of the Bible*. Grand Rapids: Kregel, 1997.

Larmer, Robert A. *The Legitimacy of Miracle*. Lanham: Lexington, 2014.

Larson, Stan. *Quest for the Gold Plates: Thomas Stuart Ferguson's Archaeological Search for the Book of Mormon*. Salt Lake City: Freethinker, 2004.

Lawrence, Paul. *The Books of Moses Revisited*. Eugene, OR: Wipf & Stock, 2011.

Lefkowitz, Mary R., and James S. Romm, eds. *The Greek Plays: Sophocles, Aeschylus, & Euripides*. New York: Modern Library, 2016.

LeMaster, James C. "Evolution's Waiting-Time Problem and Suggested Ways to Overcome It—A Critical Survey." *BIO-Complexity* 2018.2 (2018). http://bio-complexity.org/ojs/index.php/main/article/viewArticle/BIO-C.2018.2.

Lennox, John C. *Against the Flow: The Inspiration of Daniel in an Age of Relativism.* Monarch, 2015.

———. *God's Undertaker.* 2nd ed. Oxford: Lion, 2009.

Lewis, Geraint F., and Luke Barnes. *A Fortunate Universe: Life in a Finely Tuned Cosmos.* Cambridge: Cambridge University Press, 2016.

Liberty University. "ACE Interview Angus Menuge 'Human Rights.'" *YouTube*, March 20, 2015. www.youtube.com/watch?v=wvm18CH3tdw.

Licona, Michael R. *Paul Meets Muhammad: A Christian-Muslim Debate on the Resurrection.* Grand Rapids: Baker, 2006.

———. *The Resurrection of Jesus: A New Historiographical Approach.* Nottingham: Apollos, 2010.

———. "What To Say To Mormons." www.bethinking.org/mormons/what-to-say-to-mormons.

Littman, Robert J., et al. "With & Without Straw: How Israelite Slaves Made Bricks." *Biblical Archaeology Review* 40.2 (2014) 60–71. www.researchgate.net/publication/287786412_With_without_straw_How_Israelite_slaves_made_bricks.

"London Underground Overground DLR Crossrail Map." https://commons.wikimedia.org/wiki/File:London_Underground_Overground_DLR_Crossrail_map.svg.

Long Live Queen. "Queen: Flash." *YouTube* playlist, n.d., www.youtube.com/playlist?list=PLkG7CgS3OhRjxKlzqpp8nerPDpEwp5S-9.

Longman, Tremper, III. *Introducing the Old Testament: A Short Guide to the History and Message.* Grand Rapids: Zondervan, 2012.

———. "Who Wrote the Book of Genesis?" *Zondervan Academic Blog*, August 31, 2018. https://zondervanacademic.com/blog/who-wrote-genesis.

Longman, Tremper, III, and John H. Walton. *The Lost World of the Flood.* Downers Grove: InterVarsity, 2018.

Lüdemann, Gerd. *The Resurrection of Christ: A Historical Inquiry.* Prometheus, 2004.

Luskin, Casey. "'Biomimetics' Exposes Attacks on ID as Poorly Designed." www.discovery.org/a/18011/.

———. "*Phys.org*: Specialized Retinal Cells Are a 'Design Feature,' Showing that the Argument for Suboptimal Design of the Eye 'Is Folly.'" *Evolution News and Science Today*, August 8, 2014. https://evolutionnews.org/2014/08/physorg_special/.

Machen, J. Gresham. *The Virgin Birth of Christ.* London: Clarke, 1987.

Mackie, J. L. *Ethics: Inventing Right and Wrong.* Middlesex: Penguin, 1990.

Magonet, Jonathan. "Did Jephthah Actually Kill His Daughter?" www.thetorah.com/article/did-jephthah-actually-kill-his-daughter.

Maier, Paul L. "Biblical History: The Faulty Criticism of Biblical Historicity." www.equip.org/article/biblical-history-the-faulty-criticism-of-biblical-historicity.

———. "Did Jesus Really Exist?" In *Evidence for God: 50 Arguments for Faith from the Bible, History, Philosophy, and Science*, edited by William A. Dembski and Michael R. Licona, 143–46. Grand Rapids: Baker, 2010.

———. "The James Ossuary." https://www.issuesetcarchive.org/articles/bissar95.htm.

———. "Josephus and Jesus." www.namb.net/apologetics/resource/josephus-and-jesus/.

"Making the Jewish Case for Human Rights—Monsieur René Cassin." https://www. renecassin.org/making-the-jewish-case-monsieur-rene-cassin/.

"Maler der Grabkammer des Rechmirê." https://commons.wikimedia.org/wiki/ File:Maler_der_Grabkammer_des_Rechmir%C3%AA_002.jpg.

Mangalwadi, Vishal. *The Book that Made Your World: How the Bible Created the Soul of Western Civilization*. Nashville: Nelson, 2011.

Manning, Anneka. "Norwegian Almond Butter Biscuits (Serinakaker)." www.sbs.com. au/food/recipes/norwegian-almond-butter-biscuits-serinakaker.

"March Comes in Like a Lion." https://en.wikipedia.org/wiki/March_Comes_In_ like_a_Lion.

Margonelli, Lisa. "Collective Mind of the Mound: How Do Termites Build Their Huge Structures?" *National Geographic*, August 1, 2020. www.nationalgeographic.com/ news/2014/8/140731-termites-mounds-insects-entomology-science/.

Marilliononline. "Bridge (2018 Steven Wilson Remix)." *YouTube*, March 8, 2018. https://www.youtube.com/watch?v=oG6ch37V_Ug&feature=youtu.be.

Marks, Joel. "An Amoral Manifesto: Part I." www.philosophynow.org/issue80/An_ Amoral_Manifesto_Part_I?vm=r.

Marston, Paul, and Roger Forster. *God's Strategy in Human History*. New ed. Eugene, OR: Wipf & Stock, 2000.

Math Antics. "The Pythagorean Theorem." *YouTube*, May 3, 2017. https://youtu.be/ WqhlG3Vakw8.

May, Peter. "Paul at Athens." www.bethinking.org/apologetics/paul-at-athens.

McDowell, Josh. *Daniel in the Critics' Den: Historical Evidence for the Authenticity of the Book of Daniel*. San Bernadino, CA: Campus Crusade for Christ, 1979.

McDowell, Josh, and Norman L. Geisler. *Love Is Always Right: A Defence of the One Moral Absolute*. Dallas: Word, 1996.

Mckee, Maggie. "Genes Contribute to Religious Inclination". *New Scientist*, March 16, 2005. www.newscientist.com/article/dn7147-genes-contribute-to-religious-inclination/.

McGrath, Alistair E. *Dawkins' God: From the Selfish Gene to the God Delusion*. Oxford: Blackwell, 2005.

———. *Dawkins' God: From the Selfish Gene to the God Delusion*. 2nd ed. Oxford: Wiley Blackwell, 2015.

———. *Making Sense of the Cross*. Leicester: InterVarsity, 1992.

McGrew, Lydia. *Hidden in Plain View: Undesigned Coincidences in the Gospels and Acts*. Chillicothe: DeWard, 2017.

McInerny, Ralph. "Father Roger Dowling." www.detecs.org/dowling.html.

———. "Natural Law and Virtue." *The World & I Online*, January 1998. Kindle ed.

McLaughlin, Rebecca. "Richard Dawkins's Latest Case for Outgrowing God." *The Gospel Coalition*, December 4, 2019. www.thegospelcoalition.org/reviews/ richard-dawkins-case-outgrowing-god/.

Meister, Chad. *Introducing Philosophy of Religion*. Oxford: Routledge, 2009.

Men & Machines. "2019 Men & Machines Men's Breakfast with Dr John Dickson— Humilitas." *YouTube*, September 20, 2019. www.youtube.com/watch?v =MuNGhMDLcPE.

Menuge, Angus. "Reductionism, Bane of Christianity and Science." *Philosophia Christi* 4.1 (2002) 173–84.

———. "Can God Create a Rock So Heavy that He Cannot Lift It?" YouTube, Jun 12, 2013. https://youtu.be/8DB5bgjqATg.

Merriman, Helen. "The Modern Trials of theAancient Samaritans." *BBC News*, January 3, 2011. www.bbc.co.uk/news/world-middle-east-12069728.

"Merenptah Israel Stele Cairo." https://commons.wikimedia.org/wiki/File:Merenptah_Israel_Stele_Cairo.jpg.

Merz, Theo. "Men's Knitting—Is It the 'New Yoga'?" *Telegraph*, January 9, 2014. www.telegraph.co.uk/men/thinking-man/10552983/Mens-knitting-is-it-the-new-yoga.html.

Metaxas, Eric. *Miracles: What They Are, Why They Happen, and How They Can Change Your Life*. London: Hodder & Stoughton, 2015.

Meyer, Stephen C. "Can Chemistry Explain Information in DNA? A Critique of Self-organization." *YouTube*, June 2, 2016. https://youtu.be/C6G2ADJ61GA.

———. "DNA and the Origin of Life." www.discovery.org/a/2184.

———. "Evidence for Design in Physics and Biology: From the Origin of the Universe to the Origin of Life." In *Science and Evidence for Design in the Universe*, edited by Michael Behe et al., 53–111. San Francisco: Ignatius, 2000.

———. "Evidence of Intelligent Design in the Origin of Life." In *The Mystery Of Life's Origin: The Continuing Controversy*, by Charles B. Thanxton et al., 424–28. Seattle: Discovery Institute Press, 2020.

Meyer, Stephen C., et al. "The Origin of Biological Information and the Higher Taxonomic Categories." www.discovery.org/a/2177/.

———. *Science and Evidence for Design in the Universe*. San Francisco: Ignatius, 2000.

———. *Signature in the Cell: DNA and the Evidence for Intelligent Design*. New York: Harper One, 2010.

———. "Teleological Evolution: The Difference It Doesn't Make." www.arn.org/docs/meyer/sm_teleologicalevolution.htm.

Millard, A. R. "Daniel in Babylon: An Accurate Record?" In *Do Historical Matters Matter To Faith? A Critical Appraisal Of Modern And Postmodern Approaches To Scripture*, edited by James K. Hoffmeier and Dennis R. Magary, 263–80. Wheaton, IL: Crossway, 2012.

———. "Methods of Studying the Patriarchal Narratives as Ancient Texts." In *Essays on the Patriarchal Narratives*, edited by A. R. Millard and D. J. Wiseman, 43–58. Leicester: InterVarsity, 1980.

Millard, A. R., and D. J. Wiseman, eds. *Essays on the Patriarchal Narratives*. Leicester: InterVarsity, 1980.

Miller, Corey, ed. *Leaving Mormonism: Why Four Scholars Changed Their Minds*. Grand Rapids: Kregel, 2017.

Miller, Dave. "Jephthah's Daughter." http://apologeticspress.org/aparticle.aspx?cid=4709.

Mishkin, David. *Jewish Scholarship on the Resurrection of Jesus*. Eugene, OR: Pickwick, 2017.

Mon Amie. "KRISTIANSAND, Norway." *YouTube*, June 21, 2019. www.youtube.com/watch?v=f9roVod8DBo.

Monod, Jacques. *Chance and Necessity*. San Francisco: HarperCollins, 1974.

Monton, Bradley. *An Atheist Defends Intelligent Design*. Toronto: Broadview, 2009.

———. *Seeking God in Science: An Atheist Defends Intelligent Design*. Toronto: Broadview, 2009.

Moreland, J. P. "How Scientism Rules out the Presuppositions of Science." www.jpmoreland.com/2018/11/27/how-scientism-rules-out-the-presuppositions-of-science/.

———. "Intelligent Design and Evolutionary Psychology as Research Programs: A Comparison of Their Most Plausible Specifications." In *Intelligent Design: William A. Dembski & Michael Ruse in Dialogue*, edited by Robert B. Stewart, 112–38. Minneapolis: Fortress, 2007.

———. *Scaling the Secular City: A Defense of Christianity*. Grand Rapids: Baker Academic, 1987.

Moreland, J. P., and Kai Nielson. *Does God Exist? The Debate Between Theists and Atheists*. Amherst: Prometheus, 1993.

Moreland, J. P., and William Lane Craig. *Philosophical Foundations for a Christian Worldview*. Downers Grove: InterVarsity, 2003.

Morris, Leon. *Tyndale New Testament Commentaries: Luke*. Downers Grove: IVP Academic, 2008.

Moshier, Stephen O., and James K. Hoffmeier. "Which Way Out of Egypt? Physical Geography Related to the Exodus Itinerary." In *Israel's Exodus in Transdisciplinary Perspective: Quantitative Methods in the Humanities and Social Sciences*, edited by T. E. Levy et al., 101–8. Cham, Switzerland: Springer International, 2015. www.academia.edu/12144255/Which_Way_Out_of_Egypt_Physical_Geography_Related_to_the_Exodus_Itinerary.

MrShazoolo. "Atheist Refuted by Agnostic Historian (Bart Ehrman) on the Existence of Jesus." *YouTube*, December 30, 2011. https://www.youtube.com/watch?v=u9CC7qNZkOE&feature=youtu.be.

Murray, Michael J. "Belief in God: A Trick of our Brain?" www.case.edu.au/blogs/case-subscription-library/belief-in-god-a-trick-of-our-brain.

———. "God and Neuro-Science." www.reasonablefaith.org/writings/question-answer/god-and-neuro-science/.

Mykytiuk, Lawrence. "53 People in the Bible Confirmed Archaeologically." www.biblicalarchaeology.org/daily/people-cultures-in-the-bible/people-in-the-bible/50-people-in-the-bible-confirmed-archaeologically.

Nagel, Thomas. "Dawkins and Atheism." In *Secular Philosophy and the Religious Temperament: Essays 2002–2008*, 19–26. Oxford: Oxford University Press, 2010.

———. "Fear of Religion." *The New Republic*, October 22, 2006. http://keithburgess-jackson.com/wp-content/uploads/2007/04/nagel-the-fear-of-religion-2006-volume-235.pdf.

———. *The Last Word*. Oxford: Oxford University Press, 1997.

———. *Mind & Cosmos: Why the Materialist Neo-Darwinian Conception of Nature Is Almost Certainly False*. Oxford: Oxford University Press, 2012.

Nagtegaal, Brent. "Did David and Solomon Actually Exist?" *The Trumpet*, Feburary 2017. www.thetrumpet.com/14445-did-david-and-solomon-actually-exist.

Namba, Keiichi. "Self-Assembly of Bacterial Flagella." 2002 Annual Meeting of the American Crystallographic Association, San Antonio, TX.

The National Archives. "Monasteries." https://webarchive.nationalarchives.gov.uk/20180801135528/http://broughttolife.sciencemuseum.org.uk/broughttolife/people/monasteries.

National Theatre. "'Antigone': Religion and Modern Context." *YouTube*, February 4, 2013. https://www.youtube.com/watch?v=2QLcG-Tk9sU&feature=youtu.be.

Nature League. "Gregor Mendel: The Father of Modern Genetics." *YouTube*, June 13, 2019. https://youtu.be/7r__R9-eDJE.

Nelson, Paul. "Jettison the Arguments, or the Rule? The Place of Darwinian Theological Themata in Evolutionary Reasoning." www.arn.org/docs/nelson/pn_jettison.htm.

Neufeld, Thomas R. Yoder. *Recovering Jesus*. Grand Rapids: Brazos, 2007.

New Scientist. "Richard Dawkins Outgrows God." *YouTube*, September 20, 2019. https://youtu.be/qvRrQisGv8g.

Ngo Robin. "Did the Carthaginians Really Practice Infant Sacrifice?" *Bible History Daily* (blog), April 2, 2018. www.biblicalarchaeology.org/daily/ancient-cultures/ did-the-carthaginians-really-practice-infant-sacrifice/.

Nicholl, Colin R. *The Great Christ Comet: Revealing the True Star of Bethlehem.* Wheaton, IL: Crossway, 2015.

"Nidaros Cathedral." www.visittrondheim.no/nidaros-cathedral.

Nielson, Kai. "Naturalistic Explanations of Theistic Belief." In *A Companion to Philosophy of Religion*, edited by Philip L. Quinn and Charles Taliferro, 402–9. Malden, MA: Blackwell, 1997.

———. *Reason and Practice.* New York: Harper & Row, 1971.

NLA Høgskolen. "Kommunkasjon og livssyn." *YouTube*, April 14, 2016. www.youtube. com/watch?v=JmseoXLeWcM.

———. "Velkommen til NLA Høgskolen." *YouTube*, January 31, 2019. www.youtube. com/watch?v=CIAXu5E_N2g.

Noonan, Benjamin J. "Egyptian Loanwords as Evidence for the Authenticity of the Exodus and Wilderness Traditions." In *Did I Not Bring Israel Out of Egypt? Biblical, Archaeological, and Egyptological Perspectives on the Exodus Narratives*, edited by Hoffmeier et al., 49–68. Winona Lake: Eisenbrauns, 2016.

Nussbaum, Martha. "Who Is the Happy Warrior? Philosophy Poses Questions to Psychology." *Journal of Legal Studies* 37.2 (June 2008) S81–S113.

Nuzzo, Regina. "Profile of George Oster." *PNAS* 103.6 (2006) 1672–74. www.pnas.org/ content/103/6/1672.

O'Connell, Jake. "Jesus' Resurrection and Collective Hallucinations." *Tyndale Bulletin* 60.1 (2009) 69–105.

"The Odyssey and the Iliad in Just Two Minutes!" http://fettleanimation.com/odyssey- iliad-two-minutes.

Oh No, Anime! "Yoko Kanno: Musical Mastermind—Creator Spotlight." *YouTube*, March 9, 2018. https://youtu.be/_tkZJloNXWQ.

Olsen, Craig. "How Old was Father Abraham? Re-examining the Patriarchal Lifespans in Light of Archaeology." Paper presented to the Southwest Regional Meeting of the Evangelical Theological Society, March 31–April 1, 2017, Dallas Theological Seminary, Dallas, TX. www.academia.edu/33972456/How_Old_was_Father_ Abraham_Re-examining_the_Patriarchal_Lifespans_in_Light_of_Archaeology.

Orgel, Leslie E. *The Origins of Life: Molecules and Natural Selection.* New York: Wiley, 1973.

Ortiz, Stephen M. "The Archaeology of David and Solomon: Method or Madness?" In *Do Historical Matters Matter To Faith? A Critical Appraisal Of Modern And Postmodern Approaches To Scripture*, edited by James K. Hoffmeier and Dennis R. Magary, 497–516. Wheaton, IL: Crossway, 2012.

Owen, H. P. *Christian Theism: A Study in Its Basic Principles.* Edinburgh: T. & T. Clark, 1984.

———. "Why Morality Implies the Existence of God." In *Philosophy of Religion: A Guide and Anthology*, edited by Brian Davies, 648–58. Oxford: Oxford University Press, 2000.

Paparella, Emanuel. "The Medieval Monks as Preservers of Western Civilization." www.ovimagazine.com/art/2810.

Park, Nick. *Myths, Lies and Howlers from the Fringes of the New Atheism*. N.p.: Evangelical Alliance Ireland, 2019. Kindle ed.

Paterson, Keith. "Will Camel Discovery Break the Bible's Back?" *YouTube*, March 30, 2014. https://youtu.be/5B1i11P9Gbk.

Patterson, Richard D. "Victory at Sea: Prose and Poetry in Exodus 14–15." *Bibliotheca Sacra* 161 (January–March 2004) 42–54. http://faculty.gordon.edu/hu/bi/ted_hildebrandt/OTeSources/02-Exodus/Text/Articles/Patterson-Exod14-15-BS.pdf.

Pavid, Katie. "New Evidence of Ancient Child Sacrifice Found in Turkey." *Science News*, June 28, 2018. www.nhm.ac.uk/discover/news/2018/june/new-evidence-of-ancient-child-sacrifice-found-in-turkey.html.

Pennington, Jonathan. "3 Things You Didn't Know About the Sermon on the Mount." www.thegospelcoalition.org/article/3-things-didnt-know-sermon-mount/.

Penrose, Roger. *Faith, Fashion & Fantasy in the New Physics of the Universe*. Princeton: Princeton University Press, 2016.

PerHedetun. "The Catholic Church—Builder of Civilization, Episode 7: The Monks." *YouTube*, October 15, 2011. https://www.youtube.com/watch?v=iZ6zmWbiRmo.

Pettit, Harry. "Do These Ruins Prove the Biblical Story of the Exodus?" *Mail Online*, September 26, 2018. www.dailymail.co.uk/sciencetech/article-6210313/Do-ruins-prove-Biblical-story-Exodus.html.

Phad Pyakurel. "A Rotary Nonomachine." *YouTube*, November 1, 2014. https://youtu.be/lIFoMO9RO2Y.

"Philosophy Begins in Wonder." www.roangelo.net/logwitt/logwit49.html.

Pinnock, Clark, and Robert C. Brow. *Unbounded Love: A Good News Theology for the 21st Century*. Downers Grove: InterVarsity, 1994.

Pinzon, Scott. "What is Prog?" *YouTube*, May 3, 2014. https://youtu.be/RRroWZhwJBE.

Pirie, Madsen. *How To Win Every Argument: The Use And Abuse Of Logic*. London: Continuum, 2006.

Pitre, Brant. "Hatred in the Bible." *YouTube*, September 2, 2019. https://youtu.be/aMDnoAGCrRA.

———. "The Resurrection of Jesus and the Sign of Jonah." *YouTube*, November 12, 2018. https://www.youtube.com/watch?v=yCjqqtU8PR8&feature=youtu.be.

Plantinga, Alvin. *Knowledge and Christian Belief*. Grand Rapids: Eerdmans, 2015.

———. "Plantinga's Original 'Two Dozen (Or So) Theistic Arguments.'" In *Two Dozen (Or So) Arguments for God: The Plantinga Project*, edited by Jerry L. Walls and Trent Dougherty, 461–79. Oxford: Oxford University Press, 2018.

———. *Warrant and Proper Function*. Oxford: Oxford University Press, 1993.

———. *Warranted Christian Belief*. Oxford: Oxford University Press, 2000.

———. *Where the Conflict Really Lies*. Oxford: Oxford University Press, 2011.

Plato. *Euthyphro*. In *The Collected Dialogues of Plato*, edited by Edith Hamilton and Huntingdon Cairns and translated by Lane Cooper, 169–85. Princeton: Princeton University Press, 1961.

Pokrifka, H. Junia. *Exodus: A Commentary in the Wesleyan Tradition*. Kansas City: Beacon Hill, 2018.

Polkinghorne, John. *Science & Christian Belief: Theological Reflections of a Bottom-up Thinker.* London: SPCK, 1994.

———. *The Way the World Is: The Christian Perspective of a Scientist.* London: Triangle, 1994.

Pooe, Tsholofelo. "Evolution's Time Problem—Waiting for Genetic Change." https://boammaaruri.blog/2017/01/26/evolutions-time-problem-waiting-for-genetic-change.

Powell, Russell, and Steve Clarke. "Religion As an Evolutionary Byproduct: A Critique of the Standard Model." *The British Journal for the Philosophy of Science* 63.3 (2012) 457–86. https://doi.org/10.1093/bjps/axr035.

Pregilenis. "TransAtlantic—The Whirlwind: XII. Dancing With Eternal Glory / Whirlwind (Reprise)." *YouTube*, January 25, 2011. https://www.youtube.com/watch?v=ihCryXQCw8s&feature=youtu.be.

Prog Archives Music. "Bridge—Marillion." *YouTube*, November 21, 2018. https://youtu.be/R9s_8E39YX8.

Progressive Vinyl. "Transatlantic—The Whirlwind." *YouTube*, September 12, 2018. https://youtu.be/zINoI8Cvotg.

Puckett, Joe, Jr. *The Apologetics of Joy: A Case for the Existence of God from C. S. Lewis's Argument from Desire.* Cambridge: Clarke, 2013.

Pullen, Stuart. *Intelligent Design or Evolution? Why the Origin of Life and the Evolution of Molecular Knowledge Imply Design.* Raleigh, NC: Intelligent Design, 2005.

Purtill, Richard. *Reason to Believe: Why Faith Makes Sense.* San Francisco: Ignatius, 2009.

QAChristianity. "Can God Create a Rock So Heavy that He Cannot Lift It?" *YouTube*, June 13, 2013. https://youtu.be/8DB5bgjqATg.

"Quotes: Jesus' Influence on History." http://www.glenarmbaptistchurch.co.uk/quotes-jesus-influence-on-history/471.

Rashi. "Genesis Rabbah 56:8." www.sefaria.org/Rashi_on_Genesis.22.2.4?lang=bi.

Real Truth. Real Quick. "Why Did Jesus Curse the Fig Tree in Mark 11?" *YouTube*, April 6, 2018. https://youtu.be/goRMnPCpLYY.

Reardon, David C. "The Abortion and Mental Health Controversy: A Comprehensive Literature Review of Common Ground Agreements, Disagreements, Actionable Recommendations, and Research Opportunities." *SAGE Open Medicine* 6 (2018). www.ncbi.nlm.nih.gov/pmc/articles/PMC6207970/.

Reasons to Believe. "Informal Fallacies: The False Dichotomy Fallacy." *YouTube*, April 4, 2016. www.youtube.com/watch?v=3lYr4RrQ8TI.

Recht, Laerke. "Human Sacrifice in the Ancient Near East." *Trinity College Dublin Journal of Postgraduate Research* 9 (2009) 168–80. www.academia.edu/1561457/Human_sacrifice_in_the_ancient_Near_East.

"Redeem, Redemption." www.biblestudytools.com/dictionary/redeem-redemption/.

Redford, John. *Born of a Virgin: Proving the Miracle from the Gospels.* London: St Paul's, 2007.

Reeves, Mariclair A., et al. "Enzyme Families—Shared Evolutionary History of Shared Design? A Study of the GABA-Aminotransferase Family." *BIO-Complexity* 4 (2014) 1–16. https://bio-complexity.org/ojs/index.php/main/article/viewArticle/BIO-C.2014.4.

Reflexion. "Dr. William Lane Craig Gives a GREAT Analogy of the TRInity!" *YouTube*, March 21, 2012. https://youtu.be/JexU-bUY4jM.

"Richard Dawkins: 'Immoral' Not to Abort if Foetus Has Down's Syndrome." *The Guardian*, August 21, 2014. www.theguardian.com/science/2014/aug/21/richard-dawkins-immoral-not-to-abort-a-downs-syndrome-foetus.

Richards, Jay Wesley, ed. *Unapologetic Apologetics*. Downers Grove: InterVarsity, 2001.

Richardson, Bradford. "Religious People More Likely to Give to Charity, Study Shows." *Washington Times*, October 30, 2017. www.washingtontimes.com/news/2017/oct/30/religious-people-more-likely-give-charity-study/.

Richardson, R. C. *Evolutionary Psychology as Maladapted Psychology*. Cambridge: MIT Press, 2010.

RJS. "From One Couple?" www.patheos.com/blogs/jesuscreed/2015/07/02/from-one-couple-rjs/.

Rose, Hilary, and Steve Rose, eds. *Alas Poor Darwin*. London: Vintage, 2001. Kindle ed.

Rose, Steven. "Darwin, Race and Gender." *EMBO Reports* 10.4 (2009) 297–98. www.ncbi.nlm.nih.gov/pmc/articles/PMC2672903/.

Rosenberg, Alex. *The Atheist's Guide to Reality: Enjoying Life Without Illusions*. London: Norton, 2011.

Rosenfeld, Amnon, et al. "The Aucenticity of the James Ossuary." *Open Journal of Geology* 4 (2014) 69–78. http://file.scirp.org/pdf/OJG_2014031213484587.pdf.

Rossetti, Christina. "In the Bleak Midwinter." www.poetryfoundation.org/poems/53216/in-the-bleak-midwinter.

Ruse, Michael. *Atheism: What Everyone Needs to Know*. Oxford: Oxford University Press, 2015.

———. "Darwinism as Religion: What Literature Tells Us about Evolution." http://blog.oup.com/2016/10/darwinism-as-religion/.

———. "Dawkins et al Bring Us into Disrepute." *The Guardian*, November 2, 2009. www.theguardian.com/commentisfree/belief/2009/nov/02/atheism-dawkins-ruse.

———. "Evolution and Ethics." In *The Nature of Nature: Examining the Role of Naturalism in Science*, edited by Bruce L. Gordon and William A. Dembski, 855–64. Wilmington, DE: ISI, 2011.

Russell, Bertrand. "The Existence of God—A Debate Between Bertrand Russell and Father F.C. Copleston SJ." www.biblicalcatholic.com/apologetics/p20.htm.

———. *The Problems of Philosophy*. Oxford: Oxford University Press, 1980.

———. *Why I Am Not a Christian: And Other Essays on Religion and Related Subjects*. New York: Simon & Schuster, 1957.

Ryan, Christopher. "Evolutionary Psychology Deserves Criticism." *Psychology Today*, June 24, 2009. www.psychologytoday.com/gb/blog/sex-dawn/200906/evolutionary-psychology-deserves-criticism.

Ryniker, Anne. "The ICRC's Position on 'Humanitarian Intervention.'" www.icrc.org/en/doc/assets/files/other/527-532_ryniker-ang.pdf.

"Sagrada Família." commons.wikimedia.org/wiki/File:Sagrada_Fam%C3%ADlia._Façana_de_la_Passió.jpg.

Sailhamer, John. *The NIV Compact Bible Commentary*. Grand Rapids: Zondervan, 1994.

Samples, Kenneth R. "Christian Thinkers 101: A Crash Course on Mortimer J. Adler." *Reflections* (blog), December 20, 2016. https://reflectionsbyken.wordpress.com/2016/12/20/christian-thinkers-101-a-crash-course-on-mortimer-adler/.

Sanders, Fred. "What Does the Old Testament Say about the Trinity?" https://
zondervanacademic.com/blog/what-does-the-old-testament-say-about-the-
trinity.

Sanford, John, et al. "The Waiting Time Problem in a Model Hominin Population."
Theoretical Biology and Medical Modelling 12.18 (2015). https://tbiomed.
biomedcentral.com/articles/10.1186/s12976-015-0016-z.

Schirrmacher, Thomas, ed. *The Humanisation of Slavery in the Old Testament*. Eugene,
OR: Wipf & Stock, 2018.

———. "Slavery in the Old Testament, in the New Testament, and Today." In *The
Humanisation of Slavery in the Old Testament*, edited by Thomas Schirrmacher,
43–70. Eugene, OR: Wipf & Stock, 2018.

Schwartz, Glenn. *Sacred Killing: The Archaeology of Sacrifice in the Ancient Near East*.
Winona Lake, IL: Eisenbrauns, 2012.

Science Museum History of Medicine. "Monasteries." http://broughttolife.
sciencemuseum.org.uk/broughttolife/people/monasteries.

Scott, Latayne C. *The Mormon Mirage: A Former Member Looks at the Mormon Church
Today*. 3rd ed. Grand Rapids: Zondervan, 2009.

Segal, Robert A. *Myth: A Very Short Introduction*. Oxford: Oxford University Press,
2004.

Selman, M. J. "Comparative Customs and the Patriarchal Age." In *Essays on the
Patriarchal Narratives*, edited by A. R. Millard and D. J. Wiseman, 91–140.
Downers Grove: InterVarsity, 1980.

Shanks, Hershel. "First Person: Human Sacrifice to an Ammonite God?" www.
biblicalarchaeology.org/daily/ancient-cultures/daily-life-and-practice/first-
person-human-sacrifice-to-an-ammonite-god.

"Share of Adults Who Volunteered in the Last 12 Months in England from 2012/13 to
2018/19, By Religion." https://www.statista.com/statistics/420107/volunteering-
uk-england-by-religion/.

Sharp, Daniel James. "An Argument Worth Having: 'Outgrowing God' by Richard
Dawkins." *Aero*, October 21, 2019. https://areomagazine.com/2019/10/21/an-
argument-worth-having-outgrowing-god-by-richard-dawkins.

Sheiman, Bruce. *An Atheist Defends Religion: Why Humanity Is Better Off with Religion
than Without It*. New York: Alpha, 2009.

Sheldrake, Rupert. "What Will Change Everything?" www.edge.org/response-
detail/11002.

"Shell Game." www.collinsdictionary.com/dictionary/english/shell-game.

Shermer, Michael. *How We Believe: The Search for God in an Age of Science*. Rev. ed.
New York: Freeman, 2000.

Shortt, Rupert. *Outgrowing Dawkins: God for Grown-Ups*. London: SPCK, 2019.

Sinnott-Armstrong, Walter. *Think Again: How to Reason and Argue*. United Kingdom:
Pelican, 2018.

"Sixth Debate: Quincy, Illinois." https://www.nps.gov/liho/learn/historyculture/
debate6.htm.

Smith, Christian. *Atheist Overreach: What Atheism Can't Deliver*. Oxford: Oxford
University Press, 2019.

Smith, Huston. *The World's Religions: Our Great Wisdom Traditions*. San Francisco:
Harper, 1991.

Smith, Quentin. "The Uncaused Beginning of the Universe." *Philosophy of Science* 55.1 (1988) 39–57.

Smolin, Lee. *The Trouble with Physics: The Rise of String Theory, the Fall of a Science, and What Comes Next*. Boston: Houghton Mifflin, 2006.

Sophocles. *Antigone*. Translated by Dudley Fitts and Robert Fitzgerald. https://mthoyibi.files.wordpress.com/2011/05/antigone_2.pdf.

Southerton, Simon G. *Losing a Lost Tribe: Native Americans, DNA, and the Mormon Church*. Salt Lake City: Signature, 2004.

Spartakirk109. "The Real Spartacus." *YouTube*, June 17, 2013. https://youtu.be/q1-xhoJQLHU.

Stein, Robert H. *Baker Exegetical Commentaries on the New Testament: Mark*. Grand Rapids: Baker Academic, 2008.

———. *The New American Bible Commentary: Luke*. Nashville: B&H, 1992.

Stenger, Victor J. *The New Atheism: Taking a Stand for Science and Reason*. Amherst: Prometheus, 2010.

Stevenson, Charles L. "The Emotive Meaning of Ethical Terms." In *Ethics: The Classic Readings*, edited by David E. Cooper, 262–80. Oxford: Blackwell, 1998.

Stop the Traffik. "What is Human Trafficking?" www.stopthetraffik.org/about-human-trafficking/what-is-human-trafficking/.

Stove, David. *Darwinian Fairytales: Selfish Genes, Errors of Heredity, and Other Fables of Evolution*. New York: Encounter, 1995.

Strauss, Mark L. *Four Portraits, One Jesus: An Introduction to Jesus and the Gospels*. Grand Rapids: Zondervan, 2007.

Sunshine, Glenn. "Christianity and Slavery." In *True Reason: Confronting the Irrationality of the New Atheism*, edited by Tom Gilson and Carson Weitnauer, 287–302. Grand Rapids: Kregel, 2013.

Swift, David W. "The Biochemical Reasons against Genes Evolving—Introduction." https://evolutionunderthemicroscope.com/newgenes00.html.

———. "The Blind Watchmaker." https://evolutionunderthemicroscope.com/reviews01.html.

———. *Evolution under the Microscope: A Scientific Critique of the Theory of Evolution*. Stirling: Leighton Academic, 2002.

———. "Proteins Need to Fold." https://evolutionunderthemicroscope.com/newgenes02.html.

Swinburne, Richard. *The Coherence of Theism*. 2nd ed. Oxford: Oxford University Press, 2016.

———. *Does God Exist?* Oxford: Oxford University Press, 2010.

———. *The Existence of God*. 2nd ed. Oxford: Clarendon, 2004.

———. "The Justification of Theism." www.lastseminary.com/cumulative-arguments/The%20Justification%20of%20Theism.pdf.

Taliaferro, Charles. *Contemporary Philosophy of Religion*. Maiden, MA: Blackwell, 1998.

———. *Philosophy of Religion*. Oxford: OneWorld, 2009.

Tallis, Raymond. *Aping Mankind: Neuromania, Darwinitis and the Misrepresentation of Humanity*. Durham: Acumen, 2011.

Taylor, Richard. *Ethics, Faith, and Reason*. Englewood Cliffs, NJ: Prentice-Hall, 1985.

TED-Ed. "From Slave to Rebel Gladiator: The Life of Spartacus—Fiona Radford." *YouTube*, December 17, 2018. https://youtu.be/8l1NyR6UvxU.

TEDx Talks. "I Have One More Chromosome Than You. So What? | Karen Gaffney | TEDxPortland." *YouTube*, July 1, 2015. www.youtube.com/watch?v =HwxjoBQdnos.

"The Tel Dan Stela." https://commons.wikimedia.org/wiki/File:IMJ_view_20130115_ 191732.jpg.

Thaxton, Charles B., et al. *The Mystery Of Life's Origin: The Continuing Controversy.* Seattle: Discovery Institute Press, 2020.

Theißen, Günter. "Saltational Evolution: Hopeful Monsters are Here to Stay." *Theory in Biosciences* 128 (2009) 43–51.

This Morning. "Sally Phillips On Challenging Misconceptions Around Down's Syndrome | This Morning." *YouTube*, October 4, 2016. www.youtube.com/ watch?v=Cf2o4Ajn7TY.

Thompson, Damian. "If Richard Dawkins Loves Facts So Much, Why Can't He Get Them Right?" *The Spectator*, September 21, 2019. https://blogs.spectator.co.uk/2019/09/ if-richard-dawkins-loves-facts-so-much-why-cant-he-get-them-right/.

Tilley, Gerald Charles. *Defending the Christian Faith: Apologetics Essays.* 2nd ed. Tustin, CA: California Biblical University Press, 2018.

———. "The Documentary Hypothesis." In *Defending the Christian Faith*, 111–18. 2nd ed. Tustin, CA: California Biblical University Press, 2018.

Trakakis, Nick, and Yujin Nagasawa. "Skeptical Theism and Moral Skepticism: A Reply to Almeida and Oppy." *Ars Disputandi* 4.1 (2004) 222–28.

"Transatlantic—Dancing With Eternal Glory Lyrics." www.songlyrics.com/ transatlantic/dancing-with-eternal-glory-lyrics/.

Travis, Malissa Cain. *Science and the Mind of the Maker: What the Conversation Between Faith and Science Reveals about God.* Eugene, OR: Harvest, 2018.

Trigg, Roger. *Beyond Matter: Why Science Needs Metaphysics.* West Conshohocken, PA: Templeton, 2015.

UN Human Rights. "Universal Declaration of Human Rights." *YouTube*, May 15, 2017. www.youtube.com/watch?v=5RR4VXNX3jA.

United Nations. "Trafficking in Persons." www.unodc.org/unodc/data-and-analysis/ glotip.html.

"Universal Declaration of Human Rights." https://www.un.org/en/universal- declaration-human-rights/index.html.

Urbach, E. E. *The Law Regarding Slavery: As a Source for Social History of the Period of the Second Temple, the Mishna and Talmud.* New York: Arno, 1979.

van der Veen, Peter, et al. "Israel in Canaan (Long) before Pharaoh Merenptah? A Fresh Look at Berlin Statue Pedestal Relief 21687." *Journal of Ancient Egyptian Interconnections* 2.4 (2010) 15–25. https://journals.uair.arizona.edu/index.php/ jaei/article/viewFile/83/87.

Vanishing Inc. Magic. "Three Shell Game." *YouTube*, June 12, 2009. https://youtu.be/ IFLa_tl4Rko.

Venetis, Evangelos, and M. Alinia Mozdoor. "The Establishment and Development of Christianity in the Parthian Empire (1st cent.—224/6 A.D.)" www.transoxiana. org/0106/venetis-mozoor_christianity_parthian_empire.html.

Verbruggen, Jan. "5 Things You Need to Know about Camels and Biblical Accuracy." *Transformed* (blog), February 24, 2014. https://transformedblog.westernseminary. edu/2014/02/24/5-things-you-need-to-know-about-camels-and-biblical- accuracy/.

Vilenkin, Alexander. "Did the Universe Have a Beginning?" *YouTube*, June 19, 2012. http://youtu.be/NXCQelhKJ7A.

Wallace, J. Warner. "Is There Any Evidence for Jesus Outside the Bible?" *Cold-Case Christianity* (blog), October 30, 2017. https://coldcasechristianity.com/writings/is-there-any-evidence-for-jesus-outside-the-bible/.

———. "Mormonism." http://coldcasechristianity.com/tag/mormonism/.

Walton, John H. "Joshua 10:12–15 and Mesopotamian Celestial Omen Texts." In *Faith, Tradition & History: Old Testament Historiography in Near Eastern Context*, edited by A. R. Millard et al., 181–90. Winona Lake: Eisenbrauns, 1994.

———. *The Lost World of Adam and Eve*. Downers Grove: IVP Academic, 2015.

Walton, John, and J. Harvey Walton. *The Lost World of the Israelite Conquest*. Downers Grove: InterVarsity, 2017.

Walton, John H., et al. *The IVP Bible Background Commentary: Old Testament*. Downers Grove: InterVarsity, 2000.

Warburton, Nigel. *Thinking from A to Z*. 3rd ed. London: Routledge, 2007.

Ward, Keith. "Evidence for the Virgin Birth." http://christianevidence.org/docs/booklets/evidence_for_the_virgin_birth.pdf

———. *Is Religion Dangerous?* Oxford: Lion, 2006.

———. *What the Bible Really Teaches: A Challenge for Fundamentalists*. London: SPCK, 2004.

Wartick, J. W. "Book Review: 'In the Beginning God: A Fresh Look at the Case for Original Monotheism' by Winfried Corduan." https://jwwartick.com/2014/03/31/ibg-wc/.

Weiner, Noah. "The Animals Went in Two by Two, According to Babylonian Ark Tablet." www.biblicalarchaeology.org/daily/biblical-topics/hebrew-bible/the-animals-went-in-two-by-two-according-to-babylonian-ark-tablet/.

Wells, Jonathan. *Zombie Science: More Icons of Evolution*. Seattle: Discovery Institute Press, 2017.

Wenham, David. *Did St Paul Get Jesus Right? The Gospel According to Paul*. Oxford: Lion, 2010.

———. *Paul and Jesus: The True Story*. London: SPCK, 2002.

———. "The Religion of the Patriarchs." In *Essays on the Patriarchal Narratives*, edited by A. R. Millard and D. J. Wiseman, 161–96. Downers Grove: InterVarsity, 1980.

West, John G. "Debating Common Ancestry." https://evolutionnews.org/2016/05/debating_common/.

Whealey, Alice. "The Testimonium Flavianum in Syriac and Arabic." *New Testament Studies* 54 (2008) 573–90. http://khazarzar.skeptik.net/books/whealey2.pdf.

Wielenberg, Eric. "Dawkins's Gambit, Hume's Aroma, and God's Simplicity." *Philosophia Christi* 11.1 (2009) 113–28. www.academia.edu/19893604/Dawkinss_Gambit_Humes_Aroma_and_Gods_Simplicity.

Wilkins, Steve. "Introduction." In *Christian Ethics: Four Views*, edited by Steve Wilkins, 1–29. Downers Grove: InterVarsity, 2017.

Willard, Dallas. "The Three-Stage Argument for the Existence of God." www.dwillard.org/articles/individual/language-being-god-and-the-three-stages-of-theistic-evidence.

Williams, Peter J. *Can We Trust the Gospels?* Wheaton, IL: Crossway, 2018.

Williams, Peter S. "Amazing Grace." www.bethinking.org/culture/amazing-grace.

———. "Antoni Gaudí's Basílica de la Sagrada Família," *YouTube* playlist, n.d. www. youtube.com/playlist?list=PLQhh3qcwVEWhW79wlDAQi3W_GOkuP9g-R.

———. "The Archaeology of Christmas." *Christian Evidence* (blog), December 9, 2019. http://christianevidence.org/blog/entry/the_archaeology_of_christmas/.

———. "The Argument from Desire." *YouTube* playlist, n.d. www.youtube.com/playlis t?list=PLQhh3qcwVEWj3nK3TBydEVAFRtdqfrpW2.

———. "Beauty." *YouTube* playlist, n.d. www.youtube.com/playlist?list=PLQhh 3qcwVEWiL488-SGbfODhf6kLPSZbJ.

———. "A Brief Introduction to and Defence of the Modern Ontological Argument." www.peterswilliams.com/2020/01/19/a-brief-introduction-to-and-defence-of-the-modern-ontological-argument/.

———. *The Case for God.* Oxford: Monarch, 1999.

———. "Christian Prog Rock." *YouTube* playlist, n.d. www.youtube.com/playlist?list= PLQhh3qcwVEWiWOboWNjk7quRQ-XohEb5v.

———. "C. S. Lewis as a Central Figure in Formulating the Theistic Argument from Desire." *Linguaculture* 2 (2019). http://journal.linguaculture.ro/images/2019-2/ Linguaculture%202_2019_11_Peter%20S%20Williams.pdf.

———. *C. S. Lewis vs. the New Atheists.* Milton Keynes: Paternoster, 2013.

———. "'Desert Island Discs' Event with Composer Paul Mealor." http://podcast. peterswilliams.com/e/desert-island-discs-event-with-composer-paul-mealor/.

———. "Do Angels Really Exist?" www.bethinking.org/christian-beliefs/do-angels-really-exist.

———. "Does the Bible Support Slavery?" https://www.bethinking.org/bible/does-the-bible-support-slavery.

———. "The Epistle of James vs. Evolutionary Christology." *Theofilos* 9.1 (2016) 49–65. https://theofilos.no/wp-content/uploads/2019/09/2c_Academia_Williams_The-Epistle-of-James-vs.-Evolutionary.pdf.

———. "Evolution & the Waiting Time Problem." *YouTube* playlist, n.d. www.youtube. com/playlist?list=PLQhh3qcwVEWjjyp6iQmdv4fTkysKEiAtB.

———. "The Existence of Jesus." *YouTube* playlist, n.d. www.youtube.com/playlist?list =PLQhh3qcwVEWiCALtjBWyx078Dxxib4g8E.

———. "The Exodus." *YouTube* playlist, n.d. www.youtube.com/playlist?list=PLQhh3 qcwVEWjbiCIsVBzoXW4bFq72c3EJ.

———. *A Faithful Guide to Philosophy: A Christian Introduction to the Love of Wisdom.* Eugene, OR: Wipf & Stock, 2019.

———. *Getting at Jesus: A Comprehensive Critique of Neo-Atheist Nonsense about the Jesus of History.* Eugene, OR: Wipf & Stock, 2019.

———. "Heaven & Hell." *YouTube* playlist, n.d. www.youtube.com/playlist?list=PLQh h3qcwVEWiImwioEwFZIiNXYAVEQpvN.

———. "Hiromi's Playlist." *YouTube* playlist, n.d. www.youtube.com/playlist?list=PLQ hh3qcwVEWgldnKNgFFB3N4OFA-EZ3G5.

———. "In Defence of Arguments from Desire: A Second Response to Gregory Bassham." www.peterswilliams.com/wp-content/uploads/2016/11/In-Defence-of-Arguments-from-Desire_v4.pdf/.

———. "Inside the Cell." *YouTube* playlist, n.d. www.youtube.com/playlist?list=PLQh h3qcwVEWiddQNZ6pQhCtF06TPYXwKQ.

———. "Intelligent Design, Aesthetics and Design Arguments." www.arn.org/docs/ williams/pw_idaestheticsanddesignarguments.htm.

————. "Introduction to Ethics." *The Peter S. Williams Podcast*, June 7, 2017. http://podcast.peterswilliams.com/e/introduction-to-ethics/.

————. "Irreducible Complexity." *YouTube* playlist, n.d. www.youtube.com/playlist?list=PLQhh3qcwVEWh3orLA2I3KySSxU0IXAdZ3.

————. "Islam." *YouTube* playlist, n.d. www.youtube.com/playlist?list=PLQhh3qcwVEWjhD84EB0jEG5PswCOcDsmJ.

————. "Jesus the Prophesied Prophet." www.podbean.com/eu/pb-485ce-8e0119.

————. "Johann Sebastian Bach." *YouTube* playlist, n.d. www.youtube.com/watch?v=h09rZjlsyYY&list=PLQhh3qcwVEWjsZn4xCHUv7UcJljMo-GBr.

————. "Josephus on Jesus." *YouTube* playlist, n.d. www.youtube.com/playlist?list=PLQhh3qcwVEWh-7X8CFtPpH8tPwEiVcnVW.

————. "King David." *YouTube* playlist, n.d. www.youtube.com/playlist?list=PLQhh3qcwVEWjGWuucxuxxZbCVnt1cVBsB.

————. "King Solomon." *YouTube* playlist, n.d. www.youtube.com/playlist?list=PLQhh3qcwVEWi3LUPuYOTbI_hCeIimepro.

————. "Mind-Body Dualism, Free Will & Related Issues." *YouTube* playlist, n.d. www.youtube.com/playlist?list=PLQhh3qcwVEWhoMdW-hlHBPyLRWgFjzhPT.

————. "Mormonism." *YouTube* playlist, n.d. www.youtube.com/playlist?list=PLQhh3qcwVEWjOn4gyNXipluUzVuNsJjjI.

————. "Mormonism—An Introductory Critique." http://podcast.peterswilliams.com/e/mormonism-an-introductory-critique/?token=ec3e487232d37bbb7b44bb980b0f4f46.

————. "Mythology." In *The Dictionary of Christianity and Science*, edited by Paul Copan et al., 459–60. Grand Rapids: Zondervan, 2017.

————. "National Theatre, Antigone." *YouTube* playlist, n.d. www.youtube.com/playlist?list=PLJgBmjHpqgs7TVOYAmrHu1JaAcf6sA_rd.

————. "The Nativity." http://podcast.peterswilliams.com/e/the-nativity-1413287258/.

————. "The 'New Atheism.'" *YouTube* playlist, n.d. https://www.youtube.com/playlist?list=PLQhh3qcwVEWifP3P_gIS8MMsRXLOGDiG_.

————. "The Origin of Life." www.youtube.com/playlist?list=PLQhh3qcwVEWggFeEP9H7k1LyccfxzvoSr.

————. "Outgrowing God?" *YouTube* playlist, n.d. www.youtube.com/playlist?list=PLQhh3qcwVEWg5ExdpGFj2IRJpBbKvLEXQ.

————. "Paul and Jesus." *YouTube* playlist, n.d. www.youtube.com/playlist?list=PLQhh3qcwVEWhQDIEFD5W1dsmnOawCvAIU.

————. "Paul Mealor." *YouTube* playlist, n.d. www.youtube.com/playlist?list=PLQhh3qcwVEWgHI8y7_SXa3CO6GljXEJil.

————. "Perfect Being Theology." *YouTube* playlist, n.d. www.youtube.com/playlist?list=PLQhh3qcwVEWgObDfdGSUz-JGV9bFVu-sF.

————. "Philip Glass." *YouTube* playlist, n.d. www.youtube.com/playlist?list=PLQhh3qcwVEWgrtyqOFIY7j9qzzM1OlASZ.

————. "Post-Truth and Fake News." *YouTube* playlist, n.d. www.youtube.com/playlist?list=PLQhh3qcwVEWgkFUh6ZFNrcQSlQlvX4azB.

————. "Protein Synthesis." *YouTube* playlist, n.d. www.youtube.com/playlist?list=PLQhh3qcwVEWg6lDvvo2GVv2-Y_kIcpjoi.

————. "Religious Experience." *YouTube* playlist, n.d. www.youtube.com/playlist?list=PLQhh3qcwVEWjccogWzetsujJ_3BtcyLJT.

————. *A Sceptic's Guide to Atheism*. Exeter: Paternoster, 2009.

———. "Sermon: Revelation 1:1–8 (On Revealing the Trinity)." https://mcdn.podbean. com/mf/web/3w9cgh/Rev_1.mp3.

———. "Shostakovich." *YouTube* playlist, n.d. www.youtube.com/watch?v=G-FpiPWdSGA&list=PLQhh3qcwVEWiMRD-YVXLY6HC6U3Y0QW7K.

———. "Specified Complexity." *YouTube* playlist, n.d. www.youtube.com/playlist?list= PLQhh3qcwVEWiQrIEmUwrpyxVxVaZMc4i_.

———. "The Theological Roots of Science." *YouTube* playlist, n.d. www.youtube.com/ playlist?list=PLQhh3qcwVEWh3jDVYqFFzWSnTbtlUeCg3.

———. "The Trinity." *YouTube* playlist, n.d. www.youtube.com/playlist?list=PLQhh3q cwVEWhlDMYNYyenLkqdEQMMtMYo.

———. "Understanding the Trinity." www.bethinking.org/god/understanding-the-trinity.

———. "Who Designed the Designer/Caused God?" *YouTube* playlist, n.d. www. youtube.com/playlist?list=PLQhh3qcwVEWiHxfFWcRQzOZmdZV5AEHei.

Wilson, Niki. "Why Termites Build Such Enormous Skyscrapers." www.bbc.co.uk/ earth/story/20151210-why-termites-build-such-enormous-skyscrapers.

Winston, Kimberly. "'New Atheists' Emerge From 9/11." *Huffpost*, August 26, 2011. www. huffpost.com/entry/911-new-atheist_n_938356?guccounter=1&guce_referrer= aHR0cHM6Ly93d3cuZ29vZ2xlLmNvbS8&guce_referrer_sig=AQAAAE98Bp-wK9QjFeMgQDAoBGlCiNwQY4t4Fmgcs_nlzzTioYpoUXNmOYVTjTGDtlb6_ d863wFvMkvWYKITLZ2Wqc_rowoBqdWLpvPDIbXlesLoSe4fXynoF-TCCGkjxGWPD4Cj3sUCupaM1_z4wWpNmQxuZaJjjEt9f2w8iis4tfOV.

Wintour, Patrick. "Persecution of Christians 'Coming Close to Genocide' in Middle East—Report." *The Guardian*, May 2, 2019. www.theguardian.com/world/2019/ may/02/persecution-driving-christians-out-of-middle-east-report.

Wireless Philosophy. "CRITICAL THINKING—Fallacies: Straw Man Fallacy [HD]." *YouTube*, April 8, 2016. https://youtu.be/hfil34ayaEU.

———. "Introduction to Ad Hominem Fallacies." *YouTube*, January 22, 2015. https:// youtu.be/wnbK76m691I.

———. "Red Herring—Critical Thinking Fallacies | WIRELESS PHILOSOPHY." *YouTube*, December 15, 2017. https://www.youtube.com/watch?v=AfoSTrY58i4 &feature=youtu.be.

Witherington, Ben, III. "James Ossuary." http://restitutio.org/2015/10/26/james-ossuary/.

Wojciechowski, Micha. "Marriage as a (Mutual) Ownership: An Overlooked Background of Biblical Sayings on Marriage and against Divorce." *Folia Orientalia* 47 (2010) 207–14. www.academia.edu/11369497/Marriage_as_a_ Mutual_Ownership._An_Overlooked_Background_of_Biblical_Sayings_on_ Marriage_and_against_Divorce._Folia_Orientalia_47_2010_207–214.

Wolf, Jakob. "Two Kinds of Causality—Philosophical Reflections on Darwin's Black Box." *Progress in Complexity, Information, and Design* 1.4 (2002) 1–18.

Woo, Eddie. "Visual Proof of Pythagoras' Theorem." *YouTube*, January 26, 2017. https:// youtu.be/tTHhBE5lYTg.

Wright, N. T. *Judas and the Gospel of Jesus: Understanding a Newly Discovered Ancient Text and Its Contemporary Significance*. London: SPCK, 2006.

————. *Surprised by Hope: Rethinking Heaven, the Resurrection, and the Mission of the Church*. San Francisco: HarperOne, 2018.

————. "The Virgin Birth and the Constraints of History." www.abc.net.au/religion/the-virgin-birth-and-the-constraints-of-history/10098740.

Yamauchi, Edwin. "The Current State of Old Testament Historiography." In *Faith, Tradition & History: Old Testament Historiography in Near Eastern Context*, edited by A. R. Millard et al., 1–36. Winona Lake: Eisenbrauns, 1994.

Youngblood, Ronald, ed. *The Genesis Debate: Persistent Questions about Creation and the Flood*. Eugene, OR: Wipf & Stock, 1999.

Zentrum für BioKomplexität & NaturTeleologie. "A Thermodynamic Analysis of the Rarity of Protein Folds." *YouTube*, October 17, 2019. https://youtu.be/CvSpN_3tFN4.

Zimmer, Carl. "The Biologists Who Want to Overhaul Evolution." *The Atlantic*, November 28, 2016. www.theatlantic.com/science/archive/2016/11/the-biologists-who-want-to-overhaul-evolution/508712/?utm_source=fbb.